American Politics and

American Politics and Society

SECOND EDITION

David McKay

Basil Blackwell

© David McKay 1983, 1989

First published by Martin Robertson 1983
Second revised edition 1989

Basil Blackwell Ltd
108 Cowley Road, Oxford, OX4 1JF, UK

Basil Blackwell Inc.
432 Park Avenue South, Suite 1503
New York, NY 10016, USA

British Library Cataloguing in Publication Data
A CIP catalogue record for this book is available from the British Library

Library of Congress Cataloging in Publication Data
McKay, David H.
   American politics and society / David McKay.—2nd ed.
    p. cm.
   Includes bibliographies and index.
   ISBN 0–631–16781–1
   1. United States—Politics and government.   I. Title.
JK274.M514   1989
320.973—dc 19   89-93
                                           CIP

Typeset in 10 on 12pt Times
by Wessex Typesetters, a Division of The Eastern Press Ltd
Printed and bound in Great Britain by
Butler & Tanner Ltd, Frome and London

Contents

Preface to the Second Edition   viii

1   Introduction   1

The Study of American Politics   1
The Chapters to Come   6

2   Society, Economy and Political Beliefs   7

The Growth of the USA: Immigration and Demographic
    Change   7
The American Economy in Transition   13
Social Structure   15
Beliefs and Values: Dominant Ideology or Political Culture?   23
Further Reading   32

3   Constitutional Government   33

Origins   34
The American Constitution   37
Ratification   44
The Adaptive Constitution   46
Assessing the Constitution   51
Further Reading   53

*4   80,000 Governments: Federalism and Intergovernmental
    Relations*   54

Federalism in Theory and Practice   55
The Evolution of American Federalism   58

Competitive Interdependence: American Intergovernmental
   Relations since 1970   61
The Reagan Administration: Federalism Revived?   72
Is Federalism Dead?   75
Further Reading   76

5 *American Political Parties in Transition*   77

The Functions of Parties   78
Crisis and Change in the American Party System   83
Party Decline   89
Explaining Party Decline   95
Does the Decline of Party Matter?   98
Further Reading   100

6 *Political Participation and Electoral Behaviour*   101

Patterns of American Electoral Behaviour   103
Rational Voters and Inchoate Parties: Where Do We Go
   From Here?   119
Non-Electoral Political Participation   122
Further Reading   125

7 *US Legislators and their Constituents*   126

Representation and Congress   127
Congressional Elections   129
Legislators as Rational Actors   135
The Work of Members of Congress   140
Further Reading   142

8 *Congress as Policy Maker*   143

The Functions of Congress   144
The Structure of Power in Congress   145
Congress Under Fire   152
Reform and Change in Congress   160
Further Reading   167

9 *Presidential Power*   168

Formal Sources of Power   169
Informal Powers   171
The Presidency in Crisis   174

Presidential Resources 190
Assessing the Presidency: Presidential Power in the 1990s 199
Further Reading 200

10 *The Federal Bureaucracy* 201

The Federal Bureaucracy: Organization and Function 202
The Bureaucracy: How Uncontrollable? 209
The Inherent Power of Bureaucracy 210
The Bureaucratic Hydra: A Uniquely American
  Phenomenon? 211
Reform Attempts 216
Concluding Remarks – and a Word of Caution 219
Further Reading 220

11 *Organized Interests: The Real Power?* 221

Interests, Groups and Lobbyists 222
Economic Groups 224
Professional Groups 230
Promotional Groups 231
Political Action Committees 233
The Washington Lobby 236
Interest Groups: For and Against 236
Further Reading 240

12 *The Supreme Court and Judicial Politics* 241

The American Legal System 243
The Supreme Court: Decision Making 247
The Court and Political Power 254
Further Reading 267

13 *The Style and Substance of Policy Making* 269

Social Policy in America: Self Reliance and State Dependence 270
Managing Economic Change 274
Managing Foreign Affairs 289
Coda: The Future of the American Political Economy 295

Appendix *The Constitution of the United States* 300

Index 326

Preface to the Second Edition

This revised edition of *American Politics and Society* was completed on the election of George Bush to the Presidency. Few doubt that the Bush Presidency will be a difficult one. The new President follows Ronald Reagan, one of the most popular Presidents in recent American history. Bush will also inherit a generally favourable record from the Reagan years. Abroad, *détente* with the Soviet Union has progressed very satisfactorily, while at home the United States has experienced the longest continuous economic expansion in living memory. The cyclical nature of economic and political events suggests that George Bush will not enjoy uninterrupted linear progress in these vital policy areas. The budget and trade deficits seem irresolvable, while continued success with the Soviets depends largely on the fortunes of Gorbachev's plan to restructure Soviet society. Bush will, moreover, face a solidly Democratic Congress and an American public which, judging by the election turnout (the lowest since 1924) and the general tenor of the campaign, was less than enthusiastic about his elevation to the highest office in the land.

There is nothing to suggest, indeed, that the general conclusions of the first edition are any less relevant in the 1990s. The United States has a peculiarly fragmented and open political system which hardly lends itself to easy or efficient decision making. Equally serious, with the ending of American economic and military hegemony and the coming of interdependence, the pressures on political institutions to cope with change will increase.

I owe a debt of thanks to Thomas Mackie of the University of Strathclyde for pointing out errors in the first edition. Thanks also to the University of California, San Diego, whose Political Science Department provided an amenable environment for the revision of much of this book. Sean Magee at Basil Blackwell has provided advice, friendship and support throughout the history of the enterprise. Finally, thanks to Sherri Singleton who has done so much to help me really understand American society – and appreciate Californian cuisine!

Colchester, England

1

Introduction

'What do you think of our institutions?' is the question addressed to the European traveller in the United States by every chance acquaintance. The traveller finds the question natural, for if he be an observant man his own mind is full of these institutions. But he asks himself why it should be in America only that he is so interrogated. In England one does not inquire from foreigners, nor even from Americans, their views on the English laws and government; nor does the Englishman on the Continent find Frenchmen or Germans or Italians anxious to have his judgement on their politics.

James Bryce, *The American Commonwealth*

The Study of American Politics

Although Bryce's observation on the relative interest shown by different nationalities in their political institutions is no longer entirely true – the British, for example, are now deeply immersed in self analysis and self criticism – it remains the case that Americans are truly obsessed with the functioning and even viability of their political system. To the student of American politics this is a problem, for literally thousands of books on American politics exist, many of which have something important or interesting to say about the United States. Even at the level of undergraduate textbooks the choice is formidable, and almost every teacher of American politics begins his or her course with an apology for having to recommend books which provide only a particular perspective or cover only some of the ground.

Non-Americans suffer from the additional problem that the vast majority of books have been written by Americans for Americans. They therefore tend to assume a certain prior knowledge or they are tailored to the specific needs of the US educational system. The present volume was written for both a non-American and an American audience. Its approach is traditional in the sense that it covers all the main political institutions and processes of American national government. But no text on American politics can claim to be truly comprehensive; the subject is simply too vast to be covered by a single volume. This book narrows the area by concentrating on national as opposed to state and local politics (although intergovernmental relations are given special attention) and by providing extensive references to the major research findings in individual subject areas.

Perhaps the most difficult decisions facing authors of textbooks concern the relationship between factual presentation and more general comment and criticism. A book which confined itself simply to describing institutional and political processes would be dull in the extreme, while a book devoted to comment would more resemble a reflective essay than a text. The compromise reached in this volume will not please everyone, but it will, I hope, make each chapter more than a mere descriptive account. Most chapters have, in fact, a central argument or arguments around which basic facts and figures are organized. Most of these arguments relate to current controversies in the literature or ones currently debated in the broader society and polity. Naturally these controversies change as both the political agenda and the central concerns of academics change. Moreover, no book could cover all of current debate; to be both coherent and effective it has to select a particular approach based on certain normative judgements. Whether wittingly or not, all texts on American government do just this – notwithstanding that most also aim to present the reader with factual information. A good way to justify the present book's stance is to review the main objectives and orientations which other texts have taken over the last 40 years.

Three main approaches can be identified: the self-congratulatory, the critical and the functional. Let us deal with each of these in turn. Perhaps predictably, self-congratulatory texts were most influential during the 1950s and early 1960s. At that time America's dominant position in world economic and military affairs, together with relative domestic tranquillity, encouraged optimistic interpretations of American politics. Some political scientists, worried about continuing inequality in American society and the apparent failure of the political parties to provide coherent platforms for social change, were less sanguine,[1] but the general tone of the literature was optimistic. The system appeared

1   The most eloquent of the dissenting voices in this period was that of E. E. Schattsneider in his book *The Semi Sovereign People*, New York, Holt, Rinehart and Winston, 1960.

to work, albeit imperfectly. Most Americans were prosperous as never before, recent Presidents were of an acceptably high quality and, the problem of Southern racial segregation apart, few issues divided the country.

By the late 1960s all had changed. Poverty was 're-discovered' and the often serious inequalities in wealth and income in American society became increasingly obvious. The 'revolution' in civil rights was followed by racial unrest in America's cities; crime and social pathology generally were rising rapidly, and between 1963 and 1968 three of the nation's most prominent public figures were assassinated (President John Kennedy, Presidential candidate Robert Kennedy and civil rights leader Martin Luther King). Above all, the war in Vietnam had inspired fierce domestic opposition and had helped to alienate large sections of American youth from political authority. The institutional response to these events was widely perceived as inadequate. Presidents could apparently wield power in foreign affairs with relative impunity. Congressional control of the executive was hampered by fragmented decision making. The political parties, and particularly the Democrats, were internally divided, organizationally weak and often corrupt.

The subsequent events of Watergate and the Nixon Presidencies generally seemed to confirm the worst fears of many observers. If Presidents could break the law so easily and be discovered only by the chance apprehension of paid criminals in the act of breaking in to the opposition party's headquarters, then how could citizens expect to hold political authority in high regard? In response to these events and to the traumas of the 1960s, American textbooks on politics began to take on a quite different look. During the 1950s titles referring to 'American democracy' or 'government by the people' were considered adequate. By the early 1970s the emphasis had shifted to 'democracy under pressure', or 'a critical introduction'. Even those books which had established themselves as standard texts felt obliged to add chapters on race, foreign policy, or political protest. This re-appraisal was motivated not only by the functional question of how the system could be improved and institutions reformed. Many of the new texts made fundamental criticisms of American government. Some employed perspectives informed by radically different value positions. In particular, the late 1960s and early 1970s saw a new concern with the distribution of power in the United States and the consequences of this for patterns of wealth, income and racial equality. So, one of the most influential of these new books was entitled *American Politics: Policies, Power, and Change*,[2]

2 Kenneth M. Dolbeare and Murray J. Edelman, New York, D. C. Heath, 1st edn, 1971.

and contained chapters on the 'power structure' and the role of ideology in moulding the political behaviour of elites and non-elites. Interest in power was not, of course, new. More than ten years earlier pluralist political scientists had joined battle with power elite sociologists in academic debate on 'who rules America?' or in many instances 'who rules particular cities or communities?[3] The debate was never resolved because the two schools were asking similar questions inspired by quite different value perspectives on the very concept of power. What this and the later debates provoked by the troubled 1960s and 1970s did produce, however, was a much greater sensitivity to questions of equality and the distribution of power. Scholars still disagreed, but they generally became more careful in their use of language when referring to the consequences for different social groups of America's particular political and institutional arrangements. And of course no one now disputes the facts of unequal power resources, the existence of elites and masses, leaders and followers, the wealthy and the poor. Where controversy continues to rage is over the responsiveness of existing institutions to these inequalities, and over the *trade-offs* which exist between the pursuit of greater equality and other values, notably economic efficiency and individual freedom.

This brings us to the third and current emphasis of texts on American politics. During the 1970s and early 1980s the political agenda changed again, the new focus being on economic issues and the apparently intractable problem of how to achieve low rates of inflation and unemployment and high rates of growth and a balanced budget all at the same time. Blame for poor economic performance was, at first, placed on OPEC and the fourfold increase in oil prices during 1973–4. Later, however, economists and politicians began to question whether the system of public benefits which the welfare state and Keynesian economics had brought was compatible with an efficient economy. Government had, so the argument ran, become too big; too many social groups depended on public largesse; inflation was encouraged by excessive government borrowing. At the same time, all those social problems which the programmes and policies of the 1960s and 1970s had sought to solve were still very much there. Small wonder then that public and politicians began to question a system which had encouraged high spending but had produced few results. Of course, antipathy to an intrusive state role is nothing new in American history; it has been a recurrent theme, as later chapters will show. The difference by the

3 For an extensive summary and discussion of this debate, see Kenneth Prewitt and Alan Stone, *The Ruling Elites: Elite Theory Power, and American Democracy*, New York, Harper and Row, 1973.

1980s was that government expenditure had reached a high level, and, although many observers were concerned at the economic consequences of this, few could provide realistic suggestions on how, exactly, the state *could* disengage from society. Through access to Congress and political institutions at all levels, industry receives aid, old people pensions, the poor welfare benefits, farmers subsidies, the military weapons systems, and so it goes on. By the late 1980s the Iran–Contra arms deal and other cases of the abuse of power again raised the question of government accountability. The Iran–Contra affair also highlighted the extent to which the exercise of American power abroad had become an increasingly difficult and complex business.

Texts on American politics now reflect these problems. They have, in other words, become more concerned with the *functioning* of government and the policy process and how institutions might be reformed to reconcile as well as possible the conflict between efficiency and equality or between effectiveness and accountability. As a result, they are both less optimistic and less passionate than earlier generations of texts. Neither the enthusiasm for democracy prevalent in the 1950s nor the moral fervour of the 1960s is appropriate today. Instead, students are advised to counsel caution when assessing plans for institutional reform or social change.[4]

The present volume is written in much the same spirit. It emphasizes the limitations of political institutions and of recent attempts to reform them. An essentially functionalist perspective is adopted, therefore – although other values are not ignored – and a particular effort is made to explain the persistence of political and social inequalities in a society so infused with an ideology of egalitarianism and opportunity. In one quite fundamental respect, however, this book does differ from its American counterparts: it puts the American experience in comparative perspective. In other words, the criteria by which US political institutions and processes are assessed are not derived exclusively from American history or peculiarly American values. How the United States looks in terms of British and European values and perspectives is also involved. Naturally, this entails making judgements and drawing conclusions which can differ from those which American scholars might make. Hopefully, the result will be an analysis which adds new insights into the workings of American politics to add to those already provided by the vast and often impressive output of American political science.

Finally, when discussing institutions and processes, the book adopts

4 In spite of this new sober mood, almost all books on the current crisis end on a constructive if not optimistic note. This is, perhaps, related to the general tendency in American culture to stress the positive effects of social and political change.

at least a partly inter-disciplinary approach. It is not unique for this, of course. Almost all of the more influential American texts recognize that in order to understand the budgetary process or social policy it is necessary to have some grasp of economics, sociology and history. However, non-American texts on US politics have tended to take a rather narrow institutional approach to the subject, which this book consciously avoids.

The Chapters to Come

As earlier suggested, the book follows a conventional format, although the balance between different subjects and areas reflects recent developments in American society and politics. Chapter 2 is very much a background introduction which presents basic statistical information on demography, society and economy. The chapter also includes a discussion of the role of beliefs and values in American politics, and places a special emphasis on the question of whether a 'dominant ideology' prevails in the United States. Chapters 3 to 12 cover the main institutions and processes of American government with each designed to present basic information and to discuss the significance of historical trends as well as the relevance of recent research findings in political science. Special attention is paid to the role of bureaucracy and organized interests – two areas often neglected at least by non-American students of the subject. Chapter 13 has two main purposes: first, to add substance and perspective to earlier chapters by looking at the policy process in three currently crucial areas – social, economic and foreign policy; second, to discuss some of the more influential critiques of American political arrangements which recent economic and social difficulties have inspired. The general orientation of this and earlier chapters reflects my conviction that the study of political institutions can be productive only when placed in the broader social, political and economic environment. Such an approach can have costs – references to recent developments and events may lead to hasty judgements which can render a book painfully obsolete very quickly. But the cost of failing to put institutional relationships in broader context is even higher. For then the reader is condemned to an uninspired descriptive account, which is a fate I would not impose on any student of what should be one of the most interesting subjects in social science.

2

Society, Economy and Political Beliefs

It has been our fate as a nation, not to have ideologies but to be one.
Richard Hofstadter

So powerful is the dominant ideology in this country that existing economic and political arrangements frequently appear not merely as the best possible arrangements, but as the only possible ones.
Ira Katznelson and Mark Kesselman

The Growth of the USA: Immigration and Demographic Change

Until the mid-nineteenth century the United States was an 'imperialist' continental power, constantly expanding its territory by treaty, annexation and conquest. It was expansionist both in the sense that it dominated the other continental powers – Mexico, Britain, France and Spain – and in the sense that numerous native American tribes were overwhelmed by a technologically more advanced and populous society. It was, above all, America's economic might which enabled it to swallow up huge tracts of territory during this period (map 2.1). Population increases were also very considerable and did not fall below 20 per cent per decade until 1920 (table 2.1). Ever since then, the population has continued to grow rapidly and remains at over 10 per cent increase a decade – a remarkably high figure for an advanced industrial country with a small agrarian population. Both high natural increases and immigration account for this population growth although since 1971 there has been a natural *decrease* for the White population.[1] The United

1 Deaths and abortions have exceeded live births; see *Statistical Abstract of the USA, 1988*, US Department of Commerce, Bureau of the Census, 1988, table 86.

Table 2.1 Population and area, 1790–1987

| Census date | Resident population | | | | Area (square miles) | | |
| | Number | Per square mile of land area | Increase over preceding census | | Gross | Land | Water |
			Number	Per cent			
Conterminous US[1]							
1790 (2 August)	3,929,214	4.5	n.a.	n.a.	888,8111	864,746	24,065
1800 (4 August)	5,308,483	6.1	1,379,269	35.1	888,822	864,746	24,065
1810 (6 August)	7,239,881	4.3	1,931,398	36.4	1,716,003	1,681,828	34,175
1820 (7 August)	9,638,453	5.5	2,398,572	33.1	1,788,006	1,749,462	38,544
1830 (1 June)	12,866,020	7.4	3,227,567	32.5	1,788,006	1,749,462	38,544
1840 (1 June)	17,069,453	9.8	4,203,433	32.7	1,788,006	1,749,462	38,544
1850 (1 June)	23,191,876	7.9	6,122,423	35.9	2,992,747	2,940,042	52,705
1860 (1 June)	31,443,321	10.6	8,251,445	35.6	3,022,387	2,969,640	52,747
1870 (1 June)	39,818,449	13.4	8,375,128	26.6	3,022,387	2,969,640	52,747
1880 (1 June)	50,155,783	16.9	10,337,334	26.0	3,022,387	2,969,640	52,747
1890 (1 June)	62,947,714	21.2	12,791,931	25.5	3,022,387	2,969,640	52,747
1900 (1 June)	75,994,575	25.6	13,046,861	20.7	3,022,387	2,969,834	52,553
1910 (15 April)	91,972,266	31.0	15,977,691	21.0	3,022,387	2,969,565	52,822
1920 (1 January)	105,710,620	35.6	13,738,354	14.9	3,022,387	2,969,451	52,936
1930 (1 April)	122,755,046	41.2	17,064,426	16.1	3,022,387	2,977,128	45,259
1940 (1 April)	131,669,275	44.2	8,894,229	7.2	3,022,387	2,977,128	45,259
1950 (1 April)	150,697,361	50.7	19,028,066	14.5	3,022,387	2,974,726	47,661
1960 (1 April)	178,464,236	60.1	27,766,875	18.4	3,022,261	2,966,054	54,207
United States							
1950 (1 April)	151,325,796	42.6	19,161,229	14.5	3,615,211	3,552,206	63,005
1960 (1 April)	179,323,175	50.6	27,997,377	18.5	3,615,123	3,540,911	74,212
1970 (1 April)	203,211,926	57.4	23,888,751	13.3	3,618,467	3,540,023	78,444
1980 (1 April)	226,545,805	64.0	23,243,774	11.4	3,618,770	3,539,289	79,481
1987 (estimate)	243,773,000[2]	n.a.	17,227,195	n.a.	n.a.	n.a.	n.a.

[1] Excludes Alaska and Hawaii.   [2] Rounded to nearest 1000.
Source: *Statistical Abstract of the USA*, 1988, tables 1 and 2.

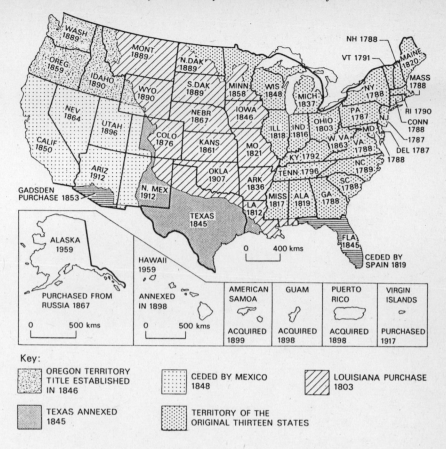

Map 2.1　The territorial expansion of the USA

Source:　Statistical Abstract of the USA, 1980, figure 7.2, p. 208.
Note:　Dates under state names denote year of statehood.

States was virtually built on an ideology of immigration, with successive generations of Americans promoting the country as a land of freedom and opportunity. The appeal was simple. Free from the corruption and oppression of Europe and rich in land and natural resources, the United States could and did absorb vast numbers of immigrants, first mainly from Britain, then from Germany, Ireland, Southern and Eastern Europe, and most recently from Asia, Mexico, Cuba, Canada, the Caribbean and other American countries. As table 2.2 shows, a high

Society, Economy and Political Beliefs

Table 2.2   Immigration, 1820–1986

Period	Total No. (1000s)	Rate[1]	Period or Year	Total No. (1000s)	Rate[1]	Year	Total No. (1000s)	Rate[1]
1820–1986	**53,122**	**3.4**	1931–1940	528	0.4	1972	385	1.8
			1941–1950	1,035	0.7	1973	400	1.9
1820–1830[2]	152	1.2	1951–1960	2,515	1.5	1974	395	1.9
1831–1840[3]	599	3.9	1961–1970	3,322	1.7	1975	386	1.8
1841–1850[4]	1,713	8.4	1971–1980[6]	4,493	2.1	1976	399	1.9
1851–1860[4]	2,596	9.3	1981–1986	3,466	2.4	1977	462	2.1
1861–1870[5]	2,315	6.4	1965	297	1.5	1978	601	2.8
1871–1880	2,812	6.2	1966	323	1.6	1979	460	2.1
1881–1890	5,247	9.2	1967	362	1.8	1980	531	2.3
1891–1900	3,688	5.3	1968	454	2.3	1981	597	2.6
1901–1910	8,795	10.4	1969	359	1.8	1982	594	2.6
1911–1920	5,736	5.7	1970	373	1.8	1983	580	2.4
1921–1930	4,107	3.5	1971	370	1.8	1984	544	2.3
						1985	570	2.4
						1986	602	2.5

[1]   Annual rate per 1000 US population. Rate computed by dividing sum of annual immigration totals by sum of annual US population totals for same number of years.
[2]   1 Oct. 1819–30 Sept. 1830.   [3]   1 Oct. 1830–31 Dec. 1840.   [4]   Calendar years.
[5]   1 Jan. 1861–30 June 1870.   [6]   Includes transition quarter, 1 July to 30 Sept. 1976.
Source: Statistical Abstract of the USA, 1988, table 131.

level of immigration continues even today with almost 3.5 million new Americans arriving in the 1981–6 period.

In comparative context this is a high figure; for no other industrial country allows such an influx. During periods of labour shortage, many European countries have encouraged some (often temporary) immigration, but none permits a continuing high level of immigration which persists even during periods of high unemployment and low rates of economic growth.[2] Not that mass immigration has gone unopposed. During and following the truly massive waves of immigration from Southern and Eastern Europe which occurred in the 1880–1910 period, opposition to what for many Americans represented an 'invasion' by alien cultures was fierce and finally culminated in the 1924 Immigration Act. This law specifically discriminated against Southern and Eastern Europe by fixing national immigration quotas favouring immigrants from Britain and Canada. Immigration fell dramatically during the 1930s and 1940s as depression and war took their toll both on economic

2   Other immigrant societies – Canada, Australia, New Zealand – have also encouraged immigration, but have generally been more selective in their policies towards newcomers, especially in recent years.

opportunity and on freedom of movement. With immigration increasing once more after 1950, criticism of the patent biases in immigration law intensified, and in 1965 a new law was adopted with fairer, more balanced quotas. Nonetheless, following amendments in 1965 and 1980, a total annual maximum of 270,000 (excluding dependants of US citizens) was set which, together with a permitted total of up to 50,000 refugees, is still a relatively high figure.

Since about 1970 the immigration controversy has been fuelled anew by substantial illegal immigration, mainly from Mexico, and by the social tensions which large numbers of Cuban and central American newcomers have brought, particularly to Florida. Illegal immigration has accelerated as poorer Mexicans have sought employment across a long and poorly policed border. Estimates of the numbers involved vary widely, but are at least in the low millions. In spite of these difficulties America's comparatively liberal attitude to immigration and the continuing belief that, at least for some, the USA should be a land of opportunity and freedom, still strikes many non-Americans as remarkable.

As the country and economy have grown, so both the composition and spatial distribution of the population have changed. Obviously with mass immigration during the nineteenth and early twentieth centuries the country became more ethnically diverse, and although these earlier immigrants are now generally assimilated into American society, many retain some national, ethnic or religious identity which has its origins in Europe. More recently, immigration and high relative birth rates have led to substantial increases in the Black and Hispanic populations. By 1985 some 16.9 millions (7.1 per cent) of Americans were Hispanic (mainly Mexican, Puerto Rican and Cuban) and 28.9 million (12.1 per cent) were Black. In the case of the Hispanic population, a linguistic as well as ethnic dimension is involved, for Spanish is the mother tongue for many, and in some areas, notably California and the South West, demands for an official bilingualism grow stronger from year to year.

America today is a highly urban society, with more than 70 per cent of the population living in cities with populations over 2500 in 1980. A more meaningful measure of urbanism is, perhaps, the number of people living in metropolitan areas, and in 1985 no less than 76.5 per cent of the population were classified thus.[3] One interesting post-1970 trend has been an increase in rural living. Between 1970 and 1980 non-metropolitan areas grew by 17.1 per cent while metropolitan areas grew by just 10 per cent. These new rural dwellers are not, in the main,

3 According to the census category Standard Metropolitan Statistical Area (SMSA). Such areas do contain some 'small' communities because jurisdictional fragmentation ensures that large conurbations contain numerous governmental units.

farmers, but people seeking a new lifestyle away from the crowded cities and suburbs. Indeed the growth of smaller towns and rural areas is a general phenomenon in advanced industrial societies.

Nonetheless, urban areas are still growing, although not in a uniform or even manner. The inner or central areas of the older industrial cities continue to decline, although during the 1980s a number of these cities

Table 2.3 Population change in the nation's 20 largest metropolitan areas, 1970–1986

Metropolitan statistical area[a]	1970 population (1000s)	1970 rank	1980 population (1000s)	1986 population (1000s)	1986 rank	% change	
						1970–80	1980–6
New York	18,193	1	17,539	17,968	1	−0.4	0.4
Los Angeles	9,981	2	11,498	13,075	2	1.4	2.1
Chicago	7,779	3	7,937	8,116	3	0.2	0.4
San Francisco	4,754	6	5,368	5,878	4	1.2	1.5
Philadelphia	5,749	4	5,681	5,833	5	−0.1	0.4
Detroit	4,788	5	4,753	4,601	6	−0.1	−0.5
Boston	3,939	7	3,972	4,056	7	0.2	0.3
Dallas	2,352	12	2,931	3,655	8	2.2	3.5
Houston	2,169	13	3,101	3,634	9	3.6	2.5
Washington DC	3,040	8	3,251	3,563	10	0.7	1.5
Miami	1,888	16	2,644	2,912	11	3.4	1.5
Cleveland	3,000	9	2,834	2,766	12	−0.6	0.4
Atlanta	1,684	18	2,138	2,561	13	2.4	2.9
St Louis	2,429	11	2,377	2,438	14	−0.2	0.4
Pittsburgh	2,556	10	2,423	2,316	15	−0.5	−0.7
Minneapolis	1,982	15	2,137	2,295	16	0.8	1.1
Seattle	1,837	17	2,093	2,285	17	1.3	1.4
Baltimore	2,089	14	2,200	2,280	18	0.5	0.6
San Diego	1,358	21	1,862	2,201	19	3.2	2.7
Tampa	1,106	26	1,614	1,914	20	3.8	2.7

[a] These cities cover metropolitan areas, not just central cities, so 'New York' refers to the New York/New Jersey/Long Island area.
Source: Statistical Abstract of the USA, 1988, table 34.

experienced a revival of their downtown areas. As table 2.3 shows, there have been some quite dramatic changes in the distribution of population among the largest metropolitan areas. Two broad trends can be discerned. First, the very rapid growth of the Southern and Western cities and the relative decline of the Northern cities. This is, of course, part of the 'Sunbelt/Snowbelt' divide much talked of in the 1970s. Second, since 1980 there are clear signs of revival among some of the older metropolitan areas with the New York, Philadelphia, Boston and St Louis areas showing renewed growth. At the same time, some of the Sunbelt cities' growth rates began to slow – although admittedly from a very high level.

By the late 1980s some commentators were characterizing the United States as having a 'bi-coastal' economy with booming East and West coasts and a relatively depressed Mid West. Such labels are probably premature, however. What we can say is that although many Northern and Eastern states and cities are booming there is a continuing general drift of population to the Sunbelt. At the same time, local and regional economies are vulnerable to the vagaries of economic change with those areas which are most dependent on a single industry (agriculture, oil, steel) being the most likely to be the victims of a boom/bust cycle.

Americans are also getting older. The percentage of over 65-year-olds in the population has increased dramatically over the last 60 years as medical care has improved and the birth rate has fallen. In 1920 only 4.7 per cent of the population were over 65, but by 1985 this figure had risen to 11.9 per cent. Both the size of the Sunbelt and the 'ageing of America' have important political consequences which later chapters will catalogue.

The American Economy in Transition

From very humble beginnings the American economy had grown to the world's largest by the end of the nineteenth century, and by 1945 the United States had established an effective global hegemony in economic affairs. America's *per capita* income was easily the highest in the world for a large country, and the economy had achieved a remarkable degree of self sufficiency. By the late 1980s the economy had grown to a staggering 4 trillion dollars and *per capita* income exceeded $14,000 (in 1988). As the economy has grown so there has been a shift, first out of agricultural employment to manufacturing and, most recently, out of manufacturing into service industries. By 1984 only 3 per cent of the labour force were employed in agriculture – even though the USA is the world's largest food producer. Of the non-agricultural labour force those employed in goods-related jobs (mining, construction and manufacturing) fell from 37.7 per cent in 1960 to 26 per cent in 1985, while service sector jobs increased to over 70 per cent of the total. With most Americans working in the service sector, talk of a post-industrial society is not entirely misplaced[4] – although it is only through great productivity advances in agriculture and manufacturing that the economy is able to sustain such a diversity of service sector jobs.

In spite of these advances, the American economy began to experience difficulties in the early 1970s. Some of these derived from world economic problems, but others were a result of peculiarly American circumstances. Very generally US productivity increases did not keep pace with those of major competing countries. Concern at the apparent 'de-industrialization' of the US increased preceptibly during the early 1980s as unemployment rose and industrial output fell. However, since 1982 the economy has recovered well, with both unemployment and inflation falling rapidly (table 2.4), and US productivity rates improving

Table 2.4   US unemployment and inflation, 1960–1988

	Annual percentage change in the consumer price index	Unemployment (percentage of total civilian workforce)
1960	1.6	5.5
1965	1.7	4.5
1970	5.9	5.0
1975	9.1	8.3
1980	13.5	7.2
1982	6.1	9.7
1984	4.3	7.5
1986	2.0	7.0
1988	4.2[1]	5.3[2]

[1]   To September.   [2]   To October.
Source: OECD *Economic Outlook*, vol. 42, December 1987. For 1988, *The Economist*, 12–18 November 1988.

in relation to other countries', with the notable exception of Japan. But much of the new growth is in the service sector, which has generated mainly low-paid unskilled jobs. By the late 1980s it was broadly accepted that recovery had also been aided by excessive government borrowing and an inflow of foreign capital attracted by high interest rates. As we will discover in later chapters, governments have become increasingly involved in the economy both by attempting to pull broad levers of macro-economic management and through more detailed micro-intervention into the activities of individual sectors, regions and corporations. By 1985, 36.7 per cent of GNP was accounted for by public spending – a very high figure in historical perspective, although, as can

4   See Daniel Bell, *The Coming of Post Industrial Society*, London, Heinemann, 1974, for a discussion of this theme.

Table 2.5   Government outlays as a percentage of GNP: selected countries 1975 and 1985

Country	Total expenditure	
	1975	1985
US	34.6	36.7
Japan	27.3	32.7
Germany	48.9	47.2
France	43.5	52.4
UK	47.5	47.7
Italy	43.2	58.4
Canada	40.1	47.0

Source: OECD, *Economic Outlook*, vol. 42, December 1987.

be seen from table 2.5, a lower figure than for any comparable country, except Japan. So, although government now plays a more intrusive role, the United States remains a country where, in comparative terms, the market and large corporations continue to play the major part in the distribution of resources. However, in the US defence spending takes a high percentage of GNP (and an increasing one since 1980). We will return to these themes in later chapters.

One final point on the economy is that, with the relative decline of American hegemony, the United States has become more interdependent with the economies of other countries. Over 23 per cent of GNP is now accounted for by exports and imports, up from only 10 per cent in 1960. No administration can afford, therefore, to ignore the rest of the world. American governments and corporations have a direct interest in maintaining a stable and prosperous international trading environment. Indeed, the relative decline of American economic power and military influence has put new pressures on US domestic institutional arrangements. Later chapters will examine this problem in some detail.

Social Structure

One of the most fundamental questions in social science is the relationship between social structure and political activity. In most countries social class, religion, language or region are important determinants of how people think and behave in relation to political authority. The purpose of this section is, therefore, to provide some background on American society as a prelude to our later analysis of political attitudes and behaviour.

The study of social class in the USA is often influenced by the absence of a coherent working-class or socialist political movement. Americans are supposed to be essentially middle-class eschewing both the working-class and aristocratic values associated with many European countries. By many objective indicators the United States should, indeed, have a predominantly middle-class culture. In 1985 55 per cent of all workers were in white-collar jobs, of whom over 50 per cent were classified as professional, technical, managerial or administrative. Only 33 per cent of all workers were in blue-collar jobs, with a further 16 per cent in service[5] and farm employment. Americans are also highly educated and enjoy a very high level of home-ownership, two indicators commonly employed to measure social class. In 1983 72 per cent of all 18-year-olds had achieved a high school certificate, and of these approximately 30 per cent went on to complete a four-year undergraduate degree, a very high percentage in cross-national context. As notable are the housing figures, over 60 per cent of all housing units being owner-occupied. Another measure of the middle-class nature of American society is the high level of stock (share) ownership in corporations. No less than 1 in 5 American families owns stock, dramatically more than in most developed countries, although most stockholders own less than $10,000's worth of equity.

Yet some sociologists have questioned these 'objective' indicators, arguing that the relationship between employed and employer is little different for white- and blue-collar workers.[6] Moreover, these figures tell us nothing about the distribution of wealth and income, or about the continuing existence of many truly poor Americans. In fact most measures place the United States at or near the bottom end of income and wealth inequalities, when comparisons across countries are made (figures 2.1 and 2.2). Moreover, calculations by the Urban Institute and the Institute for Research on Poverty have shown that recent tax cuts for the better-off combined with cuts in some of the federal welfare programmes will have the effect of increasing inequality further.[7] Estimating the number of poor people in the USA is difficult. Poverty is a relative concept and it is extraordinarily hard to measure accurately. The *official* measure in 1986 was an annual income of less than $11,000 for a family of four, and the federal government acknowledges that 12

5   This is a narrower category than that implied by service *sector*, and includes workers in catering and domestic service.
6   For a discussion of this point see Ira Katznelson and Mark Kesselman, *The Politics of Power*, New York, Harcourt Brace Jovanovich, 2nd edn, 1979.
7   As reported in Joel Havemann, 'Sharing the wealth: the gap between rich and poor grows wider', in *The National Journal*, vol. 43, 23 October 1982.

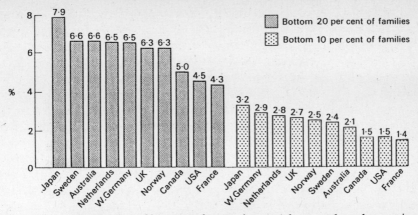

Figure 2.1   Distribution of income: after-tax income shares, selected countries, early and mid-1970s

Figure 2.2   Percentage of wealth held by top 1–2 per cent of total householders, selected countries

Source: Reproduced from Magaziner and Reich, p. 25.
Notes: 1   Derived from estate inventories, 1972.   4   Derived from 1972 data.
2   Derived from income, 1969.   5   Derived from 1975 data.
3   Derived from 1965 data.

per cent of the total population (about 30 million people) could be classified as poor by this measure (table 2.6).

Table 2.6   Percentage of all families below poverty level, 1960–1986

1960	20.7
1965	15.8
1970	10.9
1974	9.9
1978	10.0
1980	11.5
1982	13.6
1984	13.1
1986	12.0

Source: *Poverty in the United States*, 1986, US Department of Commerce, Bureau of the Census, 1988.

As can be seen from table 2.6, the poverty rate declined rapidly during the 1960s and then rose to a peak of over 13 per cent during the recession of the 1980s. With economic recovery it has again declined, but not to the low levels of the early 1970s. No matter which way it is measured one thing is certain: America does have a large population of poor people, not perhaps poor in the sense of living below subsistence level, but certainly poor in the sense of having little hope of full-time, secure employment and access to good housing and an acceptable living environment.

Of course poverty is not randomly scattered throughout the country. Its incidence is highest in the Southern states and in rural and inner-city areas. Blacks, Hispanics and one-parent families headed by women are also greatly over-represented among the poor. Indeed, the Black population is particularly badly off in spite of the enactment and often rigorous enforcement of civil rights laws. As table 2.7 shows, the Black/White/Hispanic differential in income and education, and according to other important measures, is very considerable. Moreover these groups, and especially Blacks, have made little progress in narrowing these differentials over the last 30 years.

Gender forms the basis of further inequalities, with women generally receiving lower pay and having fewer career opportunities than men. As table 2.8 shows, however, American women's participation in the labour force has been increasing more rapidly in the United States than in most comparable countries. Women remain economically subordinate to men, but their position is changing rapidly. As will be shown in later

Table 2.7   Social and economic characteristics of the White, Black and Hispanic populations, 1986

	Total population (%)	White (%)	Black (%)	Hispanic (%)
Years of school completed				
Elementary 0–8	13.3	12.5	19.2	36.8
High school 1–3	11.9	11.3	18.5	14.7
High school 4	38.4	39.0	35.6	28.4
College 1–3 years	16.9	17.1	15.8	11.6
4 years or more	19.4	20.1	10.9	8.4
Employed	60.7	61.5	54.1	58.5
Unemployed	4.6	4.0	9.2	6.9
Female householder with children	9.6	7.3	27.9	16.3
Family income				
less than $10,000	13.3	11.2	30.6	25.3
$10–$25,000	31.0	30.4	36.3	38.3
more than $25,000	55.7	58.5	33.1	36.6

Source: Statistical Abstract of the United States, 1988, table 43.

Table 2.8   Labour force participation rates, by sex, and females as per cent of total labour force, selected countries, 1970–1986

| | Labour force participation rates[1] | | | | | | Females as per cent of total labour force | | |
| | Female | | | Male | | | | | |
Country	1970	1980	1986	1970	1980	1986	1970	1980	1986
United States	50.4	61.3	66.5	90.1	87.8	87.2	36.7	41.9	43.8
Canada	41.1	57.8	64.3	87.1	87.5	86.5	32.2	40.0	42.9
France	47.5	52.5	57.2	86.9	83.4	78.2	36.6	40.1	42.7
Italy	29.1	39.2	42.0	82.0	81.2	77.7	27.1	33.4	35.8
Japan	55.4	54.9	57.4	89.4	89.0	87.5	39.3	38.7	39.8
Sweden	60.6	75.7	80.5	90.6	89.8	87.5	39.5	45.2	47.3
United Kingdom	53.5	61.7	63.5	96.1	91.5	87.3	36.2	40.3	42.0
West Germany	48.1	50.0	51.4	92.5	83.6	79.2	35.9	37.8	39.0

[1]   Labour force of all ages as per cent of population, 15–64 years old.
Source: Statistical Abstract of the US, 1988, table 1402.

chapters, this fact has had important political as well as economic consequences.

In spite of these inequalities, most of which have been characteristics of American society for many generations, class and, to some extent, even race have not emerged as major social cleavages in American politics. True, there have been occasions when at least the embryo of a national working-class or populist movement could be identified. And in particular geographical areas, class-based parties have achieved some considerable success. But their impact has been limited. Compared with the effects of radical movements on the national politics of other countries, it has been slight. Scholars have pondered long and hard as to why this should be so. As later chapters will show, institutional arrangements, particularly federalism and the electoral system militate against minority and radical political parties. Probably more important is the absence of a feudal and aristocratic past, with all the deeply rooted social cleavages which such arrangements imply. Related is what has been called a dominant ideology of equality and liberty, with its promise of unlimited opportunity and social mobility.[8] Certainly the United States has in the main been a remarkably successful country economically. Even by the mid-nineteenth century the American standard of living exceeded that of Britain, then one of the most affluent of the old European powers. Combined with bountiful and cheap land, this must constitute at least part of the explanation for the failure of socialism.

Nonetheless, rapid urbanization and industrialization had their social costs, just as they did in other countries,[9] and the economy has by no means always performed well. During the Great Depression, for example, the level of social distress among both working- and middle-class people was very high, as it is for some social groups in the late 1980s. Given this, many historians and social scientists are obliged to fall back on the explanations based on beliefs, values and ideology, when accounting for the absence of a powerful socialist party, which is a subject we will return to later.

Some scholars have argued that a repressive state (mainly at the state and local levels) in cooperation with repressive private (corporate) power prevented the emergence of a radical trade union and socialist movement during the late nineteenth and early twentieth centuries. But

8   The classic statement of this position is Louis Hartz, *The Liberal Tradition in America*, New York, Harcourt Brace Jovanovich, 1955. See also Seymour Martin Lipset, *The First New Nation*, London, Heinemann, 1964.
9   For a graphic account of conditions in Chicago at the turn of the century see Upton Sinclair, *The Jungle*, New York, New American Library, 1964.

comparisons with equivalent events in Europe appear seriously to weaken this argument. There certainly was repression in the USA, but its character was essentially fragmented, erratic and uncoordinated, compared with what were often quite Draconian and highly centralized measures employed by European governments. The repression argument is convincing as far as the Black population is concerned, however. Until the 1960s, American Blacks suffered from what was effectively an apartheid system in the Southern states, and as already established, even today their socio-economic status remains low. However, although the political behaviour of the Black population is distinctive (as chapter 6 will show), Black separatist or nationalist movements have never achieved any significant success. Along with other ethnic minorities, Blacks have tended to mobilize politically within the context of established institutions and political parties. This is not to deny the importance of an ethnic dimension to politics; within the Democratic party, for example, and at the level of local politics, ethnicity has been and continues to be a significant voting and organizational cue. But the United States has never nurtured an ethnic politics based on separatism or a complete rejection of the dominant 'American' values and political institutions.

Americans are a highly religious people – more so indeed than the populations of most comparable countries (table 2.9). There is also a multiplicity of religions, sects and denominations, and some commentators have argued that religion has been a prime source of the 'creedal passion' associated with various reform movements in American history.[10] Yet in spite of this and the clear links between religion and politics, religion has not constituted a major social division in American society equivalent to the role played by denomination in Ireland, Holland, Belgium or even Germany. Like ethnicity, religious differences are important in the United States but they have, more often than not, been subsumed under a dominant set of peculiarly *American* beliefs, values and institutions.

Region has played a somewhat different role in American history. From the very beginning the South was culturally and economically separate from the rest of the United States, and although a rising sense of national identity strengthened North–South linkages during the 1820–50 period, this was shattered by the Civil War and its aftermath. Only very slowly between 1865 and 1960 was the South reincorporated into the mainstream of American society. The South's distinctiveness was,

10 For a good discussion, see Samuel P. Huntington, *American Politics: The Promise of Disharmony*, Cambridge, Mass., Harvard University Press, 1981, chapters 1, 2, 5 and 6.

Table 2.9   Religious commitments in the 1970s, selected countries (per cent)

	Religious beliefs very important[a]	Believe in God[b]	Believe in life after death[c]
United States	58	94	71
Canada	36	89	54
Italy	36	88	46
Benelux	26	78	48
Australia	25	80	48
United Kingdom	23	76	43
France	22	72	39
West Germany	17	72	33
Scandinavia	17	65	35
Japan	14	44	18

[a]   Question asked: 'How important are your religious beliefs – very important, fairly important, not too important, or not at all important?'
[b]   Question asked: 'Do you believe in God or a universal spirit?'
[c]   Question asked: 'Do you believe in life after death? Do you believe that there is life after death?'
Source: Surveys in 1974–5 by Gallup International Research Institute for non-US countries and in 1978 by the American Institute of Public Opinion (Gallup), Princeton Religion Research Center, and the Gallup Organization, Inc., for the United States. Reported in *Public Opinion* 2 (March/May 1979), pp. 38–9. Reproduced from Huntington, *American Politics: The Promise of Disharmony*, Cambridge, Mass., Harvard University Press, 1981, p. 156. Reprinted by permission.

of course, based on its slave and later segregationist economy which produced a system of social stratification with no parallel in the rest of the country.[11] It was also a one-party region dominated by racist and often corrupt local and state Democratic parties. But the South was different in other ways. Until the post-1945 period it was predominantly rural and poor. Immigrants avoided the region; industrial and infrastructure investment was sparse; change came only slowly. Not until what had effectively become an economic and social backwater was jolted by the rapid economic growth of the 1950s and 1960s and by an increasingly strident civil rights movement, did Southern society begin to change. Since 1960, in fact, many Southern states have been transformed by migration, urbanization and economic growth. To the casual visitor many parts of the South are today indistinguishable from the rest of the country. Democratic party hegemony has broken down, although, the Black population apart, the region remains essentially conservative. But old style Southern society has by no means disappeared, especially

11   The best characterization of Southern society remains W. J. Cash, *The Mind of the South*, Harmondsworth, Middlesex, Penguin, 1973, p. 19.

in the poorer, less developed states (notably Arkansas, Mississippi and Alabama). Racism still exists, as does a peculiarly 'unamerican' resistance to change. But the South can no longer lay claim to the very special and separate status which for so long distinguished it from the rest of the country.

Beliefs and Values:
Dominant Ideology or Political Culture?

One of the most enduring debates in social science concerns the relationship between the public's beliefs and values and political authority. Liberal scholars label these beliefs 'political culture', or 'a historical system of widespread, fundamental, behavioural, political values actually held by system members (the public)'.[12] Political culture therefore embraces the dominant pattern of beliefs and values, which are acquired and modify and change as a result of a complex process of socialization and feedback from the political system. In other words, individual citizens acquire attitudes towards politics through learning from parents and their environments (socialization), and these adapt and change as political authorities produce particular responses or policies over time (feedback). Political culture is made up of the sum of individual beliefs and values and, crucially, it is essentially *independent* of political authority. In some systems it may be incompatible with prevailing political institutions – as in pre-revolutionary Mexico or Weimar Germany – in which case regime change occurs. In other systems, the political culture supports and succours the political system. Liberal scholars invariably label the American system thus. Politics and political culture may change in the USA, but they tend to be mutually supportive. Regime change is extremely unlikely in such a situation.

Advocates of the 'dominant ideology' position take a quite different stance. To them public beliefs and values are imposed from above by those in positions of power. Beliefs constitute an *ideology*, therefore, whose function is to legitimate the prevailing system of political authority and economic organization. This radical, often Marxist perspective, identifies the United States as a country where the dominant ideology is particularly powerful:

The dominant ideology is more powerful in the United States than

12   Donald J. Devine, *The Political Culture of the United States*, Boston, Little, Brown, 1972, p. 17.

in any other capitalist democracy. Most political debates in the
United States take place within the framework of this ideology, a
situation related to the absence of a broadly based working class
movement pressing for fundamental change. So powerful is the
dominant ideology in this country that existing economic and
political arrangements frequently appear not merely as the best
possible arrangements but as the only possible ones.[13]

These two apparently incompatible positions are not as far apart as
they may seem, for when American beliefs are examined, both liberals
and radicals accept the importance of similar public attitudes and
values. Samuel Huntington has summed these up as 'liberty, equality,
individualism, democracy and the rule of law under a constitution'.[14]
Unfortunately we do not have the space in this chapter to do complete
justice to what exactly these values mean in the American context, but
we can summarize what is a very large body of research as follows:

Liberty

Survey research from the 1950s and early 1960s found a high level of
support among Americans in favour of *general* statements of free speech
and opinion (for example, 'people who hate our way of life should still
have a chance to talk and be heard'), but much lower support for *specific*
statements (for example, 'a book that contains wrong political views
cannot be a good book and does not deserve to be published').[15]
Moreover, the level of support for specific freedoms was much higher
among elites (political influentials) than among the mass public. This
disjunction between general and specific support is not exclusively
American; citizens of many countries would answer positively to general
statements advocating freedom. Clearly freedom of expression is not
an absolute value, and there have been times in American history when
public tolerance of 'unamerican' values has been very low. The red-
baiting periods following the First and Second World Wars demonstrated
just how limited freedom could be in the United States.[16] And until the

13 Katznelson and Kesselman, *The Politics of Power*, p. 29.
14 Huntington, *American Politics*, p. 14.
15 More than 80 per cent of respondents to a 1962 survey agreed with the first question,
and just 50 per cent with the second, Herbert McCloskey, 'Consensus and ideology in
American politics', *American Political Science Review*, vol. 8 (1964), tables 2 and 3. This
article also contains a good summary of the literature on this subject.
16 See Seymour Martin Lipset and Earl Raab, *The Politics of Unreason: Right Wing
Extremism in America, 1790–1970*, Chicago, University of Chicago Press, 1978.

mid-1960s the attitude of white Americans in the South towards the Black population was the very antithesis of libertarian.

Since the 1960s, however, there is evidence of some important changes. Racial tolerance has generally improved, and attitudes towards 'unamerican' beliefs (communism, atheism) have become more liberal (table 2.10).

Table 2.10 Changing American attitudes towards conformity

Percentage who say	Attitudes towards (%)			
	Communists		Atheists	
	1954	1972–3	1954	1972–3
Should be allowed to speak in our community	28	57	38	66
Book should not be removed from public library	29	58	37	71
Should be allowed to teach in college or university	6	38	12	42

Source: James A. Davis, 'Communism, conformity, cohorts and categories: American tolerance in 1954 and 1972–3', *American Journal of Sociology*, vol. 81, November 1975, p. 506.

In spite of these changes, antipathy to 'non-American' values clearly remains, so it would be quite misleading to characterize the United States as a country where 'freedom of expression' or 'liberty' is assigned an inviolate status.

Three final qualifications need to be added to this conclusion, which should serve as a warning against simple over-generalizations in this area. First, as later chapters will show, there have been quite dramatic advances in the legal protection of all individual rights, and especially freedom of expression over the last 30 years. Not all these advances have been simply procedural; objectively American citizens, newspapers, and other media enjoy much more freedom than they used to. As this development can often cause governments and officials serious difficulty and embarrassment, it seems to contradict the more reductionist of the 'dominant ideology' positions. Second, the American political system is uncommonly fragmented and devolved. Some of the worst examples of the infringement of individual freedom have occurred within *local* jurisdictions with the open acquiescence of local populations. This applies particularly to racial questions and criminal procedural rights. As society has become nationalized, so such activity has become more difficult to get away with. Although this development could be interpreted as part of the advance of a 'dominant ideology', it is difficult to make the connection between less repressive local polities and the particular interests of national political authorities or corporations. Third, if we expand liberty or freedom to include economic individualism or the freedom to accumulate wealth, then there is no doubting that the United States is a free country. We will return to this theme later.

Equality

Early foreign observers of the American scene, from de Tocqueville to Dickens and Bryce, noted the remarkable absence of deference to position or status in the United States. 'Equality of estimation' is what Bryce called it, or the tendency of Americans to treat each other as equals, whatever their education, occupation or social class. This remains broadly true – although, of course, European countries have been moving in the same direction. 'Equality' was one of the earliest rallying cries of Revolutionary America, but from the very beginning it implied an equality of opportunity rather than equality of condition. The argument ran something like this: provide equal status for all citizens (except slaves, of course) under the law and every individual would be capable of achieving self fulfilment. As the country developed, so it became accepted that the pre-condition for equality of opportunity was a certain standard of education. Consequently, education achieved – and retains – a very special status in American social policy. Almost alone among the major social services, there is a broad consensus that education should be provided out of public rather than private funds.

Supporters of the dominant ideology position claim that the constant stress on equality of opportunity helps legitimize what is a very unequal society. Originally the emphasis was on the frontier and unlimited land. More recently the appeal has shifted to education and all the benefits this can bring. By constantly reassuring the population that everyone can succeed given personal effort and a good educational base, the citizenry are, so the argument runs, being duped into accepting the system. No doubt there is something to this – certainly Americans continue to believe that their economic position (or the position of their children) will improve[17] – but such a perspective fails to distinguish between equality before the law and the material or economic benefits

17 For example, in a 1982 poll 51 per cent believed their children would be better off than themselves, only 36 per cent thought they would be worse off; 70 per cent of the respondents considered themselves better off than their parents. If anything, Blacks were more optimistic than Whites, *Public Opinion*, vol. 5, no. 3, June/July 1982, pp. 24–5.

which equality of opportunity can bring. The former, which is close to equality of dignity or esteem, is highly developed in the United States and recognized as an important element in citizenship. Legislation designed to prevent unfair or unequal treatment by private and public authorities is far-reaching and, compared with similar laws in other countries, is quite rigidly enforced. In recent years discrimination against women and racial minorities has been the main focus of these laws, but the idea that all citizens, irrespective of background, should be treated equally is deeply entrenched.

Individualism

Nothing more accurately seems to represent Americanism than a stress on individual rather than collective action. Trade union membership is low in the USA, collectivist political parties of the left (and also of the right) have failed to win mass support, and the society is infused with a degree of self reliance which is rarely found in other countries. This spirit of self reliance has its roots in the puritanism which flourished in both colonial and post-colonial America, and it remains a potent force as public antipathy to 'welfare scroungers' and a surprisingly wide acceptance of job insecurity shows. So, as far as distribution of resources is concerned, Americans prefer private to public institutions. Indeed, the 'state' as such is held in quite low esteem compared with its status

Table 2.11   Individual freedom v. duty to the state

The individual owes his first duty to the state and only secondary to his personal welfare (1960) (per cent)

	USA	UK	West Germany	Italy	Mexico
Agree	25	38	41	48	92
Disagree	68	55	45	32	5
Don't know, etc.	7	7	14	20	3

Source: ICPR, reproduced from Donald J. Devine, *The Political Culture of the United States*, Boston, Little, Brown, 1972, p. 93.

in other countries (table 2.11). Unfortunately social surveys have tended not to ask more sophisticated questions in cross-national context, so one must be wary of inferring that Americans are always antipathetic to state-provided goods and services. If anything, the evidence suggests that when the question is couched in general terms, Americans show antipathy to government provision, but when asked about specific programmes such as social security, health care or education, they show a high level of support.[18] Perhaps this is not unsurprising given the much more visible role that governments, and especially the federal government, now play in economy and society.

America's anti-statist tradition has a number of roots, and there is no time for an extensive discussion here. We should note, however, that this liberal tradition has at least in part depended on the continuing success of capitalism. From beginnings where self reliance and economic individualism were the very essence of the new society (a point to be developed in chapter 3), capitalism flourished as in no other country, and not until the 1930s did it need sustained support from government. Industrialization, infrastructure development and urbanization were predominantly market phenomena. Of course government played a role, but mainly in response to the needs of capitalism, not as a leader and director of investment and resources. Even today when government intrudes into almost every aspect of society, it is treated with suspicion by many Americans. Again, it is very difficult to separate out the extent to which economic individualism has been 'imposed' on the American people by the needs of capitalism, from broader historical/cultural forces such as the absence of a feudal tradition and the fact that many Americans have benefited from economic development.

One final point on individualism. Some observers make the mistake of inferring a general *cultural* individualism when noting the undoubted prevalence of *economic* individualism in the United States. Yet as our discussion of freedom and references to religion suggest, Americans are often influenced by collectivist thinking. Whether it be McCarthyism, fundamentalist Christianity or a sometimes violent rejection of outsiders from carefully protected local communities, there is no shortage of examples of Americans moving, sometimes blindly, in masses. By this measure the society is almost certainly less individualist than British or French society, although, to repeat the point, collectivist action of this sort usually embraces only a small section of American society at any one time, or occurs at the local rather than national level.

Democracy and the rule of law

If democracy is defined in terms of a simple devotion to *majoritarianism*

18   See the *General Social Surveys, 1972–80*, Cumulative Codebook, National Research Center, University of Chicago, 1980, Questions 62–5, and 213–15 for details.

then there is no doubting that Americans believe in it. Majority opinion carries a weight and independent value in the US which is unusual elsewhere. This translates not only into a broad acceptance of the legitimacy of elections and, at the state and local levels, referenda. It also means that on occasion ill-judged policies and programmes have been adopted following a surge of (often populist) moral fervour. Such was the case with prohibition and, arguably, some of the tax cutting measures of the 1978–81 period.[19]

As far as general political arrangements are concerned, American attitudes present us with something of a paradox, for they combine strong support for the Constitution and the system as such with considerable disillusionment with particular processes and institutions. One of the first and most impressive of the political culture studies discovered that Americans were overwhelmingly supportive of the political system and Constitution compared with other countries.[20] True, this survey dates from the early 1960s when people were generally more optimistic about society, but there is still evidence that Americans believe their system to be basically sound (few want to emigrate, most greatly admire the Constitutional framework). However, since the mid-1960s, increasing numbers of people have become disillusioned with the party system, the Presidency, Congress and the federal bureaucracy.

As can be seen from figure 2.3, confidence in government reached a low by 1980 following the events of Vietnam, Watergate and the Iranian hostage crisis. With the Reagan presidency, some confidence returned – but not to the levels of the 1960s. But too much can be read into these figures. Citizens may be disillusioned with particular institutions, governments or politicians, but they are not *alienated* from the system in a way which threatens the regime.[21] The institutions and processes which succour American democracy and the rule of law are highly respected. If anything, recent evidence of declining trust in government reflects an increasing sophistication among voters who are now making more conscious connections between what parties and politicians promise and how they perform. Chapter 6 will deal with this point in some detail.

19   Starting with California's Proposition 13, many states and localities passed laws limiting property, sales and income taxes during this period. By 1982, however, these same laws were considered by many to be contributing to state and local fiscal problems or to low quality public services.
20   Eighty-two per cent of respondents said they were proud of their constitution and governmental system, compared with 46 per cent of the British, 7 per cent of West Germans and 3 per cent of Italians, Gabriel A. Almond and Sidney Verba, *The Civic Culture: Political Attitudes and Democracy in Five Nations*, Boston, Little, Brown, 1965, table 1, p. 102.
21   See Jack Citrin, 'The political relevance of trust in government', *American Political Science Review*, vol. 68, September 1974, for a discussion of this point.

Figure 2.3   Distrust of government in the United States, 1952–1984

Source: Reproduced from Gabriel A. Almond and G. Bingham Powell, Jr., *Comparative Politics Today: A World View*, Glenview, Illinois, and London, Scott Foresman, 1988, figure 3.3.

Claims that the system is essentially stable appear to be supported by the relative absence of regime-challenging parties and protest movements in American history. The Civil War apart, most protest activity has been inspired by single issues (civil rights, the Vietnam War) or has been accommodated within existing parties and institutions.[22] Radical critics are quick to point out that this is because truly revolutionary movements have been nipped in the bud by an unholy alliance of corporations and government. But much more repressive tactics have been employed in other countries to no avail. Why should much less extensive measures have been so successful in America?

More convincing perhaps is the claim that, unable to mobilize politically against the dominant ideology, increasing numbers of Americans have turned to anomic violence and anti-social behaviour. There can be no doubting that America is a violent society (more than 17,000 people were murdered in 1985 alone) but it is extraordinarily difficult to make clear causal connections between this sort of pathology and political values and institutions. Violence and crime have always been a part of what was for many generations a frontier society. What we can conclude is that until the 1960s (and possibly beyond), violence and

22   See Alec Barbrook and Christine Bolt, *Power and Protest in American Life*, Oxford, Martin Robinson, 1980.

intimidation in the South were part of a Southern social structure built on racism and exploitation. Obviously this was as much a political as social or economic phenomenon. As significant is the increasing incidence of random violence and serious crime among the racial and ethnic minorities of America's inner cities. It seems absurd to argue that these people are not politically excluded, isolated and socially alienated. If the dominant ideology thesis carries any conviction, it does so with respect to the inner-city poor. For them, the optimism, materialism, and egalitarianism which continue to dominate political discourse and which are encouraged by the highly commercial media, must seem either an irrelevance or must serve as a diversion from their plight.

We can conclude that both the dominant ideology and political culture perspectives carry some conviction. But the dominant ideology view is, with the possible exception of its effects on the new poor of America's cities, difficult to demonstrate as valid, while the political culture approach tends to understate the extent to which those in positions of political power can manipulate the mass public. Few dispute, however, that there is such a thing as the 'American creed' or 'American ideology', and that it has been uniquely effective in overpowering other systems of beliefs and values. Samuel Huntington has made this point well:

It is possible to speak of a body of political ideas that constitutes 'Americanism' in a sense which one can never speak of 'Britishism', 'Frenchism', 'Germanism' or 'Japanesism'. Americanism in this sense is comparable to other ideologies or religions. 'Americanism is to the American', Leon Samson has said, 'not a tradition or a territory, not what France is to a Frenchman or England to an Englishman, but a doctrine – what socialism is to a socialist'. To reject the central ideas of that doctrine is to be un-American. There is no British Creed or French Creed; the Académie Française worries about the purity of the French language, not about the purity of French political ideas. What indeed would be an 'un-French' political idea? But pre-occupation with 'un-American' political ideas and behavior has been a recurring theme in American life. 'It has been our fate as a nation', Richard Hofstadter succinctly observed, 'not to have ideologies but to be one'.[23]

23 Huntington, *American Politics*, p. 25.

Further Reading

For a truly comprehensive statistical background, see the annual *Statistical Abstract of the United States*, US Department of Commerce, Bureau of the Census. A good summary of the dominant ideological position is presented in Ira Katznelson and Mark Kesselman, *The Politics of Power*, New York, Harcourt Brace Jovanovich, 2nd edition, 1979. For a political culture perspective see Donald J. Devine, *The Political Culture of the United States*, Boston, Little, Brown, 1972. For a comparative perspective on the political culture view see Gabriel A. Almond and G. Bingham Powell, Jr., *Comparative Politics Today: A World View*, Glenview, Illinois, and London, Scott Foresman, 1988. The classic statement of the liberal view is Louis Hartz, *The Liberal Tradition in America*, New York, Harcourt Brace, 1955. Two stimulating critiques of recent developments in American society and economy, one written from a radical and the other from a conservative perspective, are Thomas Ferguson and Joel Rogers, *Right Turn: The Decline of the Democrats and the Future of American Politics*, New York, Hill and Wang, 1986; and Samuel P. Huntington, *American Politics: The Promise of Disharmony*, Cambridge, Mass., Harvard University Press, 1981.

3

Constitutional Government

The American Constitution is the most wonderful work ever struck off at a given time by the brain and purpose of man.

W. E. Gladstone

Good government should be sufficiently neutral between the different interests and factions to control one part of the society from invading the rights of another, and at the same time sufficiently controlled itself, from setting up an interest adverse to that of the whole society.

James Madison

Almost all governments pay formal allegiance to a written or (more rarely) unwritten constitution, but in few countries is the constitution a real and continuing constraint on the exercise of power. Even more rarely do constitutions survive political and social changes, invasions and wars. The American Constitution is unusual, both because it has remained almost unaltered since its ratification in 1789, and because it continues as a major source of authority in the political system. Indeed, even the most cursory examination of America's basic political institutions – Congress, Presidency, federalism, the electoral system – instantly shows the influence of the Constitution. To the foreign observer, the apparent resilience of the Constitution and constitutionalism is one of the most remarkable features of American politics, and one which requires some explanation. Among the most important questions raised by this phenomenon are: Why has the Constitution been amended so little through history? Has it been a major contributor to political and social stability? What real influence does it have today? In particular, does it remain an independent source of political power, or has it simply been interpreted in a way which reflects a pattern of political and economic power which would in any case have prevailed?

Before we tackle these questions it is necessary to approach the crucial issue of why the Constitution took the shape that it did.

Origins

Most dramatic regime changes following a revolution or war are quite easy to explain. France in 1789 was seething with discontent at a corrupt and insensitive monarchy. Russia in 1917 was long overdue for a revolution to sweep away an archaic, semi-feudal order. And the numerous colonial wars of independence in the post-1945 period were predictable, given the rapid political and economic changes which the Second World War had precipitated. The American Revolution fails to fit any of these neat stereotypes, however. In fact, by some definitions it was not a revolution at all. Many of the citizens of the 13 colonies considered themselves 'true born Englishmen' who, being increasingly denied the rights which they thought all free English deserved to enjoy, were entitled to challenge the 'illegitimate' exercise of power by George III. They saw their task, therefore, as one of asserting independence from a regime which had betrayed its own principles. Moreover, unlike most revolutionary wars, the War of Independence and the eventual emergence of a new constitutional system had few immediate consequences for the distribution of wealth, power and status. If anything, it reinforced trends already underway. It was essentially a conservative revolution which, in marked contrast to parallel events in France, did not lead to new class divisions in society. This is not to say that radical or revolutionary elements were absent. They were very much present, but the real power remained in the hands of a solid middle-class and professional property-owning elite.

The unusual nature of these events stems from the unique characteristics of American colonial society. From the very beginning, the British Americans had displayed a marked degree of independence and self-sufficiency. In the 13 colonies, and especially in New England, the local community became virtually the only meaningful level of government – and even then government is far too strong and modern a label to attach to what were remarkably successful self-governing entities. Sam Bass Warner has captured the spirit of these seventeenth-century communities very well:

> For a generation or two, medieval English village traditions fused with a religious ideology to create a consensus concerning the religious, social, economic and political framework for a good life.

Each of several hundred villages repeated a basic pattern. No Royal statute, no masterplan, no strong legislative controls, no central administrative officers, no sheriffs or justices of the peace, no synods or prelates, none of the apparatus typical of government then or now.[1]

Although such communities were partly transformed by economic development and population increases during the eighteenth century, the essential independence of the colonies continued to be expressed through local governments and, later, colonial assemblies whose activities were largely tolerated by Crown appointed governors. Admittedly, considerable variation existed between different colonies – and particularly between the plantation and slave economy of the South, and the more diverse agrarian and mercantilist economy of the North – but each colony respected the independence of the other.

This description implies a colonial rule which was essentially distant and benign, and such indeed was the case until the 1760s when the English, acting under a monarch determined to assert his power over increasingly corrupt and strident Whig interests at home, decided to exercise much greater control over the colonists. All goods imported to the colonies had to pass through British ports, a tax (stamp duty) was imposed on all legal documents and newspapers, a revenue tax was levied, and colonial assemblies were prohibited from issuing their own paper currency. These economic restrictions were viewed by the colonial elites as an outrageous infringement of basic rights. During the eighteenth century the idea that men possessed certain inalienable rights spread rapidly under the influence of the social contract theorists (Locke, Rousseau) and pamphleteers (Thomas Paine), and became particularly popular in a colonial America infused with a spirit of liberty and independence. Life, liberty and property were rights which governments were obliged to protect through the representation of the people in parliaments and assemblies. And should those assemblies fail to fulfil their contractual obligations to the people, then elections would ensure the incumbency of new representatives charged with carrying out the people's wishes. A monarch exercising executive power outside any representative mechanism was clearly not legitimate.

While this rather sophisticated view of events was probably held only by educated elites, the smallholders and artisans who made up the bulk of the population did have some notion of individual rights and were, by any European standard, highly independent and assertive. Indeed,

1 Sam Bass Warner, *The Urban Wilderness: A History of the American City*, New York, Harper and Row, 1972, p. 8.

for more than 100 years up to the Revolution, acts of political (usually mob) violence were quite common, as they were in England. Most people with some stake in society – a farm or other property, or a valuable manual or intellectual skill – were quite used to resorting to extra-legal methods should their grievances be ignored by established political channels.[2] Given this tradition, a growing sense of being 'American' which economic growth and better communications had brought, and the sudden change in English policy, outbreaks of armed resistance were almost to be expected. In 1774 the colonial assemblies sent delegates to a national Continental Congress – the first real assertion of national independence by the colonists. By 1775 fighting had broken out in Massachusetts, and in 1776 the Continental Congress adopted the Declaration of Independence which, with stirring rhetoric, marked the true beginnings of the United States:

> We hold these truths to be self-evident, that all men are created equal, that they are endowed by their Creator with certain unalienable rights, that among these are life, liberty, and the pursuit of happiness; that to secure these rights, governments are instituted among men, deriving their just powers from the consent of the governed; that whenever any form of government becomes destructive of these ends, it is the right of the people to alter or to abolish it, and to institute new government, laying its foundation on such principles, and organizing its powers in such form, as to them shall seem most likely to effect their safety and happiness.

For the next five years, the colonists successfully fought their revolutionary war against the British, and in 1781 established a new system of government under the Articles of Confederation. In effect this – the first American Constitution – was little more than a formal recognition of the Continental Congress. A congress was created, but no executive or judiciary. The new government was very much a confederation: individual states retained considerable autonomy giving to the Congress only limited powers – namely to declare wars, establish treaties, regulate weights and measures, oversee Indian affairs, run a post office and establish an army and navy. Crucially, no mandatory power to raise taxes was established. Instead, Congress had to rely on voluntary subventions from the state legislatures. Also, each state could issue its own paper money and generally regulate commerce within its boundaries.

2   See John C. Wahlke (ed.), *The Causes of the American Revolution*, Lexington, Mass., D. C. Heath, 1973.

Such a weak, leaderless system of government could not last long, especially in the face of a number of very urgent problems confronting the new nation. Revenue needed to be raised nationally to provide a common defence. Some central control of the currency and the enforcement of contracts needed to be created, and a common external tariff was needed to protect American goods from cheap British imports. Moreover, the war had widened the gulf between the better-off who had lent money to finance the fighting and a growing debtor class who had mortgaged small farms and houses to raise incomes in the face of economic dislocation. In 1786 a small rebellion had broken out in Massachusetts, a state where the law on debtors was particularly harsh, when Daniel Shays led over 1000 men to block the proceedings of the state's high court.

Although quickly put down, Shays's rebellion served to remind the better-off that the new Congress was ill-equipped to provide some degree of national economic security and uniformity. Prior to the rebellion a number of attempts had been made to strengthen Congress, and a convention to discuss trade problems had met at Annapolis, Maryland, in 1786. Although only five states attended, a resolution to meet in Philadelphia with the more ambitious aim of constitutional revision had been agreed at the convention. Shays made such a meeting that much more imperative, and during the summer of 1787, 55 delegates assembled in Philadelphia charged with the momentous task of producing new constitutional arrangements for the United States.

The American Constitution

While the 55 delegates – the Founding Fathers – were obviously not operating in the absence of political and economic constraints, they were able genuinely to combine normative judgements on what best would make for a good system, with provisions imposed on them by political necessity. They were not, in other words, engaged in the exercise of naked political power. Nor were they obsessed with retributive measures against past masters. And unlike many twentieth-century harbingers of regime change, their actions were not informed by a single, closed ideology. Instead, they could afford to compromise, to show pragmatism and to draw on a number of political theories and constitutional arrangements at that time commonly discussed by the educated and liberal-minded.

The Founding Fathers were certainly educated, about one half having college degrees – a very high proportion for that time. They were also established (and comparatively young) men of property and status – merchants, lawyers, planters, doctors, intellectuals. George Washington presided over the meetings, although he played virtually no role in the proceedings. Inviting Washington – who came only reluctantly – was a clever ploy, as he was the one figure almost universally respected in the new nation. The real driving forces behind the convention and its proceedings were James Madison of Virginia, a brilliant young politician who had helped to write Virginia's constitution, and Alexander Hamilton from New York, one-time aide to Washington during the war, who had helped set up the Annapolis convention.

As delegates from the state legislatures, the Founding Fathers were not directly elected by the people – indeed one state, Rhode Island, was not even represented, dominated as it was by a disgruntled debtor class. In one curious respect, this lack of a universal popular mandate gave them some extra freedom, for, meeting in secret, they could eventually produce a document as a *fait accompli* and then lobby hard for its acceptance by the states. As we will see, this in effect is precisely what they did.

What were the main influences on the Framers? Four main ideas stand out: social contract theory, representation, the separation of powers and federalism. We have already mentioned the idea of the social contract, with its provision of obligation on both governed and governors. Although central to the thinking of Hobbes and Rousseau, it was Locke's vision of the social contract which most influenced the Founders. To Hobbes, the contract was a very one-sided affair where the people traded their freedom for the security which a strong state would bring. Rousseau's contract was far more idealized and democratic, involving as it did the identification and implementation of the general will of the people. Locke, in contrast, made *representation* the central canon of his ideal society. Citizens, or those with a stake in society, men of property, were entitled to a government which would champion their natural rights. Through representative institutions – free elections and assemblies – the people could hold the rulers accountable for their actions. Obedience to the law (the people's side of the contract) was, therefore, conditional on the government fulfilling its side of the contract – the guarantee of life, liberty, and property.

Representative government carries with it other notions, notably majority rule and the implication that there are clear limits to democracy. Both were accepted by the Founding Fathers, and their limits on democracy were, by modern standards, quite severe. Only the lower house of the legislature, the House of Representatives, was to be elected directly by the people (Article 1, Section 2).[3] Senators were to be nominated by the state legislatures (Article 1, Section 3), and the President was to be elected by an electoral college, the members of which were to be appointed by the state legislatures (Article 2, Section 1). The Framers' very limited acceptance of democracy reflected their fear of unbridled majority rule. If the people could vote for all the main officers directly, it raised the spectre of an insensitive – and possibly tyrannical – permanent majority capable of riding roughshod over the minority. As Thomas Jefferson had noted some years before the convention, 'an elective despotism was not the government we fought for.'[4] Note also that the electoral qualifications of those who could vote for the House of Representatives were to be determined by the state legislatures (Article 1, Section 2). In most cases this meant a very limited suffrage consisting of property-owning males. None of this was incompatible with popular sovereignty or a republican form of government. Sovereignty resided in the people (albeit a minority of them) not in a monarch or emperor. And this, together with the majoritarian provisions in the Constitution, guaranteed a republican system.

The Framers were not only worried about the possibility of tyranny by the majority; they were also aware of the dangers of concentrating too much power in any one institution. A powerful executive suggested monarchial or despotic leadership. A powerful legislature carried with it the possibility of rule by an insensitive majority. A device existed to overcome these dangers – the separation of powers. Borrowing in part from the ideas of the French philosopher Baron de Montesquieu, who greatly admired what he thought was a division of powers in the English system, the Framers went about a deliberate separation of authority between legislature, executive and judiciary. Congress was accordingly given a separate power base (or constituency) from the Presidency, and although the judiciary was not given the quite awesome power of judicial view it was later to assume, Supreme Court and other federal judges were to be appointed by the President. However, the precise jurisdiction of the courts, as well as the final say on the appointment of judges, were accorded to Congress (Article 3).

To ensure a division of power between the major institutions, a system of *checks and balances* was introduced. So both houses of the legislature had to approve a bill, but the President could exercise a veto

3 The full text of the Constitution is given in Appendix 1, pp. 300–25.
4 Quoted in T. Mason (ed.), *Free Government in the Making*, New York, Oxford University Press, 3rd edn, 1965, p. 165.

over it. The Senate and House of Representatives could, in turn,
override a veto if two thirds of the members of both houses voted for it
(Article 1, Section 7). Congress was also given some control over
executive appointments, which had to be filled with the 'advice and
consent' of the Senate (Article 2, Section 2). These checks and balances
should not imply an *equality* of power and authority between the
institutions. There is no doubt that the Framers intended the Congress,
and in particular the House of Representatives, to be the key *source* of
policy. This is clear from Article 1, Section 8, which enumerates the
powers of Congress. As these included fiscal, monetary and regulatory
powers, as well as the authority to raise armies and declare war, they
were, in contemporary terms, quite comprehensive. Significantly, the
directly elected chamber, the House of Representatives, was given
special responsibility for revenue bills (Article 1, Section 7) thus reflecting the popular demand ('no taxation without representation') that the
'people's branch' should be directly accountable to the voters on taxation
matters.

Executive and judicial branches were, in contrast, given few specific
powers, although the dictum that the 'executive power shall be vested
in a President,' (Article 2, Section 1) leaves open the question of where
executive power begins and ends. Congress was, then, expected to be
the source of most legislation, but its power would be checked both
internally (via bicameralism) and by the President. These checks are
essentially negative in nature, suggesting that the Framers had a greater
fear of the abuse of power than an inability to exercise it. We have
already mentioned the fear of democracy, majority rule, and a despotic
executive. In addition some of the Framers were deeply suspicious of
the machinations of groups, parties or 'factions'. James Madison, in
particular, feared that government might become the creature of some
class or special interest. He eloquently outlined his position in *The
Federalist*:[5]

> Among the numerous advantages promised by a well constructed
> Union, none deserves to be more accurately developed than its
> tendency to break and control the violence of faction . . . By a
> faction, I understand a number of citizens, whether amounting to
> a majority or minority of the whole, who are united and actuated
> by some common impulse of passion, or of interest, adverse to the

5 *The Federalist* papers written mainly by Madison and Hamilton were published after
the convention as a tract to persuade some of the states to accept the Constitution. They
are a remarkable collection of essays which reflect some of the most crucial debates of
the convention.

rights of other citizens, or to the permanent and aggregate interests of the community. There are two methods of curing the mischief of faction: The one, by removing its causes; the other by controlling its effects. There are again two methods of removing the causes of faction: the one, by destroying the liberty which is essential to its existence; the other by giving to every citizen the same opinions, the same passions and the same interests.[6]

Madison is in no doubt that the only solution is to control the effects of faction. Liberty is essential and where it exists factions will exist, and giving an equal voice to every citizen can be achieved only in a democracy. Democracy is impractical and dangerous except in very small communities. This leaves the control of faction to a republican form of government, or the sort of representative system with a limited suffrage, some indirect elections, a separation of powers and the operation of checks and balances, which was eventually adopted.

The convention was no means united on basic constitutional arrangements. Alexander Hamilton feared that without a strong executive, few of the nation's pressing problems would be solved. Madison, in contrast, feared both a strong executive and an overbearing legislature. More generally, the larger states (Virginia, Massachusetts, Pennsylvania) favoured a strong central government (whether dominated by Congress or not) while the smaller states, fearing an encroachment by the more populous areas, favoured more decentralized arrangements. In fact, debates on federalism and the delineation of powers between centre and periphery were among the most acrimonious at the convention. For in addition to the small/large state dichotomy, there was the thorny problem of the very different interests represented by the Southern as opposed to the Northern states. Following intense debate between those wanting a strong federal government (the so-called Virginia Plan) and those demanding decentralized power (the New Jersey Plan), a compromise was reached by giving the Senate a representative base founded on territory rather than population (two Senators from each state, Article 1, Section 3). The House was to be elected on a population basis and (a further compromise) given special powers over federal revenues.

The distinctive economy and culture of the South posed a potentially even greater problem and was eventually resolved only by the unsavoury expedient of counting slaves as three-fifths of a free person for the purpose of representation in the House and in distributing federal taxes.

6 *The Federalist*, no. 10, in *The Federalist Papers*, New York, Mentor Books, 1961, pp. 77–8.

Of course this did not mean that slaves played any part in the political process. They did not. Many Northern delegates disliked this compromise, but accepted it knowing that the South would not tolerate any serious incursion into its slave-based economy. The South was also an exporter of cotton and other agricultural produce and had much less interest in the protectionist policies which Northern politicians favoured. To safeguard their position, Southerners demanded that a two-thirds majority be required to ratify treaties in the Senate. In this way, it was hoped that trade agreements favouring the North would be avoided.

These controversies over the status of the South and large versus small states should not obscure the fact that the Framers were obliged to create some sort of federal system. After all, the convention was made up of representatives of the states, and the war had been waged against a strong central government. A unitary system in the style of England was completely unacceptable to most delegates. What eventually transpired was a highly flexible federalism. Indeed, reading the Constitution it is not at all clear where federal power begins and ends, which gives at least great potential power to the centre.

The genius of the Constitution was that although it was the first written constitution ever to be adopted by a country, and although it propounded the virtues of a republican form of government – a radical idea, indeed, in the late eighteenth century – it remained intrinsically *conservative* in content and implication. The Founders, and particularly the most influential and able of them, Madison and Hamilton, were hardly social visionaries. Instead their hopes for the New Country were tinged with caution and not a little pessimism about man's greed and selfishness. As Madison put it:

> As there is a degree of depravity in mankind which requires a certain degree of circumspection and distrust, so there are other qualities in human nature which justify a certain portion of esteem and confidence.[7]

As with most educated eighteenth-century men, the essentially inegalitarian view that there are worthy and unworthy, talented and talentless, wise and stupid men in the populace, prevailed. The President was to be elected by an electoral college made up, it was hoped, of wise, educated and established citizens, free from the rabble-rousing and instant judgements which democratic processes inspired. Senators too, were expected to be elder statesmen elected by their peers for a leisurely six years and able, therefore, to hold in line a potentially capricious and

7 *The Federalist*, no. 55, p. 346.

unruly lower house. What the Framers hoped for, therefore, was firm, cautious and responsible government. The Constitution was designed to provide the basic framework for such a system of stable and limited political power. It was also intended to stand the test of time – an objective which was greatly aided by a cumbersome amendment process. Amendments have to be proposed by a two-thirds vote in both houses of Congress and then ratified by three-quarters of the state legislatures or by a ratifying convention in two-thirds of the states. Alternatively a national convention at the behest of two-thirds of the state legislatures can propose an amendment which in turn can be ratified by Congress or by a ratifying convention (Article 5). The first method (Congress proposing, the state legislatures ratifying) has become the normal amending mechanism, and it is testimony both to the flexibility of the Constitution and to the difficulties inherent in the amending process that, between 1791 and 1982, there have been only 16 amendments.

Reflecting on the personal interest which the Framers had in a successful economy and on the pressing economic problems which the Articles of Confederation had patently failed to solve, some commentators have claimed that the whole exercise in Philadelphia was motivated by economic interest rather than the higher ideals of liberty, republicanism and civic virtue.[8] While there is certainly something to this, it seems odd that the fundamental disagreements on major questions which did occur involved delegates with an equal stake in economic sucess. Virtually *all* the delegates were men of property, so the more reductionist of the economic theories of the Constitution should predict no real disagreement on basic principles. Yet those who voted against the Constitution had just as much a stake in prosperity and stability as those who voted for it.[9] A more persuasive way to characterize the Framers' motivations is to accept that they were indeed troubled by economic dislocation and the ever present threat of uncontrolled democracy, but differed markedly on which system would best overcome these problems. Crucially these differences were not only instrumental and pragmatic. Delegates also differed *intellectually* and represented more than one political philosophy and conception of human nature.

8 The classic statement of this view is Charles Beard's *Economic Interpretation of the Constitution of the United States*, New York, Macmillan, 1913 (paperback, 1961).
9 As established by Forrest McDonald, *We the People – The Economic Origins of the Constitution*, Chicago, University of Chicago Press, 1958.

Ratification

Fearful of failure, the Framers wrote into the Constitution the requirement that ratification could be achieved by just nine of the 13 states, and then by special state conventions rather than the (often untrustworthy) state legislatures. The Framers also labelled themselves *Federalists*, thus imposing on opposition groups the unattractive sobriquet 'Anti-Federalist'. Opposition was, in fact, fragmented, coming as it did mainly from the more remote rural areas. There was a geographical split, but not a North/South one. Instead, it was the commercial interests of the coastal areas, the larger towns and cities and the big landowners of the South who supported ratification. The Anti-Federalists were concentrated in 'the part most remote from commercial centres, with interests consequently predominantly agricultural. It included fractious Rhode Island, the Shays regions of Massachusetts and the centre of a similar movement in New Hampshire'[10] (see map 3.1).

Federalist lobbying in favour of the Constitution was intense and inspired the first truly national political debate in the United States. Very generally, the Anti-Federalists complained that the Constitution was insufficiently democratic and that it implied a strong and domineering central government. Complaints that individual rights were not specifically guaranteed by the Constitution were also common, and in order to ensure ratification in some states, the Federalists accepted that a Bill of Rights would be added as soon as the first federal government was established. Between 1787 and 1789, state conventions, one after the other, voted for ratification. Success was assured when the New York convention eventually ratified by a margin of three votes. The Federalists won because they were better organized, had all the leading politicians and statesmen behind them, and because the Anti-Federalists were obliged to fight a negative campaign, a return to the Articles of Confederation being their only immediate alternative to the Constitution. In order to appease the remaining Anti-Federalists the first Congress quickly voted for 10 amendments, which, once ratified by the states in 1791, became the Bill of Rights. Interestingly, a number of additional amendments failed in Congress or during ratification, almost all of which would have made the system more democratic. One proposed that the electorate should issue binding instructions to their

10 O. G. Libby, quoted in J. C. Clark Archer and Peter J. Taylor, *Section and Party*, Chichester, John Wiley, 1981, p. 49.

Map 3.1   The geography of ratification

Source: O. G. Libby, as reproduced in J. C. Clark Archer and Peter J. Taylor *Section and Party*, Chichester, John Wiley, 1981, p. 50. Reprinted by permission of John Wiley & Sons Ltd.

Congressmen, thus turning them into delegates. Another suggested that there should never be less than one Congressman for every 50,000 inhabitants. The mind boggles at the consequences for American politics if either or both of these proposals had been adopted.

The Adaptive Constitution

Change by amendment

No constitution can elaborate the precise relationship between institutions and political forces. If it attempts to do so it runs the danger of being ignored. Successful constitutions must, therefore, be flexible and open to varying interpretations. In some ways, the shorter and vaguer the document the better. Completely unambiguous statements lead to rigidity and can render a constitution unworkable. The US Constitution is free of all these faults. It does, of course, lay down certain guidelines and rules, but it says remarkably little about the precise powers of the main institutions, or about how authority should be shared between federal and state governments. When a comparison is made between the United States of 1789 (3.5 million people, agrarian, confined to the East Coast) and the United States of the late 1980s (243 million people, highly industrial, a continental and world power) the true success of the Constitution can be appreciated. For virtually the same document applies today as applied nearly 200 years ago. Moreover, if we examine the 16 Amendments[11] which have been accepted in this period, their significance is almost certainly not as great as the changes in interpretation to which the Constitution has been subjected.

Of the 16 Amendments, some are relatively trivial, two were devoted to the adoption and subsequent rejection of prohibition, and the remainder are devoted either to electoral questions or to limiting and expanding the role of the federal government.

Amendments affecting elections

The first important amendment here was the 12th which was adopted in 1804 to simplify the election of the electoral college, which in turn elects the President. As mentioned earlier, the Founding Fathers hoped that a group of elder statesmen (the electoral college) would choose the President, but with the emergence of competing political parties it soon became obvious that the college had become highly partisan. In 1800 the vote in the college was a tie between Thomas Jefferson and Aaron Burr. When the vote was referred to the House of Representatives it took numerous ballots to decide the eventual winner (Jefferson). The

11   Excluding the first 10 Amendments (The Bill of Rights).

12th Amendment ensured that any election in which a candidate received less than a majority of the electoral college would then be decided in a run-off election in the House of Representatives. Votes for President and Vice-President were combined. Previously the college had elected the two officers separately. Gradually between 1800 and 1832 the state legislatures voted to provide for the direct popular election of members of the electoral college. Surprisingly, this system persists. Americans still do not vote directly for a Presidential candidate, but for members of the college. Moreover, it is a *winner-take-all* mechanism, so that the candidate who gets a majority of votes in a particular state wins *all* that state's electoral college votes. What determines the number of electoral college votes in a state? Each state simply has one vote for each Representative and Senator which means that the votes are distributed roughly in proportion to population (the number of representatives in any state changes regularly in accordance with population shifts (see chapter 7, and as there are only two Senators per state this introduces a small bias in favour of low population states). The major criticism of this system is that it is possible for a candidate to win the electoral college vote, but receive fewer popular votes than another candidate. Just this happened in 1824, 1876 and 1888, although it has not occurred since. Another criticism focuses on the danger of electoral college members failing to vote for the candidate mandated by the electorate. Again, this has happened on rare occasions, but it has never been critical.

Clearly the electoral college system favours the larger states. If a candidate wins just seven states: New York, California, Texas, Pennsylvania, Illinois, Michigan and Ohio, he amasses 211 votes even if he wins by only a narrow margin in each of these states. And only 270 electoral college votes are needed for victory. Talk of reforming the system is never far from the surface in the United States, and the mechanism probably persists because there are only two main parties,[12] and some bias in favour of big population centres does compensate for other biases in the system in favour of smaller states and rural areas.

Almost all the other amendments affecting elections have been designed to expand the electorate or to hold elected officials more accountable or responsive to the public (table 3.1). These changes,

12 Should no candidate receive a majority in the college – a likelihood if the USA had a multi-party system – then the House of Representatives chooses the President on the basis of *one vote* per state delegation. This massive bias in favour of the small states would not be tolerated for long were the system put to the test (although it did occur twice in the nineteenth century). In recent years the USA has only rarely produced a serious third party candidate, and few have accumulated electoral college votes.

Table 3.1   Constitutional amendments affecting elections

Amendment	Purpose	Proposed	Adopted
12	Reform of electoral college	1803	1804
15	Voting rights extended to all races	1869	1870
17	Direct election of Senators	1912	1913
19	Voting rights extended to women	1919	1920
20	'Lame duck' session of Congress abolished[a]	1932	1933
22	Presidents limited to two terms	1947	1951
23	Voting rights extended to residents of District of Columbia	1960	1961
24	Voting rights democratized – abolition of poll tax	1962	1964
25	Reform of Presidential succession in case of disability	1965	1967
26	Voting age lowered to 18	1971	1971

[a]   This changed the date of new Congressional sessions from March to January to shorten the period during which the old Congress could act.

together with the abolition of property qualifications for voting at the state level during the first part of the nineteenth century have, in total, greatly increased the democratic element in the Constitution.

Amendments affecting the powers of the federal government

In one sense, changes in electoral qualifications were to be expected as the democratizing trends of the nineteenth and twentieth centuries took hold. If this is so, it would also be unsurprising if the Constitution had been frequently amended to expand the powers of the federal government. Yet as table 3.2 shows, only three amendments have had this purpose, the 13th to assert federal power over those states practising slavery, the 14th imposing the Bill of Rights on the states and the 16th establishing the power to introduce a national income tax. And of these three, the 14th Amendment was not, in fact, applied to the states until the twentieth century.[13]

13   Proof of the problems involved in amending the Constitution is provided by the failure to adopt the Equal Rights Amendment (equal opportunity for women, see Appendix 1, p. 325). Originally proposed in 1972, the amendment was three states short of ratification by the end of the original deadline in 1979. Although extended by a further three years, the amendment remained three states short in 1982, in spite of broad popular support. The Reagan Administration was not sympathetic to the amendment, and it was not renewed.

Table 3.2   Amendments affecting the powers of the federal government

Amendment	Purpose	Proposed	Adopted
11	Limited federal courts' jurisdiction over suits involving the states	1794	1798
13	Abolished slavery	1865	1865
14	Extended due process of Bill of Rights to the states	1866	1868
16	Established power to introduce a national income tax	1909	1913

Change by interpretation

Much more important have been changes in Constitutional interpretation which owe more to the development of American society and economy than to the wording of the Constitution as such. We can identify four such changes:

1   The assertion of federal over state power.
2   The assertion of executive over legislative power.
3   The emergence of the Supreme Court as the final arbiter of the Constitution.
4   The growing protection of individual rights under the federal government.

Each of these four will be dealt with in detail in later chapters. For now it is enough to point out the first two were certainly not intended or envisaged by the Framers, the third probably was, and the fourth has developed in a way which could not possibly have been predicted in 1787.

Although the Constitution is ambiguous on the question of federal/state relations, there can be no doubt that the relationship which had developed by the 1970s was light years away from anything the Framers could have intended. Today the federal government intrudes into almost every facet of economic and social life, leaving to the states very little that *constitutionally* they can call their own except perhaps their territorial integrity. In 1791 it was broadly expected that the 10th Amendment's dictum: 'The powers not delegated to the United States by the Constitution, nor prohibited by it to the States, are reserved to the States respectively, or to the people', would leave the states unequivocally in charge of a number of governmental functions. As the next chapter will demonstrate, this was not to be.

Similarly, Congress was expected to be the major source of legislative initiative, while the President implemented laws with prudence and efficiency. The late twentieth-century reality is very different. For while Congress does play a greater role in policy initiation than most national legislatures, and is indisputably a powerful and independent institution, it has forfeited the lion's share of the legislative function to the President and to an awesomely large and complex executive branch.

The reasons why government has become larger, more centralized and concentrated in executive rather than legislature will be addressed in detail in later chapters. But these trends have occurred in almost all countries with rapid economic and social development, the mobilization of populations by parties and groups and the corresponding increase in demands placed on all governments, particularly those with the greatest potential for resource distribution and regulation – central governments.

In 1803 the Supreme Court asserted the power of judicial review, or the right to declare any act of Congress or action by the executive branch as incompatible with the Constitution and therefore illegal. Actions by states can also be struck down by the Supreme Court. Although used sparingly at first, this power has been utilized with increasing frequency, and as we will see in chapter 12, has had profound consequences for the working of the political system. Although some of the Founders may have envisaged the Court playing the role of final arbiter of the Constitution, none could have foreseen the intimate involvement of the nation's highest court in such questions as abortion, electronic bugging and political party campaign finance.

Finally, citizens' right to free speech, assembly, religion, and privacy, and to 'due process' and the equal protection of the laws have slowly been extended to apply to the states. This is crucial, for slavery was an institution protected by state governments and constitutions. Following the Civil War, the 13th and 14th Amendments swept away slavery and, in theory, discrimination. However, the Supreme Court failed to enforce the 14th Amendment in the South until after the Second World War, so allowing the perpetuation of segregation and the worst sort of racial discrimination. Deference to states' rights extended to other areas such as standards of occupational safety, employment conditions and criminal justice. So for many Americans, civil rights and liberties were anything but 'God given rights'. Only under federal legislation did they exist, and until the twentieth century the federal government played only a small role in the lives of individual citizens. Beginning in the 1930s and accelerating between 1945 and 1970, this anomalous situation was slowly corrected, with the Supreme Court insisting in case after case that the Bill of Rights and 14th Amendment apply to all American governments, whatever their status. So in cases involving national security, privacy, racial, religious and sex discrimination, and the administration of justice, the Supreme Court has insisted that all authorities have an obligation to heed constitutionally defined rights. Of course this does not mean to say that the Court has always favoured the individual rather than government – although in recent years more often than not it has. Changes in official attitudes to civil rights and liberties parallel the growth of government noted earlier. As governments at all levels have increasingly intruded into the lives of individuals, so the need for protection from arbitrary governmental authority has grown. As we will discover in chapter 12, governments – and especially federal governments – have also been active in controlling the abuse of individual rights by *private* bodies, in particular corporations. It seems highly unlikely that the Framers could have foreseen that the question of individual rights would have become part of a complex web of interaction between myriad private and public institutions and individuals.

Assessing the Constitution

Some of the most dramatic changes in American government and society over the last 200 years have involved institutions and political processes not even referred to in the Constitution. Parties emerged during the early years of the nineteenth century as the major agents of political mobilization. Interest groups have grown in number and influence until today some commentators seriously argue that they are the true sources of political power and influence. Similarly the nationally organized media equipped with formidable electronic resources can play a critical role in swaying political opinion. Does this mean that the Constitution is of relatively little importance? Not at all, for all these changes have had to be accommodated within certain institutional limits which the Constitution imposes. Political and economic changes have indisputably altered the relationships between institutions and the broader society, but they have not been transformed in such a way that the document has ceased to have meaning. Congress remains separated from the Presidency. Interest groups, Presidents, individual citizens, the media – even foreign governments – have to accept that the independent power of Congress can and frequently does thwart Presidents. The Courts are also independent and have shown, especially in the last 40 years, that President and Congress must sometimes tread warily when exercising their powers. States, too, remain important political units – although, as we will discover in the next chapter, their relationship with the federal government is now more one of interdependence than autonomy.

Criticisms of the modern Constitution usually concentrate either on the continuing political hiatus between executive and legislature, or on the progressive weakening of the states in relation to the federal government. The first of these will become a constant theme in later chapters, and there is little doubt that American Presidents are, in comparison with most industrial countries, uncommonly constrained by the essentially negative power of Congress. But as we will see, American government is not only fragmented by the separation of powers. Getting policy efficiently formulated and implemented is also affected by the complexity of the executive branch and, simply, by the many competing interests in American society which have created and nurtured so many access points to those with political power. It seems reasonable to infer that this would have happened whatever the precise constitutional arrangements in force.

Arguments suggesting that the decline of the states' legal autonomy is in part attributable to the Constitution's failure to define precisely where state sovereignty begins and ends are less persuasive. Such a strict delineation of powers would have been inflexible and ultimately unworkable, and in any case the states were admirably independent until this century. The gradual erosion of their legal powers is not, therefore, a matter so much of constitutional failure as it is a consequence of the states' inability to deal with the pressing social and economic problems which industrialization and other changes brought. Any assessment of the Constitution has to recognize that, as with any constitution, its continuing influence is ultimately dependent on those in positions of political power accepting its legitimacy. Had its provisions proved a major threat to power-holders, it would have been ignored or radically amended. No doubt the Founding Fathers recognized this and, anticipating problems, deliberately opted for a short and rather vague document which would stand the test of time. But this would hardly have been enough had America been torn by fundamental divisions based on class, ethnicity, language or religion. The Framers knew that good government was all about the business of reconciling differences between competing groups and interests in society, and no doubt they were aware that the United States would experience social and political conflict of varying intensity. But the conflict between North and South apart – and this very nearly put paid to the Union – the United States has been remarkably unaffected by fundamental political divisions. Free from a feudal past and lacking deeply rooted religious, ethnic, linguistic and, after the Civil War, regional divides, the country was able to accommodate quite extraordinary economic and demographic changes within a single, almost unchanging, constitutional structure. Above all it is this relative consensus on political fundamentals amid rapid change that has allowed what is in any case a brilliantly adaptive Constitution to survive.

This does not mean to say that the Constitution will continue for ever, of course. And there are more than enough critics who claim that the basic division of power between legislature and executive is inappropriate for the sort of efficient policy making needed to run an economically powerful late twentieth-century world power. Whether this is true, later chapters will reveal. But whatever the charges, the Constitution is under no imminent threat either from domestic political conflict or from radical amendment. According to the simple measure of its ability to survive, therefore, it must be deemed a success.

Further Reading

Among recent interpretations of the origins and consequences of the pre- and post-revolutionary periods, two stand out: Bernard Bailyn, *The Ideological Origins of the American Revolution*, Cambridge, Mass., Harvard University Press, 1967; Garry Wills, *Inventing America*, Garden City, New York, Doubleday, 1978. For a textbook account of the Constitution, see Edward S. Corwin, *The Constitution and What it Means Today*, Princeton, New Jersey, Princeton University Press, 14th edition, 1978. For a non-American history of the period, see M. J. Heale, *The Making of American Politics*, London, Longman, 1977.

4

80,000 Governments: Federalism and Intergovernmental Relations

Over the past decade and a half, a new system of domestic government has emerged in the United States – one whose degree of complexity and interdependency, extent of inter-level contacts and constraints, and vastly expanded scope of intergovernmental financing and servicing arrangements are in marked contrast to the simpler, more separated features of its predecessor patterns of the nineteen fifties and certainly of the nineteen twenties.

David B. Walker, Assistant Director,
Advisory Commission on Intergovernmental Relations

This Nation has never fully debated the fact that over the past 40 years, federalism – one of the most essential and underlying principles of our Constitution – has nearly disappeared as a guiding force in American politics and government. My administration intends to initiate such a debate . . .

Ronald Reagan

To the European student of American government, the practice of federalism presents itself as something of a conundrum. On the one hand is the extraordinary variety of contrasting public policies displayed by the states. Most states levy an income tax, but ten do not; most have capital punishment, but 12 do not; state mandated land-use planning is light years away from the policy agenda in Texas – a state which prides itself on its free market in land – but in Oregon and Hawaii state planning is a fact of life. In California the possession of marijuana is no longer a criminal offence; in Missouri it *is* a major offence, carrying with it a stiff prison sentence. On the other hand, American observers repeatedly tell us that federalism is dying – or is even dead; that the federal government has effectively usurped the powers of the states and now plays the dominant role in American government. Federalism, so we are told, has been transformed from a system of shared sovereignty with each level of government supreme in its own sphere and converted into a complex web of intergovernmental relations where political and economic forces, not constitutional imperatives, are the key variables.[1] A major purpose of this chapter is to explain the apparent paradox of continuing state variety and increasing federal power. To achieve this, special attention will be paid to what has been called 'fiscal federalism' or the financial relations between different levels of government. As will be shown, such an approach focuses attention not only on federal–state relationships, but also on *local*–state and *local*–federal links. Finally, some reference will be made to the Reagan administrations' attempts to revive the institution of federalism.

Federalism in Theory and Practice

It was not so long ago that Europeans viewed the federal arrangements of the United States with a combination of distanced interest and condescension. A constitutional division of powers between centre and periphery might, so the argument ran, suit such large and diverse countries as the United States, but they were clearly inappropriate for homogeneous countries like Britain and France, with their centralized metropolitan political cultures based on dominant capital cities. For social reformers, federalism was viewed with particular scepticism. How, after all, could resources be distributed from rich to poor areas and from the haves to have-nots of society in the absence of a powerful central government operating unhindered by 'regressive' state governments? Critics pointed to the stark inequalities of American society which seemed so often to correlate with state boundaries – abject poverty in Mississippi and Alabama, an easy affluence in Connecticut and Wisconsin.

In recent years, however, the institution of federalism has experienced something of a revival. Centralized governments have been criticized as spendthrift and insensitive, and federalism has been cited as a compromise solution to the claims by increasing numbers of regions and ethnic minorities in a variety of countries for more autonomy. To the critic of the over-centralized state, federalism's advantages seem obvious. Local and regional cultural, political and economic characteristics can

1 See Michael Reagan and John Sanzone, *The New Federalism*, New York, Oxford University Press, 2nd edn, 1981.

be preserved; government can be brought 'closer to the people'; and central power can be limited by ensuring that the administration of a whole range of domestic policies is conducted at the state and local level. Federalism is, of course, much more than the mere devolution of powers which, to a greater or lesser extent, exists in all states, unitary and federal. *Dual sovereignty* is the central theoretical condition for federalism. This involves not just the sharing of policy responsibilities between different levels of government, it additionally *guarantees* constitutional integrity to state governments. No federal government can abolish its constituent states as a British government can, theoretically at least, abolish all its local governments. Naturally the crucial question is: Which powers should reside in the state governments and which in the federal government? Historically under 'classic' or 'dual' federalism,[2] defence and foreign affairs together with some aspects of financial management have been considered federal government responsibilities, while most domestic policies – education, roads, welfare, the administration of justice – have been allocated to state and local governments.

Few constitutions, however, specify precisely which policy areas should be the responsibility of different levels of government. Article 1, Section 8 of the US Constitution, for example, does enumerate the powers of Congress, but it does not do so in a way which unambiguously defines the federal role. Congress is given the power to regulate inter-state commerce, but what does this mean: The regulation of inter-state transport? The movement of manufactured goods across state boundaries? The regulation of banking across state lines? The regulation of those aspects of *intra*-state commerce which are affected by *inter*-state transactions? Or what? Clearly what Congress does here and what remains a state responsibility is left undefined by the Constitution.

In reality the delineation of the federal and state roles has been left to judicial interpretation and to the ways in which the courts have reacted to shifting political and economic environments. As was pointed out in chapter 3, workable constitutions have to be flexible and open to new interpretation, and any attempt to lay down in a permanent fashion the limits to federal or state powers would be doomed to failure. As we shall see, for federalism the cost of flexibility has been the gradual and steady erosion of the states' powers by the federal government.

In strict constitutional terms, the states are guaranteed just four things: equal representation in the Senate (Article 1, Section 3); the right to jurisdictional integrity (Article 4, Section 3); the right to a

2 For a discussion of the operation of dual federalism see Morton Grodzins, *The American System*, Chicago, Rand McNally, 1966.

republican form of government (Article 4, Section 4); and protection against invasion and domestic violence (Article 4, Section 4). What in reality they have retained in addition to this has varied with the historical period and a whole range of economic, social and political forces. They remain an important level of government, not just for constitutional reasons, but also because they are a convenient jurisdictional base for a range of powerful actors and interests in contemporary America. Political parties, for example, are organized on a state rather than a national basis – a fact which gives the states a key role in nominating Presidents and in electing Congressmen and Senators. We will elaborate on this point later, but for now it is important to stress that local as well as state governments are important power bases in the American system. Localism is as strong in the USA as in any country and this in spite of the weak constitutional position of local governments (in theory, they are constitutionally subordinate to state governments). The power of local governments is reflected in their resilience. In spite of the many pressures to consolidate into larger units – pressures which exist in all industrial countries – the number of local units in the USA remains

Table 4.1   Types of government, USA, 1967–1987

Type of government	1987	1977	1967
Total	83,217	79,913	81,299
US Government	1	1	1
State governments	50	50	50
Local governments	83,166	79,862	81,248
County	3,042	3,042	3,049
Municipal	19,205	18,862	18,048
Township	16,691	16,822	17,105
School district	14,741	15,174	21,782
Special district	29,487	25,962	21,264

Source: 1987 Census of Governments, Preliminary Report, Bureau of the Census, 1987, table A, p. 1.

high (table 4.1). Note also the *variety* of local units which derives from variations in state law. Twenty states, for example, have townships which generally have the powers of municipalities but which, unlike municipalities, cover areas irrespective of population concentrations. Special districts which continue to increase in number have been created to perform a specific local function such as fire protection, soil conservation, water supply or sewerage. They are legally separate from, although almost always linked politically to, municipal and county governments.

In recognition of the weakness of classic or dual federalism, and of the strength of local governments, some commentators have argued that, rather than become involved in arcane discussions on the constitutional status of federalism, it is now more appropriate to talk of *intergovernmental relations* (IGR).[3] Such a focus obliges the student to examine the political and economic relationships between different levels of government – a focus largely adopted by this chapter.

To understand why the federal role has increased so rapidly and why, as a constitutional concept, federalism has declined in importance, it is necessary to examine the historical evolution of IGR in the USA.

The Evolution of American Federalism

Opting for a federal rather than a unitary or confederate system of government in 1787 was understandable. Government under the Articles of Confederation had been minimal. A weak Congress (there was no executive branch) was obliged to rely on the cooperation of 13 near-independent states. In economic affairs this proved almost impossible and internal tariff barriers, together with the absence of a common currency, rendered the new Republic almost impotent against the economic might of Britain. If a confederate system, relying on the cooperation of constituent states was unworkable, the other most tried alternative, unitary government, was inappropriate for historical and political reasons. It was, after all, the centralized and highly insensitive power of England which had prompted the revolt of the colonies. Each colony had in addition its own traditions and history which might have been threatened by a centralized system. Finally, unitary government was associated with a strong executive – not a feature likely to endear the system either to the artisans and smallholders who made up the bulk of the American population or to those sections of the elite who supported Madison's notion of limited government.

A federal system involving the sharing of authority between central authority and constituent states was a natural compromise. Hence the Constitution gave to the federal government authority to raise armies, to tax, and to regulate interstate commerce – powers that were notably absent under the Articles of Confederation – while the individual traditions of the states were protected both by the checks and balances imposed on the central institutions of Congress and Presidency and by

3 This abbreviation is taken from Deil S. Wright, *Understanding Intergovernmental Relations*, North Scituate, Mass., Duxbury, 1978.

the 10th Amendment.[4] The fundamental problem which federalism attempts to solve – the tension between central authority and local autonomy – is still very much with us today. In the late eighteenth century, however, this tension took on a very different form from that presently at work in the United States. Then, a strong federal government was needed for two purposes: to defend the young republic against a hostile outside world and to provide an open and orderly market for the free exchange of goods and services within the borders of the new nation state. At all levels government's role was limited and, although some conflict between state and federal governments existed, it rarely reached the point where it intruded greatly into citizens' lives. In an agrarian and small town society characterized by poor communications and a strong tradition of localism, the federal government was a remote and, in terms of people's everyday dealings, a relatively minor authority. Today, in contrast, federal, state and local governments intrude into almost all areas of social life through a bewildering array of policies and programmes. It is not surprising, therefore, that federal–state–local relations today are very different from those of late eighteenth-century America. Initially, debate was concentrated on the *regulatory* powers of the federal government – and especially the extent to which federal law was *supreme* in the regulation and promotion of commerce. By the mid-nineteenth century, with the emergence of slavery as a national issue, the role of the federal government in protecting the rights of citizens was added to the policy agenda. These issues remain an important part of current debate on federalism, but they have been overshadowed by the vastly enhanced spending power of the federal government. An examination of the more celebrated Supreme Court cases on federal–state relations confirms these shifts in emphasis. Prior to the Civil War, the most significant cases concerned such things as the right of the federal government to establish a national bank (*McCulloch* v. *Maryland*, 1819) and to run ferries between New York and New Jersey (*Gibbons* v. *Ogden*, 1824). Later the Court led by Chief Justice Taney resolutely defended the right of the states to permit slavery – a right promptly removed by the War and the subsequent 13th and 14th Amendments. Between 1870 and 1938, the Court resisted attempts by the federal government to regulate industrial and commercial life – although anti-monopoly laws were upheld and a federal income tax was eventually approved through constitutional amendment (16th Amendment, 1913). With the exception

4 'The powers not delegated to the United States by the Constitution, nor prohibited by it to the States, are reserved to the States respectively, or to the people.'

of the income tax question, which did inspire a vociferous debate on the role of the federal government, the period up to 1933 was characterized by a general agreement that the states were the proper level of government for most domestic policy formulation and implementation. Federal government power was on the increase, but Presidents and Congresses generally accepted that *direct* intervention by the government in the economic and social life of the nation was undesirable.

All changed with the depression of the 1930s and the advent of the New Deal. From 1933 the federal government began to legislate in a variety of new areas from social security to public works. In reaction to what it saw as an unlawful interpretation of the Commerce Clause and Necessary and Proper Clause, the Court struck down much of this new legislation in the name of the states' rights. Had the decisions in such cases as *Schechter Corporation* v. *the USA* (1935) and *USA* v. *Carter Coal Company* (1936) prevailed, Roosevelt's New Deal would have been in serious trouble, and only a last minute change in Court opinion prevented a constitutional crisis. (See chapter 12, p. 256.)

Since this famous turnabout, the executive and judicial branches have been in approximate agreement over the economic role of the federal government in American society. Conflict has not disappeared from debate on federalism, however. The civil rights issue, in particular, inspired intense dispute between the states and all branches of the federal government during the 1950s and the 1960s. While state (and more recently local) resistance to federal civil rights laws and judicial decisions should not be underestimated, scholars have probably been right in emphasizing that conflict as such is not now the main characteristic of American federalism. Morton Grodzins was the first to recognize the cooperative nature of federalism in the 1940s and 1950s. Using the metaphors of layer cake and marble cake to characterize conflictual and cooperative federalism, Grodzins identified the crucial transition of federalism from the intergovernmental antagonisms of the nineteenth century to the mutual interest and collaboration typical of the late 1930s to the late 1950s period.[5] Economic distress and external threat combined to transform the role of the federal government during this period. Lower level governments responded to national emergency not with antagonism but in a spirit of cooperation and consensus. Since the late 1950s, however, federalism has developed further, and cooperation is certainly not the main characteristic of intergovernmental relations today. Now, with the proliferation of programmes and policies at all levels of government, a much more confused and fragmented situation

5   Grodzins, *The American System*.

exists. Various scholars have attempted to describe this in terms of a single metaphor or characteristic.[6] The task is not easy, however, because of the sheer complexity of the IGR system. What follows is an attempt to unravel this complexity by explaining why the number of programmes and policies has increased so dramatically and by giving some specific examples of how governments interact today.

Competitive Interdependence: American Intergovernmental Relations since 1970

The reasons why the federal role has increased over time are complex. Most relate to the close connection between administrative and political centralization and what has been called the nationalization of economic and social life.[7] It is easy to be overdeterministic in this area – certainly the causal lines run in many directions. The evolution of mass-based political parties nominating Presidents with national appeals was no doubt both an effect and a cause of the increasingly nationalized nature of economic life during the late nineteenth and early twentieth centuries. As corporations began to organize on national lines, so the need for national standards and regulations grew. Demands for minimum standards of (say) food processing or for fair competition required the sort of political mobilization which could come only from mass-based political parties. As these strengthened, so the need for better and more centralized organization on the part of commerce and industry to combat (or cooperate with) the federal government emerged. The growth of news dissemination inevitably aided this process, especially after the introduction of radio and television.

While all these forces were important, the main impetus to the growth of federal power came from two rather different sources – economic depression and war. As we noted earlier, it was the programmes of the New Deal and the massive military spending on the Second World War which transformed the federal role. As can be seen from table 4.2 public spending as a percentage of GNP increased from just 10 per cent in 1929 to 23 per cent in 1949, and the federal share of this expenditure increased from 2.6 per cent to 16 per cent – much of it, after 1939, as a

6 Deil Wright, for example, has described the period since 1960 in terms of 'picket fence' federalism, but it seems doubtful that this produces the accurate image which the layer and marble cake metaphor invoked. See Wright *Understanding Intergovernmental Relations*, p. 41.

7 See the collection of essays edited by Theodore Lowi and Alan Stone, *Nationalizing Government: Public Policies in America*, Beverly Hills, Sage, 1978.

Table 4.2   Government expenditures, from own source, selected years 1929–
1987

Calendar year	Total public sector	Federal government	Total state–local government	State government	Local government
As a percentage of GNP					
1929	10.0%	2.6%	7.4%	2.0%	5.4%
1939	19.3	9.9	9.4	4.1	5.4
1949	23.0	16.1	6.9	3.4	3.5
1959	26.6	18.5	8.1	3.8	4.3
1969	30.1	19.8	10.3	5.3	4.9
1979	30.6	20.8	9.9	5.8	4.1
1981	33.0	23.0	9.9	5.8	4.1
1983	34.9	24.5	10.4	5.9	4.5
1984	33.9	23.7	10.1	6.0	4.2
1985	34.9	24.6	10.4	6.2	4.2
1986	35.1	24.4	10.7	6.3	4.5
1987[e]	34.9	23.7	11.3	n.a.	n.a.
Percentage distribution by level of government					
1929	100.0%	26.0%	74.0%	20.2%	53.8%
1939	100.0	51.1	48.9	21.0	27.8
1949	100.0	70.0	30.0	14.7	15.3
1959	100.0	69.5	30.5	14.4	16.1
1969	100.0	65.9	34.1	17.7	16.4
1979	100.0	67.8	32.2	18.8	13.3
1981	100.0	69.9	30.1	17.6	12.6
1983	100.0	70.2	29.8	17.0	12.8
1984	100.0	70.1	29.9	17.6	12.3
1985	100.0	70.3	29.7	17.6	12.1
1986	100.0	69.4	30.6	17.9	12.7
1987[e]	100.0	67.7	32.3	n.a.	n.a.

[e] = estimated.
Source: Adapted from Advisory Commission on Intergovernmental Relationships
(ACIR), *Significant Features of Fiscal Federalism*, Washington DC, 1987, 1988, table 1.
For full notes on these data, see originals.

result of increased defence spending. The other most startling trend
shown in table 4.2 is the dramatic relative decline in local government
spending since 1929. Since that year local government's share of all
spending has declined from 53.8 per cent to 12.7 per cent. Of course
this is in effect the corollary of an increased federal role. The New Deal
and the Second World War added new responsibilities to government
which local and state governments were either unwilling or unable to
take on. But table 4.2 is misleading on the declining role of local
government, for if we take into account *intergovernmental transfers* a

Table 4.3 Government expenditures, after intergovernmental transfers, selected years 1929–1987

Calendar year	Total public sector	Federal government	Total state–local government	State government	Local government
As a percentage of GNP					
1929	10.0%	2.5%	7.5%	2.1%	5.4%
1939	19.3	8.8	10.5	3.3	7.2
1949	23.0	15.3	7.8	3.0	4.8
1959	26.6	17.1	9.5	3.4	6.1
1969	30.1	17.7	12.4	4.5	7.9
1979	30.6	17.6	13.1	5.0	8.1
1981	33.0	20.2	12.8	5.0	7.8
1983	34.9	22.0	12.9	5.1	7.8
1984	33.9	21.3	12.6	5.1	7.5
1985	34.9	22.1	12.8	5.2	7.7
1986	35.1	21.9	13.2	5.4	7.9
1987[e]	34.9	21.4	13.5	n.a.	n.a.
Per capita, in constant (1982) dollars					
1929	$585	$146	$439	$124	$315
1939	1,059	481	578	180	397
1949	1,711	1,135	576	220	357
1959	2,440	1,570	869	309	560
1969	3,599	2,120	1,479	534	946
1979	4,343	2,491	1,853	710	1,142
1981	4,654	2,845	1,809	712	1,098
1983	4,878	3,073	1,804	712	1,093
1984	5,006	3,149	1,857	752	1,113
1985	5,267	3,334	1,933	786	1,155
1986	5,394	3,367	2,027	825	1,213
1987[e]	5,475	3,357	2,118	n.a.	n.a.

[e] = estimated.
Source: ACIR, *Significant Features*, adapted from table 2.

rather different picture emerges. As table 4.3 shows, a good chunk of increased federal spending derives from transfers to state and local government. State governments in turn have transferred increasing amounts to local governments. Hence, after transfers, a full 7.9 per cent of GNP was accounted for by local government spending in 1980, a significantly higher figure than as recently as 1959. Table 4.3 also reveals the massive increase in real spending at all levels of government between 1929 and 1981. Again, while the federal share has generally increased, the absolute level of state and local spending also increased. Perhaps most dramatically, apart from the 1929–39 period, real federal domestic spending experienced its largest boost during the 1969–79 period, and this followed a considerable expansion of federal state and local spending between 1959 and 1969. Clearly, forces other than depression and war account for the increasingly important role of governments during this 20-year period. Note also the levelling off – and even the small decline in some years – in spending by all levels of government after 1981. Earlier we mentioned how American federalism of the 1940s could be characterized as cooperative in nature, there being relatively little conflict between different levels of government. Governments and the public were generally agreed on the need for intervention to solve pressing problems. The 1960s and 1970s were quite different. Consensus on the nature and extent of government intervention largely broke down; jurisdictions were in competition with one another for federal or state aid; and, above all, governments became economically and politically *interdependent.*

A major spur both to increased federal spending and to producing qualitative changes in intergovernmental relations was the growth of federal grants in aid to state and local governments. There are two distinctions within any intergovernmental transfer system which must be drawn if the system is to be understood. First, it is necessary to distinguish between grants and payments which are paid *directly* to the population by the federal government and those which are paid to lower level governments. The former – in the USA such things as social security,[8] Medicare,[9] agricultural subsidies – do constitute a major part of federal spending. Grants to states and localities include both aid which goes directly to individuals through state and local governments – welfare is the most important item here – and aid for programmes such as urban renewal and highways, where the state or local government constitutes the final stage in the transfer transaction. Table 4.4 makes some of these distinctions by breaking down federal budget outlays for the 1959–87 period. Note the rapid rise in grants to state and local government between 1969 and 1975, and their subsequent decline after 1980. The 'payments for individuals' category includes both social security and welfare payments. As we will see, however, the levelling off in this category after 1980 is mainly accounted for by cuts in welfare (which is channelled through the states) rather than cuts in social security and other benefits which go direct to individuals. Finally, note that

8 In the USA, social security applies specifically to *contributory* benefits such as unemployment, old age and disability allowance. *Welfare* applies to non-contributory maintenance benefits (the equivalent of British supplementary benefits).
9 Medicare is the national health allowance scheme for the old introduced in 1965. It is mainly contributory, whereas Medicaid, a similar scheme for the poor, is not.

Table 4.4   Percentage distribution of federal budget outlays, 1959–1987

Year	Amount (billion $)	Constant prices (1982 $)	% distribution					
			Defence	Total non-defence	Payments for individuals	Grants[1]	Other	Net interest
1959	92.1	*	49.1	50.9	20.6		19.7	10.7
1960	92.2	*	48.9	51.9	21.9		18.3	10.8
1965	118.4	*	40.1	59.9	24.6		25.7	9.7
1969	184.5	*	43.9	56.1	28.6	6.9	1.7	6.9
1971	211.4	509.4	39.8	61.2	35.5	8.5	14.9	6.7
1975	326.2	586.0	27.3	72.7	45.4	10.0	14.5	6.9
1979	493.6	660.0	24.1	75.9	45.7	10.9	14.5	8.3
1980	579.6	699.1	23.5	76.5	46.5	9.8	14.8	8.9
1982	617.8	745.7	24.9	75.1	47.8	6.7	12.7	11.4
1984	666.5	789.9	26.8	73.2	46.7	6.2	11.2	13.0
1985	734.1	848.0	27.0	73.0	44.7	6.0	12.2	13.6
1986	769.1	866.2	28.0	72.0	45.0	6.0	10.9	13.6
1987e	842.4	862.3	28.1	71.9	45.5	5.3	11.4	13.4

e   estimated
*   not available
[1]   Grants to state and local governments
Source: *US Budget in Brief 1982 and 1988*, Washington DC, US Government Printing Office, table 2, p. 77 (1982) and p. 99 (1988).

government expenditure has continued to rise because of sizeable increases in defence expenditure and net interest since 1980. A clue to the rapid rise in grants in aid to lower-level governments during the period 1969–75 is the increase in general purpose block grants after 1972. Indeed, the second crucial distinction in IGR is between *block* grants which are general appropriations given to states and localities, and *categorical* grants which are given for specific programmes and policies and which often have strings attached. For example, the Urban Renewal Programme introduced in 1949 was categorical: it allocated monies to local governments specifically for the financing of downtown renewal. From 1954 until 1974, this money was available only if recipient governments abided by a 'workable programme' or general plan of how new development would fit in with existing housing and other facilities.[10] Since 1974, however, Urban Renewal, along with a number of related programmes have been replaced by Community Development Block Grants which carry considerably fewer restricting regulations. The Community Development Block Grant was just one of a series of block grants introduced by the Nixon and Ford administrations between 1970 and 1976. President Nixon was the architect of the main block grant scheme, General Revenue Sharing, introduced in 1972, the history of which tells us a great deal about American intergovernmental relations in the 1970s.

Table 4.3 confirms that the 1960s as well as the 1970s were a period of rapidly rising federal expenditure. Many of the programmes through which this money was spent were associated with Lyndon Johnson's Great Society: model cities (1966) to reinvigorate inner-city areas; mass transit (1966) to provide cities with more efficient public transport; subsidized housing for 'moderate' and lower income families (1968); Medicare and Medicaid (1965), and a whole host of smaller social welfare and other policies. In addition, the Great Society period witnessed an expansion of *existing* programmes[11] – Urban Renewal, public housing, welfare, social security. Many of these programmes – and especially the newer ones – had two features which, although not new, became much more pronounced during the 1960s. There was, first, the tendency for them to by-pass the states and transfer monies directly to local governments. The states had long been identified as 'regressive'

10 For a history of the Urban Renewal Programme see the collection of essays edited by Jewell Bellush and Murray Hausnecht, *Urban Renewal: People, Politics and Planning*, New York, Anchor, 1967.
11 The 1960s saw a particularly rapid increase in welfare spending. For a discussion of the causes of this, see Frances Fox Piven and Richard Cloward, *Regulating the Poor*, New York, Pantheon, 1971.

or 'backward' participants in the social reform process.[12] Dominated by rural conservatives, state legislatures tended not to favour social reform measures. Given this, the Great Society's focus on aid to local governments was understandable. Second, it was within the jurisdictions of local, not state, governments that the social problems which inspired increased federal aid existed. Urban problems – racial conflict, inner-city decay, crime, poor housing, poverty – began to dominate the policy agenda during these years.

Small wonder that these new emphases, together with burgeoning civil rights legislation, bothered both fiscal conservatives and defenders of classic federalism. By-passing the states was bad enough, but when this was combined with huge increases in government expenditure, it appeared to many that not only federalism but America's free enterprise tradition was withering away. It was in this context that the Nixon administration came into office in 1969. The new administration was broadly sympathetic to the conservative position, and was also eager to respond to the growing sentiment that government – and especially the federal government – was getting too big; that federal bureaucrats were interfering in the everyday lives of people. Nixon's response was, first, to disband or reduce some of the more criticized Great Society programmes, and second to introduce General Revenue Sharing and other block grant programmes. We now know that the closure of such agencies as the Office of Economic Opportunity (OEO), a major instrument in Johnson's War on Poverty, was largely symbolic in nature. OEO was never a big spending agency, and its closure meant little, especially as many of its programmes were transferred to the Department of Health, Education and Welfare (HEW). Meanwhile, many other categorical programmes continued to expand.

Revenue Sharing was the major plank in Nixon's 'New Federalism'. Its rationale was simple. Instead of having a mass of categorical programmes with all their Washington and field bureaucrats, why not give a lump sum to the states and localities which they could then spend as they wished? This would cut out the bureaucrats and, given the right formulae, remove what was perceived to be the bias in federal programmes in favour of the larger cities. It would also ensure that the

12   A reputation which was reinforced by the depression of the 1930s which exposed the inadequacy of existing state welfare provision. See Walter I. Trattner, *From Poor Law to Welfare State*, New York, Free Press, 2nd edn, 1979. Even after the passage of the 1935 Social Security Act, provisions in the law requiring welfare funds to be distributed on a matching basis, with the federal government agreeing to match whatever states were willing to put up, resulted in massive discrepancies in welfare assistance. In 1977, for example, *per capita* expenditure on welfare in Arizona was $55, whereas in New York State it was $297.

states, who were to receive the lion's share of revenue sharing, would be re-established as a major level of government. In addition to revenue sharing, other block grant programmes would be introduced to consolidate confusing arrays of categorical grants. The spirit of what the President wanted was well reflected in a Presidential radio address on 21 October 1972:

> Do we want to turn more power over to bureaucrats in Washington in the hope that they will do what is best for all the people? Or do we want to return more power to the people? It is time that good, decent people stopped letting themselves be bulldozed by anybody who presumes to be the self-righteous moral judge of our society. In the next four years, as in the past four, I will continue to direct the flow of power away from Washington and back to the people.

In his subsequent State of the Union Message, he added:

> [Revenue Sharing] would reverse the flow of power resources from the states and communities to Washington, and start power and resources flowing back from Washington to the states and communities and more important to the people all across America.[13]

Although Revenue Sharing was enacted into law in 1972 and soon became a $6 billion a year programme, and although Community Development Block Grants and other block grant initiatives followed, Nixon's New Federalism achieved almost none of its objectives. As we noted, spending continued to increase rapidly. Categorical programmes continued to mushroom parallel to Revenue Sharing. And while federal civilian employment did not increase during these years, state and local employment increased very rapidly, largely as a result of increased federal aid.[14] Moreover, a mass of new regulatory federal programmes assured the continued rise in federal 'interference'. Finally, rather than the big cities and poorer localities declining in importance as recipients of federal aid, they actually received more and more money from the federal government. The Nixon and Ford administrations' failure to make the New Federalism work has three interlinked causes.

1 They seriously underestimated the political strength of the agency–

---

13 Quoted in Dennis R. Judd and Frances N. Kopel 'The search for national urban policy, from Kennedy to Carter', in Lowi and Stone (eds), *Nationalizing Government*, pp. 173–4.

14 Between 1968 and 1978, federal executive branch employment decreased from 2.87 million to 2.82 million, while state and local government employment increased from 9.14 million to 12.82 million, *Special Analyses, Budget of the United States Government, Fiscal Year 1980*, table 1.4, p. 258.

client link characteristic of most categorical programmes. Federal bureaucracies have customers – local and state governments, private individuals and groups – and it is in the interest of all participants in the transfer process to see programmes flourish. Murray Edelman's reference to the symbiotic relationship which exists between these actors is apt.[15] Each needs the other and each 'feeds' off the other. Congressional subcommittees are also part of the transfer process and they too win kudos and power by maintaining and strengthening programmes. What happened after 1970, therefore, was that most categorical programmes continued to grow and many new ones – especially in the area of regulation – were added parallel to the rise of General Revenue Sharing and other general assistance programmes. Table 4.5 notes just some of the new programmes enacted between 1970 and 1976. It is a formidable list.

2   Nixon and Ford also underestimated the power resources of the intergovernmental lobby. In a 1978 article Samuel Beer referred to the rise of 'topocracy' during the 1960s and 1970s.[16] Topocracy is rule by intergovernmental officials – city managers, mayors, governors and their lobbyists. There can be little doubting the growing influence of such officials during this period, mainly through their lobbying organizations such as the National League of Cities, US Conference of Mayors, the National Governors' Conference, the National Legislative Conference, the Council of State Governments, the National Association of Counties and the International City Management Association. Through carefully cultivated links with Congressmen, Senators, federal officials and the press,[17] these organizations and others built up an intricate network of influence, any part of which could be mobilized should the need arise. When in 1974 and 1975 deep recession hit the US economy, it was the mayors and city managers who pleaded for anti-recession aid to help combat the serious fiscal difficulties being experienced by a range of localities. Their pleas were not for help for specific programmes or policies, but for general aid to meet municipal payrolls and debt interest. Such broad appeals, which carried with them the veiled threat that without help some cities would be forced into bankruptcy, proved too much for most Congressmen.[18] How, after all, could a Congressman,

15   Murray Edelman, *The Symbolic Uses of Politics*, Urbana, Illinois, University of Illinois Press, 1964.
16   Samuel Beer, 'Federalism, nationalism and democracy in America', *American Political Science Review*, March 1978, pp. 9–21.
17   For example state officials interested in urban affairs have close links with Rochelle Stanfield and Neil Peirce of the influential *National Journal*.
18   See D. Judd and F. Kopel, in Lowi and Stone (eds), *Nationalizing Government* and Theodore Lowi's first chapter, 'The Europeanisation of America?' in the same volume.

Table 4.5   Federal regulatory laws and programmes enacted since 1970

1969–70	Child Protection and Toy Safety Act
	Clear Air Amendments
	Egg Products Inspection Act
	Fair Credit Reporting Act
	Occupational Safety and Health Act
	Poison Prevention Packaging Act
	Security Investor Protection Act
1971	Economic Stabilisation Act Amendments
	Federal Boat Safety Act
	Lead-Based Paint Elimination Act
	Wholesome Fish and Fisheries Act
1972	Consumer Product Safety Act
	Equal Employment Opportunity Act
	Federal Election Campaign Act
	Federal Environmental Pesticide Control Act
	Federal Water Pollution Control Act Amendments
	Motor Vehicle Information and Cost Savings Act
	Noise Control Act
	Ports and Waterways Safety Act
1973	Agriculture and Consumer Protection Act
	Economic Stabilisation Act Amendments
	Emergency Petroleum Allocation Act
	Flood Disaster Protection Act
1974	Atomic Energy Act
	Commodity Futures Trading Commission Act
	Consumer Product Warranties Act
	Council on Wage and Price Stability Act
	Employee Retirement Income Security Act
	Federal Energy Administration Act
	Hazardous Materials Transportation Act
	Housing and Community Development Act
	Pension Reform Act
	Privacy Act
	Safe Drinking Water Act
1975	Energy Policy and Conservation Act
	Equal Credit Opportunity Act
1976	Consumer Leasing Act
	Medical Device Safety Act
	Toxic Substances Control Act

Source: Reproduced from, Lowi and Stone (eds), *Nationalizing Government*, p. 19. This list also includes some new general revenue programmes.

elected every two years in small constituencies often contiguous with a particular city or part city, be seen to refuse aid under such circumstances? By 1977 some $4.6 billion had been appropriated for anti-recession aid of one sort or another.

The intergovernmental lobby's influence was helped by two other factors. First, for structural economic reasons, lower level governments were experiencing increasing financial difficulties. New York City and Cleveland were extreme cases of a more general although not universal phenomenon – services becoming increasingly expensive to provide while the resources available to pay for them were limited. At the local level, property taxes (the equivalent of the British rates) were unpopular and inflexible. At the state level, income and sales taxes were also unpopular. Reactions by citizens to constant attempts by governments to increase these taxes was fierce. During 1978 and 1979 a variety of referenda to limit state and local taxes were successful. The most celebrated of these, Proposition 13, limited California property taxes to 1 per cent of its 1975–6 market value. At a stroke this almost halved many local governments' revenue. If local and state taxes were limited, then either services would be cut – not an easy alternative to pursue in most cases – or the federal government had to step in with aid.

Second, the American system of government seriously inhibits any attempts by a central authority to plan or control spending on particular programmes. Fragmentation between programmes and agencies at the federal level and between federal, state and local governments ensures that at any one time literally thousands of different policies are being implemented, each with its own political, interest group and bureaucratic supporters. The structure of the party system where nomination to Congress is organized on a state and local basis aids this fragmentation by insisting that Congressmen and Senators are beholden to state and local not national interests. And it is not only federal and state authorities which are legislating. Local governments, too, often have discretionary powers to legislate for their own jurisdictions.[19] Combined with a long and resilient history of localism this gives local governments considerable independence. Mayors could go to Washington not as political subordinates but as *partners* with governors and federal politicians. Small wonder that in this context it is misleading to talk of dual federalism.

3   Related was the fact that the Nixon administration had no clear conception of what the federal government's role should be. For

19   This power, first established in the 1930s, is known as Home Rule. It should, however, be emphasized that local governments make relatively few laws in comparison with state and federal governments. Their influence lies more in *political* rather than legal resources.

although Nixon was committed to devolving power to the states he was not a fiscal conservative. Only in one year (1973 for fiscal 1974) did he propose significant cuts in federal spending. During the Nixon years, therefore, a number of new programmes were legislated at the behest of the administration, while existing programmes continued to grow. Gerald Ford did attempt to hold back the tide of federal spending, but his was an emasculated presidency operating in the shadow of Watergate and obliged to confront a highly partisan Democratic Congress.[20]

Paradoxically it was Jimmy Carter who was the first President successfully to hold back federal grants to state and local governments. Carter was very much a fiscal conservative determined to reduce the federal budget deficit. Short of raising taxes the only way to achieve this was to cut back on what are often called discretionary programmes, or programmes that do not involve *entitlements* for individuals. As can be seen from table 4.4, grants to state and local governments began to level off during the late 1970s. The Carter experience demonstrated that federal aid to state and local governments was not destined to spiral ever upwards. It could be held in check – if from a high level.

We can conclude, then, that the pattern of intergovernmental relations prevailing by the early 1980s was very different from that of earlier eras. Governments of all types competed with one another for federal aid, and fragmentation within the system assured a prominent federal role. This does not, however, mean that the federal government was increasingly *dominant*. The ways in which federal aid is distributed were, and remain too political and complex to provide any one institution and political leader with complete control. Of course, the level and type of aid do vary with Congressional opinion, Presidential preference and political and economic climate.

The Reagan Administration: Federalism Revived?

In his campaign speeches and his 1981 inaugural address, Ronald Reagan made the revival of federalism a central part of his programme to rekindle traditional American values. The federal government had become inefficient, insensitive and cumbersome and, so the argument ran, should be reduced radically in size. One way to achieve this was to revive Richard Nixon's original idea and consolidate myriad categorical

20   See David McKay, *Domestic Policy and Ideology: Presidents and the American State 1964–1988*, Cambridge: Cambridge University Press, 1989, chapter 4.

grants-in-aid programmes into a number of block grants. In this way, the states would be returned to their 'rightful' position as the main source of domestic policies and programmes. Accordingly, during 1981 the administration proposed consolidating 83 categorical programmes into six human services block grants (health services, preventive health services, social services, energy and emergency assistance, local education services and state education services). The total amount of federal money involved here was $11 billion. At the same time the 1981 Budget Reconciliation Act reduced federal spending in a wide range of programmes. Some intergovernmental programmes were eliminated altogether, while others were subject to substantial real cuts (table 4.4).

Later, in 1982 the Administration presented an even more radical plan for a 'New Federalism' involving a 'swap' of the three main welfare programmes funded by the states and federal government on a matching basis. Welfare and food stamps would be taken over by the states while the federal government assumed responsibility for Medicaid (medical care for the poor). This plan was combined with a massive 'turnback' to the states of most other grant-in-aid programmes which, initially at least, would be funded by a special trust fund. In just five years, however, the fund would be wound up leaving the states in glorious isolation. In the meantime, an immediate 25 per cent cut in funding would be imposed.

The plan was greeted with almost unanimous opposition from the states, Congress and even from within the Office of Management and Budget – Medicaid was the most rapidly growing item in the federal budget. Within months the 'swap' plan was dropped as was the grandiose scheme for a near complete devolution of programmes to the states. In the event, Congress accepted some of the consolidations into block grants and some of the cuts. Generally, welfare, food stamps and capital spending programmes suffered most.

Although by 1984 the grand strategy of the New Federalism had been abandoned, Ronald Reagan had succeeded in reversing the historical trend towards ever increasing federal aid. By the late 1980s, a Democratic Congress urged on by the intergovernmental lobby began to fund programmes anew, but Reagan's impact on the agenda was considerable. How was he able to stem the flow of federal aid – especially in the light of all those factors which accounted for the explosion of aid in the 1960s and 1970s? Three points are of relevance:

1   In spite of renewed recession during the early 1980s, the fiscal position of most states and localities had improved by the time the Reagan cuts came into effect. Only the older Northern and Eastern cities continued to experience serious difficulties, and their political

influence in Washington was declining – especially as the Republicans controlled both the presidency and the Senate between 1980 and 1986.

2   The public mood had shifted away from supporting grandiose new social programmes and was strongly in favour of fiscal rectitude. Ronald Reagan was able to exploit this new mood, although, as will be shown later, he almost certainly went much further than the public were willing to accept.

3   The President's position on federal aid was simple and consistent. He wanted to rid the federal government of virtually *all* intergovernmental responsibilities, because he genuinely believed they did not work. Witness his 1980 comments on the federal urban renewal programme:

> Billions of dollars, thousands of studies, hundreds of experts – this is the formidable array of weapons the federal bureaucrats brought to the struggle to revitalize the cities. And what did it all lead to? Failure. Failure so great, so costly, so devastating in its destruction of neighborhoods – all in the name of 'urban renewal' – that it is all unbelievable. You don't need billions of taxpayers' dollars to save a city. You need a sense of purpose, some pride, some hope, and a capacity for work.[21]

Reagan was the first President in the modern era to have such a clear conception of the federal role. It was this ideological clarity that helped achieve the substantial cuts in federal funding during his first few years in office.

In spite of these successes Reagan was unable to turn the clock back to the 1950s by massively reducing federal aid. The public may be more critical of the federal government's role in this area,[22] but when it comes to specific programme cuts, the opposition forces mobilize – not always successfully – but sufficiently to prevent a transformation of the system.

21   Quoted in Richard P. Nathan, Fred C. Doolittle and Associates, *Reagan and the States*, Princeton, New Jersey, Princeton University Press, 1987, p. 48.
22   In 1936 56 per cent of a sample of voters said they preferred power to be concentrated in the federal rather than in state government. By 1981 the figure had fallen to 36 per cent. However a large majority, 76 per cent, still believed that the federal government had a responsibility for providing certain services for those who could not afford them. All figures from *Public Opinion*, vol. 4, no. 6, December/January 1982.

Is Federalism Dead?

Classical federalism, with state and federal governments each sovereign and separate in their own designated area, is very much dead – indeed, there is serious doubt that it ever applied in the United States. Cooperative federalism, which dominated intergovernmental relations from the 1930s to the 1950s, is also inappropriate as a description of the 1970s and 1980s. Competitive interdependence is a much more accurate label; but it describes federal, state and local relations not just federal–state interactions. If this is so, what is left of federalism? In strictly constitutional terms, not very much. Given the encroachment of federal powers and the relative independence of local governments, it is highly misleading to talk of shared sovereignty in the USA today. However, the states do remain important administrative and political units. As we noted at the beginning of the chapter, the states preserve variety – each continues to have its own separate legal and political system, and travelling from state to state the observer is aware of distinctive political cultures. Certainly, the states preserve a degree of local or regional political autonomy which is quite unfamiliar in unitary systems. The states are now also much more *efficient* and professional as policy makers than ever before. As state government has increased in size and status it has attracted more able personnel. Governors are of higher quality, and corruption, although still very much a part of some states' political cultures, is almost certainly less prevalent than it used to be. Finally, as suggested earlier, states now do a great deal more than they used to, not only in administering federal programmes but in running their own,[23] but the resilience and growth derive not so much from constitutional imperatives as from traditions, custom and the fact that the states remain *convenient* jurisdictions for the representation of a variety of interests.

The weak constitutional position of the states was confirmed in a landmark 1985 Supreme Court decision, *Garcia* v. *San Antonio Metropolitan Transit Authority* which permitted the federal government to regulate the wages of San Antonio bus workers. What was significant about the decision (arrived at by a five to four majority) was the rejection by the Court of any constitutional basis for this exercise of federal power. Instead the Court argued that limits to federal power 'inhered principally in the workings of the national government itself'.

23   See David McKay, 'Fiscal federalism, professionalism and the transformation of American state government', *Public Administration*, vol. 60, Spring 1982.

The full consequences of this decision will not be known until the election of a more actively interventionist federal government. Even in this event, the states will remain important administrative and political units. State law remains pre-eminent in many areas of economic and social life including industrial relations, insurance, marriage and divorce. At the same time state and local taxes are the main source of revenue for a range of distinctive state and locally provided services including transport, education and law enforcement. If anything, the role of the states has increased as federal governments have required them to participate in the implementation of federally funded or partly funded programmes. American society may be becoming more nationalized as federal standards increasingly apply. The constitutional position of the states may also be weak, but they remain highly convenient political and administrative units for the implementation of a broad range of federal and state programmes.

While federalism has been utilized by localist and anti-statist interests to inhibit the coordinating and planning role of the federal government, social reformers should be wary of criticizing the institution of federalism as such. They would be better advised to study those political and economic forces which have used federalism so successfully. The great paradox of the 1980s is that the main critics of federal power often have strong links with states and localities which are now locked into an interdependent relationship with the federal government.

Further Reading

The best general introduction to US intergovernmental relations is Deil S. Wright's *Understanding Intergovernmental Relations*, North Scituate, Mass., Duxbury, 2nd edition, 1982. For the traditional view of the transition from conflictual to cooperative federalism, see Morton Grodzins's *The American System*, Chicago, Rand McNally, 1966. Michael Reagan's *The New Federalism*, New York, Oxford University Press, 1972, 2nd edition with John G. Sanzone, 1981, is a well written account of changes in IGR during the 1960s and 1970s. For an account of the evolution of federalism from Johnson to Reagan, see David McKay, *Domestic Policy and Ideology: Presidents and the American State, 1964–1988*, Cambridge, Cambridge University Press, 1989. Richard P. Nathan, Fred C. Doolittle and Associates provide an account of the effects of the Reagan policy changes on the states in *Reagan and the States*, Princeton, New Jersey, Princeton University Press, 1987.

5

American Political Parties in Transition

A democratic society has to provide a mode of consistent representation of relatively stable alignments or modes of compromise, in its
polity. The mechanism of the American polity has been the two party
system. If the party system, with its enforced mode of compromise,
gives way, and 'issue politics' begin to polarize groups, then we have
the classic recipe for what political scientists call 'a crisis of the
regime', if not a crisis of disintegration and revolution.

Daniel Bell, *The Public Interest*

The American political party system is not an insoluble puzzle. But it
does have more than its share of mysteries. The main one, arguably,
is how it has survived for so long, or perhaps, how it survived at all,
in a difficult and complicated environment.

William J. Keefe,
Parties, Politics and Public Policy in America

To the outside observer, the American party system conjures up almost
a caricature picture of American politics. Parties appear non-ideological,
organizationally weak and in a constant state of crisis. In contrast, most
European political parties have quite vivid public images based on class,
regional, religious, linguistic, ethnic or ideological divisions. And when
new parties emerge claiming support based on social consensus rather
than cleavage (as did the British Social Democratic Party during the
early 1980s) their 'pragmatism' or even 'opportunism' is viewed with
distrust and suspicion.

While this is an oversimplified characterization of the two types of
party system, it remains broadly true that American parties cover a
much narrower band of the ideological spectrum than do their European
counterparts. They are also much less *programmatic*, offering their

supporters very general and diffuse policy options rather than the highly structured and specific policy programmes associated with European parties. What is true of almost all party systems is that they are constantly developing and adapting to rapid social and economic changes – a fact which leads so many commentators to attach the label 'crisis' to the most recent development or electoral event. The remarkable thing about the American system is that it has always had just two major parties – although not always the same two parties – competing for major offices at any one time. Moreover, these parties have been largely non-ideological in style and policy substance, and this in a country constantly being buffeted by the very major social changes which immigration, industrialization and urbanization have brought.

A large part of this chapter will be devoted to explaining why the American party system has taken this particular shape. As we shall see, however, although this system has retained its two-party, largely non-ideological status through history, it has by no means been static or unchanging. In organization and function the parties have changed quite dramatically over the last 200 years. To understand these changes it is first necessary to discuss the functions which political parties normally play in political systems.

The Functions of Parties

Although often abused by politicians and publics alike, political parties do perform vital functions in every political system, and in countries with democratic traditions they are an indisputably necessary part of the democratic process. In the American context parties perform at least five major functions.[1]

Aggregation of demands

In any society, social groups with particular interests to promote or defend need some means whereby their demands can be aggregated and articulated in government. Traditionally, political parties have performed this function – hence the association of party with particular social groups, regions or religions. In the USA parties have acquired

1 This list of functions – although not the discussion of them – is taken from Gerald M. Pomper, 'Party functions and party failures', in Gerald M. Pomper et al., *The Performance of American Government: Checks and Minuses*, New York, Free Press, 1972, pp. 46–63.

just such associations, although to a rather lesser extent than in some other countries. Hence, the Democrats became the party of Southern interests quite early in history, although by the 1930s the Democrats had also become the party of the Northern industrial working class. The Republicans emerged from the Civil War as the party of national unity and later became identified as the party most interested in defending free enterprise and corporate power, an identification which remains today.

But generally, parties in the United States have not been exclusively identified with one social group or class or one geographical region. Instead they tend to be coalitions of interests, aggregating demands on behalf of a number of social groups and regional interests. Given the relatively low level of ideological division and conflict in the USA (see chapter 2), this is, perhaps, unsurprising.

Conciliation of groups in society

Even in the most divided society some conciliation between competing or conflicting interests has to occur if government is to operate efficiently. Political parties often help this conciliation process by providing united platforms for the articulation of diverse interests. Indeed in the USA, there has hardly been a major political party which has not performed this function. In recent history, the Democrats have attempted (and until 1964 largely succeeded) in reconciling a segregationist South with the interests of Northern industrial workers. In specific elections, the particular coalition of support established is uniquely determined by contemporary issues and candidates. So in 1960 Democratic Presidential candidate John F. Kennedy managed to appeal both to the Catholic voters of the North (Kennedy was himself a Catholic) and Southern Protestants. In 1968 and 1972, the law and order issue cut across regions and classes and helped bring victory to Richard M. Nixon, the Republican candidate. By 1980 the Republicans had forged a new coalition consisting of a regional component (the West and South West), a religious component (the Fundamentalist Christian right) and an economic/ideological component (the middle classes and supporters of a 'return' to free enterprise). By conciliating such diverse groups and offering a common programme, Republican candidate Ronald Reagan was assured victory. In 1988 George Bush managed to retain the loyalty of sufficient numbers of these same groups to ensure victory.

Clearly, political parties have to appeal to a number of competing and potentially conflicting interests if they are to succeed in a country as diverse and complex as the United States. As a result, parties have tended to move towards the middle of the ideological spectrum avoiding those more extreme positions which are likely to alienate potential supporters. Noting this tendency towards moderation, political theorists have produced a more general model of party behaviour which assumes that if parties are rational and really want to win elections they will *always* move towards the centre. For only in this way can they ensure majority electoral support.[2] Whatever its merits in other countries, this theory seems particularly apt in the United States where with rather few exceptions (of which more later) parties have remained remarkably moderate.

Staffing the government

In a modern, complex society parties are a necessary link in the relationship between government and people. According to social contract theory, governments must be held accountable for their actions. If they are perceived to be failing, then the people can always replace them at election time. Unfortunately, accountability and responsiveness can never be continuous or complete except in very small societies or communities. Given this, parties provide the public with a focus for accountability. Once elected, a President appoints government officials to fill the major posts in the new administration. Not only departmental chiefs (members of the Cabinet) but also the top civil service positions are filled in the main through party linkages (see chapter 10). When judging the performance of the government, therefore, the public can look to the record of an administration united by a common party label and, presumably, a common set of policies. As the party is rooted in society via democratic party organization, staffing the government through party helps to ensure an intimate link between the implementation of policies and public preference. This at least is the theory of how party should operate in government. As we will discover later the practice is rather different. One serious practical problem occurs when party organization, rather than reflecting the interests of social groups or regions, is instead merely the vehicle for the promotion and election of a particular *candidate*. Another problem, to which we will now turn, occurs when different branches of government have different constituencies and therefore distinct party organizations.

2 Anthony Downs, *An Economic Theory of Democracy*, New York, Harper and Row, 1957.

Coordination of government institutions

As has already been noted several times in this book, American government is uncommonly fragmented. National legislature is separated from executive. Federalism adds further fragmenting influence by giving state (and through the states, local) governments considerable independence from the federal authorities. In centralized systems with cabinet government, parties actually dominate institutions. In Britain for example, powerful political party organizations nominate candidates, fight elections, and, if successful form the government out of a majority in the House of Commons. By exercising control over the party organization, governments (or oppositions) can usually ensure the obedience of individual Members of Parliament. In this sense party is hardly needed as a coordinating influence, because a system of party government prevails. In marked contrast, America's separated powers and federal arrangements greatly aggravate problems of coordination, and as numerous American political scientists have pointed out, party is the main means whereby disparate institutions can coordinate the formulation and implementation of policy.[3]

So, even if state and local government, Congress and President have different constituencies, a common party label can provide a means of communication and coordination. In fact, Democratic governors, mayors and Congressmen normally do have more in common with Democratic Presidents than with Republican Presidents – although we will discover later they often do not. Moreover, there have been periods in American history when relations between Congress and President have been greatly aided by political party ties. During the Jeffersonian period, for example, something approaching party government prevailed. More recently, Presidents Franklin Roosevelt and Lyndon Johnson (both Democrats) used party ties greatly to enhance their relations with Congress and thus erect major new social programmes.

At the state and local levels, the coordinating function of party has taken a rather different form. In the decades immediately following the Civil War, municipal and to a lesser extent state governments proved less than adequate in dealing with successive waves of immigrants from Europe. Hopelessly divided and fragmented institutionally and politically, local governments could do little to improve transport, housing and other urban facilities, or even to ensure a reasonable degree of public order. Political parties filled this void through the creation of

3 Hence the pleas for a system of 'responsible party government' in the USA. For a summary of this literature, see Austin Ranney *Curing the Mischiefs of Faction: Party Reform in America*, Berkeley, University of California Press, 1975.

the political machine – an informal 'government' based on patronage, bribery and corruption.[4] Machines depended on tightly knit grass-roots organization with the party providing ordinary citizens with direct access to the political authorities. Officials in the legitimate government gained through patronage and bribes and the party was given a guarantee of political power in return. Although hardly welfare organizations, the urban machines of the late nineteenth and early twentieth centuries did at least keep government going in the great cities by providing an essential buffer between the immigrant masses and a hostile economic and political environment.

Promotion of political stability

Parties do not always promote political stability. In many countries parties mobilize movements against existing regimes and are a major force in bringing regime change. Moreover, if *governmental* (as opposed to regime) stability is the measure, it is clear that the multi-party systems of Western Europe do anything but promote stability, as the Danish, Dutch and Italian systems testify. In 'mature' democracies, however, parties do help socialize citizens into an acceptance of the regime, if only by legitimizing national parliaments and assemblies and facilitating the peaceful transferral of power from one government to another.

For reasons which we will discuss later, America's two-party system has proved remarkably resilient, with the result that the country has never suffered the problems associated with a proliferation of organized parties. Although the causal lines are blurred it does seem reasonable to argue that American political parties have helped promote political stability. Quite frequently, for example, political movements outside the mainstream of American political life have had their policies pre-empted by one of the leading parties. This happened to the Populists during the 1890s when much of their programme was adopted by the Democrats, and to a number of left-wing parties and movements during the early New Deal period. Moreover, the two most significant third parties of the twentieth century, the Progressives and the American Independent Party grew out of existing parties and were eventually re-incorporated into them. In both cases the breakaway was led by a single charismatic figure – Theodore Roosevelt in the case of the Progressives and George Wallace in the case of the American Independent Party.

4   The classic account of the machine is by Harold F. Gosnell, *Machine Politics: Chicago Model*, Chicago, University of Chicago Press, 1937.

In fact George Wallace effectively *was* the party and without him it simply disappeared. But the crucial point is that the issues which inspired both movements – dispute over the federal government's role in economy and society and the racial integration of the South – and which the existing parties could not accommodate, did *not* lead to a permanent split in the party movement. Instead, either the Democrats and Republicans adapted to the new demands or the movements themselves were re-incorporated into the mainstream once the protest had been made.

The constantly impressive ability of American political parties to absorb potentially destabilizing social movements has no doubt contributed to the stability of the system, although the more enquiring mind could note that the two major parties have been able to perform this function only because there have been so few deep ideological divisions in American society. A more divided society could not possibly sustain such a monopoly of power shared by two such amorphous and adaptable parties.

Crisis and Change in the American Party System

At least since the early 1950s political scientists have bemoaned the decline of American political parties. The 'crisis' has been identified mainly in terms of a constant erosion of the five functions listed above. In what is already a highly fragmented political system, the decline of these functions has, so the argument runs, led to highly inefficient government ridden with indecision and confusion.

In order to understand this critique it is necessary to be familiar with the development of American political parties. Table 5.1 provides a schematic outline of their history by identifying five distinct stages of development. Such a brief summary of the parties' growth must oversimplify somewhat. In particular the outline implies that the parties have mobilized different regions and social groups in a coherent way throughout history. But this has never been the case. With the notable exception of the Civil War period, the parties have always represented broad coalitions, and they have almost always eschewed appeals to those class-based ideologies which exploit social divisions in society.

Until the early years of the nineteenth century, parties were considered useful only as temporary expedients, or as 'factions' necessary to mobilize political power in response to particular crises. As was emphasized in chapter 3, the Constitution and the political culture generally in the New Republic were deeply suspicious of political parties and their implied threat of government by factions, tyrannical majorities

Table 5.1　The development of American political parties

Period	Majority party	Minority party
1789–1800	*Federalist:* A coalition of Mercantile and Northern landowning interests led by Alexander Hamilton, George Washington and John Adams.	*Republican (the first Republican party):* A coalition of farmers and planters based in the central and southern states and led by Thomas Jefferson.
1800–56	*Democratic–Republican:* The original Republican coalition was consolidated in this period under James Madison. Later under the leadership of Andrew Jackson and Martin van Buren, the party broadened its mass appeal and was renamed the Democratic Party.	*Federalist* then *Whig:* Federalists, whigs and a number of smaller parties failed to challenge the Democratic–Republican ascendancy. Victories by the conservative Whigs in 1840 and 1848 were temporary exceptions and led to the rather inauspicious presidencies of William Harrison and Zachary Taylor, both of whom died in office.
1856–1932	*Republican:* The Civil War produced a second Republican Party championing the Unionist cause under Abraham Lincoln. Following the War, a formidable coalition of industrialists, bankers, Northern and Western farmers and some industrial workers proved formidable. Apart from Abraham Lincoln, only Theodore Roosevelt (1901–9) proved a memorable President. The era of strong local and state party organizations and machine politics.	*Democratic:* Democratic strength remained firmly rooted in the South where both poor Whites and larger landowners supported the party (those Blacks briefly enfranchised after the War supported the Republicans). The four Democratic victories of 1884, 1892, 1912 and 1916 were greatly aided by splits in the Republican ranks.
1932–68	*Democratic:* The era of the New Deal coalition, with the South, the unions, the big cities, ethnic groups and intellectuals providing a near-permanent majority in the House and the Senate. Franklin Roosevelt, Harry Truman, John Kennedy and Lyndon Johnson are all notable presidents.	*Republican:* Relegated to minority status, the Republican victories in 1952 and 1956 are attributable to the charismatic appeal of Dwight Eisenhower. Main Republican support comes from rural areas, big business, middle-class suburbanites, the West and New England.
1968–	Support for the two main political parties becomes much more volatile and unpredictable. The New Deal coalition breaks down, with the South voting Republican in Presidential and increasingly in Congressional and state elections. Some claims by 1980 of an emerging Republican majority consisting of the West, the South, big business and middle-class suburbanites. But by the end of the 1980s the Democrats remain the majority party and continue to dominate the House of Representatives and most state governments. Local and state party organization declines, but national party organization is strengthened during the 1970s and 1980s.	

and mass political action. Significantly when, under the guidance of Andrew Jackson and Martin Van Buren, mass parties did develop, they did so in a way which largely avoided the dangers foreseen by the Founding Fathers. The new Democratic Party appealed to broad principles of political equality (at least for White males) rather than to narrow class and sectional interests. It also transformed the party into a highly *instrumental* organization. For the first time the idea that working for the party could bring specific rewards for the individual became influential. So party membership and loyalty brought with it rewards or political 'spoils' of which patronage was the most important. Clearly, delivering the vote and distributing patronage required organization, and it was during this period that local and state parties acquired permanent organizations, as Michael Wallace and others have documented.[5] What united these new party organizations was a simple belief in equal opportunity for white males (and a concomitant opposition to aristocratic political values) and in the party as a distributor of spoils. Beyond this the party represented little that was tangible. Great local and regional variety was encouraged rather than tolerated.

A party based on equality and democracy (achieved mainly through the extension of the franchise) and which adopted a new instrumentalism in organization was hardly likely to undermine the Republicanism and constitutionalism which the Founding Fathers so feared would be threatened by mass parties. From the very beginning, therefore, mass political parties in the United States built their electoral competition not on appeals to class, ethnic or religious division, but rather by adapting their programmes to what was always a broad base of support for individualism and democracy. In this context the parties were also able to aid the Presidential nomination process by limiting competition and providing truly national constituencies.

As we know, this new party system was far from being completely successful. Southern Democrats were determined to champion their exclusive sectional interests, and the Civil War effectively destroyed the first mass party system. As table 5.1 shows, what emerged after the War was a dominant Republican party, again depending on a broad coalition of support. It was also during the latter half of the nineteenth century that parties became associated with corruption and the growth of the large urban political machine. Much has been written about the machine, although nobody quite captured the spirit of the period as did George Washington Plunkitt, the notorious boss of New York's

5   Michael L. Wallace, 'Changing concepts of party in the United States: New York, 1815–28', *American Historical Review* 74, 1968, pp. 453–91.

Tammany Hall. His comment that 'you can't keep an organization together without patronage. Men ain't in politics for nothin'. They want to get somethin' out of it'[6] gives some of the flavour of the time. Milton Rakove has characterized the machine in slightly more academic terms:

> An effective political party needs five things: offices, jobs, money, workers, and votes. Offices beget jobs and money; jobs and money beget workers; workers beget votes; and votes beget offices.[7]

It follows that if one party controls all the offices it effectively controls the politics in that jurisdiction. Just such a pattern emerged in numerous nineteenth-century towns and cities (and in a modified form in some states). Scholars have cited a number of reasons for the spread of machine politics, the most important being the growing need for an institution capable of integrating a diverse and ever increasing number of urban immigrants into American society. With state and local authorities unwilling or unable to provide immigrants with good government, political machines stepped in to fill the gap. The new Americans, confused, intimidated or exploited by employers, landlords or the police, could turn to party precinct captains or ward bosses for help. In return the machine demanded electoral loyalty.

Machine politics permeated party systems from the lowest ward and precinct level up to city and in some cases state committees. Figure 5.1 shows the basic party organizational structure which emerged during this period and which still holds true in most states today. As will be developed later, this structure used to be very much a 'bottom up' affair with the committees at county level and below as the key organizational units.

In spite of the emergence of a largely middle-class reform movement intent on cleansing the cities of machine politics, the machine remained an important part of the American scene until well after the Second World War. But some of the reforms introduced in the late nineteenth and early twentieth centuries did have a significant and lasting effect on American politics. A major concern of the reformers was to remove the partisan element from the electoral process. Accordingly, most of the proposed changes involved weakening the link between parties and electors. Party labels were removed from voting lists; elected mayors were sometimes replaced by city managers appointed by the local assembly; candidates were elected 'at large' or from a list covering the

6 William Riordan, *Plunkitt of Tammany Hall*, New York, E. P. Dutton, 1963, p. 63.
7 Milton Rakove, *Don't Make No Waves, Don't Back No Losers*, Bloomington, Indiana University Press, 1975, p. 42.

Figure 5.1   Party organizational structure

whole city rather than on a ward-by-ward basis, and, most significant, *primaries* were introduced in order to deny the party machines control over nominations for office. Instead, voters were given a direct say in who was to be nominated through an intra-party primary election. These and other reforms hardly transformed the American party system. At best they had a limited effect in certain areas and regions, particularly in the more populist Mountain and Western states. *Local* party machines were, in any case, the main target of the reformers for it was in the burgeoning industrial cities that the most corrupt regimes had developed.

Primary elections, however, soon affected national parties as an increasing number of states adopted them for Presidential elections. By 1916 no less than 20 states required the parties to go direct to the voters to decide the selection of delegates to the national nominating convention[8] rather than rely on party machines with party bosses deciding among themselves who should go to the convention pledged to a particular candidate.

In fact, between the 1920s and the 1960s this democratizing trend in American political parties received little fresh impetus. On the contrary, this period witnessed something of a return to old-fashioned party

8   Nominating conventions are the party conferences held during the summer preceding Presidential elections to choose Presidential and Vice-Presidential candidates. For a fuller discussion, see chapter 9.

politics. Presidential primaries declined (to a mere 16 or 17 in 1968, see table 5.2), as the nominating power reverted to the state party caucuses. And at the local level parties often found ways of by-passing the institutional obstacles to party hegemony.[9] However, it would be misleading to characterize these trends simply as a return to the old model. In many ways they were profoundly different from the late nineteenth century. Above all, after 1932 the Democratic Party emerged as the 'majority' party constructed around a seemingly invincible coalition consisting of the South, Northern industrial workers, ethnic minorities and an increasingly insecure middle class. Local, state and even national Democratic party organizations were greatly strengthened by this enduring coalition which scored victory after victory at every level of politics. But unlike the nineteenth century, these party organizations did not primarily function as intermediaries between the authorities and urban masses. By the 1930s welfare and social security reforms reduced the dependence of the poor on party workers, and government officials themselves became increasingly professional and less susceptible to bribery and corruption. Instead, parties developed into modern organizations performing, albeit imperfectly, many of the functions described above. The parties also became markedly more ideological, with the Democrats clearly emerging as the party of the left and the Republicans as the party of the right. Indeed almost all the major social and economic reforms of recent years have been initiated by Democratic administrations. While hardly socialist in conception or outcome, these have resulted in a much enhanced role for the federal government in society.

But even by the 1940s there were signs that the New Deal coalition was not completely secure. The South, in particular, found what were very hesitant steps taken by the Truman administration on civil rights unpalatable and by the 1968 election the Democratic-led integration of the South resulted in open revolt, with George Wallace leading a breakaway Southern party intent on preserving racial segregation. As important, the considerable – and very 'unamerican' – ideological cohesion of the Democratic party began to crumble as suburbanization, affluence and a changing occupational structure slowly transformed the political agenda. We will discuss the relationship between these changes and voting in some detail in chapter 6, but for now it is important to explain their effects on political parties.

9   Chicago, for example, was 'reformed', but the Mayor retained his position as 'boss' through control over the Cook County Democratic Party which contains the city of Chicago. See Mike Royko, *Boss. Mayor Richard J. Daley of Chicago*, New York, E. P. Dutton, 1971.

It it obvious that if parties are to perform their functions competently they must have some internal cohesion. Within Congress a party label must mean something more than mere nomenclature. If a common party is the major means whereby Congress and President can liaise, then President and legislators must have at least some shared policies and perspectives. When a President staffs the executive branch, he must assume that his appointees broadly share his philosophy of government. Such party cohesion must have roots in the broader society; in effect some form of party organization must exist to facilitate the exchange of ideas, and to mobilize electoral support and nominate candidates. It was the apparent erosion of cohesion and party organization from the mid-1960s that worried so many commentators. Three major questions are raised here: What was the nature of party decline? What explains it; and, more controversially, does it really matter – especially given recent evidence of some revival in the state and national parties?

Party Decline

There are a number of ways of measuring party decline, the most common of which are: membership, party identification, organization and control over candidate nominations, ideological cohesion and, of course, voting patterns. By all these measures parties have been in decline, although party membership is not a meaningful measure in the USA as it is equivalent to the simple act of registering (sometimes as a Democrat or Republican) to vote in most states. In other words, people do not *join* and pay dues in the European manner. Party identification, or the psychological attachment which individual voters have to particular parties has been weakening steadily over the last 35 years with the number of Independents[10] clearly on the rise. (See figure 5.2.)

Weaker party identification produces a much more fickle electorate prone to sudden shifts in loyalty, to ticket splitting, and to voting for individual candidates or issues rather than according to traditional party ties. Measuring changes in party organization is rather more difficult. Certainly the party machine model no longer applies. Recent research has shown that even in an archetypal machine city, elected officials no longer expect party loyalty and service in return for the patronage they dispense.[11] But the typical party organization described earlier still applies even if individual activists' motivations have changed.

10   The concept of 'independent' voter, virtually unknown in most European countries, is well established in America. See chapter 6, pp. 113–14.
11   For a general discussion, see Martin P. Wattenberg, *The Decline of American Political Parties, 1951–1980*, Cambridge, Mass., Harvard University Press, 1984.

Figure 5.2   Party identification in the United States 1952–1986

Source: Center for Political Studies, University of Michigan, National Election Studies, various years.

Party organization has always been loose in the United States, and it remains the case that the higher the level of committee the looser it becomes. Much of the essential work of fundraising and campaigning occurs at the precinct level, with the counties also playing a major role in some states. State parties vary in organizational strength. In some states (mainly in the West) state parties are quite powerful in such areas as fundraising and slating statewide candidates. Unfortunately there is no consistent pattern; much depends on the history and tradition of individual states.[12]

Until the 1970s it was normal to characterize the national party committees as little more than very loose *ad hoc* organizations which emerged every four years to help arrange the national conventions. They are very much more than this today, however. The Republican National Committee (RNC), in particular, has acquired a range of new

12   For a discussion, see John F. Bibby et al., 'Assessing party organizational strength', *American Journal of Political Science*, vol. 27, 1983, pp. 193–222.

resources and powers since the 1970s including a capacity to run direct mailing campaigns on behalf of candidates at the national and the state levels. The RNC also provides staff and technical services (polling, breakdowns of local and regional voting patterns) for candidates. Much of the impetus for this new role came from RNC Chairman Bill Brock (1977–81) who realized the potential for a national role in what had become a much more ideologically unified Republican Party. Although stronger than it used to be, the Democratic National Committee (DNC) has not assumed a similar role – probably because the Democratic Party is more fragmented than the Republican, and the ideological unity between different candidates and local parties is lower. What the DNC has initiated, however, is a series of enquiries into the presidential nominating process including how the party chooses delegates to the national convention. The first of these, the McGovern–Fraser Commission (1969), recommended that state parties change their rules so as to allow greater participation by minorities, women and the young at the convention. Two subsequent enquiries, the Mikulski Commission (1972–3) and the Winograd Commission (1975–8) further refined these rule changes. Most recently the Hunt Commission (1981–2) and the Fairness Commission (1984–5) have moved the party in a quite different direction, requiring as they did increased representation of party regulars and elected officials (the so called super delegates). The background to these changes will be discussed below.

What of the party activists themselves? Only about 2 per cent of the adult population are active participants in party organizations, almost all of which are locally based. Generally over the last few years these activists have become more candidate and issue oriented, one of their main motivations being to promote a particular candidate or to fight for just one special issue. Critics argue that these trends have weakened party organization and coherence even further.

One area where the role of party organization can be accurately measured is control over nominations. At the Presidential level, at least, the trend here was, until 1980, unequivocal. As table 5.2 shows, primaries spread to the point where, in 1980, 71 per cent of Democratic delegates to the national convention and 75 per cent of Republican were chosen or bound by primary elections. In quite dramatic fashion, therefore, the intra-party means of choosing delegates (party caucuses and conventions whose use actually increased between 1916 and 1968) were rejected, leaving this key decision to the mass of voters themselves. Since 1980 concern in the Democratic Party in particular that it was losing control of nominations led to a partial return to the caucus method (table 5.2). However even these are more open to popular

Table 5.2   Presidential primaries, 1968–1988

Party and Coverage	1968	1972	1976	1980	1984	1988
Democratic Party						
Number of states using a primary for selecting or binding national convention delegates	17	23	29	31	24	31
Number of votes cast by delegates chosen or bound by primaries	1,276	1,977	2,264	2,378	2,046	2,771
Percentage of all votes cast by delegates chosen or bound by primaries	49	66	75	71	52	66
Republican Party						
Number of states using a primary for selecting or binding national convention delegates	16	22	28	33	31	34
Number of votes cast by delegates chosen or bound by primaries	601	715	1,501	1,502	1,517	1,751
Percentage of all votes cast by delegates chosen or bound by primaries	45	53	66	75	68	77

Source: Congressional Quarterly, various years.

pressure than 'old style' party meetings. In fact by 1988 the trend towards the use of primaries was re-established. As we will discuss later, these particular changes have had particularly significant consequences for the state of the modern Presidency.

The evidence on intra-party cohesion is also pretty unequivocal. A host of surveys have shown how, since the mid-1960s, the issues which bound the New Deal coalition together – and which provided a convenient target for the Republicans – have either receded in importance or have been diluted by the emergence of other, less class-based issues. Until the mid-1970s, the major change involved the decline of economic issues in relation to 'social' issues. In 1975 Walter Dean Burnham characterized this shift in the terms shown in figure 5.3.

What Burnham was describing here was what social scientists call 'cross-cutting cleavages' or the fact that individuals and social groups often lack ideological coherence across all issues. Hence in the late 1960s many industrial workers and trade unionists remained left wing on economic or class issues, while finding themselves on the right of the political spectrum over racial questions and the Vietnam War. While figure 5.3 is now out of date, the phenomenon of cross-cutting cleavages is still very much with us. Figure 5.4 attempts to characterize the divisions of the early 1980s. Although not shown by these figures, which give no indication of the *distribution* of support for these issues, the

Figure 5.3   Cross-cutting issues in the late 1960s and early 1970s

Source: Adapted from *The American Party Systems: Stages of Political Development*, 2nd edn, edited by William Nisbet Chambers and Walter Dean Burnham, © 1975 Oxford University Press, Inc., p. 340. Reprinted by permission.

major shift from the earlier period is the emergence of a much more ideologically coherent right, organized around the Presidency of Ronald Reagan. In the early 1970s, the majority party, the Democrats, were in disarray, their support being split between the two left-hand segments of figure 5.3. By the early 1980s this division continued to affect the Democrats, and a number of commentators were claiming that the Republican right were fast assuming the status of majority party. But the Reagan victories were not to be repeated at the Congressional or state levels, and by 1988 Democratic presidential prospects improved, even though George Bush was the eventual winner. Clearly this recovery was related to the personalities of the respective candidates, but it was also related to issues. As figure 5.5 shows, by the late 1980s it was possible to make distinctions according to the public's and candidates'

Figure 5.4   Cross-cutting issues in the early 1980s

* Affirmative action, abortion, civil liberties, the environment.

association with economic/welfare state issues and social/foreign policy issues. The former refer to such questions as job security (providing a minimum notice of dismissal for laid off workers), education, training, relief for economically distressed regions and welfare reform. The latter refer to the conscience issues (abortion, civil liberties, prayers in public schools), affirmative action (civil rights enforcement), the environment, consumer protection, occupational safety, child care and selected foreign policy issues (Central America and South Africa).

Note that by 1988 the two presidential candidates were much closer together in ideological terms than was the case in 1980 or 1984. Indeed as the electorate has become more volatile and a politics of personalities rather than issues has developed, so it has become increasingly difficult to characterize the parties in terms even of a loose ideological profile. Ever more complex cross-cutting issues are leading the system further

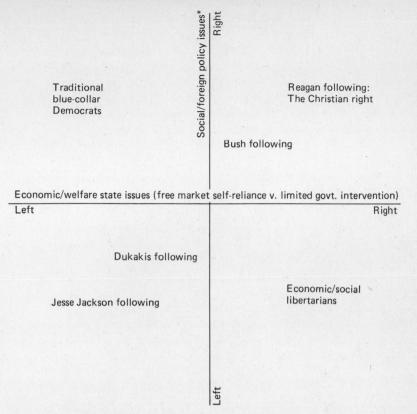

Figure 5.5　Cross-cutting issues in the late 1980s

* Affirmative action, abortion, child care, civil liberties, the environment, Central America, South Africa.

and further away from the relative ideological cohesion associated with the New Deal.

Explaining Party Decline

Reference has already been made to the social and economic changes usually invoked to explain decline. Affluence, increasing levels of education and suburbanization have produced less 'solidaristic' communities, as the sociologists put it. In other words, a political life based on an individual's place of work or neighbourhood has become increasingly irrelevant as the mobile service sector worker living in a sprawling suburb or, more recently, semi-rural area, replaces the blue-collar inner-city industrial worker as the 'norm' in American society.

This new, essentially middle-class citizen has acquired a political life defined not just in terms of occupation or geographical location, but also in terms of his or her individual preferences, prejudices and particular interests. In response to this much more complex and less categorizable voter, the parties have themselves changed, becoming even less programmatic and ideological. But in trying to be all things to all citizens, parties have become progressively less appealing. It stands to reason that a class- (or region-, or religion-) based party can have instant attraction to voters whose lifestyles and occupational interests coincide closely with those represented by party policies. A more amorphous, non-ideological party is rarely as appealing and always runs the risk of alienating a particular section of society should it commit itself to a specific policy.

But we should counsel caution in accepting this sociological analysis. Many groups – and particularly ethnic and racial minorities – remain 'solidaristic', concentrated as they are in ghettos and in lower paid manual jobs. More importantly, this analysis suggests some simple past when American political parties represented 'left' and 'right' in society with reasonable coherence. But as repeatedly pointed out in this chapter, this has never been the case. Parties have always been essentially non-ideological and even the New Deal Democratic Party was marked by a degree of internal dissension and compromise over policies which would be unusual in European class-based parties.

A related explanation for the decline of parties concentrates less on societal changes and more on the performance of government itself. Hence the 'overload' thesis argues that the increasing democratization of American society has placed an excessive load on what is in any case a complex decision-making system. Unable to cope with the array of competing demands placed on them, institutions have increasingly come under fire from a disenchanted public. Indeed, during the early 1970s a burgeoning literature on declining trust in government hinted that public disillusionment with political institutions posed a threat to democracy itself.[13] Although this particular argument is now largely discredited, it remains the case that parties continue to take much of the blame for public disenchantment with politics. For to repeat the point, it has been the failure of parties to provide coherent programmes, to staff the government, to help smooth relations between Congress and President which, so the criticism goes, accounts for the failure of successive administrations to solve America's problems.

13   For a discussion of this literature, see David McKay, 'The United States in crisis: a review of the political literature', *Government and Opposition*, vol. 14, no. 3, Summer 1979.

Paradoxically, attempts within the parties to improve their perform-ance may actually have aggravated the situation. By the mid-1960s activists in both parties, but particularly from within the ranks of the Democrats, became increasingly disillusioned with the undemocratic nature of intra-party decision making. Both parties were dominated by age cohorts recruited during the New Deal period – male, White, middle-aged and middle-income (upper middle-income in the case of the Republicans). The new activists, most of whom were strongly committed to the 'new' issues of the 1960s – social reform in the case of the Democrats, economic liberalism with the Republicans – slowly but surely began to take over local and state party organizations. In doing so they insisted on more open decision-making structures and better access by under-represented groups – within the Democratic Party, Blacks, women, the poor and younger people. It was this quite virulent intra-party reform movement which paved the way for the spread of primary elections and for new rules at nominating conventions favouring delegates from under-represented groups (as recommended by the 1969 McGovern–Fraser Commission). As we have mentioned, the spread of primaries actually weakened both parties as the crucial power of control over nominations passed directly to the voters. And more open conventions led, in the case of the Democrats, to party opinions and policies seriously out of tune with those supported by the 'typical' Democratic voter. Hence the now famous 1972 Democratic convention was dominated by new 'social issue' delegates (see bottom left quadrant of figure 5.3) who nominated a candidate, George McGovern, with very little support from traditional 'economic issue' Democrats.[14] Since 1972 the Democrats have modified the party rules so as to permit a less rigid selection of delegates and to ensure some representation of party regulars and elected officials (the so-called super delegates), but in one important sense the change was permanent, for the events of the late 1960s and early 1970s reduced the influence of regular activists in myriad state and local parties. In their stead, a new breed of party volunteers had taken over many party organizations. Paradoxically, this new type of activist was *more* middle-class than the people they replaced, in spite of the fact that the changes were themselves inspired by calls for equal opportunity and greater representation of the poor and minorities. The explanation here is simple: people who *volunteer* their services and who care about issues are usually educated, competent and well informed. Many of the old style party workers were recipients of party patronage

14   See Jeane Kirkpatrick, *The New Presidential Elite*, Russell Sage, Twentieth Century Fund, 1976.

or had become active during the 1930s and 1940s when there was a clearer relationship between party and class. As a result, the old style Democratic activists, although White, male and middle-aged, were decidedly less well educated and generally of lower socio-economic status than the new style party workers who replaced them.

Unravelling cause and effect when explaining party decline is difficult. The rise of the social issue during the 1960s resulted in large part from changes in American society, although also from the way in which the Vietnam War was being conducted. Parties and political institutions were profoundly affected by these changes and, once affected, in turn influenced the public's perception of the performance of government. This complex interaction of institutions and society is, of course, a continuous process and it may well be that, not only in the USA but in other mature democracies, the age of the highly organized and effective political party is over. A crucial question is raised by this prospect: can liberal democracy function properly without strong political parties?

Does the Decline of Party Matter?

To the more pessimistic observers, the fact of party decline is incontrovertible. Pointing to the indicators discussed above, they reluctantly accept the demise of the parties, warn of the deleterious consequences and plead, somewhat forlornly, for party revival, or more 'consensual' institutions.[15] In essence, weak parties erode the vital five functions discussed earlier. Presidential/Congressional liaison becomes difficult, Presidents have few cues to guide them when appointing officials, a Presidential nominating process outside the control of party boosts 'media created' candidates who may be skilful at winning primaries but rarely make good Presidents. Above all, political competition based on special interests or causes, rather than on broadly contrasting party programmes, results in a politics of confusion and waste. Certainly, examples – and sometimes dramatic examples – of all these maladies can easily be found in recent American politics.

Before we accept the critique in full, however, we should note the following. First, amid all the furore over disintegrating parties, not a single third party has emerged with even the semblance of electoral

---

15   Two eloquent essays on this theme are Samuel P. Huntington, *American Politics: The Promise of Disharmony*, Cambridge, Mass., Harvard University Press, 1981, and Ranney, *Curing the Mischiefs of Faction*.

strength.[16] The institutional obstacles in the way of third parties in the USA are well known[17] and continue to apply. But a much more significant obstacle is the continuing distaste among the American electorate for parties based on class, region, religion, ethnicity or a single ideology. Second, it may be that the parties have *not* declined in the sense that they have ceased to be important *in government* or to be an indicator of electoral behaviour. Instead they have *changed*, and today perform rather different functions or perform traditional functions in a different manner. Indeed, recent research shows that state and national party organizations have in some respects been strengthened in recent years.[18]

For the very same forces which precipitated the reforms of the early 1970s also set in motion a period of soul searching which is still very much with us. As earlier noted, the Democrats have launched a series of enquiries into the Presidential nominating process, and as will be elaborated in chapter 7, disquiet with the ways in which Democratic candidates are selected remains. National parties are now stronger, but their authority in part depends on the support of incumbent Presidents. This is one reason why the Republican National Committee was able to achieve so much during the 1980s compared with its Democratic counterpart.

Recent party revival is not equivalent to the party strength associated with smoke-filled rooms and party machines, but more, not fewer, people are now actively involved in party organizations. Party activists may be motivated more by issues or candidates than by party loyalty – in any case nothing new in American politics – but the label 'Democrat' or 'Republican' continues to mean something to most Americans. That this is so is amply demonstrated by the continuing importance of party label in congressional elections – very few candidates dare to call themselves independent. Research has also revealed that the electorate, rather than being *alienated* from the parties, increasingly view them

16 Excluding George Wallace and his American Independent Party which, as emphasized, was a single issue and ephemeral phenomenon. In 1980 independent candidate John B. Anderson managed to attract 7 per cent of the vote.
17 The US electoral system puts additional burdens on third parties, for all states require a minimum number of registered voters to sign a petition before a party can field a candidate. Also, acquiring strength in one state or region – the usual pattern for American third parties – is rarely enough to ensure national impact. Victory in a Presidential election is achievable only via mass national support, and without at least the prospect of winning at this level, third parties cannot hope to be taken seriously.
18 See Malcolm E. Jewell and David M. Olson, *American State Political Parties and Elections*, Holmewood, Illinois, Holmewood Press, 1978; Cornelius P. Cotter and John F. Bibby, 'Institutional development of parties and the thesis of party decline', *Political Science Quarterly*, vol. 95, 1980.

neutrally. They continue to see important differences between them but, crucially, find it difficult to link these differences to the policies of particular candidates.[19] So rather than the parties disintegrating into a 'shambles', they have become even looser coalitions of diverse interests. In some ways they have gained organizational strength, particularly at the national level. But their control over candidates and nominations has weakened.

All this implies that, should politics again crystallize around a few central issues, the parties are poised to resume the role they played during the New Deal period. They are not about to disappear. On the contrary, they continue to function in the erratic, confusing and often inefficient manner which is the hallmark of the American system.

Further Reading

The best historical (but analytical) account of American parties is William Nisbet Chambers and Walter Dean Burnham (eds), *The American Party Systems: Stages of Political Development*, New York, Oxford University Press, 1975. See also David R. Mayhew, *Placing Parties in American Politics*, Princeton, New Jersey, Princeton University Press, 1986. Critiques of the reforms of the early 1970s include Austin Ranney, *Curing the Mischiefs of Faction: Party Reform in America*, Berkeley, University of California Press, 1975. More optimistic views are presented by Gerald M. Pomper (ed.), *Party Renewal in America*, New York, Praeger, 1980. A good recent account of party decline is Martin P. Wattenberg's *The Decline of American Political Parties, 1952–1984*, Cambridge, Mass., Harvard University Press, 1986. One of the better textbook treatments of parties is William J. Keefe, *Parties, Politics and Public Policy in America*, Washington DC, Congressional Quarterly Press, 5th edition, 1988.

19   Martin P. Wattenberg, 'The decline of political partisanship in the United States: negativity or neutrality?', *American Political Science Review*, vol. 75, 1981.

6

Political Participation and Electoral Behaviour

Elections commit the people to a sense of responsibility for their own betterment . . . It seems clear that they are essential to us as props of the sentiment of legitimacy and the sentiment of participation.

W. J. M. Mackenzie, *Political Studies*

There is currently a widespread sense, shown by public opinion surveys and complaints by informed observers, that the American electoral system is in trouble. Some believe that this trouble is minor and can be dealt with through moderate reforms; others think it goes deep and requires extensive political surgery, perhaps accompanied by sweeping changes in the larger social order.

A. James Reichley, *Elections, American Style*

America's claim to status as a democratic country depends almost entirely on the nature and extent of public participation in political life, and from the earliest years of the Republic there has been dispute and controversy over what, precisely, participation means. To the educated eighteenth-century man, 'democracy' was equivalent to a republican form of government which limited electoral participation to those with an established stake in society – White men of property. Any further extension of participation raised the spectre of rule by the mob and the eventual breakdown of civil society. In contrast, many artisans and small farmers, especially in the North East, were imbued with a more egalitarian brand of democracy which implied participation by a much wider electorate. Slowly, during the nineteenth and twentieth centuries, this egalitarian spirit gained ascendancy over the more elitist views of the Founding Fathers.

Today, the degree of electoral participation would truly shock eighteenth-century man. Measured in terms of the number of public offices open to electoral choice, the United States is the most democratic of countries. In total some 526,000 posts are elected, from the humblest local officials to local and state judges, mayors, councillors, governors and legislators to the Vice-President, President, and members of the US Congress. In addition, many Americans vote in primary elections to nominate which party candidates will stand in the election proper. Many states and localities have also introduced a number of devices associated with populism or direct democracy. Hence, some citizens vote in referenda, or in initiative and recall elections all of which are designed to give the voter a direct say in policy making.[1] Further, there are no formal barriers to the participation of any particular social group. Property and taxpaying restrictions were abolished by the 1830s, effectively enfranchising all adult White males. Women won the right to vote in national elections through the passing of the 19th Amendment in 1920. Formal restrictions on Southern Blacks' electoral participation were swept away by the 1965 Voting Rights Act and by a number of Supreme Court decisions. Finally, the 26th Amendment, ratified in 1971, reduced the minimum voting age to 18.

By the simple measure of electoral access, therefore, there is no doubting the democratic nature of the American system. Yet as our discussion of political parties revealed, there is very much more to participation than mere access to elections. More important are questions of *choice* and *control* over government policy. Many people ask whether the United States can be 'truly' democratic when electoral turnout is so low and when the choice offered by elections is so narrow. Others probe further and claim that in modern complex societies elections must, by their very nature, be but limited means of control over governments and bureaucracies. The remainder of this chapter will be devoted to these and related questions. The first section will concentrate on electoral behaviour – why Americans vote as they do, what sort of choice they are offered by the electoral process, and how patterns of behaviour have changed over time. The second section will introduce a discussion of non-electoral participation which will be continued in later chapters.

1   Recalls enable the electorate on presentation of a minimum number of signatures to hold a special election to recall an official from office. Initiatives are similar devices enabling the electorate by petition to vote directly on a proposal (such as tax change) rather than go through the local or state legislature. Initiatives are, in fact, a type of referendum and are often referred to as such.

Patterns of American Electoral Behaviour

Basic questions

Observers of voting behaviour usually first ask the simplest and most obvious question, 'Who has voted for which party'? So we are used to reading opinion poll findings which indicate that support for a particular party has risen or fallen or that some region, ethnic or social group has shifted its allegiance away from or towards a party. Survey or poll data can be an invaluable aid when answering these questions, and have helped to establish some very general norms or expectations about people's voting behaviour. So, table 6.1, showing the distribution of votes by social group over the 1980, 1984 and 1988 Presidential elections, confirms tendencies which apply in most democratic countries: older, higher socio-economic status, White voters tend to be more conservative (i.e. vote for Reagan and Bush) than younger, lower status, ethnic minority voters. Table 6.1 also reveals patterns which may be peculiarly American: Jews and Roman Catholics are more liberal than Protestants; the West and South of the USA appear markedly more conservative than the East. But even these general trends provoke a number of deeper questions. What precisely, is meant by conservative and liberal in the American context? To what extent does the *party* as opposed to candidates and issues determine voting behaviour? It must be that the balance of influence shifts quite markedly between the three, for in 1984, of those considering themselves Democrats, 75 per cent voted for Walter Mondale, compared with 67 per cent voting for Jimmy Carter in 1980 (table 6.1). Yet, Ronald Reagan amassed *more* votes in 1984 than in 1980. Other questions arise. Why are Blacks so overwhelmingly Democratic in their loyalties? What accounts for the regional variations in voting behaviour? We will return to these questions in detail later, but for now it should be noted that American voting behaviour seems considerably more complex than electoral participation in other countries. In many European countries, for example, class, regional ethnic or religious divisions are quite clearly defined and can act as accurate predictors of voting intentions.[2] In the USA, however, the political parties are loose coalitions and ideological and other social cleavages are relatively weak, so analysing who votes and why can be

2 Although even in Europe, traditional voting patterns are breaking down in many countries. For a review see David Butler, Howard R. Penniman and Austin Ranney (eds), *Democracy at the Polls: A Comparative Study of Competitive National Elections*, Washington, American Enterprise Institute, 1981.

Table 6.1   1980, 1984 and 1988 Presidential votes, by groups

Group	1980 vote (%)			1984 vote (%)		1988 vote (%)	
	Reagan	Carter	Anderson	Reagan	Mondale	Bush	Dukakis
All	51	41	7	59	40	53	45
Men	55	36	7	62	37	57	41
Women	47	45	7	56	44	50	49
Whites	55	36	7	64	35	59	40
Blacks	11	85	3	9	89	12	86
Hispanics	33	59	6	37	61	30	69
18–29 years old	43	44	11	59	40	52	47
30–44 years old	54	36	8	57	42	54	45
45–59 years old	55	39	5	59	39	57	42
60 and older	54	41	1	60	39	50	49
White Protestant	63	31	6	72	27	66	33
Catholic	49	42	7	54	45	52	47
Jewish	39	45	15	31	67	35	64
White Fundamentalist Christian	63	33	3	78	22	81	18
Union Household	43	48	6	46	53	42	57
Less than high-school education	46	51	2	49	50	43	56
High-school graduates	51	43	4	60	39	50	49
Some college	55	35	7	61	37	57	42
College graduates	52	35	11	58	41	56	43
East	47	42	9	52	47	50	49
Mid-west	51	40	7	58	40	52	47
South	52	44	3	64	36	58	41
West	53	34	10	61	38	52	47
Republican	86	9	4	93	6	91	8
Democrat	26	67	6	24	75	17	82
Independent	55	30	12	63	35	55	43
Liberal	25	60	11	28	70	18	81
Moderate	48	42	8	53	47	49	50
Conservative	72	23	4	82	17	80	19
Professional or manager	57	32	9	62	37	59	40
White collar	50	41	8	59	40	57	42
Blue collar	47	46	5	54	45	49	50
Unemployed	39	51	8	32	67	37	62
Under $12,500 income	42	51	6	45	54	37	62
$12,500–24,999	44	46	8	57	42	49	50
$25,000–34,999	52	39	7	59	40	56	44
$35,000–50,000	59	32	8	66	33	56	42
over $50,000	63	26	9	69	30	62	37

Source: New York Times/CBS Poll, reported in the *New York Times*, 10 November 1988, p. B6. 1988 data are based on an exit poll of 11,645 voters. Don't knows and no answer responses are excluded. Figures do not always add up to 100 because of rounding.

that much more difficult. We can broadly categorize the Democrats as the liberal or even 'left' party and Republicans as the conservative or 'right' party, but when the whole range of candidates in each of these parties is examined, there are numerous exceptions even to this generalization. To complicate matters further, federalism and the separation of powers have spawned myriad elections and distinctive levels of government, each with a different constituency. At the national level this shows itself most graphically in the relationship between Presidential and Congressional elections. Individual Congressmen are beholden to their own constituents whose interests may be quite separate from those of the national electorate responsible for electing the President. Admittedly, it is probable that a successful party at the Presidential election will also at least be partly successful at the Congressional level, but there is no guarantee that this will be so, especially in recent years. In 1972, for example, the near landslide victory of a Republican President, Richard Nixon, was not accompanied by any significant inroads by his party into the Democratic majorities in both Houses of Congress. The pattern was similar in 1984. Ronald Reagan won a landslide triumph, but the Democrats lost few House seats and actually gained a few in the Senate.

A second question raised in any simple description of voting behaviour is: Who actually votes? A wealth of social science and professional opinion poll research enables us to make quite accurate assessments of electoral participation patterns.[3] Very generally people of higher socio-economic status (a combination of income, occupation and education) vote and participate in other political activities to a much greater extent than people of lower socio-economic status. The relationship between voting and age is a little more complex, with participation rising from a low at 18 to a peak during middle age and then declining gently in later middle and old age. Until the late 1960s one of the most dramatic differences in participation was between Black and White Americans. Until the civil rights legislation of the mid 1960s, very few Southern blacks were able to register to vote (for example in 1964 a mere 7 per cent in Mississippi) and among those registered, actual turnout was low. Since the 1965 Voting Rights Act, however, registration has steadily increased, and by 1980 the percentage of Blacks registered to vote was only 10 per cent below the figure for Whites. Black turnout remains generally lower than that of Whites, but mainly because a disproportionate number of Blacks are of low socio-economic status.

3   See in particular Sidney Verba and Norman H. Nie, *Participation in America: Political Democracy and Social Equality*, New York, Harper and Row, 1972.

Finally, turnout among women is slightly lower than for men (in Presidential elections about 51 per cent of men always vote and only 48 per cent of women). However, the gap has been closing and compared with differences based on socio-economic status and age, voter participation rates between men and women are comparatively close.

A third basic question is: How many of the people actually vote? In the USA turnout is notoriously low for all elections. Even the contest perceived by most people as the most significant – electing the President – hardly inspires a high level of mass participation. Since 1960 turnout has been declining, and now rarely exceeds 55 per cent for Presidential elections and 50 per cent for Congressional contests (table 6.2). In 1988, turnout sank to below 50 per cent – the lowest for a Presidential election since 1924. At the state and local levels turnout is even lower and can fall as low as 20 per cent. This seeming political apathy has long puzzled and disturbed American political scientists. Explanations usually fall into one of two categories – institutional and non institutional. The institutional barriers to voting are, in fact, considerable, although claims that the formidable *number* of elections reduces turnout are probably erroneous. After all, turnout at Presidential elections remains low in spite of their relative infrequency and the disproportionate amount of publicity and attention paid to them by political parties and the media. More significant are America's voter registration laws. Under the laws of individual states voters must themselves make the decision to register and most states apply minimum residency requirements. Although for Presidential elections this requirement has been reduced by Congress to only 30 days, the fact remains that in a mobile, open society many people fail to register or to register in time. Indeed only about 71 per cent of eligible voters were registered in 1980.[4] Unlike most European countries, there is no automatic nationally organized compulsory registration system, and recent studies have shown that were such a system introduced, turnout may increase by between 10 per cent and 12 per cent.

Non-voting may also be linked to the fact that the US has a first-past-the-post single member district electoral system rather than one based on proportional representation (PR). By closely relating votes cast to representation in assemblies, PR 'wastes' few votes. Under a single member district system, however, voters know that in many constituencies their vote will make no difference because of the large majority enjoyed by one party. Their incentive to vote is, therefore, reduced.

But these institutional factors provide only a partial explanation for

4   Of a sample of voters, *New York Times/CBS News Poll*, 1 November 1980.

Table 6.2   Turnout in Presidential and House elections, 1930–1988 (percentage of voting age population)

Year	Presidential elections	House elections
1930	–	33.7
1932	52.4	49.7
1934	–	41.4
1936	56.9	53.5
1938	–	44.0
1940	58.9	55.4
1942	–	32.5
1944	56.0	52.7
1946	–	37.1
1948	51.1	48.1
1950	–	41.1
1952	61.6	57.6
1954	–	41.7
1956	59.3	55.9
1958	–	43.0
1960	62.6	58.5
1962	–	45.4
1964	61.9	57.8
1966	–	45.4
1968	60.9	55.1
1970	–	43.5
1972	55.4	50.9
1974	–	36.1
1976	54.4	49.5
1978	–	35.1
1980	53.4	48.1
1982	–	37.7
1984	53.3	47.4
1986	–	33.4
1988	49.1	N.A.

Source: Norman J. Ornstein, Thomas E. Mann, Michael J. Malbin, Allen Schick and John F. Bibby, *Vital Statistics on Congress*, 1987/88 edition, Washington DC, American Enterprise Institute, table 2.1. Data for 1988 from *The New York Times*, 10 November 1988, p. B6.

American non-voting. For uniquely among developed democracies, the rate of voter participation has been declining rapidly in the US. Very broadly, two schools of thought have attempted to explain this: the sociological and public choice. Public choice theorists argue that it is simply not rational to vote when the choice offered by the parties is so limited. Certainly the relative absence of well-defined and deep-rooted social cleavages articulated by class, ethnic or regionally based parties reduces the direct and immediate interest the voter has in ensuring that 'his' or 'her' party is represented in government. American parties and candidates rarely promise social revolution; nor do they often promise to defend well defined sectional, class, religious or ethnic interests. Moreover recent research has shown that citizens often vote *retrospectively*; or they decide to vote for party A rather than party B by judging an incumbent's past performance – usually in terms of whether the party's period in office has increased the voter's real income. As Morris Fiorina and others have shown, it is increasingly difficult to make this calculation when party programmes are so diffuse and when the appeal to voters is by individual *candidates* rather than parties.[5] This more atomized, individualized politics may account for the decline of voting among all social groups since 1960 (table 6.3).

Table 6.3   Voter turnout rates in Presidential and off-year elections, by occupation, male labour force, 1964–1980

Occupational category	Turnout rate, presidential years		Per cent decline,	Turnout rate, off-years		Per cent decline,
	1964	1980	1964–80	1966	1978	1966–78
Middle-class and white collar	**83.2**	**73.0**	**12.3**	**68.7**	**58.9**	**14.3**
Professional and technical	84.7	77.0	9.1	70.1	62.7	10.6
Managers (excluding farm)	82.8	72.6	12.3	68.9	57.9	16.0
Farm owners and managers	84.7	76.1	10.2	71.0	64.4	9.3
Sales and clerical	81.3	67.8	16.6	66.3	54.3	18.1
Service occupations	**72.8**	**53.0**	**27.2**	**57.9**	**43.6**	**24.7**
Manual (excluding service)	**66.1**	**48.0**	**27.4**	**50.6**	**35.1**	**30.6**
Craft and skilled workers	72.2	53.6	25.8	56.7	40.6	28.4
Semiskilled operatives	63.5	44.7	29.6	48.3	32.1	33.5
Labourers (excluding farm)	57.7	41.4	28.2	41.1	28.1	31.6
Farm labourers	44.6	35.0	21.5	32.7	24.4	25.4
Unemployed	**56.9**	**38.1**	**33.0**	**42.7**	**25.9**	**39.3**
Total	73.0	58.1	20.4	58.9	45.2	23.3

For clarifying notes, see original.
Source: Reproduced from Walter Dean Burnham 'The turnout problem' in A. James Reichley (ed.), *Elections, American Style*, Washington DC, Brookings, 1987, table 5.4.

The sociological school argues, simply, that poorer, less well educated citizens vote less than richer, better educated citizens. Table 6.3 certainly confirms this, with more than 50 per cent of manual workers apparently excluded from voting altogether. Again this is a unique American phenomenon. In other democracies the (much smaller) number of non-voters is drawn from all social groups, with few citizens caught in a

5   Morris P. Fiorina, *Retrospective Voting in American National Elections*, New Haven, Yale University Press, 1981.

pattern of permanent non-voting.[6] Non-voting among lower status groups can also be linked to rational expectations. Their sense of political effectiveness tends to be lower because they are poorer and, as important, they find it difficult to identify with a party which fails to appeal to voters on class lines. Significantly, the party which used to project such an appeal, the Democratic Party, has moved further and further away from class-based politics with the decline of the New Deal coalition and the rise of candidate- and issue-based politics.

Concern about non-voting in the United States is compounded by the fact that an increasingly educated and sophisticated population should have led to increased rather than decreased electoral participation. This phenomenon, above all, confirms the public choice theorists' claims that voters cannot easily make rational decisions when faced by inchoate parties and a politics based on individual office holders unable to offer effective programmes of social and economic change.

'The American Voter' model and the New Deal coalition

During the 1950s and early 1960s a number of studies were published whose findings established a 'model' of American voting behaviour. The unique contribution of this work was to explain the voting of individual citizens in terms of *psychological* orientations. By asking survey respondents how they felt about parties, candidates and issues and then relating these sentiments to actual political behaviour it was possible to build up a cognitive picture of how individuals thought about politics. The results were surprising, to say the least. In a more recent study, Nie, Verba and Petrocik[7] summarized the findings thus:

> The American public had a remarkably unsophisticated view of political matters characterized by an inability to consider such matters in broad abstract terms . . . Citizens had inconsistent views when one looked across a range of issues . . . Most Americans had strong, long term commitments to one of the major political parties

6   For a full discussion, see Walter Dean Burnham, 'The turnout problem', in A. James Reichley (ed.), *Elections, American Style*, Washington DC, Brookings, 1987.
7   Norman H. Nie, Sidney Verba and John R. Petrocik, *The Changing American Voter*, Cambridge, Mass., Harvard University Press, enlarged edn, 1979, chapter 2. The main works summarized were: Angus Campbell et al., *The American Voter*, New York, John Wiley, 1960; Gabriel Almond and Sidney Verba, *The Civic Culture*, Princeton, New Jersey, Princeton University Press, 1963; Robert A. Dahl, *Who Governs?* New Haven, Yale University Press, 1961; David E. Apter (ed.), *Ideology and Discontent*, New York, Free Press, 1964.

and this commitment served as a guide to their political behaviour
. . . Citizens felt relatively satisfied with the political system and
relatively efficacious.

Very few – a mere 2.5 per cent of the *American Voters'* sample –
were categorized as ideologues, or people who thought about politics
in abstract terms. Most evaluated candidates and parties in terms of the
benefits they brought to social groups (42 per cent) or in terms of the
'nature of the times' (24 per cent). In other words most voters had little
sense of 'left' and 'right' or the role that parties and candidates might
play in moving society in a particular direction. Instead, immediate or
recent events or simple promises by politicians to lower taxation, say,
or to increase social spending influenced voters. Reinforcement of this
analysis was provided by studies showing that voters were often
inconsistent in their views across issues. Some citizens favouring
increased social spending also wanted a reduced role for government in
society; anti-communists were not always in favour of an increased role
for the United States as international policeman. Most importantly of
all, when attitudes on all issues were examined it was not possible to
find any pattern consistent with a coherently thought out ideology,
whether liberal, conservative, socialist or whatever.[8]

The image projected, therefore, is one of a rather ill-informed voter
who thinks rather little about politics. However, in one important
respect American voters were found to be consistent: in their attachment
to political parties, voters displayed enduring loyalties. Labelling this
phenomenon *party identification*, voting analysts discovered that people
acquired a positive or negative psychological attachment to a party early
in childhood which remained with them throughout their lives. In
essence citizens were *socialized* by family and other social cues into
thinking of themselves as Democrats or Republicans, a phenomenon
which may account for the fact that 78 per cent of respondents to a
1958 survey had the same party identification as their parents.[9] Not all
voters were found to be strong party identifiers. Some identified
less clearly with a party, while others considered themselves either
independent or independently supportive of one or other of the parties
(figure 6.1).

We will discuss this changing pattern of party identification later, but
for now note the consistency of Democratic support which constitutes a
clear majority for most of the period. As these figures are for voting in

8 Philip Converse, 'The nature of belief systems in mass publics', in Apter, *Ideology
and Discontent*, p. 543.
9 *The American Voter*, p. 147.

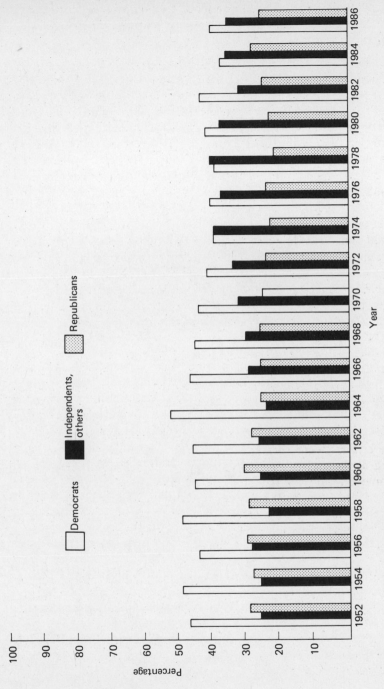

Figure 6.1 Party identification, 1952–1986 (Michigan Surveys)

Source: Reproduced from Paul Allen Beck, 'Incomplete re-alignment: The Reagan legacy for parties and elections', in Charles O. Jones, *The Reagan Legacy: Promise and Performance*, Chatham, New Jersey, Chatham House, 1988, figure 5.4.

Presidential elections they raise an interesting question: How is it that the Republicans managed to win in 1952, 1956, 1968, 1972, 1980, 1984 and 1988 (table 6.4) given the inbuilt Democrat majority implied by the preponderance of Democratic identifiers?

In answering this question political scientists at first stressed that party identification was very much a psychological orientation to politics. There may be elections when voters deviate from their normal identification because of the particular appeal of the candidate (as was the case in the 1950s with Dwight Eisenhower) or because of the importance of certain issues (for example law and order in 1968). Obviously, however, the Democratic majority must come from somewhere; it cannot be purely psychological. The answer is that there have been certain periods in American history when rapid social and economic changes have forged new political coalitions. During these periods orientations towards parties change as the parties themselves come to represent an emergent social group or region. By implication, during these years of turbulence, the voter is indeed guided by the issues and by objective economic and social circumstances. Political scientists have called such transitions periods of *re-alignment* when new electoral majorities are built. Between 1896 and 1928 the Republican Party reigned supreme. Urbanization, depression, the naturalization and integration of new immigrant groups and the emergence of an organized working class transformed party politics during the 1920s and early 1930s, however, and culminated in the resounding Democratic victory of 1932 (table 6.4). From the late 1920s the Democrats became the party associated with the urban working class, trade unions and the underprivileged. The near invincibility of what was to be called the New Deal coalition was assured because of the support guaranteed by the traditionally Democratic South. By the mid-1930s the intellectual establishment and many members of an insecure middle class had joined the coalition resulting in the *maintaining* elections of 1936, 1940, 1944 and 1948. Not until incumbent Democrats (most notably Harry Truman) began to support civil rights for Southern Blacks did the first cracks in the majority appear (in 1948).

The Republican victories of 1952 and 1956 were, according to the scholars, *deviating* elections. In other words, the Democrats remained the 'natural' majority party, but the specific circumstances of these elections allowed the Republicans to triumph. Eisenhower was an avuncular, charismatic war hero; in contrast, Adlai Stevenson, the Democratic candidate, projected an aloof, intellectual and narrowly Eastern establishment image. This personality contrast was, above all, responsible for the Republican victories. Significantly, these successes were only partly repeated at the Congressional level. Following Republican victories in 1946 and 1952, after 1954 Congress was firmly controlled by the Democrats.

The decline of partisanship and the New Deal coalition

This neat and appealing theory of electoral behaviour seemed to be reinforced by the 1960 and 1964 Presidential elections. Democratic victories returned, with the Republicans reverting to their normal status as the minority party. However, from about 1964 onwards a number of developments appear which in total present a rather serious challenge to the accepted theory. In particular we note the following:

Partisanship declines   A popular interpretation of Richard Nixon's victory in 1968 was that it heralded a new Republican majority.[10] More citizens were suburban, middle class and conservative, so the Republicans should find themselves ascendant. Moreover, the South, so long solidly Democratic, could no longer tolerate the integrationist policies of Democratic Presidents.

Superficially, the 1972 election seemed to reinforce these trends (table 6.4). Yet 1968 and 1972 were not classic *re-aligning elections* like 1932. The number of Republican party identifiers far from increasing decreased slightly during these years (table 6.3) and the Democrats retained their dominance of Congress. Similarly at the state level there was little evidence of an unstoppable Republican surge. Note, however, that Democratic Party identification also declined during the 1960s. This fact, together with the rise of Independent identifiers has led some commentators to speculate that what was occurring was party *de-alignment*, or the slow demise of party identification as a key indicator of political preference.

By 1986, this process of de-alignment seemed to have stabilized (figure 6.1), but at the same time neither party had recaptured the centre stage in the way in which the Republicans did after 1896 or the Democrats did after 1932.

Another indicator of declining partisanship is 'ticket splitting' or the tendency for voters to divide their loyalties between candidates of

10   See, in particular, Kevin Phillips, *The Emerging Republican Majority*, New York, Doubleday Anchor, 1970.

Table 6.4 Presidential election results, 1928–1988

Year	Presidential candidates	Party	Electoral vote	Popular vote	Percentage share	No. of states won[a]
1928	Herbert Hoover	Republican	444	21,392,190	58.2	42
	Alfred E. Smith	Democratic	87	15,016,443	40.8	6 (all Southern)
	Norman Thomas	Socialist	0	267,420	1.0	0
32	Franklin D. Roosevelt	Democratic	472	22,821,857	57.3	42
	Herbert Hoover	Republican	59	15,761,841	39.6	6 (all North Eastern)
	Norman Thomas	Socialist	0	884,781	2.2	0
36	Franklin D. Roosevelt	Democratic	523	27,751,597	60.7	46
	Alfred M. Landon	Republican	8	16,679,583	36.4	2 (Maine and Vermont)
	Norman Thomas	Socialist	0	187,720	0.5	0
40	Franklin D. Roosevelt	Democratic	449	27,244,160	54.7	38
	Wendell L. Wilkie	Republican	82	22,305,198	44.8	10
	Norman Thomas	Socialist	0	99,557	0.2	0
44	Franklin D. Roosevelt	Democratic	432	25,602,504	52.8	36
	Thomas E. Dewey	Republican	99	22,006,285	44.5	12
	Norman Thomas	Socialist	0	80,518	0.2	0
48	Harry S. Truman	Democratic	303	24,179,345	49.5	32
	Thomas E. Dewey	Republican	189	21,991,291	45.1	12
	J. Strom Thurmond	States' Rights Dem.	39	1,176,125	2.4	4 (all Southern)
	Henry A. Wallace	Progressive	0	1,157,326	2.4	0
	Norman Thomas	Socialist	0	139,572	0.2	0
52	Dwight D. Eisenhower	Republican	442	33,936,234	55.2	40
	Adlai E. Stevenson	Democratic	89	27,314,992	44.5	8 (all Southern)
56	Dwight D. Eisenhower	Republican	457	35,590,472	57.4	41
	Adlai E. Stevenson	Democratic	73	26,022,752	42.0	7 (all Southern)
60	John F. Kennedy	Democratic	303	34,226,731	49.9	23[b]
	Richard M. Nixon	Republican	219	34,108,157	49.6	26

Year	Candidate	Party	Electoral votes	Popular vote	%	States
64	Lyndon B. Johnson	Democratic	486	43,129,484	61.1	46
	Barry M. Goldwater	Republican	52	27,178,188	38.5	5 (Southern and Arizona)
68	Richard M. Nixon	Republican	301	31,785,480	43.3	32
	Hubert M. Humphrey	Democratic	191	31,275,166	42.7	14
	George C. Wallace	American Independent	46	9,906,473	13.5	5 (all Southern)
72	Richard M. Nixon	Republican	520	47,169,911	61.3	49
	George McGovern	Democratic	17	29,170,383	37.3	2 (DC and Massachusetts)
	John G. Schmitz	American	0	1,099,482	1.4	0
76	Jimmy Carter	Democratic	297	40,830,763	50.1	24
	Gerald R. Ford	Republican	240	39,147,973	48.0	27
	Eugene J. McCarthy	Independent	0	756,631	1.0	0
80	Ronald Reagan	Republican	489	42,951,145	51.0	46
	Jimmy Carter	Democratic	49	34,663,037	41.0	5
	John B. Anderson	Independent	0	5,551,551	7.0	0
84	Ronald Reagan	Republican	525	54,450,603	59.2	49
	Walter Mondale	Democratic	13	37,573,671	40.8	2 (DC and Minnesota)
88	George Bush	Republican	426	47,917,341	54.0	40
	Michael Dukakis	Democratic	112	41,013,030	46.0	11

a From 1960 includes Alaska and Hawaii. From 1964 includes Washington DC.
b 15 electoral college votes were cast for segregationist candidate Harry F. Byrd, including 8 in Mississippi which he effectively 'won'.

Table 6.5　Ticket splitting between Presidential and House candidates, 1900–1984

Year	Districts[a]	Districts with split results[b]	
		Number	Percentage
1900	295	10	3.4
1904	310	5	1.6
1908	314	21	6.7
1912	333	84	25.2
1916	333	35	10.5
1920	344	11	3.2
1924	356	42	11.8
1928	359	68	18.9
1932	355	50	14.1
1936	361	51	14.1
1940	362	53	14.6
1944	367	41	11.2
1948	422	90	21.3
1952	435	84	19.3
1956	435	130	29.9
1960	437	114	26.1
1964	435	145	33.3
1968	435	139	32.0
1972	435	192	44.1
1976	435	124	28.5
1980	435	143	32.8
1984	435	196	45.0

[a]　Before 1952 complete data are not available on every congressional district.
[b]　Congressional districts carried by a presidential candidate of one party and a House candidate of another party.
Source:　Ornstein, Mann, Malbin, Schick and Bibby, *Vital Statistics on Congress*, 1987/88 Edition, table 2.14.

different parties. As can be seen from table 6.5, ticket splitting has risen dramatically since the 1950s. By 1984 no less than 45 per cent of Congressional districts produced a split result on voting for Presidential and House candidates. A similar pattern has emerged for statewide offices (elections for Senators, governors, state legislatures) in a number of states and regions.

Candidate and issue voting increases　A natural corollary to a decline in partisanship is that citizens (or at least those of them who vote) are using some other criterion when making a decision on who to vote for. Candidates and issues had always played some part in the voting calculus, of course, but from the 1960s they began to play a much more prominent role. It also follows that if people are voting for individual candidates or for particular issues, the electorate is much more sophisticated than implied by the *American Voter* model. Indeed, in their 1976 work, *The Changing American Voter*, Nie, Verba and Petrocik discovered that from about 1964 voters showed a significantly increased consistency in their views on domestic and foreign policy issues. Unlike the rather unthinking citizen portrayed by *The American Voter*, the public appeared more able to see the connections between issues, parties and candidates and to view the world in terms of broad ideological categories such as 'liberal' or 'conservative'. Certainly, Presidential elections took on a more ideological stance after 1964. The Goldwater–Johnson contest of that year was clearly a conflict between conservative and liberal, as were the later contests between Humphrey, Nixon and Wallace and, more especially, between McGovern and Nixon. In 1976 there was a marked decline in ideological voting, almost certainly because the two candidates projected rather bland images and few issues clearly divided them. 1980 saw a return to a clear-cut choice, however, with the conservative Ronald Reagan facing in incumbent President, Jimmy Carter, identified – albeit reluctantly on his part – with the liberal cause. 1984 also presented a clear-cut choice, with Ronald Reagan appealing directly to the right and Walter Mondale to liberals and the left. In 1988, however, the two candidates were much closer together on basic issues. So much so, in fact, that George Bush worked hard to label Dukakis a 'liberal' so as to secure the conservative vote.

Declining partisanship and the rise of what has been called 'issue voting' raises a number of questions. One of the most important of these we addressed in the last chapter – the failure of the political parties to exploit the new interest in politics by providing coherent and ideologically consistent programmes to the electorate. Indeed to a European observer the combination of more ideological voters but declining parties and partisanship should be slightly baffling. Surely parties should be stronger in such a context? But as was pointed out in chapter 5, the complexity of the issues dominating the political agenda together with recent changes in American society, have made it impossible for the parties to know what to say and to whom. Recall that in order to win, American political parties have to build broad coalitions of support. And research has shown that although there has been a rise in ideological thinking among some of the electorate, it hardly dominates. The price of presenting to voters an unequivocally ideological programme was revealed in 1972, when George McGovern's evangelizing liberalism was rewarded by a landslide victory for his Republican opponent. So, rather than parties and issues coinciding and thus strengthening partisanship, the opposite has been happening. Issues and individual candidates have gained importance independently of parties and have often done so in a way which seriously damages a party's fortunes. Hence in 1968 and 1972 Vietnam and the 'social issue' dominated – a combination of law and order, civil rights and civil liberties. Liberals within the Democratic party found themselves seriously at odds with some of the traditional Democratic supporters on these questions. Southerners were conservative on civil rights and a large number of blue-collar workers were consistently conservative on Vietnam and the social issue. This combination helps explain Richard Nixon's victories in 1968 and 1972. Nixon's success seemed to herald the beginning of the end for the New Deal coalition. At the level of Presidential elections the South was moving rapidly into the Republican camp, and the now dominant social issue divided rather than united Democrats.

Some have argued that Ronald Reagan's 1980 and 1984 victories were in a different category. He won, so the theory goes, because his economic policies coincided nicely with what the electorate wanted. Disillusioned with high levels of public spending, and inflation the public had acquired an *ideological* aversion to big government. Ronald Reagan's promise of a new prosperity based on free-market principles offered an irresistible alternative. Concomitant with the success of this issue appeal came a revival of the Republican Party, and because the Party became identified with 'Reaganomics' some commentators claimed that a permanent re-alignment was under way.

Yet as figure 6.1 shows, the number of Republican identifiers did not increase markedly either in 1980 or in 1984. Moreover, the public's attitudes on economic issues are not as unambiguously ideological as the more optimistic of the Republican supporters claimed. Of course everyone wants a healthy economy, but if the price of low inflation – the major objective of Reagan's programme – is high unemployment then large sections of Republican support are likely to fall away. This is exactly what happened during the 1982 mid-term elections when Republican candidates associated with the administration's economic policies fared particularly badly. President Reagan's 1984 victory was no doubt attributable to a number of factors including his personal popularity. But few commentators doubt that the rapid recovery of the economy in 1983 and 1984 was crucial. All this suggests that 1980 and 1984 were far from being re-aligning elections. Much the same could be said for the 1988 contest, when the Democrats made further inroads into the House and Senate while once again losing the Presidency.

This accepted, figure 6.1 presents a vivid picture of a Democratic

Party whose support has been waning in relation both to Independents and to Republicans. Democrats continue to represent the largest single block of voters, but their earlier position of dominance is over. In some states and regions, particularly in the South, the Republicans have made major inroads into Congressional, state and local politics. By 1988 22 of the Nation's 50 governors were Republicans and 40 per cent of the state legislatures were controlled by the Grand Old Party (GOP). Put another way, instead of a clear re-alignment in favour of one party or another, the Democrats and Republicans are much closer to a position of equality than they used to be.

Rational Voters and Inchoate Parties: Where Do We Go From Here?

The most intractable problem for the American voter is making a choice between parties which offer little in the way of ideologically contrasting programmes of social and economic change. Faced with this choice – or lack of choice – voters increasingly vote for candidates as individuals – either in terms of their personality appeal and appearance or in terms of how they stand on particular issues. As suggested, such an electoral strategy is far more complex and confusing than one where voter decisions are determined by identity with an ideologically coherent political party. The rational voter will assess candidates *as individuals* rather than in terms of party label. Such was clearly the case with many Reagan supporters. Numerous nominal 'Democrats' voted for Reagan because they liked him and because they liked his stand on a range of issues.

But, as shown in chapter 5 issues in American politics do not cluster together in an ideologically coherent manner. Instead, they cut across those strata in society – social class, region, religion – which have traditionally formed the basis of party support. As a result, the American voter tends to be mobilized by strong, appealing candidates such as Ronald Reagan, or he/she is unexcited by the whole electoral race. In 1988, for example, the electorate seemed singularly unenthused by the two candidates for President, George Bush and Michael Dukakis. On the issues, they could see little between them, and neither man had the charismatic appeal of a Ronald Reagan.

All of this amounts to a serious problem for democratic theory. It is at least feasible to expect parties presenting coherent programmes of change to be held accountable by the electorate. The voter can, after all, test the party's performance in government against electoral promises. Individual candidates however can hardly be expected to do this. If they are elected on personality and appearance alone then no programmatic element can exist. If candidates do take stands on issues, then at most levels of government they cannot directly translate issue promises into policy changes. What difference can one member of Congress make to the rate of inflation, for example? Only Presidents (and possibly governors) can be expected to deliver electoral promises, but most recent Presidential candidates, including both the 1988 contenders, deliberately avoided taking clear issue stands because they knew that the electorate is divided on most issues in highly complex ways. As a result, the electorate has little incentive either to vote or to take much interest in politics.

Further trends in the American electorate

While this general problem applies, the electorate is not a broad undifferentiated mass; changes in voting alignments continue to occur, the most important of which are listed below.

1   Younger voters are even less attached to traditional party cues than older voters. As each age cohort moves up, therefore, the electorate is likely to become even less partisan, more unpredictable and less likely to participate in elections. This is not so much a sign of apathy as an indication among the best educated under-30 age cohort in American history that they simply do not find it rational to take much interest in politics.

2   A 'gender gap' has emerged among voters in Presidential elections. In the last three elections more women voted Democratic than should have been expected from national trends. This applied with particular force in 1980 when women split their vote 47–45 per cent between Reagan and Carter, compared with a 56–36 per cent margin for men, and in 1988 when the split was 50–49 per cent for Bush, compared with 57–41 per cent among men. Younger, single women are especially prone to vote Democratic, reflecting, perhaps, an antipathy towards the tendency for Republican candidates to be conservative on a range of issues affecting women (abortion, child care, the Equal Rights Amendment, affirmative action).

3   Region is a much less accurate guide to voters than it used to be. During the first half of this century the South was solidly Democratic, and until the 1930s New England was solidly Republican. Today the South is more Republican than Democratic, not just at the Presidential but increasingly at the state and local levels as well. The region is far from being solidly Republican however, even if it is conservative.

The West also tends to be Republican and conservative, although this applies only erratically in the Pacific states (Washington, Oregon and California) where the personality of particular candidates is often a better indicator of their success than their ideological position.

Northern and Northern Eastern states are more Democratic and liberal – as should be expected from their industrial past. But even here Republicans have done well in Presidential elections. In 1984, of course, Democratic candidate Walter Mondale lost all but one state (Minnesota) and the District of Columbia. In 1988, however, the Democrats showed considerable strength in the Mid West, and to a lesser extent in the West. What the 1988 result did confirm is that only one major region now seems irrevocably in one camp at the Presidential level: the South.

4   Finally, we should note the very high and consistent support for the Democrats among black and some other minority voters. In 1984 a staggering 89 per cent of Blacks[11] voted Democrat, 4 per cent up on 1980 and against the national trend (table 6.1). Two conclusions can be drawn from these figures. Either the vast majority of Blacks perceive themselves to be the direct beneficiaries of Democratic policies, or they display a remarkable sense of group solidarity. On the former point, Democrats are more supportive of the civil rights and welfare policies from which many Blacks benefit. But by no means all Blacks are direct beneficiaries of these policies, and the high support for the Democrats implies that the party is always unambiguously in favour of welfare and civil rights, which is certainly not the case. More feasibly, most Blacks feel a strong sense of racial solidarity and vote Democrat because they know that many of their number are more likely to benefit from Democratic policies than from Republican measures. No other social group of significant size shows such solidarity, which speaks volumes for the very special and troubled status of Blacks in American history and present-day society.

We can conclude then, that, minority groups apart, the behaviour of the American electorate is now much more volatile and difficult to predict than during the 1950s and 1960s. Voters are also more sophisticated, better informed and make their electoral choices according to rational criteria – such as candidates' stand on issues. Unfortunately, however, the political parties are less able to provide the voters with clear choices based on coherent programmes of social and economic change. Given that individual candidates either cannot deliver on issues or are reluctant to commit themselves for fear of defeat, voters' interest

11   Other minorities, including Hispanics also support the Democrats, but not to the same extent as Blacks. See table 6.1.

in politics and in voting is probably lower than at any point since the 1920s. Most observers agree that this is not the hallmark of a healthy democracy.

Non-Electoral Political Participation

As earlier implied, elections must by their very nature represent limited means of control over those forming and implementing policy. A considerable degree of centralized political power is necessary even for a relatively low level of economic efficiency and social justice. With centralized power, individual citizens casting their votes in periodic elections can only hope to exercise an occasional veto influence over those at the apex of the constitutional system. This applies even in state and local elections where voters, although closer to the office holders, are still several steps removed from day-to-day decision making.

But elections are just one of a number of means whereby citizens can influence the decision makers. As table 6.6 shows, participation extends to a number of other activities, particularly those associated with the local community. Historically, the local community was the primary focus of political life with both formal and informal access to local officials being the very essence of American democracy. In many respects this holds true today with some 30 per cent of a sample of citizens having worked on community problems and 20 per cent having contacted a local official (table 6.6). For most Americans, then, non-electoral participation involves contact with local officials or community leaders over such questions as school management, zoning,[12] public works projects and law enforcement. This is a continuing, constantly changing interactive process. It is also perceived by all parties to be highly legitimate, and local policies *are* created, modified and vetoed through citizen involvement. Of course this process is not equivalent to direct or pure democracy. The earlier noted biases against participation by lower income groups, women and ethnic minorities remain, and virtually no apparently local policy issue is entirely local today. Federal and state funding of local programmes ensures that local political activity is but one of a number of influences at work. Nonetheless, the importance of local community activity should not be underestimated – especially in the light of the very high percentage of citizens (14 per cent) who

12   Zoning is equivalent to local land-use planning powers in European countries and involves the division of land into different use-types: residential, industrial, commercial, recreational.

Table 6.6   Percentage engaging in 12 different acts of political participation

Type of political participation	Percentage
1 Report regularly voting in Presidential elections	72
2 Report always voting in local elections	47
3 Active in at least one organization involved in community problems	32
4 Have worked with others in trying to solve some community problems	30
5 Have attempted to persuade others to vote as they were	28
6 Have ever actively worked for a party or candidate during an election	26
7 Have ever contacted a local government official about some issue or problem	20
8 Have attended at least one political meeting or rally in last three years	19
9 Have ever contacted a state or national government official about some issue or problem	18
10 Have ever formed a group or organization to attempt to solve some local community problem	14
11 Have ever given money to a party or candidate during an election campaign	13
12 Presently a member of a political club or organization	8

Number of cases: weighted   3,095
unweighted   2,549

Source: *Participation in America: Political Democracy and Social Equality* by Sidney Verba and Norman H. Nie, New York, Harper and Row, p. 31. © 1972 Sidney Verba and Norman H. Nie. Reprinted by permission of Harper and Row Publishers, Inc.

have directly helped *form* a group or organization to solve a local community problem (table 6.6).

There are two further varieties of political participation which table 6.6 either excludes or refers to only obliquely. The first involves the activities of national interest groups. As chapter 11 will show, there is hardly an area of economic or social life that is not influenced by interest groups. How representative or democratic groups are is a point we will cover later, but as earlier implied, interest group membership and loyalties do cut across party allegiances, so their activities must be considered an additional part of the representative process.

Second, there are all those political actions usually viewed as external to the established channels of political access: demonstrations, marches, boycotts and, more rarely, acts of political violence and terror. Clearly the latter are evidence of the breakdown of democratic processes, and at the national level, at least, have been remarkably rare in the USA. In recent history they have been confined to the actions of isolated individuals (assassinations, hijacks) or have been precipitated by a single, sometimes ephemeral issue (the Vietnam War, Black rights). At the local level the picture is somewhat different. Until the 1960s political violence was a relatively common feature of some parts of Southern society, with the black population being the victims of often systematic intimidation and random violence. Rarely, however, has local political violence been motivated by a desire for regime change. More often the motivation has been the assertion of authority over a politically and socially subordinate minority group. Often, these illegal acts were implicitly endorsed by the legitimate authorities.

More difficult to evaluate are acts of political protest – demonstrations, marches, boycotts, political strikes. These are very much a part of American life and at certain times have played a crucial role in politics. Starting in the 1940s and reaching a crescendo in the early 1960s these were precisely the methods successfully employed by the civil rights movement, a fact which must help explain the greater sympathy shown

Table 6.7   Protest attitudes by race

Percent of Buffalo, New York, citizens who say it is wrong to	Whites	Blacks
Go with a group to protest to a public official	19	8
Attend protest meetings	29	8
Join in a protest march	52	14
Join in public street demonstrations	62	21
Riot if necessary to get public officials to correct political wrongs	83	62

Source: Adapted from Lester W. Milbrath and M. L. Goel, *Political Participation*, 2nd edn, New York, Rand McNally, 1977, p. 15.

by the Black community for these types of political activity (table 6.7).

Other than civil rights, however, it is difficult to find an issue where protest was both successful and broadly accepted as legitimate, and even the civil rights movement helped inspire the urban riots of the 1960s which aroused bitter controversy and, eventually, a 'backlash' from many Whites. This is not to deny that protest has been influential. In many instances – over unemployment in the 1930s and the Vietnam War in the 1960s – clearly it has. But it is almost impossible to *measure* its influence, or in some cases, to judge whether it actually helped or hindered the cause in question.

What we can conclude is that protest is very much a last resort. Only when the unambiguously legitimate means of access are either unavailable or exhausted do individuals and social groups take recourse to protest. In some cases, such as Southern Blacks in the 1950s and early 1960s, they had no choice because within Southern states normal channels of access were closed. But even in this example, the movement needed and received vital support from established political actors and institutions in the North. In other cases – protest over the Vietnam War, nuclear energy, the use of abortion, for example – some argue that direct political action was illegitimate because normal channels of access were available and the democratic process took its course. This last point demonstrates nicely the problems involved in discussing political participation. As emphasized, 'the democratic process' – whether electoral or through interest group activity – must always be an imperfect representative mechanism. Some individuals and social groups will win or lose more than others; some have disproportionately greater access and hence greater political power than others. What is perhaps remarkable about the American system is that in spite of the obvious biases in the system in favour of certain interests and classes, there is a broad acceptance of basic constitutional arrangements. Protest and political violence are comparatively rare. Most Americans accept the legitimacy of the established channels of political access – elections and the activities of interest groups.

Further Reading

The best analysis of political participation in the USA is Sidney Verba and Norman H. Nie, *Participation in America: Political Democracy and Social Equality*, New York, Harper and Row, 1972. For a discussion of changes in electoral behaviour, see Norman H. Nie, Sidney Verba and John R. Petrocik, *The Changing American Voter*, Cambridge, Mass., Harvard University Press, enlarged edition, 1979. The classic statement of the voter as rational actor is Morris P. Fiorina's, *Retrospective Voting in American National Elections*, New Haven, Yale University Press, 1981. For accounts of the crisis of participation in the late 1980s, see A. James Reichley (ed.), *Elections, American Style*, Washington DC, Brookings, 1987. Presidential elections are fully covered by Nelson Polsby and Aaron Wildavsky, *Presidential Elections*, New York, Scribner's, 7th edition, 1988.

7

US Legislators and their Constituents

Congress has declined into a battle for individual survival. Each of the Congressmen and each of the Senators has the attitude: 'I've got to look out for myself'. If you remember the old best advice you ever had in the Army, it wound up with: 'Never Volunteer.' This applies to Congress, and so we have very few volunteers. Most of them are willing only to follow those things that will protect them and give them the coloration which allows them to blend into their respective districts or their respective states. If you don't stick your neck out, you don't get it chopped off.

Senator William B. Saxbe (Republican, Ohio), quoted in David Mayhew, *Congress, The Electoral Connection*

The US Congress is usually – and accurately – referred to as the most powerful legislature in the world. While a common trend in other democratic countries has been the rise of powerful executives and the relative decline of assemblies and parliaments, the Congress has been remarkably successful in maintaining its independence from executive influence. This is not to deny that the powers and functions of Congress have changed over time. Clearly they have, and the particular way in which the institution operates today is very different even from 20 years ago. But throughout its history, Congress has remained an essentially autonomous institution. Even during periods of executive ascendancy – most recently during the Johnson years – Congress never became the mere instrument of Presidents.

The independence of Congress derives in part from its constitutionally defined powers and in part from the particular way in which the American party system has evolved. Constitutionally, Congress was given three main powers, all of which remain important today. First, all legislative power is vested in the House of Representatives and the

Senate, and within this broad function Congress is given special powers to appropriate monies, to raise armies and regulate interstate commerce. Second, Congress has a constitutionally established right to declare wars and ratify treaties. Finally, the Senate is empowered to approve appointments by the President to the judiciary and executive branch and the House can impeach executive officers for wrong-doing. In addition, from very early in its history, Congress established the right to oversee and investigate the behaviour of the executive. In total these powers are awesome, especially when it is remembered that originally Congress was expected both to initiate and to approve legislation. As with other legislatures around the world, Congress has largely (although by no means entirely) forfeited the responsibility for initiating legislation to the President. Unlike most other assemblies, however, Congress retains an independent power to approve legislation, appropriate monies and generally oversee the executive branch.

The simplest explanation of this autonomy is the distinctive constituency base which individual members of Congress enjoy. In contrast to parliamentary systems, the electoral fortunes of Presidents and legislators are not directly linked. Presidents can, and often do, face a legislature dominated by a party other than their own. But this constitutional arrangement has been reinforced by the nature of the American party system. It is certainly possible to imagine a system characterized by bicameralism and the separation of powers where political party ties are strong and the electoral fortunes of legislators are interdependent with those of the executive. Only rarely has this been the case in the history of the United States. Much more common is a very loose party relationship between the President and members of Congress, with the legislators remaining essentially independent.

Representation and Congress

The sort of party government associated with parliamentary systems greatly restricts the representative function of individual legislators. In Britain, for example, the individual member of Parliament is largely tied, through party discipline in the House, to the policies of either government or opposition. Crucially, his or her electoral survival depends on an official party endorsement.[1] So while MPs may exercise some independent pressure on party leaders or governments, it is limited. Clearly, this close organic link between executive and legislator

1   Only very exceptionally do British MPs survive the removal of party endorsement; they may survive on personal appeal for one election, but rarely longer.

limits the representative function of MPs. The electorate may benefit, at least in theory, from the coherent programmes and policies which party government produces, but the interests of individual constituencies do tend to become subordinated to national policy objectives. Curiously, British MPs are quick to insist that they come closest to what is called *trustee* representatives, that is, they are elected by the people on trust to exercise their own judgement. They are not *delegated* to carry out a specific programme, to the letter, and without discretion. In reality they are closer to being *party* delegates than trustees. Members of Congress are patently not delegates either in the sense of being slaves to a party programme or in the sense that they are mandated by their constituents to carry out specific policies. Indeed, the idea of a representative being a direct delegate of the people has relatively few applications in modern industrial societies. In small communities – and possibly in early New England town meetings – such a concept has meaning. But no member of Congress can accurately and continuously carry out the wishes of diverse and volatile electorates. Even if he or she knew what the electorate wanted, the individual member of Congress has but limited powers to influence what is a complex national policy process.

In truth, members are much closer to being trustees of their electorates. They are elected on the promise that they will exercise their judgement on behalf of their constituents' interests. And should they fail in the opinion of the electorate to defend and promote these interests, they are punished in subsequent elections. If members of Congress are not delegates, neither are they representative in the *microcosmic* sense. In fact by this measure they could hardly be less representative. An overwhelming majority of Senators and Representatives are White, middle-aged, middle-class and male. In the 100th Congress (1987–8) no fewer than 246 of the 539[2] members were lawyers, with a further 170 identified as businessmen or bankers. Very few (25) were women or members of ethnic minorities (22 were Black).

To claim that members approximate most closely to a trustee form of representation is accurate, but tells us very little about the precise linkages between legislators, constituency and party, and how these have changed over time. Over the last 20 years, for example, it is commonly asserted that party has weakened its influence on members even further, with constituency pressures in the ascendant. The remainder of this chapter will be devoted to these questions and also to a preliminary discussion of the links between constituency influences on

2 There are 435 members of the House of Representatives, 100 Senators, 3 delegates (District of Columbia, Guam, Virgin Islands) and a Resident Commissioner from Puerto Rico. The latter four cannot vote on the floor but can serve as committee members.

members of Congress and their work within the House and the Senate.

Congressional Elections

Representatives are elected every two years, Senators every six (with one third elected every two years). This simple fact helps account for what are some starkly contrasting trends in the electoral dynamics of the two Houses, but there are also some common trends. Let us examine these first.

The spread of direct primaries

As with Presidential elections, primaries are now the major means whereby members of Congress win their party's nomination for office. One major consequence of the demise of party conventions (the standard nineteenth-century form of nomination) has been to weaken the role of political parties in the nomination process. By being able to appeal directly to the electorate, the Senator or Representative now owes much less allegiance to local and national party figures.

Democrat dominance

In spite of several Republican Presidential victories, Democrats continue to dominate the House (table 7.1) and, until 1980, the Senate. And even the 1980 Senate results, with the Republicans holding 55 seats to the Democrats' 45, hardly reflected the landslide victory enjoyed by Ronald Reagan. In 1984, the Democrats actually increased their number to 47 – again in spite of the President's sweeping victory. Following the 1986 mid-term elections, the Democrats recaptured the Senate by a margin of 53 to 47, a lead which they consolidated in 1988 by increasing their majority to 55–45. The major reason for this pattern is the continuing majority of the Democratic identifiers in the population (see chapter 6, figure 6.1). Although this majority has decreased recently, it has not been accompanied by a Republican surge sufficient for us to talk of a re-alignment of voters. The Democrats also benefit from being the majority party in another sense. For in single member district first-past-the-post electoral systems majority parties usually score more constituency victories than would be expected from their aggregate popular vote (table 7.1). Democrats also dominate state legislatures

Table 7.1 National popular vote and seats won by Democrats, House of Representatives 1946–1986

Year	Per cent of all votes	Democratic seats
1946	44.3	43.3
1948	51.6	60.6
1950	48.9	54.0
1952	49.2	49.1
1954	52.1	53.3
1956	50.7	53.8
1958	55.5	64.9
1960	54.4	60.0
1962	52.1	59.4
1964	56.9	67.8
1966	50.5	57.0
1968	50.0	55.9
1970	53.0	58.6
1972	51.7	55.8
1974	57.1	66.9
1976	56.2	67.1
1978	53.4	63.7
1980	50.4	55.9
1982	55.9	61.8
1984	52.1	58.2
1986	54.5	59.3

Source: Ornstein, Mann, Malbin, Schick and Bibby, *Vital Statistics on Congress*, 1987/88 edition, table 2.2.

which are responsible for drawing up the boundaries of Congressional districts. Although the Courts have been active on the question of malapportionment (chapter 12 pp. 250 and 262), a considerable amount of discretion remains – especially over the *shape* of constituencies rather than the balance of population between districts.

Regional convergence

While at the Congressional level the Democrats continue to do better than would be expected from Presidential election results, they have lost what was the solid support of the Southern states. As we noted in the last chapter, the electorate is now more volatile and no one region can be labelled as unequivocally Republican or Democratic. In the House regional party solidarity has tended to break down, with Southern Democrats and Mid-Western and North East Republicans declining in relation to representation from other regions. Similar, although not identical, trends have occurred in the Senate.

The importance of money

For both Senators and Representatives, money has become a crucial resource in Congressional elections. With voters acting in response to the appeal of individual candidates rather than to parties, both incumbents and challengers must ensure that the voters know who they are and what their record is. This translates into buying television time for advertisements as well as spending money on mailings, meetings and other attention-seeking devices.

At one time the personal efforts of candidates in raising money were less important than winning the party endorsement or the endorsement of the big corporations and labour unions. Large donations from such sources could help clinch the election of a particular candidate. However, with declining partisanship and the passage of the Federal Election Campaign Act (FECA) in 1974, candidates have been forced to rely more and more on their own capacity to raise funds or to persuade others to contribute to their campaigns. FECA was designed to reduce candidate dependence on money, but in many respects it has increased it (figure 7.1). Why is this? In part because the Supreme Court struck down a central provision in the Act which limited contributions by candidates, and in part because the law encouraged the growth of Political Action Committees (PACs). Although PACs are limited to giving $5000 per candidate per campaign they contributed 37 per cent of all campaign financing in 1984. Individuals are limited to $1000 per candidate, but there are no limits on what candidates themselves can spend on their campaigns.

Figure 7.1 tells only part of the picture, because under FECA, the rules for national party contributions 'on behalf of' candidates – i.e. not going directly or exclusively to a particular candidate's campaign – are much looser than for individual or PAC contributions. There are limits on this so-called coordinated spending, but by exploiting the law to the full, national party committees can contribute up to $73,620 to a House candidate and $1.73 million to a Senator from the most populous states.[3] These loopholes give to the well organized Republicans an enormous advantage. In 1984, for example, the Republican National

3 Gary C. Jacobson, *The Politics of Congressional Elections*, Boston, Little, Brown, 2nd edn, 1987, p. 69.

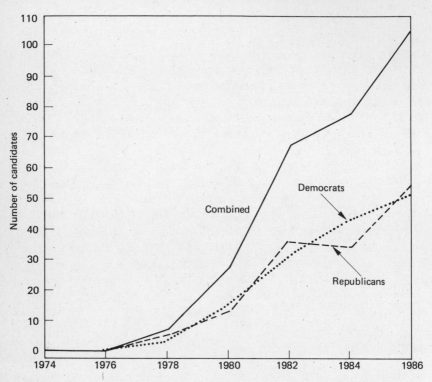

Figure 7.1   House candidates who spent more than $500,000, 1974–1986

Source: Ornstein, Mann, Malbin, Schick and Bibby, figure 3.2.

Committee raised $246 million, compared with a mere $66 million raised by the Democrats.[4]

These common trends can be contrasted with the rather different patterns which apply to incumbency and turnover of members between the two Houses. As table 7.2 shows, of those seeking re-election to the House, a remarkably high and generally rising percentage are re-elected (90 per cent in 1984). Incumbency clearly has its advantages. The contrast with the Senate is considerable, where in 1980 only 53 per cent of those seeking re-election were successful – although note the increase in incumbency over the last six years (table 7.3). What accounts for this

4   Jacobson, *The Politics of Congressional Elections*, p. 69.

Table 7.2   House incumbents re-elected, defeated or retired, 1946–1986

				Sought re-election			
						Re-elected	
Year	Retired[a]	Total	Defeated in primaries	Defeated in general election	Total	Percentage of those seeking re-election	Percentage of House membership
1946	32	398	18	52	328	82.4	75.4
1948	29	400	15	68	317	79.2	72.9
1950	29	400	6	32	362	90.5	83.2
1952	42	389	9	26	354	91.0	81.4
1954	24	407	6	22	379	93.1	87.1
1956	21	411	6	16	389	94.6	89.4
1958	33	396	3	37	356	89.9	81.9
1960	26	405	5	25	375	92.6	86.2
1962	24	402	12	22	368	91.5	84.6
1964	33	397	8	45	344	86.6	79.1
1966	22	411	8	41	362	88.1	83.2
1968	23	409	4	9	396	96.8	91.0
1970	29	401	10	12	379	94.5	87.1
1972	40	390	12	13	365	93.6	83.9
1974	43	391	8	40	343	87.7	78.9
1976	47	384	3	13	368	95.8	84.6
1978	49	382	5	19	358	93.7	82.3
1980	34	398	6	31	361	90.7	83.0
1982	40	393	10	29	354	90.1	81.4
1984	22	409	3	16	390	95.4	90.1
1986	38	393	2	6	385	98.0	88.5

[a] Does not include persons who died or resigned from office before the election.
Source: Ornstein, Mann, Malbin, Schick and Bibby, *Vital Statistics on Congress 1987/88*, Washington DC, American Enterprise Institute, table 2.7.

difference? Most important is the relative status of the two Houses. Senators are elected for six years; they represent whole states – which can mean over 26 million people in the case of California, and being a Senator can lead to higher things, certainly a Cabinet post and possibly even the Presidency. In contrast, House members are elected every two years, they represent relatively small constituencies (around half a million people) and the rewards of office are modest. Above all, Senate elections are more exposed to voters' perceptions of the quality of individual candidates. A good image or a sound record can overcome national and local trends in favour of one party or the other. While Senate seats are more competitive, the advantages of incumbency are apparent. Not surprisingly fewer Senators voluntarily retire than Representatives. For some members of the lower house, a seat is simply

Table 7.3 Senate incumbents re-elected, defeated or retired, 1946–1982

Year	Retired[a]	Sought re-election				Re-elected as % of those seeking re-election
		Total	Defeated in primaries	Defeated in general election	Total re-elected	
1946	9	30	6	7	17	56.7
1948	8	25	2	8	15	60.0
1950	4	32	5	5	22	68.8
1952	4	31	2	9	20	64.5
1954	6	32	2	6	24	75.0
1956	6	29	0	4	25	86.2
1958	6	28	0	10	18	64.3
1960	5	29	0	1	28	96.6
1962	4	35	1	5	29	82.9
1964	2	33	1	4	28	84.8
1966	3	32	3	1	28	87.5
1968	6	28	4	4	20	71.4
1970	4	31	1	6	24	77.4
1972	6	27	2	5	20	74.1
1974	7	27	2	2	23	85.2
1976	8	25	0	9	16	64.0
1978	10	25	3	7	15	60.0
1980	5	29	4	9	16	55.2
1982	3	30	0	2	28	93.3
1984	4	29	0	3	26	89.6
1986	6	28	0	7	21	75.0

[a] Does not include persons who died or resigned from office before the election.
Source: Ornstein, Mann, Malbin, Schick and Bibby, *Vital Statistics on Congress 1987/88*, Washington DC, American Enterprise Institute, table 2.8.

one rung on a long career ladder – whether in or out of politics.

Given the personalized nature of Congressional electoral politics, how do members reconcile their commitment to campaigning and winning re-election on the one hand and their obligations to public policy making on the other? To answer this question we have to look more carefully at the work of members and in particular at the sort of strategic choices they face, when seeking election or re-election.

Legislators as Rational Actors

Senators and Representatives' determined efforts to get elected or re-elected essentially involve an interaction between the candidate and the constituency. While not unimportant, party ties and contacts have long since ceased to dominate the nomination and campaign process. But this electoral interaction is not simply one of candidate projection and media promotion. Members are also required to tend to the needs and interests of their constituencies – a job which in the American context is both complex and demanding.

Political scientists have attempted to characterize these efforts in terms of rational choice analysis. David Mayhew, for example, in his stimulating and influential book, *Congress: The Electoral Connection*,[5] argues that members of Congress are mainly motivated by one thing: re-election. Almost all their behaviour inside and outside Congress is shaped by this simple drive. A major *a priori* assumption here is that members *can* affect their re-election chances. While Mayhew accepts that there are limits to what a Representative or Senator can do to please his or her constituents – no individual legislator can, after all, banish unemployment or solve the budget deficit problem – he does identify three broad strategies which can improve re-election chances. He or she can, first, advertise by spreading his or her name and reputation and generally creating a favourable image. Exposure on television and in the local press can be important, and unlike the Washington/New York press, local newspapers are generally sympathetic to members of Congress.[6] Sometimes members go to unusual lengths in their efforts at self-promotion. Mayhew reports Charles Diggs Jr. (Democrat, Michigan) as running a radio programme with himself as 'combination disc jockey–commentator and minister', and Daniel Flood (Democrat, Pennsylvania) apparently is 'famous for appearing unannounced and often uninvited at wedding anniversaries and other events'.[7]

Probably more significant is *credit claiming*, or convincing constituents that the member has 'delivered the goods'. This is nothing new, of course. Indeed, 'pork barrel' politics is part of American folklore. Pork barrel politics almost always involves particular rather than collective benefits to constituents. It would be very difficult for an individual

5 New Haven, Yale University Press, 1974.
6 While there are no genuinely national newspapers in the USA, the *New York Times*, *The Wall Street Journal* and *Washington Post* act as forums for national debate.
7 Both quotes from David Mayhew, *The Electoral Connection*, New Haven, Yale University Press, 1974, p. 51.

member of Congress to claim credit for having reduced the rate of inflation, which everyone benefits from. Much more likely is he or she to benefit from helping direct federal investment (for example on a military installation or community development project) to his or her constituency. As we shall see later, the internal structure of power in Congress, not least the absence of strict party discipline facilitates just such distributions.

Finally, members benefit from *position taking* or being identified positively in the minds of constituents with a particular policy position. A predominantly Roman Catholic or Fundamentalist Christian constituency would be gratified by public pronouncements or actual legislative action by their Congressman against abortion. New York's large Jewish community would expect their Congress person to take a pro-Israeli stance, and so on. Most recently, legislators have formed caucuses to promote or defend a particular constituency interest. Typical examples are the House Automobile Task Force and the Steel Caucus, both of which have striven to counteract economic decline in these industries.

Senators and Representatives have always tended their constituencies, but in recent years the pressures to do so have increased considerably. We have already noted the decline of political party influence – one potentially major bulwark against an intimate constituency/legislator relationship. Less obvious is the impact of a number of political and technological changes on the information flow between the electorate and member. On the members' side, free mailing privileges, together with computerized mailing lists, enable legislators not only to send out a vast volume of letters (Senate offices, for example, send out about 1 million letters a month),[8] but also to *target* mail to particular groups of constituents. So if a legislator wants to publicize his anti-abortion stand to all Roman Catholics and Born Again Christians in his district he can do so. He can even hone down the target group to a particular neighbourhood or block. On the constituents' side, interest groups and political action committees increasingly 'rate' the legislative voting record of individual members. These group ratings enable groups and, via publicity back home, constituents, to identify their members as 'liberal', 'conservative', pro- or anti-environmental protection, labour, affirmative action or whatever.[9]

8   See Michael J. Robinson, 'Three faces of Congressional media', in Thomas E. Mann and Norman J. Ornstein (eds), *The New Congress*, Washington DC, American Enterprise Institute, 1981, pp. 55–96.
9   An excellent and comprehensive sample of ratings can be found in Michael Barone and Grant Ujifusa, *The Almanac of American Politics 1988*, Washington DC, Barone and Co., 1988.

Predictably, Senators are less exposed to such highly focused pressures than are Representatives, but Mayhew contends they are just as instrumental in their quest for re-election as House members. There is undoubtedly a great deal of validity to the rational choice approach. Any observer of the Washington scene would have to concede that members are increasingly preoccupied with constituency matters. Richard Fenno, who spent several months with Congressmen as a participant observer, dubbed these activities 'home style'.[10] Fenno also noted another phenomenon, however, which does cast some doubt on the rational choice thesis. The longer House members remained in Congress, the more concerned they became with Washington affairs and the less diligent they became in their pastoral constituency work. The implication here is that there are forces at work in the lives of members of Congress other than the simple drive to win re-election. It may be, of course, that these other forces complement rather than compete with constituency pressures. Most voters have very little knowledge of what Representatives and Senators actually do in Washington. And given that the electorate is not so naive as to expect an individual member to transform society, a steady flow of positive messages linked to advertising, credit claiming and position taking may be enough to convince voters that 'their' Representative or Senator is doing a good job.

Undoubtedly there are a number of activities important to the legislators which do not seriously conflict with constituency duties. On some issues – especially foreign policy or technical financial questions – constituents do not have well formed opinions. Yet if members devote themselves to such issues, possibly they are at least indirectly neglecting their re-election chances by not putting their time to the most effective use. The rational choice theorists' answer here is simple: members devote time to non-constituency questions because the internal dynamics of the House (or Senate) demand it. As separate and individual political actors they can achieve very little for the voters. So in order (say) to ensure the siting of a federal installation in their constituency, they are obliged to form *coalitions* with other members. Naturally, coalition formation involves give and take. It is necessary for a legislator to spend time on apparently nonrelevant legislative activity, in order to win support on those issues which are directly relevant. This is called *logrolling* or the bargaining, vote trading and exchange of favours which has long been a characteristic of Congress. As long ago as 1885 Woodrow

10   Richard E. Fenno Jr., *Home Style: House Members in their Districts*, Boston, Little, Brown, 1978.

Wilson, then an academic observer of Congress, noted:

> It is principally in connection with appropriations that what has come to be known in our political slang as 'log-rolling' takes place. Of course the chief scene of this sport is the private room of the Committee on Rivers and Harbors, and the season of its highest excitement the hours spent in the passage of the River and Harbor Bill. 'Log-rolling' is an exchange of favors. Representative A is very anxious to secure a grant for the cleaning of a small watercourse in his district, and representative B is equally solicitous about his plans for bringing money into the hands of the contractors of his own constituency, whilst representative C comes from a seaport town whose modest harbor is neglected because of the treacherous bar across its mouth, and representative D has been blamed for not bestirring himself more in the interest of schemes of improvement afoot amongst the enterprising citizens of his native place; so it is perfectly feasible for these gentlemen to put their heads together and confirm a mutual understanding that each will vote in Committee of the whole for the grants desired by the others, in consideration of the promise that they will cry 'Aye' when his item comes on to be considered.[11]

Today, of course, it is not the Committee on Rivers and Harbors, but any one of the 127 standing workgroups (committees and sub-committees) in the Senate and 159 in the House which dominate day-to-day legislative business (figures are for the 98th Congress, 1983/4).[12] We will return to log-rolling and the work of Congressional committees later. For now it is important to stress that although persuasive, the rational choice view of the work of Congress has its limitations. It assumes that legislators can know what the interests of his or her constituency are. Often this is difficult. Some districts are socially, ethnically and economically diverse. A Senator from Washington State may not need any prompting when voting on legislation affecting the two industries – lumber and aerospace – which dominate that state. But it is much more difficult for Senators from California, representing diverse and politically volatile populations, to respond in this way.

More serious is the implication in the rational choice approach that members of Congress are mere automatons responding to constituency

11 Woodrow Wilson, *Congressional Government*, New York, Meridian Books, 1956, p. 121.
12 Ironically, however, 'water' continues to generate a mass of pork barrel legislation, mainly because dams and other water projects are widely supported by rural Congressmen and by the Army Corps of Engineers who build them.

demands. There is no place for ideology, party or individual preferences. Yet a wealth of empirical evidence exists to suggest that at one point or another in a legislator's life all of these can be – and usually are – important. As suggested, party influences are weak by European standards, but that does not mean they do not exist. Democrats have some policy positions and perspectives in common, as have Republicans. The next chapter will show, indeed, how party leadership within each House can be crucial in determining the outcome of legislation. Similarly, appeals by a President to his fellow party members in Congress can be effective. Lyndon Johnson used the Democratic majorities in the House and Senate to great effect when pushing through his Great Society social and civil rights programmes. More recently, Ronald Reagan appealed directly to party solidarity when endeavouring to persuade the Republican Senate to support his economic reforms in 1981–2. Assured of Republican minority support in the House, victory there was sealed by the additional support of conservative Democrats.

The existence of 'conservative' and 'liberal' groupings shows the importance of ideology. In itself this need not be significant – members may after all be simply mirroring their constituents' view – but constituencies are not always easily labelled conservative or liberal, and it is not uncommon for an established conservative or liberal member to represent a constituency which cannot accurately be described as either. Legislators are also influenced by other members and by their staff. In other words, in the context of a legislative process which is both fragmented and complex, they are exposed to a number of pressures and influences. Constituency demands may be on the ascendant but this does not mean that we should reduce the role of legislators to the vote-getting machines implied by some political scientists.

In sum, members are exposed to many influences. Given the importance of their constituents' preferences in deciding their electoral survival, it is unlikely that members will do anything directly to antagonize the voters. And, if particularly vulnerable or in a marginal seat, they may indeed devote all their energies to re-election. For some, and particularly members of the Senate, however, political life becomes much more complex, with constituency, party, committee, interest group and ideological pressures competing for the members' favour.

The Work of Members of Congress

The changing pattern of influence on members has had important consequences on the internal structure of power in each House – and these changes will be analysed in the next chapter. A useful way to link discussion of the activities of members outside and inside the legislature is to examine the typical workload of legislators and the support in staff, offices and other services provided for them.

Clearly Representatives and Senators are not 'lobby fodder' as British MPs are often labelled. They have little choice but to take note of the needs and demands of their constituents and to act on them. Part of this function involves formulating and monitoring a mass of complex legislation. Given the sheer volume of legislation (some 25,000 bills are introduced every session, but only about 600 become law) most members specialize in a particular policy area, often but not always related to their constituents' interests. Senator William Fulbright, for example, was for many years Chairman of the Senate Foreign Relations Committee. In this job he took a predominantly liberal stance, especially on the conduct of the Vietnam War – not a strategy which was linked in any obvious way to the interests of his rural and conservative constituency, Arkansas. Most of the crucial legislative work is conducted in the committees and subcommittees, yet as table 7.4 shows, Representatives spend rather little of their awesome 11-hour day directly on committee work. The remainder is devoted to a number of tasks – but in particular answering mail and consulting with aides. To assist the legislator perform all these functions, Congress has voted for itself a quite extraordinary number of services. Office space, furnishings, stationery and postal allowances are generous. And all communication with constituents, primarily by mail, is free for Senators, and Representatives are given generous mailing privileges. All of these benefits pale into insignificance compared with the provisions made for Congressional staff. In 1983, a staggering 25,000 people worked for Congress including, in the House, 7606 personal aides and in the Senate 4059. So each Representative has approximately 17 people working for him or her, and each Senator enjoys the assistance of no fewer than 40 aides. Some of these positions are secretarial, but many are professionals including some (about two for each member in the House and five in the Senate) directly assigned the job of drafting and amending legislation.[13] In addition 2000 staff

13 See Michael J. Malbin, 'Delegation, deliberation, and the new role of Congressional staff', in Thomas E. Mann and Norman J. Ornstein (eds), *The New Congress*, Washington DC, American Enterprise Institute, 1981, pp. 134–77.

Table 7.4   A Representative's average day

	Minutes	Hours
In the House chamber		2.53
In committee/subcommittee work		1.22
Hearings	26	
Business	9	
Mark ups	42	
Other	5	
In his/her office		3.19
With constituents	17	
With organized groups	9	
With others	20	
With staff aides	53	
With other Representatives	5	
Answering mail	46	
Preparing legislation, speeches	12	
Reading	11	
On telephone	26	
In other Washington locations		2.02
With constituents at Capitol Hill	9	
At events	33	
With leadership	3	
With other Representatives	11	
With informal groups	8	
In party meetings	5	
Personal time	28	
Other	25	
Other		1.40
Total		11.16

Source: US House of Representatives, Commission on Administrative Review, *Administrative Reorganization and Legislative Management*, 95th Congress, 1st session, 1977, H. Doc. 95–232: pp. 18–19.

work for House committees and over 1200 for Senate committees. Over the last 20 years there has been a rapid increase in the number of subcommittees, reflecting both an increase in the legislative workload and the increasing independence of members of Congress, and staffs have risen correspondingly. Finally, members benefit from the work of a number of support agencies such as the Library of Congress (over 5400 staff) and the General Accounting Office (5300). Of course these support agencies are rarely directly involved in legislation, but their presence does reinforce the claim that, probably uniquely among world assemblies,[14] Congress has acquired a formidable permanent bureaucracy.

So we can conclude that the typical member is a man or woman under pressure. But American national legislators are also uncommonly independent of party and executive, and to help them perform their legislative duties and retain this independence, they are uniquely privileged with staffing and other bureaucratic support. But the important questions remain. How does Congress influence the policy process? To what extent does it check executive power? Most important, is Congress truly the 'people's branch' in the sense that it expresses the democratic wishes of the population?

Further Reading

David Mayhew's *Congress: The Electoral Connection*, New Haven, Yale University Press, 1974, catalogues the ways in which members of Congress tend to their constituencies. *Home Style*, Boston, Little, Brown, 1978, by Richard E. Fenno Jr. is a book rich in anecdote on the same theme. Congressional elections are examined in Gary C. Jacobson, *The Politics of Congressional Elections*, Boston, Little, Brown, 2nd edition, 1987. An overview of Congress is provided by Barbara Hinckley, *Stability and Change in Congress*, New York, Harper and Row, 4th edition, 1988.

---

14   Michael Malbin notes that the next most heavily staffed legislature is the Canadian Parliament, with a mere 3300 staff, Mann and Ornstein (eds), *The New Congress*, p. 135.

8

Congress as Policy Maker

Let me say this about Congress . . . A Congress is not a President . . . A Congress should not be a President . . . A Congress should be nothing more, nothing less than what it is: a reflection of the will of our people and the problems that disturb them and the actions they want taken. The Congress ought to improve its ability to serve that function.

Senator Edmund S. Muskie (Democrat, Maine),
quoted in John L. Steele (ed.), *The Role of Congress II: Study of the Legislative Branch*

It is impossible for either the internal or the foreign policy of great states to be strongly and consistently carried out on a collegial basis. Collegiality unavoidably obstructs the promptness of decision, the consistency of policy, the clear responsibility of the individual, and ruthlessness to outsiders in combination with the maintenance of discipline within the group.

Max Weber, *Theory of Social and Economic Organizations*

As was stressed in chapter 3, Congress was originally intended to be the key institution in the federal government. It was only through Congress that the people were given a direct control over policy. Members of the House of Representatives were directly elected, Senators, President and Vice-President were not. Moreover Congress was meant to formulate and pass laws – the President's main job being merely to implement them. Popular control of government was of course limited by the Presidential veto and the territorial base of appointed Senators. But it was the House of Representatives which controlled the purse strings and it was Congress as a whole which stood, as legislature, at the apex of the constitutional system.

The actual functioning of the institution never quite worked as intended. During the first thirty years of the nineteenth century state legislatures voted to adopt the direct election of the President, and as the country grew and demands on government increased, President and executive took on the major responsibility for formulating legislation. This trend has occurred in almost every country and is an almost inescapable consequence of the vast information and manpower resources available to modern executive bureaucracies, but not to legislatures. Yet unlike some national legislatures, Congress retains formidable power. It remains an indisputably important actor in the policy process. It is also an institution whose powers and internal operations are constantly changing. The main purpose of this chapter is to analyse the nature and significance of these changes so that an accurate understanding of the policy-making role of Congress in the 1980s and 1990s can be achieved.

The Functions of Congress

As indicated in chapter 7, the first and most general function of Congress is one of representation. At its simplest this means that members of Congress are held accountable for their actions through the electoral process. In complex societies the citizen/representative relationship must necessarily be limited, however, so when we talk of the 'representative function of Congress' we are actually referring to a number of different functions, most of which are at least one removed from the direct influence of the voters. So the business of formulating and passing laws – the legislative function – involves constant interaction between members, and between members and staff, interest groups, executive officials, the courts and the media. Clearly the individual voter's influence in this process is limited, although as we have already established, the constant threat of electoral defeat does oblige US legislators to tend to the general pastoral needs of their constituencies. A second major function of legislatures, and especially the Congress, is to oversee the executive branch. Constitutionally and by convention, Congress has a number of established oversight powers. It controls finance, so appropriations bills originate in the House of Representatives and have to be approved by both Houses. As we will develop later, it is the President who initially produces the annual budget, so the appropriations process is an opportunity for Congress to approve, modify or criticize the executive's spending plans and also to monitor them during implementation. The Senate also approves Presidential appointments, and both Houses have power to investigate inefficiency or wrong-doing in the executive branch. Finally, Congress has the power to veto all administrative reorganizations in the executive branch. Before we look at these functions in detail, it is necessary to outline the formal structure of power in the two Houses.

The Structure of Power in Congress

Two major foci of power exist – committees and party leadership. Table 8.1 lists the standing committees and subcommittees of the 100th Congress, together with their chairmen. Committees have always been central to the business of legislation in Congress and if anything their importance has increased over the years. As table 8.1 shows, the permanent committees are distinguished by function, and as government has become more complex, so the number of committees and subcommittees has proliferated. Consolidation and reorganizations do occur, but it is never long before the need for another work-group emerges. Both internal and external pressures are at work to increase this need. Internally, individual legislators build reputations by specializing in a particular subject. Often this specialization is linked to constituent needs. Moreover, Congress's own bureaucracy has to match developments in the executive branch, and as departments and agencies have increased in number and function, so Congress has been obliged to respond. Often this is a two-way street. Members' career and constituency needs may benefit from executive fragmentation which legislation often encourages.

It is in the committees that the business of framing, amending and rejecting legislation occurs. Most committees *authorize* legislation while others provide funds to *finance* programmes. Hence the Appropriations, House Ways and Means, Senate Finance and the Budget Committees are concerned with approving income (taxation) and expenditure bills. We will examine the budgetary process in more detail in chapter 13. By no means are all committees equal in power. The above-named finance committees are particularly prestigious and influential, especially so in the case of the House Appropriations Committee (which is the source of all appropriations bills), the House Ways and Means and Senate Finance Committees (which are responsible for tax bills) and the Budget Committees. Of the authorizing committees, the Senate Foreign Relations is of central importance in foreign policy, while the Agriculture, Banking and Judiciary Committees are prominent in both Houses. An equivalent hierarchy applies to most subcommittees with, for example, the House Appropriations Subcommittee on Defense being

Table 8.1   Senate and House: standing committees and subcommittees, 100th Congress, 1987–1988

Senate committees	Chairman (all Democrats)	Number of subcommittees
Agriculture, Nutrition and Forestry	Patrick Leahy Vermont	7
Appropriations	John Stennis Mississippi	13
Armed Services	Sam Nunn Georgia	6
Banking, Housing and Urban Affairs	William Proxmire Wisconsin	4
Budget	Lawton Chiles Florida	None
Commerce, Science and Transportation	Ernest Hollings S. Carolina	8
Energy and Natural Resources	J. Bennett Johnson Louisiana	5
Environment and Public Works	Quentin Burdick North Dakota	5
Finance	Lloyd Bentsen Texas	7
Foreign Relations	Claiborne Pell Rhode Island	7
Governmental Affairs	John Glenn Ohio	5
Judiciary	Joseph Biden Delaware	6
Labor and Human Resources	Edward Kennedy Massachusetts	6
Rules and Administration	Wendell Ford Kentucky	None
Veterans' Affairs	Alan Cranston California	None
Small Business	Dale Bumpers Arkansas	6

House committees	Chairman (all Democrats)	Number of subcommittees
Agriculture	Eligio De La Garza Texas	8
Appropriations	Jamie Whitten Mississippi	13
Armed Services	Les Aspin Wisconsin	7
Banking, Finance and Urban Affairs	Fernand St Germain Rhode Island	8

House committees	Chairman (all Democrats)	Number of subcommittees
Budget	William Gray Pennsylvania	8*
District of Columbia	Ronald Dellums California	3
Education and Labor	Augustus Hawkins California	8
Energy and Commerce	John Dingell Michigan	6
Foreign Affairs	Dante Fascell Florida	8
Government Operations	Jack Brooks Texas	7
House Administration	Frank Annunzio Illinois	6
Interior and Insular Affairs	Maurice Udall Arizona	6
Judiciary	Peter Rodino New Jersey	7
Merchant Marine and Fisheries	Walter Jones N. Carolina	6
Post Office and Civil Service	William Ford Michigan	7
Public Works and Transportation	James Howard New Jersey	6
Rules	Claude Pepper Florida	2
Science, Space and Technology	Robert Roe New Jersey	7
Small Business	John La Falce New York	6
Standards of Official Conduct	Julian Dixon California	None
Veterans' Affairs	Sonny Montgomery Mississippi	5
Ways and Means	Dan Rostenkowski Illinois	6

* Task Forces.
Source: Congressional Quarterly.

markedly more important than the subcommittee responsible for the District of Columbia. Because the House of Representatives is a larger and, by tradition, a more formal body than the Senate, the number of complex rules have been formulated to govern day-by-day business. The Rules Committee is responsible for interpreting these regulations and in particular for helping to decide which bills, and in what form, come before the floor of the House. This power to withhold bills or to allow them to proceed only if certain amendments or provisions are omitted or included gives the Rules Committee considerable political clout. Indeed during the late nineteenth and early twentieth centuries, the Rules Committee was at the very centre of Congressional power. Today, although it continues to perform a gatekeeper function, it is less powerful, in part because the House is less formal than it was (of which more later) and in part because the Committee tends to be the voice of the majority party leadership rather than being an independent source of power in Congress.

Clearly, membership of committees is an important determinant of the status and influence of individual Representatives and Senators, and accordingly the processes whereby members are selected to sit on committees and eventually selected as chairmen have long been the subject of debate and controversy. The most basic rule is that the party with a majority in the Chamber automatically achieves a majority in the committees, with the minority party represented in rough proportion to its delegation in the Chamber as a whole. Committee and subcommittee chairmen are drawn exclusively from the majority party. In both House and Senate, members are allowed to sit on a maximum of two committees, although House members assigned to the important Rules, Ways and Means and Appropriations Committees are not normally permitted further assignments. In both Houses party committees selected by party caucuses (meetings of all party members in each House) choose the members of the standing committees. This process is predictably political, with seniority, experience, reputation and connections being the main determinants of assignments. Since the 1950s the Senate has ensured that all freshmen (new) Senators are given at least one major committee assignment (the so-called 'Johnson Rule' introduced under the influence of the then Senator majority leader, Lyndon Baines Johnson). By winning prestigious committee jobs, members can enhance their institutional reputations, gain access to legislative programmes of direct interest to their constituents, and, occasionally, attract national attention.[1] During the first two years of the 1980–4 Reagan adminis-

1   See Richard Fenno Jr., *Congressmen in Committees*, Boston, Little, Brown, 1973, for a vivid account of committee politics.

tration, for example, Congressman James R. Jones (D. Oklahoma) assumed a pivotal position as Chairman of the House Budget Committee. Although he opposed many of the Administration's economic policies, Jones was able to straddle party positions by proposing alternative, but by no means opposite, policies and by maintaining a friendly relationship with Pete Domenici, the Republican Chairman of the Senate Budget Committee.

Within individual committees and subcommittees status is no less important, with the chairman of each work-group at the very top of the pecking order. Both ranking within committees and the assertion of power by the chairman over committee members is largely determined by seniority. Until the early 1970s the seniority rule was condemned by liberals because of the enormous advantage it gave to the solidly Democratic – but racist and conservative – one-party South. Indeed, the caricature image of elderly white-haired Southerners lording over all and sundry on Capitol Hill was not far from the truth, as such figures as Richard Russell of Armed Services, Russell Long of Finance and James Eastland of Judiciary in the Senate and Carl Vinson of Armed Services, and Howard Smith of Rules in the House, testified.

Chairmen were, and indeed still are, powerful because of their control of the agenda. They can decide the order in which bills are discussed, the timing of committee meetings, the frequence of public hearings and the management of bills on the floor of the House. They used also to have a major say in the number and composition of subcommittees, together with the selection of subcommittee chairmen. Since the early 1970s a number of reforms have removed committee chairmen from the very pinnacles of power, although they remain very powerful members of Congress. But they now no longer have control of the work and membership of subcommittees which, as we will expand upon later, have considerable independent influence. Moreover, seniority is not now the only criterion for advancement within committees. In 1975 the House Democratic caucus, caught up in a general atmosphere of reform, removed three of the most powerful committee chairmen at a stroke (Wight Patman of Texas – Banking and Currency, W. R. Poage of Texas – Agriculture, and F. Edward Hébert of Louisiana – Administration). In fact, seniority remains central to any promotion within committees. The crucial difference now is that chairmen are obliged to treat subcommittee chairmen (and committee members generally) more as equals than as feudal vassals. This is part of a general democratization and dispersal of power in both the House and (to a lesser extent) the Senate which we will return to later. Seniority is much less criticized now because the one-party nature of the South has changed. The region is more competitive, and many seats, especially in the Senate, turn over more frequently.

In addition to the standing committees in each House, a number of other work-groups exist, the most important of which are the Conference Committees. These are, simply, *ad hoc* bodies created to reconcile the differences that occur in the House and Senate versions of the same piece of legislation. Membership is drawn from those members in each House who have been most closely involved with the legislation – usually the relevant committee members – who then vote *en bloc* so as to represent the wishes of their Chamber. A great deal of politicking goes on in conference with bills often amended considerably, and not always in line with the wishes of the House or Senate as a whole. Conference decisions can, however, be rejected by a subsequent vote on the floor of each Chamber and sent back to the committee. (See figure 8.1 p. 154.) In addition, *ad hoc* committees can be formed by the Speaker of the House to reconcile standing committees with overlapping jurisdictions, and select committees appointed by presiding officers can be created in either House to expedite a particular problem, often in association with a Congressional investigation. In recent years, for example, select committees on ageing and intelligence have been formed in both Houses. Such committees have to be renewed every two years and they cannot report legislation to the floor. In most cases select committees emerge as a forum for airing currently controversial issues.

The second focus of power in Congress is the party leadership. In the House the key figures are the Speaker and Minority Leader, and the key groups are the party caucuses, in particular the majority party caucus. The Speaker of the House used to have quite awesome formal power. Until 1911, he was also Chairman of the Rules Committee and he appointed committee chairmen. This combination enabled Speakers to control the flow of legislation on to the floor. Concentration of such power in the personage of one particularly assertive Speaker, Joseph Cannon, led to a revolt in 1910–11 which resulted in the removal of the Speaker's control of the Rules Committee and of committee assignments. But the Speaker retains considerable authority. He continues to help control the flow of legislation, recognizes who is to speak on the floor, can create *ad hoc* committees, gives advice on assignments to conference and select committees, helps in assigning bills to committees and he votes in the event of a tie. While the Speaker has the greatest formal power of any individual in the House, his potential informal power is much greater. As both leading parliamentarian and party leader he can become a crucial link between other centres of power – particularly committee chairmen – as well as be the person most able to muster often disparate party forces behind a particular bill or the programme of a President. Whether these powers are utilized to the full depends on the personality, capabilities and political skills of the incumbent.

In recent years, for example, the office has come full circle as incumbents have changed. Between 1940 and 1960 the office was dominated by the forceful and highly political Sam Rayburn (with breaks in 1947–8 and 1953–4 when the Republicans had a majority in the House). Between 1961 and 1978 first John McCormack and then Carl Albert became Speakers, neither of whom had the skills or the charisma of Rayburn. Between 1978 and 1986 the highly partisan and politically astute Thomas (Tip) O'Neill partly returned the office of Speaker to its former glory. O'Neill's personality was ideally suited to the brokerage politics of the House, and he was aided by the 1975 reforms which gave to the Speaker the power to appoint Democratic members of the Rules Committee and to the Democratic Steering Committee, which assigns new committee members within the Party. Given the Democratic dominance of the House, these amounted to considerable powers. On his resignation in 1986, O'Neill was replaced by Jim Wright of Texas, a long-time O'Neill supporter and until 1986 Democratic House Majority Leader.

After the Speaker, the most important offices are the majority and minority floor leaders, who are elected by the party caucuses and whose main job is to monitor and organize party business on the floor of the House. In fact the Minority Leader is often a more crucial figure than the Majority Leader, largely because the Speaker is the effective majority spokesman. Robert Michel (pronounced 'Michael'), the most recent Minority Leader, saw his position and importance increase when the Republicans controlled both the Senate and the Presidency between 1980 and 1986. Finally, both parties appoint whips to help control floor business. These are in no way equivalent to British Parliamentary whips; they have no effective sanctions at their disposal to oblige members to toe the party line (if there is one!). Instead their job is to persuade, negotiate, bargain and cajole members into broad agreement on particular items of legislation.

During the 1970s the House Democrats strengthened the organization of the whipping system in order to counter the ongoing trend towards decentralization in the chamber. Under the guidance of Tip O'Neill these measures were to meet with some success during the 1980s.

The party caucus meets infrequently and then usually to agree in procedure rather than to discuss substantive policy issues. As important today are the informal caucuses which have emerged over the last 20 years. Most important are the Democratic Study Group representing liberal Democrats, the Southern caucus, or 'Boll Weevils', which crosses party lines and is generally conservative in orientation, and the equally conservative Republican Study Group.

Leadership in the Senate roughly parallels that in the House, but there are some important differences. Unlike the House, the presiding officer, the Vice-President of the United States, has few powers. Neither, indeed, has the President Pro-Tem who normally presides over day-to-day business. Real power lies with the majority and minority leaders, although even they can often do little to control the behaviour of just 100 fiercely independent Senators. Again, much depends on the personality of the incumbents. Some Majority Leaders such as Lyndon Johnson (1955–60) built reputations as power brokers, as did a recent incumbent, Republican Howard Baker, whose management of the Republicans' fragile majority in 1981–5 showed great political skill. Robert Dole of Kansas, who succeeded Baker in 1985, had to use all his political skill to hold together an even narrower Republican majority until the Democrats regained control of the Senate in 1986. In contrast to Johnson and Baker, some recent Leaders such as Mike Mansfield (1961–78) and Robert Byrd (1977–81 and 1986–8) have either been unwilling or less able to assert authority over fellow party members.

So far in our discussion we have concentrated on describing the formal powers of committees and party leaders. This tells us little about the dynamics of the policy-making process, however, and how the institution can be assessed in terms of its performance and effectiveness. One way to examine these questions is first to look at the validity of the *criticisms* which have been directed at Congress over recent years, and then to discuss the reform measures adopted in response to these criticisms.

Congress Under Fire

At least since the Second World War Congress has been the subject of sometimes intense criticism. Very generally we can divide these criticisms into broad categories – those which are historically specific and those which identify structural features of Congress which persist through time. Of course, the two sets of critiques are related, especially as the institution is constantly changing, but this simple distinction does facilitate a more subtle understanding of how the institution works.

1 *Perhaps the most common and persistent criticism is that Congress is*

fragmented and unresponsive; that it is not a 'coherent' policy-making body but instead a forum for the defence and promotion of disparate, unrelated interests. That the policy-making process in Congress is fragmented cannot be disputed. Power is dispersed to committees and subcommittees and the legislative process itself is cumbersome. When a bill is introduced it faces a formidable number of potential veto points before it actually becomes law, and this is true even of those bills which are part of the President's programme, have substantial support in Congress, and are recognized as important public questions. Figure 8.1 shows the major obstacles that confront any bill when introduced into Congress. Committee action is the most difficult stumbling block, with only about 10 per cent of bills actually reported out. The Presidential veto is a much rarer barrier, but it is frequently exercised on important items of legislation and is now used more than during the 1950s or 1960s. Even less common are successful attempts to override a veto. The President can also exercise a *pocket veto* by failing to sign a bill passed within the last 10 days of a legislative session.

Figure 8.1 also omits reference to the Senate *filibuster* – a debating device which, although used infrequently, has ended the life of several controversial bills. Filibustering is the practice, allowed only by Senate rules, of speaking in unlimited debate and eventually forcing the opposition to back down. During the 1950s and 1960s many civil rights bills were killed by this method, with segregationist Southern Senators speaking for many hours against the reform measures. A device does exist for ending a filibuster known as a *cloture* (or closure) rule; this can be invoked to end debate if three-fifths of the Senators agree. Between 1917 (when the Cloture Rule was introduced) and 1980, 159 cloture votes were taken, of which 49 were successful. Since the 1970s cloture has been voted much more frequently and is now successful in about 50 per cent of cases.

In the House, the Rules Committee can constitute a further barrier to the passage of a law. Until 1975, Southerners dominated the Committee and frequently refused to grant rules to bills they disliked, irrespective of the support the measures may have won in the legislative committees. Again liberal, and especially civil rights legislation was the victim. In 1975, however, the Democratic caucus voted to give the Speaker the power to appoint Rules Committee members. As a result, although the Committee can still stop bills, it acts more in accordance with the general wishes of the House – and particularly with the relevant legislative committee – than before. Interestingly, debate on the floor used to be one of the least significant aspects of the legislative process, for by the time a bill reached this stage it was already roughly in its

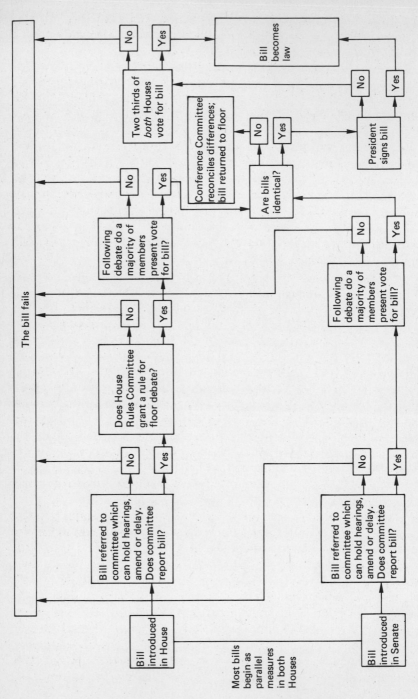

Figure 8.1 How a bill becomes law: the obstacle course for legislation in Congress

final form. Recent reforms, however, have increased floor activity with individual legislators now more able to attach riders and amendments to bills. Floor *votes* can also be crucial, of course.

Figure 8.1 gives the slightly misleading impression that bills either proceed past a number of legislative hurdles or are simply killed off. The reality is that most bills are non-starters because they lack the support of key members – although some are initiated simply to attract public attention to an issue – and the remainder embark on a course which is beset with problems and pitfalls. But these do not always involve the possibility of a sudden death. As likely are the possibilities of amendment and delay. Delay can occur at almost any stage of the process, but it is in the committees that bills most often become buried, sometimes never to reappear. Given that Congress has a heavy workload and is constantly under pressure, delaying a bill is often an expedient course to follow. For a bill's supporters, including Presidents, this can be highly frustrating.

Few bills emerge from Congress in the precise form that they entered. They are amended – sometimes dramatically – from their original form, and this amendment process is the very essence of Congressional politics, for it is by changing the detailed provisions of bills that Congressmen can indulge in *log-rolling*, or the exchange of favours which is so crucial to their electoral survival. So items are added to or deleted from bills in accordance with bargains struck between key legislators, usually within, or between committees. Committee hearings, open to public scrutiny, also allow organized interests to air their views and generally to advertise particular points of view. And of course executive departments and agencies usually have a crucial interest (with positions to defend or promote) in the detail of legislation. Finally, committees may compete one with the other, for as can be inferred from the list of committees in table 8.1, there are a number of areas where overlapping jurisdictions occur.

When all these influences are at work, as they are in major items of legislation, the potential for delay, obstruction and even confusion, can be appreciated. A classic example of what can happen to a vital piece of legislation is provided by President Carter's energy programme introduced in Congress in 1977. Carter's programme, involving as it did changes in oil and gas pricing and taxation, conservation in homes and factories and an increase in coal consumption, automatically concerned several Congressional committees (Finance, Ways and Means, Interior, Banking, Currency and Urban Affairs plus a number of subcommittees), but also members from competing constituencies (the energy rich West versus the energy poor North East), the oil, gas and coal interests, and organized consumer interests intent on higher taxes for the then highly profitable oil companies. After a long and sometimes acrimonious process, the bill failed. And this in spite of the importance of the issue, general public support for energy reforms, President and Congress controlled by the same party, and determined efforts by the House Speaker, Tip O'Neill, to drive the legislation through.[2] To be fair, President Carter's liaison with Congress was poor, but there have been remarkably few occasions when a major legislative package has not been delayed or obstructed by Congress. The early New Deal and Great Society (89th Congress, 1965–6) periods are usually mentioned as the notable exceptions (see chapter 13). Some have argued that the first two years of the Reagan administration were also characterized by a responsive and responsible Congress, but the President by no means had it all his own way, and by the end of 1982, Congress began to assert a more independent position, especially on economic policy.

Perhaps, indeed, Congress should assert its independence. How else, after all, could it be responsive to the demands of public opinion and voters? There are two answers to this question. The first, which is highly controversial, is the simple fact that in a complex and pluralistic society beset with urgent domestic and international problems, democratically elected executives should not have to face open resistance from the legislative branch. Executives in most Western states are relatively free from such pressures, and may be, as a result, more able to respond effectively to crisis. We will return to this contentious point in chapter 13. The second response is more relevant to the argument in this section: fragmentation of power in Congress, multiple veto points and open access by myriad interests to centres of power render the institution *inefficient.* In other words it cannot be responsive because its decision-making structure is clumsy, slow and confused. When it does appear to 'work', it is to resist change and pander to special rather than collective or public interests. Our brief survey of the legislative process suggests that there is considerable truth to this charge. Certainly more than one generation of House and Senate members have been aware of it, for they have repeatedly attempted to reform the institution. Before we examine these reforms, we should mention some of the other criticisms levelled at Congress.

2   *Congress has failed to perform the oversight function effectively.* In

2   Appreciating the jurisdictional battles which the legislation would inspire, O'Neill actually created an *ad hoc* committee to handle the bill, consisting of key members from the relevant standing committees. O'Neill's ploy worked, but the resulting bill was quite incompatible with the Senate version. Events in the Senate went rather differently, with petty amendments, filibustering, and jurisdictional disputes dominating.

addition to passing legislation, Congress is charged with the job of
overseeing the executive or holding the President, executive departments
and agencies accountable for their actions. The appropriations process
in part involves this job and this will be dealt with elsewhere (chapter
13, pp. 274–89). In addition Congress is responsible for monitoring
executive appointments, holding formal investigations into the executive
branch, and, as a last resort, it has the authority to impeach executive
officers. The Constitution requires the Senate to approve Presidential
appointments, but it is not a power which the Senate has used in the
strictly 'moral' sense, i.e. rooting out inefficient, incompetent or corrupt
appointees. As often, Senators are concerned to ensure that incumbents
in the more than 1500 major posts subject to Senate confirmation are
men and women who are sympathetic to the legislators' political or
constituency interests, or who are likely to defend an organized interest
(such as labour or business) which Senators are known to identify with.
The appointment process is, in other words, not unlike the legislative
process – it is highly politicized and subject to similar constituency
interest group pressures.[3] Only rarely are appointees rejected or obliged
to withdraw. In 1977, for example, only ten appointees were rejected
or had to withdraw – the highest in the whole post-1961 period – out of
a total 1529 nominations.[4] So Congress is accused of two failings in this
area. First it favours many appointees not because they are likely to
serve the public interest, but because they will support particular or
special constituency and group interests. And second that, independently
of this problem, it has failed to root out some of the more obvious and
colourful examples of incompetent Presidential nominations. The Nixon
administration was littered with such cases. But even the Carter
Presidency was able to produce its Bert Lance (the Budget Director
who was eventually obliged to resign following exposure of illegal
banking practices). Most recently, the Reagan administration has also
had its share of dishonest or incompetent appointees including James
Watt who was obliged to resign as Secretary of the Interior and Raymond
Donovan who was indicted while Secretary of Labour on fraud and
larceny charges. While all this is true, Congress does now examine the
records of the most senior nominees more carefully than in the past.
This is particularly true of Supreme Court nominees who have the
potential to shift the ideological complexion of the Court on a range of
sensitive issues. Such perceptions certainly applied to Robert H. Bork,
Reagan's 1987 nominee to the Court, who was opposed by the wide

3 For an excellent analysis of this subject, see G. Calvin Mackenzie, *The Politics of
Presidential Appointments*, New York, Free Press, 1981.
4 Ibid., table 8.1, p. 177.

margin of 58 to 42 Senators. Reagan's second nominee for the vacant position, Douglas H. Ginsberg, was obliged to withdraw following an admission that he had smoked marijuana while at law school. Eventually the President nominated a 'safe' candidate, Anthony Kennedy, who was quickly confirmed by the Senate.

The investigative power of Congress consists of investigations by the standing committees, the work of special or select committees created for the specific purpose of enquiring into a particular problem, and the work of the General Accounting Office (GAO). GAO auditing of the executive spending is a continuous process, with the Office reporting its findings to Congress. Congress can also require the GAO to investigate a particular programme or agency at any time. Standing committee investigations involve public hearings into alleged executive inefficiency or wrong-doing. One of the most famous was the Army–McCarthy hearings by the Senate Government Operations Permanent Investigations Subcommittee into communist influence in the Army, the CIA and Department of State. Subcommittee Chairman Joseph McCarthy became notorious as a red-baiter in this role, and his unfair and intimidating methods led eventually to his censure by the Senate in 1954.[5]

More typical are the several instances when Congress has created a select committee specifically to investigate a subject of public concern. In recent years, for example, the Senate Select Committee on Campaign Practices – known popularly as the (Sam) Ervin Committee after its Chairman – won great public attention through its enquiries into the Watergate scandal. This in turn spawned further investigations into the security agencies (FBI, CIA, Defense Intelligence) the legality of whose activities had been questioned during the Watergate exposures. In 1987 the Reagan Administration was also investigated by Congressional select committees set up in each house to investigate the origins and management of the Iran–Contra affair. In this case the House and the Senate decided to conduct joint hearings into the affair. Other notable Congressional investigations include enquiries into racketeering in trade unions, safety in atomic power stations, the conduct of the Vietnam War and standards in the pharmaceutical industry.

Note that it is not only government activities which come under Congressional scrutiny – although it is usually investigations into the executive branch which arouse the most feeling and controversy. The reason for this is simple: investigations (and oversight generally) raise

5 The institution of red-baiting, if not the actual practice, continued with the work of the House Unamerican Activities Committee (later the Internal Security Committee) until its abolition in 1975.

awkward questions about where executive power begins and ends. With the rise of big government and the vast bureaucracy which accompanies it, Congress has found it increasingly difficult to perform the oversight function because it has limited access to exactly what goes on within the executive. Information is a valuable commodity and one jealously guarded by Presidents and their bureaucrats. Even though Congress can subpoena witnesses and documents, Presidents have repeatedly refused or been extremely reluctant to hand over information. In recent years they have claimed 'executive privilege' to certain information. Unfortunately this concept has no clear constitutional status, so the legality of withholding information remains an open question. Since Watergate and Richard Nixon's unprecedented reluctance to furnish evidence to Congressional committees (he withheld information at least 19 times on matters unrelated to Watergate), Presidents have been more pliant. But as the Iran–Contra affair confirmed, the executive continues to hold the trump card because the sheer volume and technical complexity of documentation often makes it difficult for a hard-pressed committee even to know what to ask for.

Finally, Congress has the power to impeach executive officers. Impeachment is a formal accusation of wrong-doing which the House of Representatives carries out, while the Senate actually tries and convicts impeached officials. But on only 12 occasions has the House used this power, and on only four has the Senate convicted. One President, Andrew Johnson, was formally impeached although the Senate failed to convict, and of course the House Judiciary Committee voted articles of impeachment against Richard Nixon, who resigned before further action could be taken. Again, Congress has been accused of tardiness and indecision in this general area. The main criticism is that the impeachment process is so cumbersome and formalized that it is rarely used. Critics also point to the continuing evidence of executive wrong-doing which shows that impeachment is not an adequate deterrent. (Although the cumbersome impeachment process has also been praised for preventing hasty and partisan attacks on individual officials and politicians.)

In addition to these structural criticisms, Congress is at any one time criticized for its specific failure to deal with a contemporary crisis or problem. Or, observers infer that a structural feature of the institution is permanent when it is only temporary. So in the ten years following the Second World War it was common to accuse Congress of excessive partisanship. And indeed the red-baiting committees of the late 1940s and early 1950s did in part represent Republican attempts to indict the activities of past or present Democratic administrations. By the late 1950s and early 1960s the charge was somewhat different: Congress was dominated by conservative, segregationist Southerners. Following the reforms of the 1970s, the criticism has shifted once again. Now the accusation is that Congress is the creature of increasingly vocal and influential special and public interest lobbies. This is hardly a new accusation, however, and it is one we will return to in chapter 11. These shifting criticisms show not only that the policy agenda is constantly changing, but also that the institution is too. Some of these institutional changes result from conscious reforms adopted in response to the catalogue of criticisms outlined above.

Reform and Change in Congress

The major criticisms of Congress prevalent in the late 1960s and early 1970s stressed two failings: legislative business was dominated by a few senior committee chairmen; and in its dealings with the executive, Congress was failing to provide either realistic policy-making alternatives or to check the burgeoning growth of executive power. Commentators had long noted that, if these problems were to be solved, political party organizations in the two Houses would have to take the lead. Indeed if we think in terms of centralizing and decentralizing influences, party and party leadership are clearly centralizing forces, while the committee structure essentially disperses power. Party voting has not been strong in Congress since the 1890–1910 period, when over half the roll calls (votes on the floor) involved 90 per cent of one party voting differently from 90 per cent of the other.[6] As table 8.2 shows, even by the weakest measure of party unity – the percentage on which a majority of voting Democrats opposes a majority of voting Republicans – less than half of the roll-call votes in the 1954–83 period show any party cohesion – although some recovery of party solidarity is evident between 1983 and 1986. And even on these occasions only between approximately 50 per cent and 80 per cent of members from the same party voted together.[7] Note also that what little party unity there was declined markedly in the House from the mid-1960s to the early 1970s. But this simple index hardly gives an accurate picture of the frustration which most members increasingly felt at the way in which a few often conservative chairmen

6   John F. Bibby, Thomas E. Mann and Norman J. Ornstein, *Vital Statistics on Congress 1980*, Washington DC, American Enterprise Institute, p. 97.
7   Ibid., table 8.4.

Table 8.2   Votes in Congress showing party unity, 1954–1986 (per cent of all votes)

Year	House	Senate
1954	38	47
1955	41	30
1956	44	53
1957	59	36
1958	40	44
1959	55	48
1960	53	37
1961	50	62
1962	46	41
1963	49	47
1964	55	36
1965	52	42
1966	41	50
1967	36	35
1968	35	32
1969	31	36
1970	27	35
1971	38	42
1972	27	36
1973	42	40
1974	29	44
1975	48	48
1976	36	37
1977	42	42
1978	33	45
1979	47	47
1980	38	46
1981	37	48
1982	36	43
1983	56	44
1984	47	40
1985	61	50
1986	57	52

Data indicate the percentage of all recorded votes on which a majority of voting Democrats opposed a majority of voting Republicans.
Source: Congressional Quarterly Almanac, various years.
Reproduced from Ornstein, Mann, Malbin, Schick and Bibby, *Vital Statistics on Congress* 1987/88 Edition, table 8.3.

dominated committee business and the legislative agenda. By the early 1970s this frustration had reached such a point that a number of sweeping reforms were introduced, reaching a crescendo in 1975 following the election of the unusually liberal post-Watergate Congress in 1974. The major changes were:

1 In 1970 the House ended non-recorded teller voting and switched over to electronic voting on all roll calls. As a result the *number* of roll calls increased dramatically from 177 in 1969 to 541 in 1978.

2 In 1973 all bill drafting in committee was opened to public scrutiny, so exposing to organized interests and constituents the precise policy preference of members.

3 The Democratic caucus in the House voted in 1971 to permit 10 or more members to demand a special vote on a disputed committee chairman assignment. In 1975 all nominees for chairmen were subject to an automatic secret ballot by caucus members.

4 Also in 1975 the caucus voted to give the Speaker the power to appoint Rules Committee members, subject to caucus approval.

5 Since 1973 all Democratic House members have been guaranteed a major committee assignment and since 1974 committee assignments have passed from the Ways and Means Committee (traditionally dominated by Southerners) to the party's Steering and Policy Committee.

6 Subcommittees have been greatly strengthened and increased in number by a number of measures, beginning with the 1970 Legislature Reorganization Act. In 1973 the subcommittes were provided with a 'Bill of Rights' which gave to the full committee caucus the power to set subcommittee jurisdictions and select chairmen. Subsequently, subcommittees have been allocated extra staff.

7 Although the number of formal changes in the Senate have been fewer than in the House, reforms have taken the same general direction and in some cases have been quite radical. Committee meetings have been opened up to the public, the Democratic caucus's power has been strengthened in relation to the nomination of committee chairmen, and it is now much easier to end a filibuster than it was in the early 1970s. Also, the committee structure has been rationalized with the number of committees reduced and some overlapping jurisdictions eliminated.

All these reforms were designed to speed up the legislative process and to weaken the entrenched power of committee chairmen. By so doing, members hoped to make Congress a more effective policy-making body and therefore enhance its position in relation to the executive. In fact, in the wake of the abuse of executive power represented by the conduct of the Vietnam War and Watergate, Congress passed a number of laws specifically designed to curb such excesses and to strengthen the legislative branch. The two most important of these measures were the following.

The 1973 War Powers Act

Overriding a Presidential veto, Congress acted in 1973 to limit President's ability to conduct war without the prior approval of Congress. Under this law the commitment of US armed forces could occur only if Congress declared war or authorized the use of forces or if the President acted in a national emergency. During emergency actions, Presidents were required to win Congressional support after 60 days, and a further 30 days could be granted. After the 90-day period Congress could act to stop the use of troops in a law which is not subject to a Presidential veto.

The 1974 Budget and Impoundment Control Act

A perennial complaint of Congress watchers in the post-war period was the failure of the institution to match the executive's budget-making capacity. Presidents presented annual budgets which had effectively become national policy programmes. Congress, in contrast, seemed unable to see the budget as a coherent whole. Indeed it dealt with finance in an incremental, piecemeal way, reflecting the fragmentation characteristic of bicameralism and the appropriations process. The 1974 Act attempted to compensate for these problems by creating budget committees in each House and a Congressional Budget Office to provide specialized technical information for both chambers and allow Congress to compete with the President as budget maker.

We will expand on executive/Congressional relations in chapters 9 and 13. But for now, what have been the main effects of these reforms? Little was expected from them as they were being adopted; by the early 1980s, however, they had helped to contribute to what are now recognized as profound changes in the institution, as titles such as *The New Congress* and *The Decline and Resurgence of Congress* suggest. The main changes can be summed up quite simply: power in Congress is now even more dispersed than it used to be, but the institution is more professional, more concerned with the details of the legislative process and with oversight of the executive. Finally Congress is still essentially a conservative body – although not in the same ways as before.

The reform movement was fuelled by two main forces – the increasing electoral independence of individual members from party and regional ties which a more rapid turnover of members and other changes had produced, and the already noted disillusionment with the institution's ability to deal with executive power. Chapter 7 showed just how much constituency pressures have increased and how electoral success now depends less on traditional party organization and more on personal resources. In order to 'deliver the goods' to constituents, members needed two things: more control within Congress over legislation and more control over the executive policy-making process. The reforms have gone a long way towards the achievement of both objectives. Almost every legislator now has a power base in Congress, with the proliferation of near-independent subcommittees facilitating this dispersal of authority. The erstwhile czars of Capitol Hill – individual committee chairmen – have been replaced by myriad centres of power with individual legislators even better placed to defend and promote constituent and pressure group interests.

In one sense Congress is more efficient – for although no more bills are passed, those that are tend to be more complex and comprehensive (figure 8.2). In addition committees do expedite bills more rapidly than before. But subcommittee proliferation has cancelled out many of the rationalizations, and scheduling bills on the floor is now a more complex and cumbersome process than ever before. In other words, Congress remains an institution where blockages, delays and vetoes can happen at several stages in the legislative process. As a result it retains an inbuilt conservative bias – it is easier to prevent things happening than to pass bills. The increase in the number of 'omnibus' bills (figure 8.2) represents an attempt to please as many members as possible. But each of these bills is passed only after an enormous amount of members' time and effort has been spent on them. In other words, coalition building – always a defining characteristic of Congress – has assumed an even greater importance during the 1980s. Partly as a result of this institutional characteristic, although also because of the electoral changes outlined in chapter 7, a conservative coalition continues to exercise considerable influence. Until the early 1970s this consisted of Southern Democrats and Northern Republicans. Today it consists of Southern Democrats and Republicans from every region. President Reagan's quite impressive legislative successes in economic policy during 1981 and 1982 were

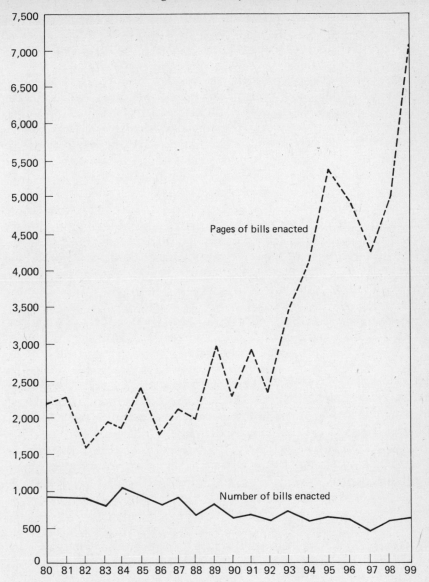

Figure 8.2 Public bills in the Congressional workload, 80th–99th Congresses, 1947–1986

Source: Ornstein, Mann, Malbin, Schick and Bibby, *Vital Statistics on Congress*, 1987/88 Edition, figure 6.9.

possible only because this coalition was able to organize support in both Houses behind the President's programme. He was, of course, aided by a Republican controlled Senate until 1986 (which has, independently of party, become more conservative in recent years). But victory in the House testifies to the strength of the coalition.

Yet we should be wary of inferring too much from Reagan's early successes. Congress today almost certainly reflects the moods and wishes of the nation more accurately than for many years. This is a direct result of a new, much more intimate Congressman/constituency relationship and the easier access to legislators which organized interests now enjoy. During the 1978–81 period, public opinion appeared to move to the right and Congress accurately mirrored this trend. But as we have already established, the American electorate is now highly volatile and issues are much less susceptible to a simple identification on a left/right political continuum than they used to be. Indeed, after 1981 Congress showed increasing resistance to the Administration's attempts to cut domestic spending. By the late 1980s Congress and President had reached a near *impasse* on this question. We should also be cautious about assuming that because Congress appears to pander to *particularistic* interests in American society (individual constituents and organized interests) rather than to the *public* interest, it is always incapable of effective collective action. On rare but important occasions it has shown unexpected resolve. In 1985 both houses passed the Gramm, Rudman–Hollings Deficit Reduction Act which bound President and Congress to successive reductions in the budget deficit (for details see chapter 13, pp. 287–8). A year later Congress passed the most sweeping overhaul of the American tax system in modern history.

Clearly the House and Senate can respond to outside pressures or to perceptions that the collective interest must take precedence over particular interests. Indeed, recent small signs of party revival (table 8.2) may help such reactions. Unfortunately, however, collective action of this sort is rare. In its everyday business, special and particular interest dominates, for the central dilemma for Congress in the 1980s and 1990s is, in fact, the same dilemma of the 1950s and 1960s: building coalitions in a highly fragmented institution involves many trade-offs with costs in terms of time, coherence and efficiency mounting steadily as the legislative process lumbers on. If anything, these costs have increased with recent reforms as the number of power centres has multiplied. And although reform was initiated through party mechanisms, political party influence on legislation remains weak. Given the ever more serious economic and international problems confronting the United States, the need for decisive and coherent policy making is now greater than ever. If Congress can contribute relatively little in this area, then this role must be played by that institution traditionally associated with national leadership – the Presidency.

Further Reading

Among volumes on change in Congress, the best are: Barbara Hinckley, *Stability and Change in Congress*, New York, Harper and Row, 4th edition, 1988; Thomas E. Mann and Norman J. Ornstein (eds) *The New Congress*, Washington DC, American Enterprise Institute, 1981, and James L. Sundquist, *The Decline and Resurgence of Congress*, Washington DC, Brookings, 1981. The classic work on committees is by Richard Fenno Jr., *Congressmen in Committees*, Boston, Little, Brown, 1973. For a good analysis of Congressional leadership, see Robert Peabody, *Leadership in Congress*, Boston, Little, Brown, 1976. Facts and figures on the institution can be found in Congressional Quarterly's *Inside Congress*, Washington DC, latest edition, 1988, and also in Ornstein, Mann, Malbin, Schick and Bibby, *Vital Statistics on Congress*, 1987/88 Edition, American Enterprise Institute, 1987. For an account of how some Senators attract national attention and prominence, see Stephen Hess, *The Ultimate Insiders: US Senators in the National Media*, Washington DC, Brookings, 1986.

9

Presidential Power

The modern Presidency of the United States, as distinct from the
traditional concepts of our highest office, is bound up with the survival
not only of freedom but of mankind . . . The President is the unifying
force in our lives . . . The President must possess a wide range of
abilities: to lead, to persuade, to inspire trust, to attract men of talent,
to unite. These abilities must reflect a wide range of characteristics:
courage, vision, integrity, intelligence, sense of responsibility, sense
of history, sense of humour, warmth, openness, personality, tenacity,
energy, determination, drive, perspicacity, idealism, thirst for information, penchant for fact, presence of conscience, comprehension of
people and enjoyment of life – plus all the other, nobler virtues
ascribed to George Washington under God.

Nelson A. Rockefeller, *Unity, Freedom and Peace*

The saddest life is that of a political aspirant under democracy. His
failure is ignominious and his success is disgraced.

H. L. Mencken

These two quotations pinpoint the central dilemma of the modern
Presidency: in the American political system the President is the only
national unifying force. He has, therefore, both awesome responsibilities
and awesome power. But in recent years few incumbents have possessed
the qualities necessary to carry out the job efficiently and responsibly.
Every President between the mid-1960s and 1980 was associated to a
greater or lesser extent with failure. Lyndon Johnson was broken by
the Vietnam War and Richard Nixon by Watergate. Gerald Ford was
little more than a caretaker President and Jimmy Carter had been
judged indecisive and politically inept. Although it is too early to make
a final assessment of Ronald Reagan, he will probably not be deemed

one of the great Presidents. In 1988 neither candidate for the office inspired much confidence among the voters, and the eventual winner, George Bush, lacks the charisma and authority associated with great Presidents.

Curiously, this association of the office with mediocrity and the abuse of power is comparatively recent. Most texts on American government written during the 1950s and 1960s saw little wrong either with the nature of the office or with recent incumbents.[1] In retrospect the mid-century Presidents – Franklin Roosevelt, Harry Truman, Dwight Eisenhower and John Kennedy – do seem impressive figures. So what has happened since? There are three possible answers to this question which will constitute the major part of discussion in this chapter. First, it could be argued that an accumulation of changes in American society and polity have made the job almost impossible to perform satisfactorily. Second, the process whereby Presidents are recruited may have changed in ways which preselect inappropriate Presidential candidates. Third, it could be simply that different – and inappropriate – personality types have occupied the office in recent years. Before we examine these claims in detail, it is necessary briefly to outline the formal and informal sources of Presidential power and to trace the growth of the modern Presidency.

Formal Sources of Power

To a European observer, one of the most remarkable features of the American political system is the concentration of governmental functions in one institution, the Presidency. The Constitution is partly responsible for this, for it assigns to the Presidency the roles of chief executive (Article 2, Section 1), commander in chief of the armed forces (Article 2, Section 2), chief diplomat (or the power to make treaties, Article 2, Section 2, chief recruiting officer to the executive and courts (Article 2, Section 2) and legislator (by making recommendations to Congress, Article 2, Section 3, and exercising the veto power under Article 1, Section 7). As was emphasized in chapter 3, the Framers did not expect the President also to become *chief* legislator, but over the last 100 years he has assumed this crucial function. Finally, the President is Head of State, so must carry out all those diplomatic and ceremonial duties normally performed by constitutional monarchs (in Britain, the Netherlands) or Presidents (in Israel, India and Italy).

1 For a good review of this 'textbook' view of the Presidency see Thomas E. Cronin, *The State of the Presidency*, Boston, Little, Brown, 2nd edn, 1980, chapter 2.

Given this panoply of powers it is not surprising that we automatically think of periods in American history in terms of incumbent Presidents. The first years of the Republic are inseparable from the personality and influence of George Washington. Andrew Jackson's Presidencies are closely associated with the democratization of American politics and the rise of a modern two-party system. Abraham Lincoln's personal conduct of the Civil War effectively shaped a whole era in American history, while Woodrow Wilson was the first President to elevate the United States on to the world diplomatic and military stage. Since the New Deal period – itself synonomous with the personage of Franklin D. Roosevelt – every President has made a lasting imprint on both American and world politics. Of course Presidents are constrained, sometimes seriously, by a number of domestic and international forces, but within the United States, the chief executive is the natural and immediate focus of attention. As we saw in chapters 7 and 8 it would be difficult to consider Congress a natural leader or decision maker. If anything, the opposite is true. Federalism fragments political power and authority even further, leaving the Presidency (and on rather rare occasions, the Supreme Court) as the sole unifying and centralizing influence in the system.

During the nineteenth and early twentieth centuries, it was the constitutionally assigned powers in military, foreign and diplomatic policy which tended to raise the visibility of the office. Indeed, through exercising these powers some Presidents greatly expanded and even exceeded the constitutional authority. In 1803 Thomas Jefferson authorized the purchase of the Louisiana Territories from France (see map 2.1, p. 9) without consulting Congress. Abraham Lincoln's conduct of the Civil War was almost authoritarian, involving as it did a blockade of the South, the suspension of *Habeas Corpus* and unauthorized increases in the size of the army and navy. Much later Woodrow Wilson asked for, and was given, broad powers under the 1917 Lever Act to seize factories and mines and fix prices to help the war effort. But government, and especially the federal government, played a relatively minor part in economic and social life during this period. An assertive Congress could, and often did, dominate the political agenda. Without the vast bureaucratic and logistical resources of the modern executive, those Presidents lacking political skills or unfortunate enough to preside over particularly difficult domestic events such as the recriminations and confusion charateristic of the post-Civil War period, were truly secondary political figures. From the New Deal period onward, no President has been able to take the back stage because the demands on the office have multiplied so dramatically.

All of the constitutionally assigned powers of the Presidency have been asserted as never before. Sincle World War II, commander in chief has meant control over several million men and women under arms and literally the power of life and death over mankind. As chief executive, modern Presidents are responsible for numerous programmes and policies affecting every aspect of society. As chief legislator, the President takes to Congress a package of programmes, together with budget requests, which effectively mould the national political agenda. As we catalogued in chapter 4, the rise of federal grant programmes has meant that even local governments – those bodies so free from central control in the early Republic – now depend in part on the President's policies. Of course the President is constrained when performing these functions, and of course every industrial country has been required to centralize power in executives and greatly to expand the role of government. However, no Western country has acquired such formidable military and strategic power as has the USA, and in none has the role of state been transformed in quite the way as in America. The USA is, after all, the country where the state has traditionally been weak in relation to society; where the market was considered the most appropriate mechanism for distributing resources (chapter 2, pp. 27–8). Yet by the 1980s more than 30 per cent of national income was accounted for by government spending, and in some areas of economic and social life, the federal government had become a major source of income and support for large numbers of individuals, sub-national governments and corporations. It could be argued that American institutional arrangements, especially federalism and the separation of powers, are ill suited to the sort of efficient and effective policy making needed in modern industrial society. If this is so, it increases the pressures on the executive even more, for to repeat the point, only the Presidency has a truly national constituency and only the Presidency is the natural coordinator and organizer of national policy.

Informal Powers

Given the President's position at the apex of the constitutional system, it is not surprising that the office has also attracted a number of informal powers or influences additional to those constitutionally assigned. These include his position as party leader, and as national and world leader. All three can provide Presidents with valuable extra resources, but they can also burden the office with extra duties and responsibilities. Being party leader certainly sounds grandiose and impressive enough – and in the British system, for example, being both Prime Minister and party leader is indeed a great political advantage. But as we have seen, American political parties are fragmented and weak. Only very rarely in recent history have Presidents been *guaranteed* party support in Congress, and lucky is the President who knows he can count on the support of governors, mayors and other party leaders in the federal system. This accepted, weak party ties are almost certainly better than none at all and Presidents do use party connections to rally support (if not always successfully) during the nomination process and at mid-term elections. Party is also the vital cue available to Presidents when they make appointments to the executive branch. Without the myriad party contacts at congressional, state and local events, it would be difficult to fill all the 50,000-plus jobs which are nominated annually. Presidents also use this process to pay off debts for electoral and other services rendered.

Americans expect something more than the efficient execution of policy from their Presidents; they also expect them to embody the spirit of the nation or, in Clinton Rossiter's term, to be the 'voice of the people'.[2] It should not be forgotten that the United States has relatively few symbols of national unity, such as the monarchy in Britain or a long-established culture rooted in language and custom as in France. In some respects the institution of the Presidency helps fill this gap by providing Americans with a sense of national identity. When, at press conferences, an aide announces the entrance of 'The President of the United States', he is presenting a national symbol as well as chief executive, and the simple words of the announcement carry with them an almost religious respect that is notably missing when a British Prime Minister or German Chancellor appears in public.

In recent years, Presidents' role as national leaders has been reinforced by America's emergence as a world power, a fact amply demonstrated by President Kennedy's famous speech at the time of the Cuban missile crisis:

> Let no one doubt that this is a difficult and dangerous mission on which we have set out. No one can foresee precisely what course it will take or what costs or casualties will be incurred. Many months

2   In the heady optimism of the late 1950s Clinton Rossiter's famous essay *The American Presidency*, New York, Harcourt Brace Jovanovich, 1960, listed five informal powers, some of which now look unachievable, if still sought after: (1) voice of the party; (2) voice of the people; (3) protector of the peace; (4) manager of prosperity; (5) world leader (pp. 4–25).

of sacrifice and self-discipline lie ahead – months in which both our patience and our will will be tested, months in which threats and denunciations will keep us aware of our dangers. But the greatest danger of all would be to do nothing. The path we have chosen for the present is full of hazards, as all paths are; but it is the one most consistent with our character and courage as a nation and our commitments around the world. The cost of freedom is always high – but Americans have always paid it. And one path we shall never choose, and that is the path of surrender or submission.[3]

Such stirring rhetoric may seem inappropriate in the 1980s, but Presidents continue to project themselves as the spirit of the nation, as an examination of Jimmy Carter's speeches on energy or Ronald Reagan's on virtually every subject would show. In other words, Presidents attempt to project themselves as defenders of the *public interest*. In contrast to the fragmentation and particularism of Congress and the federal system, they alone claim to see policy in terms of what is in the interest of the whole country. In this sense, they attempt to elevate themselves above party, special interests and even ideology. Of course they do not always succeed – indeed few recent Presidents have even come close to succeeding – but they are constantly striving for this very special status, and almost certainly the American public expect their Presidents to play this part. Indeed, the public are dramatically more aware of the Presidency (including the Vice-President) than other public offices, and this consciousness is acquired early in life (table 9.1).

Table 9.1 Awareness of political leaders on the part of adults and children, 1969–1970

Office	Percentage correct by age		
	Adult	17	13
President (Nixon)	98	98	94
Vice-President (Agnew)	87	79	60
Secretary of State (Rogers)	16	· 9	2
Secretary of Defense (Laird)	25	16	6
Speaker of the House (McCormack)	32	25	2
Senate Majority Leader (Mansfield)	23	14	4
At least one Senator from own state	57	44	16
Both Senators from own state	31	18	6
Congressman from own district	39	35	11

Source: Fred Greenstein, 'What the President means to Americans', in James Barber (ed.), *Choosing the President*, Englewood Cliffs, New Jersey, Prentice-Hall, 1974, p. 125.

3 Quoted in Robert F. Kennedy, *Thirteen Days*, Harmondsworth, Middlesex, Penguin, 1970, p. 37.

As world leaders, some recent Presidents have had to attenuate their styles and rhetoric in line with the relative decline of American power. But they retain a special status in the international system. Certainly what Presidents say and do is significantly more important than the speeches and deeds of British and Japanese Prime Ministers, German Chancellors and French Presidents. This crucial international status adds yet another dimension to Presidential power, and also to the pressures of the office.

The Presidency in Crisis

Presidential selection

Returning to our original questions, it seems reasonable to hypothesize that the crisis of the modern Presidency is one of recruitment. It may be simply that the wrong men are being selected for the job. What is the nature of the Presidential nomination process? And why is it now the subject of such criticism? We can divide Presidential elections into four distinct phases: pre-primary, primary, convention and campaign.

Pre-Primary It is often quipped that no sooner is a President elected than he has to start running for his second term. Although an exaggeration, this is not so far from the truth, for any candidate with even the slightest hope of winning nomination must plan his campaign several years ahead. In his build-up for the 1976 campaign, Jimmy Carter cultivated newspaper editors and political commentators more than a year before the convention. His strategy was simple: he had to raise his public visibility in order to neutralize the 'Jimmy who?' reaction whenever his name was uttered. Ronald Reagan announced himself more than two years before the 1980 election and by late 1982, ex Vice-President Walter Mondale was already grooming himself for the 1984 contest. In 1985, Vice-President Bush was beginning to build an organization ready for 1988, and Jesse Jackson announced his candidacy for 1992 immediately after the 1988 contest. Merely announcing early guarantees nothing, of course. Much depends on the political resources, reputation, experience and skill of the candidate. The times are also important. Jimmy Carter's extraordinary journey from obscurity to President between 1972 and 1976 owned much to the prevailing disillusionment with 'Washington' and established party candidates. More typically, candidates must win the support of key political figures if they are to have any chance. In 1980 Ronald Reagan was endorsed by many of the leading Republicans and 'king makers' of the political right; Gerald Ford notably lacked such support and was well advised to make an early retreat from the race. Edward Kennedy, in contrast, had failed to win the unequivocal endorsement of the Democratic establishment but soldiered on nonetheless. In 1984 Walter Mondale did win support from established sections of the Democratic Party which almost certainly helped him to create the image of front runner very early in the campaign. An incumbent President naturally enjoys a huge advantage in winning his party's nomination, and there is no instance in recent years of a President who wants to stand failing to secure nomination.

Curiously, few incumbent Vice-Presidents have been *elected* President in American history. George Bush was to prove an exception in part because he won the support of many leading Republicans early in Reagan's second term.

The Primaries   There was a time when a candidate with strong intra-party support could avoid the primary circuit. In 1968, for example, only 49 per cent of the votes cast by delegates at the Democratic convention were decided by primary election, the remainder were in the pocket of party caucuses. By 1976 this figure had risen to 75 per cent, thus making it absolutely essential for candidates to run in the primaries (see table 5.2, p. 92). So Hubert Humphrey's strategy of depending on his very considerable Democratic Party connections was successful in 1968, but suicidal even four years later when he entered the primaries late and was effectively beaten before the convention. Following reforms in the Democratic Party, the number of primaries was reduced in 1984 but increased again in 1988, so that today no candidate can afford to ignore them.

Today there are at least 31 primaries in the Democratic Party and 34 in the Republican, starting with New Hampshire in February and concluding with California and a number of other states in early June.[4] Unfortunately, the precise technicalities of primaries defy simple description because each state decides the timing, voter eligibility and general organization of its primary elections. The most important formal distinction is between *closed primaries* operative in most states, which are open only to registered party members, and *open primaries* where voters can vote for either party, but not both, by asking for that party's ballot at the polling station. They do not, in other words, have to be

4   Puerto Rico is effectively first with its Republican primary scheduled in February, but it is not a meaningful guide to trends on the continental USA.

registered as Democrats or Republicans to vote in that party's election. In those states without primaries for Presidential nominations (all states have some form of primary for statewide elections) party caucuses decide delegate selection. Over the last 20 years, primaries have become more important not only because they have increased in number, but also because changes in party rules have had the effect of binding delegates more closely to candidates. Moreover the partial switch back to caucuses in the Democratic Party in 1984 did not signal a return to 'old style' party politics. For most of the new caucuses are very open and are as binding on delegates as primaries. There was a time when bargaining on the convention floor resulted in delegates switching their allegiance, so making the convention a key decision maker in the nomination process. Today the primaries and caucuses proper play this role.

As candidates *must* enter the primaries they must have the political and financial and even physical resources to endure the long series of campaigns involved. They must also have the *time*, for staging a series of primary campaigns is effectively a full-time job. As will be developed later, this fact alone may preselect certain sorts of candidates. Recent elections have also shown how important it is for candidates to make a good start. There is what might be called a 'media bandwagon effect', where a particular candidate is identified as a winner and this itself provides an essential impetus to his campaign. This may constitute a disadvantage for candidates with key support in those large industrial states whose primaries come relatively late. Some commentators have even gone so far as to claim that Iowa (an early party caucus state) and New Hampshire (the first primary) hold the key to the fortunes of candidates – and these are hardly representative areas of the United States. Certainly Jimmy Carter did well in early contests in 1976 and 1980, which helped him to head off opponents with support in larger states. And in 1980 George Bush's late victories in such states as Michigan meant little when Ronald Reagan had already won most of the early primaries and therefore had accumulated a formidable number of delegate votes. Even if candidates do not win all the early primaries, they must at least enter and perform reasonably well. Such was the case with the successful nominees in 1988, George Bush and Michael Dukakis.

The Nominating Conventions   To foreigners, nothing better represents the sheer theatre of American politics than the nominating conventions. During the summer before the election several thousand party delegates meet to chose their Presidential and Vice-Presidential candidates in an apparently crazy few days of party festival. Although policy is discussed at conventions, they are more of a media event, where candidates and their supports strive to achieve maximum public exposure. There was a time when the conventions actually chose candidates for the general election, with several ballots required before a majority (until 1936 two-thirds in the Democratic convention) of all the delegates could agree on a candidate. During this period conventions were an accurate reflection of the vote trading and coalition formation typical of American politics generally. They were, in other words, highly political, involving deals, bargains and periodic deadlocks as party bosses switched their blocks of delegate votes or opted for a compromise candidate. In recent elections, however, the winning candidate is almost certainly identifiable before the convention begins as the primaries effectively decide the contest.

The spread of primaries was part of a general party reform movement prevalent in the late 1960s and 1970s. In the case of the Democrats, calls for reform were greatly aided by the events at the 1968 convention in Chicago when an old style party organization nominated Vice-President Hubert Humphrey, a candidate associated with organized labour and Lyndon Johnson's conduct of the Vietnam War. But this was the period when the social issue (the war, minority rights, the liberalization of society) was in the ascendant, and traditional Democratic Party organizations were notably unsympathetic to the new movement. Following violent scenes outside the convention hall when the young, radicals and other excluded groups demonstrated against the old style machine politics, the Party was plunged into a turmoil of recriminations.[5] The upshot was the appointment of a commission (the McGovern–Fraser Commission) to recommend changes in delegate selection. Since then the Party has never been free of commissions, reforms and debate on how best to organize itself.

McGovern–Fraser resulted in two major changes. From 1972, representation at conventions from minorities and under-represented groups – Blacks, women, youth – was greatly increased. Second, a system of proportional representation was recommended for primary elections. Previously, the persion winning the primary took all the delegate votes ('winner take all'). McGovern–Fraser recommended that the delegates given to a candidate should be in proportion to his share of the vote. Between 1972 and 1984, the rules were modified further following the advice of further commissions, most notably the Hunt

5 For a graphic description of these harrowing events and the contrast with the Republican convention of that year, see Norman Mailer, *Miami and the Siege of Chicago*, London, Weidenfeld and Nicholson, 1968.

Commission which reported in 1982. From 1980 a minimum of 20 per cent cut-off point was established in the primaries to discourage frivolous candidacies. (It has since been set at a minimum of 15 per cent. The original McGovern–Fraser idea of quotas for under-represented groups has been replaced with affirmative action requirements,[6] and beginning in the early 1970s the rules governing selection of delegates to party caucuses have been gradually modified to 'open up' meetings and committees to rank and file members.

Very generally, these reforms (which are paralleled in an attenuated form in the Republican Party) have involved the struggle between old style party professionals and a new breed of party activists which was discussed in chapter 6. As we established, the new party activists have generally won out, yet it would be misleading to argue that somehow party influences are stronger as a consequence. In fact the opposite is true. Because delegates are now primarily chosen in primaries and are almost always tied to particular candidates, the voters, not party activists, decide the nomination. And given the rise of candidates' own vote-getting organizations, this effectively relegates political parties to a minor position in the nominating process. As James W. Caeser has put it:

> Over the past fifteen years the nominating process has . . . been transformed from a mixed system, in which control over the nomination was shared by the people and the party organizations, to what can be termed a plebiscitary system in which the key actors are the people and the individual aspirants. Along with the emergence of this new institutional form has come a new method of generating support in presidential campaigns: 'popular leadership', or the attempt by individual aspirants to carve out a personal man's constituency by their own programmatic and personality appeals and by the use of large personal campaign organizations of their own creation. At the nomination stage, this form of leadership takes place entirely without the filter of traditional partisan appeals, as the nomination race is in effect a national non-partisan contest.[7]

Not only has the drive for more democratic procedures in party

6 In the American context affirmative, action means a determination to increase the representation (in employment, access to housing and other services) of women and minorities. It can mean quotas, but as often is interpreted as taking positive action to help the under-represented.
7 James W. Caeser, *Presidential Selection: Theory and Development*, Princeton, New Jersey, Princeton University Press, 1979, p. 5.

nominations weakened the influence of party, it has also failed to correct the non-representativeness of convention delegates. In 1972, the delegates were certainly younger and more radical than in 1968, but in ideological and programmatic terms they were *not* typical of the average Democratic voter.[8] By 1980, Democratic delegates were markedly more female and Black than before, but they were also more middle-class and had fewer links with industrial trade unions and traditional Democratic Party organizations and stronger links with the growing public sector unions. Increasing disquiet within the Party has moved some leading Democrats, including Terry Sanford, the ex-Governor of North Carolina, to call for a return to party control over nominations.[9] Indeed in March 1982 the Democratic National Committee accepted the recommendations of the latest commission to investigate the nomination process (the Hunt Commission). The major changes recommended were:

1   a shortened primary season:
2   reform of the rule whereby delegates are bound or committed to candidates;
3   an increase in the number of delegates at the convention drawn from party and elected officials – a reform designed to increase peer group review of candidate selection.

In the event, the primary season was shortened by just five weeks (state laws, not party rules decide the timing of primaries). However, in 1984 and again in 1988 about one-seventh of all delegates to the convention were reserved for party and public officials and, as mentioned, caucuses replaced primaries in several states. Most observers agree that these changes did little to alter the fundamental nature of the nomination process. Although a 'traditional' candidate, Walter Mondale, was nominated, Gary Hart, a 'new style' candidate, very nearly beat him. And the candidacy of civil-rights activist, Jesse Jackson, who did well in many primaries, showed how the system was basically unchanged since 1980. In 1988, neither of the two frontrunners were old style party candidates. Jesse Jackson's impressive showing in the primaries and caucuses came to nothing, not because Michael Dukakis had won the support of the party regulars (which he had), but because Dukakis won more primaries and caucuses than Jackson and therefore came to the

8   See Jeane Kirkpatrick, *The New Presidential Elite*, New York, Russell Sage, Twentieth Century Fund, 1976.
9   *A Danger of Democracy: The Presidential Nominating Process*, Boulder, Colorado, Westview, 1981.

convention with enough delegate votes to ensure victory.

The campaign   Before the campaign proper starts, nominated candidates have to choose their Vice-Presidential running mates. Unlike most recent activity on the floor of the convention hall, this remains a highly political process. Nominees use the opportunity to heal political wounds or to balance the ticket geographically or ideologically. In 1960 John Kennedy's choice of Lyndon Johnson helped to smooth relations between the two main contenders for the nomination; it also balanced the ticket between the urbane Catholic North Easterner and the more populist, Protestant Southerner. The choice is a crucial one, for although the office of Vice-President is not itself very important, no fewer than five of the last nine Vice-Presidents eventually became Presidents themselves (Harry Truman, Lyndon Johnson, Richard Nixon, Gerald Ford and George Bush). Occasionally things go terribly wrong. George McGovern's initial choice of Thomas Eagleton in 1972 had to be changed with indecent haste once it was revealed that Eagleton had received psychiatric treatment. In 1980, Ronald Reagan's first preference, Gerald Ford, proved politically tactless when Ford, not unsurprisingly, laid down certain conditions for acceptance including a demand that the Vice-President should be more an executive partner than subordinate. In 1984 Democratic Vice-Presidential candidate Geraldine Ferraro was constantly dogged by revelations of her husband's financial wrongdoings. In 1988 George Bush's choice of Dan Quayle, the junior senator from Indiana, was greeted with surprise and incredulity among Republicans and Democrats alike. Quale apparently did little to balance the ticket in geographical or ideological terms. Quale, in addition, proved an inept and inexperienced campaigner. After a few weeks, the Bush organization was obliged to shunt Quale off into political sidings where any damage he might do would be kept to a minimum.

Both the pre-convention and post-convention campaigns are expensive. Advertising, and particularly television advertising, takes the lion's share. Indeed spending on television has risen almost exponentially since the first major exposure of candidates during the 1960 campaign, when John Kennedy confronted Richard Nixon in live debates. What effect it has on the voters is, however, an open question. Some evidence exists to suggest that general television advertising has little, most voters apparently acquire positive or negative impressions towards candidates quite early on and then their perceptions are based on performance rather than image.[10] What advertising and the Presidential debates

10   Thomas E. Patterson and Robert D. McClure, *The Unseeing Eye: The Myth of Television Power in National Elections*, New York, Putnam, 1976.

almost certainly do do, however, is *reinforce* public perceptions of candidates. In 1988, for example, the Bush campaign's efforts to label Dukakis as a liberal who was soft on law and order, almost certainly confirmed in the minds of many voters – Republican, Democratic and Independent – what they had suspected. No candidate can afford to drop his guard, therefore; television is widely perceived as important even if its effects are difficult to measure.[11]

For most candidates a high level of public exposure is maintained by constant travel, usually by air, but still a candidate may hire a train to re-enact the famous whistle stop tours of an earlier era. Incumbent Presidents standing for re-election are usually less eager to engage in constant public image-building. They do, after all, enjoy the advantages of incumbency and can exploit their established position as statesmen. In 1972, for example, Richard Nixon appeared in public infrequently and relied instead on the prestige of the Presidential office when appealing to the voters.[12] Whatever the campaign strategy, all candidates continue during the last two or three months before the election to build political bridges, and to strengthen the coalition of support they must already have established to have won the nomination. To a European observer, the campaigns are remarkably free from reference to specific programmes and policies. Indeed candidates score points against opponents or make reference to very broad issues and ideological labels. Michael Dukakis was condemned by George Bush as inexperienced and incapable of upholding American power and prestige abroad. Dukakis in turn criticized Bush for his insensitivity to the needs of ordinary citizens. Attacking opponents may not be the only focus. Reagan promised in 1980 to 'get America back to work'. Richard Nixon in 1968 pledged that he would pursue 'peace with honour' in Vietnam. As we have already noted, the whole of the campaign, pre- and post-convention, has increasingly become an exercise dependent not on traditional party organization, but on *personal* party organization and in some cases simply on personal followings. Again, this demonstrates the general trend towards essentially non-partisan elections, the implications of which we will discuss later.

11   For an account of Presidential communications, see Robert P. Hart, *The Sound of Leadership: Presidential Communication in the Modern Age*, Chicago, University of Chicago Press, 1987.
12   And also, as we now know, on the illegal activites of CREEP (the Committee to Re-elect the President).

Presidential selection: faults and foibles

Writing in 1981 and making direct comparisons with the selection process for British Prime Ministers, Anthony King listed eight apparently serious flaws in the 1980 Presidential selection process. It is worth repeating these:

1 The two winners in the United States had entered politics in middle age, and neither had very much experience of government . . .
2 Neither winner in the United States had ever served in any capacity in the national government, whether in Washington or overseas. Moreover, at the time of their nomination, neither held any public office whatsoever . . .
3 The candidates in the United States were assessed and voted upon by party activists in some states but mainly by voters in primary elections. No special weight was attached to the views of those who had worked with the candidates or had had a chance to observe them at first hand . . .
4 The campaigns of would-be Presidential nominees in the United States last for a very long time.
5 Campaigns for Presidential nominations in the United States involve an enormous amount of wear and tear on the part of the candidates and their families . . .
6 The campaigns in the United States cost enormous sums of money, and the candidates and their staffs have to devote a great deal of time and effort to raising money.
7 The process of selecting Presidential candidates in the United States is by no means an exclusively party process . . .
8 Electoral considerations may have loomed large in the minds of many of the party regulars who attended party caucuses in 1976 and 1980, but they probably figured scarcely at all in the minds of most voters in the primaries.[13]

Many of the charges have already been implied in earlier sections. In sum, they add up to a serious indictment of recent party reforms and also of those reforms in campaign finance which have almost certainly weakened candidates' ties with party organizations. Under the 1971 and 1974 Federal Election Campaign Acts, primary candidates receive matching federal funds up to a maximum of around $15 million (in

13 Anthony King, 'How not to select Presidential candidates: a view from Europe', in Austin Ranney (ed.), *The American Elections of 1980*, Washington DC, AEI, 1981, pp. 315–20.

1984). During the campaign proper a further subsidy is available provided candidates do not spend more than this from money raised from other sources. National and state local party committees can also spend a limited amount on the campaign. Crucially, candidates have to raise most of this money from large numbers of individual contributors. Voters can contribute no more than $1000 to candidates per election (primary and general election) and only $250 of this qualifies for matching funds. Following a 1976 Supreme Court decision (*Buckley* v. *Valeo*) no limit exists on what candidates can themselves spend on their own campaigns. Although these reforms have reduced the dependence on a few large contributions they have also reduced candidate dependence on grass-root party activists and organizations. So according to the critique, candidates are out of touch with the 'real' world of party organization and with day-to-day governmental activity.

Ronald Reagan and (in 1976) Jimmy Carter were 'unemployed' middle-aged (or even elderly) men with no experience of Washington and the wider international community. In 1988 Michael Dukakis was in incumbent governor, but again he lacked any Washington experience. They owed their success to an undisputed political acumen devoted to winning their party's nomination. This involved mobilizing a personal party following and exploiting the uniquely open – even populist – nature of the 'new' American nomination process. As the critique bluntly asserts, such a system encourages the candidates of a breed of politicians – the 'unemployed', wealthy, ambitious and instrumental – who are much less likely to make good Presidents than those tested by peer group pressures and the rigours of many years' experience in high office.

There is, without doubt, a great deal of truth to these charges. Certainly, few successful European leaders have assumed office with as little experience of the world of high politics as did Ronald Reagan or Jimmy Carter. But we should be wary of extrapolating from such small a sample; the same accusation would, after all, be difficult to level at the other three 'failures' among recent Presidents – Lyndon Johnson, ex-Senate Majority Leader and Vice-President; Richard Nixon, ex-Congressman, Senator and Vice-President; and Gerald Ford, ex-House Minority Leader and established party man. In 1988 the American people elected a man of very broad experience, for George Bush had not only been Vice-President for eight years, he had also been a Congressman, Chief of the CIA and the US Ambassador to the United Nations.

Of course at least three old style party candidates (Hubert Humphrey, Gerald Ford and Walter Mondale) did *lose* elections, which may vindicate the charges, but then so did George McGovern in 1972 (very much a non-party candidate) and Jimmy Carter in 1980 (an incumbent President with all the advantages that should bring). Final judgment on the Reagan Presidency should be reserved until a later date. But during his first term he used his party connections in the House (via Bob Michel, the Minority Leader) and in the Senate (through Howard Baker, the Majority Leader) to great effect. This performance is not quite what should be expected from a man whose election depended on popular appeal rather than party connections, and who had no experience of 'high politics' before coming to Washington.

Nevertheless, we can conclude that the American Presidential selection process is far from ideal and has no doubt contributed to a succession of less than impressive Presidents. But the very considerable problems associated with the office in recent years also have their origins in forces beyond the technicalities of the selection process, and it is to these we must now turn.

The Presidency and structural changes in American society

As suggested, reforms in the selection process reflect deeper changes in the party system and in American society generally. It could well be argued that, almost irrespective of the quality of President, these and other developments have together made the job of chief executive much more difficult than ever before. We can identify three such developments, each of which has added to the burden of office.

The decline of party and the rise of issue politics In one sense condemnation of recent Presidential candidates because they have lacked close party ties and have failed to subject themselves to party peer group review is unfair, for if traditional party organizations have declined, candidates cannot be expected to have utilized this particular route to nomination. Once in the White House, however, the real problems of trying to govern in the absence of unifying party forces becomes painfully apparent. In chapter 5 we listed the functions of political parties, and among the most important were the provision of institutional cohesion and a means to staff the government. Jimmy Carter is usually quoted as the classic case of a President who failed on both counts, largely because he came to Washington with very limited executive experience (as Governor of Georgia) and with few connections in the traditional world of the Democratic Party (the unions, the big cities, the North Eastern establishment). As a result, so the argument runs, his liaison with Congress was poor and his ability to fill key posts with the right men and women, wanting. Certainly, Carter had a rough time with Congress and was not personally inclined to create and nurture relationships with Congressional leaders. But he was not unique in experiencing difficulties with Congress. As we saw in chapter 8, *all* Presidents have had such problems, including John Kennedy and even Franklin Roosevelt, both of whom had strong party contacts and support. The difference now is that Congress is even more fragmented and party leadership even weaker than it used to be. The coalition building that is essential for legislative success is now correspondingly more difficult.

Worse still, the political vacuum left by the parties has in part been filled by 'issue politics', or the mobilization of political resources around particular issues and ideas. We will examine this phenomenon in more detail in chapter 11, but even the most casual observer of the American political scene will be aware of the rise of the minority caucuses, pro- and anti-abortion leagues, women's caucuses, the nuclear freeze movement, the conservative coalition and so on. Each of these movements has its Congressional supporters and advocates within administrations and state governments. Issue politics have been aided by the growth of political action committees (PACs) devoted to ensuring the success of 'their' men or women in Congress or the defeat of their opponents. In 1982, for example, it is estimated the NICPAC (the National Conservative Political Action Committee) spent $214,000 trying to unseat the supposedly 'liberal' Senate Minority Leader, Robert Byrd, and $526,000 to defeat the more transparently liberal Edward Kennedy. PACs help build Congressmen's independence from party and administration, and therefore make the President's job that much more difficult.

Issue politics has had a more subtle effect on the political agenda, however. For when policy is defined in terms of discrete issues or one-dimensional ideologies (such as 'conservatism'), the effect is to fragment decision making throughout the political system. Within the executive departments and agencies each issue or position has its supporters, so compounding the already problematical business of getting bureaucrats to implement policy (of which much more later). In sum, in the absence of strong party linkages. Presidents increasingly lack ideological and organizational 'connective tissue' when performing their duties – a fact which puts even more of a premium on the skills and political acumen of individual incumbents.

The Nationalization of Politics and Society　With improved communications and the spread of governments' responsibilities, the United States has become a much more centralized society over the last 30–40 years. Information is disseminated centrally by the three major television networks (NBC, CBS, ABC) and by the news services and syndicated columns of major newspapers and cable TV networks. Economically, society is more centralized and nationalized with giant corporations providing the same goods and services uniformly throughout the country. It follows that the demands on governments have been centralized, with Washington increasingly the focus of political activity. Chapter 4's discussion of intergovernmental relations showed how state and local governments have become more interdependent with the federal government in recent years. And the same is true of unions, corporations, farmers and almost all those interests in society affected by federal government spending, regulation and arbitration. Naturally, the President is a major focus of all this attention, for he frames most major laws, draws up the budget and has the responsibility for implementing all laws. As chief executive, the President has to manage the vast bureaucracy responsible for these tasks, a bureaucracy which in terms of powers and complexity has grown considerably.

The Relative Decline of American Economic and Political Power
Although not always true, it does seem reasonable to suppose that governing is easier when a country's economy is growing in real terms and its status and power abroad are in the ascendant. Both applied in the case of the United States between 1942 and 1965. Between then and 1982, American international economic and military might experienced relative decline. Perhaps it is not entirely coincidential that the earlier period was associated with the era of 'successful' Presidents, while the latter has witnessed the incumbency of executive 'failures'. While it would be foolhardy to accept this argument in full – was Harry Truman, after all, a 'success' and was Ronald Reagan a 'failure'? – there is no question that the management of the economy and the exercise of military and diplomatic power abroad are *more likely* to be difficult during periods of relative decline.

The Vietnam War was the first major demonstration of the limits to American military power and it effectively broke one President (Lyndon Johnson) and led another (Richard Nixon) to commit a series of illegal acts, including the secret bombing of Cambodia and the unauthorized surveillance of opponents of the war. More recently, Jimmy Carter's handling of the Iranian hostage situation dominated the final year of his Presidency, and provided a poignant reminder of the limitations of American might. For recent Presidents, ventures abroad have been problematical, for nothing increases Presidential popularity more instantly than successful – or even unsuccessful but bold – military and diplomatic forays overseas. John Kennedy's popularity soared during the Cuban Missile Crisis, as did Jimmy Carter's following the signing of the Begin/Sadat/Carter Camp David accords in 1979 and Ronald Reagan's after the US invasion of Grenada and the bombing of Libya. When the USA is apparently 'humiliated' abroad as, eventually, with Vietnam, the hostage incident in Iran and perhaps over American inability to stop the spread of left-wing activity in Central America, it puts pressure on Presidents to do something about it. Whether the resulting actions are in the public interest or in the interests of world peace are, of course, another matter.

At home, managing the many distributional questions which are the very essence of the chief executive's job is obviously more difficult when the economy is stagnating or when, even if the economy is growing, the budget deposit is rising. In his book the *Zero Sum Society*,[14] Lester Thurow identifies this as the key problem of modern society. In other words, when the national cake stays the same size or when federal spending is constant, distributional questions become a zero sum game; when one person gains another must lose, because there is a strict limit to the total amount of resources available. So if more women are employed fewer men must be, or if South Carolina receives an increase in federal aid, other states must suffer a decrease. Of course in reality the number of decision points in the distributional system means that it is more complex than this. Even so, no single individual is more centrally placed to make these distributional decisions than is the President. He is responsible for producing an annual budget amounting to over $1000 billion, and for ensuring that this money is properly spent on literally thousands of programmes. Congress is, of course, also involved in this process and when it comes to contested distributions the courts become key actors. But neither Congress nor the courts are as politically visible as the President. Only the President is perceived as national leader and defender of the public welfare. Small wonder, then, that recent Presidents have experienced such difficulties, both in domestic policy and with defence spending, which naturally affects the amount available for domestic programmes. Add to this zero sum problem the increasingly strident demands of the single issue lobbies, and the potential for conflict and failure can be appreciated. So no recent President has been able to balance the budget (in 1986 Ronald Reagan, a fiscal conservative, presided over a deficit of more than $180

14   Harmondsworth, Middlesex, Penguin, 1981.

billion), or has come anywhere near satisfying the demands of the social groups. Take Ronald Reagan's 1981 tax cut measures. As passed by Congress, the cuts had a number of divisive consequences. They gave those earning between $15,000 and $20,000 a year (a majority of wage-earners) only $6 extra a week. But for the rich the benefits were sizeable – $90 a week for those earning $100,000 a year, $257 a week for the super-rich in the $200,000-plus class. Organized labour was offended by this apparently unfair package, especially as it was accompanied by cuts in welfare and social security benefits. Together with tax cuts on corporate profits and increases in defence spending, this combination obliged Reagan to claw back some of the cuts with tax hikes during 1983. So the President's radical changes, which had been central to his 1980 electoral platform, ended up satisfying almost nobody. Between 1983 and 1988 the quite dramatic recovery of the American economy certainly helped Ronald Reagan's popularity, but the basic distributional problem of how to cut expenditure and not offend almost anybody remains.

In effect, these changes in society and politics have made the country less easy to govern. Pressures on the central institutions are greater while the ability to respond effectively has been weakened. For the Presidency this unfortunate combination has been particularly serious and helps explain the waxing and waning of Presidential power over the last 20 years. The era of the 'Imperial Presidency' coincided with the tail end of American hegemony, and also, of course, with the incumbency of two especially imperious Presidents. By the mid-1960s the office had grown enormously in power, and the pressures imposed by the Vietnam War and a declining economy tested the office to the full. The potential for the abuse of power was considerable. Unfortunately for the American people Lyndon Johnson and, particularly, Richard Nixon fell to this temptation. The real importance of the Nixon period is not that the President, along with many of his aides and cabinet officers, broke the law, but that the chief executive wielded power in such a way that raised very serious questions on where, exactly, Presidential power began and ended.

Richard Nixon impounded funds appropriated by Congress for programmes he disliked (Impoundment is the setting aside by the executive of funds appropriated by Congress). Towards the end of his Presidency he was exercising the veto power extensively and few of his vetoes were overridden by Congress. He invoked 'executive privilege' to justify the withholding of information from Congressional investigative committees and he nominated a number of men to official posts who were unqualified or otherwise unsuitable. Even before Watergate, Congress began to fight back, notably by rejecting two of his more outrageous Supreme Court nominees (see chapter 12, p. 259). In 1972 the Congress attempted to control the President's discretion to make executive agreements – effectively treaties with foreign powers which could be concluded, sometimes in secret, without consulting the Senate. Under the Case Act all such agreements have to be submitted to Congress. More far reaching was the 1973 War Powers Act passed by Congress over a Presidential veto which put limits on the President's power to commit troops overseas (see chapter 8, p. 163). In 1973 Congress also insisted that the President's Director and Deputy Directors of the vital Office of Management and Budget be subject to Senate confirmation.[15]

Following Watergate, Congress asserted its power even more vigorously – in part because Watergate had precipitated a landslide victory for the Democrats in the 1974 mid-term elections. The Budget and Impoundment Control Act of 1974 obliges the President to report 'recission' to Congress when funds appropriated remain unspent. Congress then has to approve recission within 45 days. The same law created the Budget Committees in Congress to enable the legislature to play a more constructive part in the budget process (see chapter 13, pp. 282–4).

As can be seen from table 9.2 Gerald Ford exercised the veto on major bills frequently and was overriden by Congress on no less than seven occasions. Note also the general tendency for the veto to be applied more frequently and in particular to appropriations and foreign policy bills which in the past almost never attracted the Presidential veto. This reflects the much more difficult environment in which today's Presidents have to work. Sometimes this means facing a Congress controlled by the opposition's party. Equally often it means the fundamentally irreconcilable interests represented by a fragmented Congress on the one hand and the President on the other.

Finally in 1976 Congress put considerable limits on the President's power to declare emergencies and assume special powers. Under the National Emergies Act of 1976, Congress can terminate a declaration of emergency and all declarations must be reported to Congress, together with legal justifications for them.

Following the adoption of all these measures and the incumbency of an unusually unassertive President, Jimmy Carter, Presidency watchers began to talk of the *decline* of Presidential power and the resurgence of Congress. As we saw in chapters 7 and 8 there can be no doubting that Congress has become more rather than less difficult for Presidents to

15 The best history of the Nixon era is Jonathan Schell, *The Time of Illusion*, New York, Vintage, 1975.

Table 9.2   Major bills vetoed, 1933–1986

President	Total	Number involving appropriations	Number involving foreign and foreign economic policy	Major vetoes per year in office	Number overridden
Roosevelt	2	0	0	0.16	2
Truman	6	0	0	0.8	5
Eisenhower	2	2	0	0.25	1
Kennedy	0	0	0	0	0
Johnson	0	0	0	0	0
Nixon	13	10^1	1^4	2.4	4
Ford	11	10^2	1	4.4	7
Carter	5	2^3	2	1.3	1
Reagan	10	6	4	1.7	3^5

[1]   Excludes HR 7447 (1973) appropriations bill with a rider prohibiting use of funds for bombing of Cambodia.
[2]   Excludes S 2662 (1976) involving $3.1 billion for arms sales and military aid. Veto was justified on foreign policy rather than fiscal grounds.
[3]   Excludes HR 7584 (1980) involving $9 billion appropriations for State, Justice and Commerce. Veto was exercised because of attachment of an anti-busing rider.
[4]   Excludes 1973 War Powers bill which is coded as of major constitutional import rather than as a challenge to specific aspect of foreign policy.
[5]   Excludes S 1128 (1986 Clean Water bill) which as HR 1 was easily overridden in February 1987 by the new Democratically controlled Congress (401–26 and 86–14).
Source: David McKay, 'Presidential strategy and the veto power: a reappraisal', *Political Science Quarterly*, 1989, table 5. For a definition of major bills, see original.

deal with. However, Presidents retain an enormous fund of resources on which to draw. The next section concentrates on those resources not covered in earlier sections and on the ways in which successive Presidents have adapted to the pressures and problems associated with the office.

Two main resources can be identified – the public and the Presidential bureaucracy – to which a third, conceptually distinct resource, personality, can be added.

Presidential Resources

The Public

It may seem paradoxical in the light of the foregoing discussion to view the public as a resource. Yet under many circumstances it can be just that. As national leaders, Presidents can make direct appeals to the public through press conferences and special televised announcements. In some instances this amounts almost to a limited form of direct democracy. In 1981 and 1982, for example, Ronald Reagan made specific appeals to the public on television that they should write to their members of Congress expressing support for the President's economic policies. Both the tax and spending cuts were passed by narrow margins and it seems reasonable to assume that Reagan's pleadings had some effect – especially as many members cannot afford to ignore a sudden influx of constituency mail. Later in his Presidency, Reagan used the public resources to help win support for a number of foreign policy initiatives including the invasion of Grenada, the bombing of Libya and the arms limitation agreement signed with the Soviet Union. Appeals to the public are not always successful, of course, as Richard Nixon's sometimes painful public attempts to hide his guilt over Watergate demonstrated. But earlier in his Presidency, Nixon had made highly effective use of this resource through his carefully constructed public lectures on American disengagement from Vietnam.

Although still a potentially powerful weapon, the public appeal resource is beset with problems and pitfalls. As was established in chapter 6, the American electorate is now highly volatile. Together with a growing cynicism about public institutions, not least the Presidency,[16] this had made the President's public appeals more risky than they used to be. During Ronald Reagan's first two years, it seems reasonable to infer that the public were willing to provide support during what was effectively a 'honeymoon' period. Following the mid-term elections when the Democrats made deep inroads into the conservative coalition in the House, such support will probably become more grudging with, possibly, the balance of public opinion, shifting to the Congress rather than the President. This accepted, no other national institution – Congress, party, courts – can use the media quite like the President. He is, after all, just one man with a special national status. Given all the problems of governing in the 1980 and 1990s, Presidents will continue to make direct appeals to the public, for it is one of the few, if imperfect,

16 Both during and immediately after Watergate public rating of the office sank to a new low with, in 1974, only 13 per cent expressing 'a great deal of confidence in the executive branch'. Quoted in Louis W. Koenig, *The Chief Executive*, New York, Harcourt Brace Jovanovich, 5th edn, 1986, p. 102. Since the mid-1970s public confidence in the office has increased a little, but ratings of individual Presidents have generally been low. Comparing Reagan with his predecessors, after 12 months in office, around 55 per cent of the public approved of the way he was handling his job as President, compared with 68 per cent for Eisenhower, 77 per cent for Kennedy, 69 per cent for Johnson and 61 per cent for Nixon. Both Ford (46 per cent) and Carter (52 per cent) fared badly by comparison (*Public Opinion*, Vol. 4, No. 6, December/January, 1982, pp. 30–1). Between 1982 and 1985 Reagan's popularity increased, only to decline following the revelations of the Iran–Contra affair in 1986 and 1987. By the end of his second term, however, Reagan had re-established his reputation with the public. President Bush started his term in office with higher ratings than most of his predecessors.

means whereby the fragmenting influences in American politics can be overcome.[17]

Bureaucracy

As the job of President has become more demanding, so incumbents have adapted their administrative resources accordingly. All Presidents have had a *Cabinet* composed mainly of departmental heads at their disposal, but as we will see, the Cabinet is but one of a number of administrative devices available, most of which have been introduced during this century to help Presidents formulate and execute policy. In 1921 the Bureau of the Budget (now called the Office of Management and Budget) was established to help the President prepare the budget and coordinate spending policies. As can be seen from figure 9.1, since then a number of other agencies have been created which collectively are known as the Executive Office of the President (EOP) (formally established by Franklin Roosevelt in 1939). Quite distinct from the Cabinet, the Executive Office consists of about 2000 individuals directly accountable to the President. This figure includes about 500 people who actually work in the White House as personal aides to the President – the White House Office in figure 9.1. How Presidents actually use the EOP, and in particular the White House staff, has aroused bitter controversy over the last 20 years. A major criticism, inspired mainly by Watergate, has concerned the extent to which the staff has grown in recent years and has increasingly insulated Presidents from public opinion and political reality. A related theme centres on whether any personal bureaucracy can be an adequate adminstrative tool against the vast resources of executive departments and agencies and against a fragmented but powerful Congress.

There can be no disputing that some Presidents have used their staffs unwisely. Richard Nixon, in particular, relied heavily on just a handful of personal aides, eschewing most Cabinet officers, Congressional and party leaders. Three of his closest aides, John Ehrlichman, Bob Haldeman and Ron Zeigler, became so effective in acting as the President's mouthpieces that they earned the sobriquet 'The Berlin Wall'. And in the Carter Presidency Stewart Eisenstadt, the domestic policy adviser, almost assumed the status of policy initiator and spokesman. During the second Reagan administration Donald Regan guarded his position

17   For a comprehensive account of how Presidents use the public resource, see Sam Kernell, *Going Public*, Washington DC, Congressional Quarterly, 1986.

Figure 9.1   The Executive Office of the President, 1989

[a] Formally incorporated into the Executive Office in 1939.
Source: Adapted from *US Government Manual 1987/88*, Washington DC, US Government Printing Office, 1987, p. 86.

as Chief of Staff jealously until he was forced to resign over the Iran–Contra Affair. Not that these are historically isolated examples. This century there are at least three other instances of staffers assuming national prominence and even notoriety as 'the powers behind the throne'.[18] Critics have argued that the very considerable power of personal staffs is undemocratic – they are, after all, unelected and few are subject to Senate confirmation. Personal staffs – and modern Presidents all have domestic, economic and foreign policy advisers, a press secretary, legal counsel, and staff responsible for liaison work with Congress – often overlap with members of other agencies within the EOP. Hence Presidents' national security advisers are also members of the National Security Council, a body consisting among others of the President, Vice-President and Defense and State Secretaries set up by Congress in 1947 to help the formulation of foreign policy and aid crisis management. In some instances, the National Security Adviser becomes more important than the Secretary of State, as was clearly the case with Henry Kissinger before he effectively 'deposed' the incumbent, William Rogers, and assumed the office of Secretary of State himself during Nixon's second term. Similarly the Director of the Office of Management and Budget can become a key figure, for the OMB is responsible for monitoring the spending of the various executive departments. In 1980 Ronald Reagan's choice of Director, David Stockman, a bright young ex-Congressman, designed to ensure that the OMB Director would have direct responsibility for handling the budget and the cuts to be imposed on many of the departments and agencies.[19] In this sense, the OMB and its director resemble, although they are by no means identical to, the British Treasury and Chancellor of the Exchequer.

How Presidents use the EOP and especially their personal staff varies greatly from administration to adminstration. Until Watergate it was common to contrast Franklin Roosevelt's style of creating an atmosphere of constructive competition, with aides deliberately positioned to provide contrasting information and advice, with Eisenhower's tendency to delegate responsibility and Kennedy's emphasis on intelligence and *esprit de corps*.[20]

Since Watergate, however, there is evidence that whatever management strategy is adopted by Presidents, they will experience serious command problems. Certainly, Presidents have felt obliged to innovate

18   Colonel House with Woodrow Wilson, Harry Hopkins with Franklin Roosevelt and Sherman Adams with Dwight Eisenhower.
19   Significantly since 1973 the Director of OMB has been subject to Senate confirmation.
20   An excellent account of how different Presidents have used their staff is Richard Tanner Johnson's *Managing the White House*, New York, Harper and Row, 1974.

and reorganize the executive branch to improve management. Some Presidents have adopted 'chiefs of staff' specifically to help management of the White House – although two recent incumbents in this position, Bob Haldeman of Watergate fame and Hamilton Jordan in the Carter White House, whose private lifestyle attracted some attention, have not been the best advertisements for the job. Ronald Reagan appointed Martin Anderson as chief of the Office of Policy Development, a new unit replacing the Domestic Policy Office and embracing some responsibility for economic affairs. Anderson had a special status within the White House, particularly in helping smooth relations between Cabinet members. However he left the White House after only a short period, and instead three of President Reagan's other staffers – Chief of Staff James Baker, President's Counsel Edwin Meese and Deputy Chief of Staff Michael Deever – acquired a special status and became more centrally placed than other staffers or individual departmental secretaries. All three had left the White House in 1985, however, when ex-Treasury Secretary Donald Regan took over as Chief of Staff.

As mentioned earlier, Regan was obliged to resign in 1987 and was replaced by the more politically astute ex-Senate majority leader, Howard Baker. Indeed, Reagan's use of the EOP changed quite dramatically between his first and second terms. In his first term he relied on at least three chief advisers and in his second, just one (apart from his wife, who played an active role throughout). While praised for his management style in the first term, he was condemned for his failure to oversee the detail, and sometimes even the main thrust, of policy in the second. The Iran–Contra débâcle resulted in part from this failing. A more radical ploy has involved attempts to institutionalize the delegation of power through strengthening the Cabinet. Although every President has had a Cabinet, the Constitution unambiguously assigns executive power to the President, so whether the device is used or not is a matter of great discretion. Its membership consists of the heads of the executive departments plus individuals assigned by the President himself. Re-invigorating the Cabinet is a natural option for Presidents to choose, because a major part of executive leadership involves control and management of the vast federal bureaucracy. Much of the work of personal staff involves liaison with this bureaucracy, and the closer the communications and finer the line of command, the better. So Presidents Nixon, Carter and Reagan pledged that they would strengthen their Cabinets. Nixon patently failed to do this, but Carter did in fact use the Cabinet quite frequently, as did Ronald Reagan. Indeed, during his first year in office President Reagan convened his Cabinet no less than 37 times, a very high figure in historical perspective. It is doubtful that this has smoothed relations between the White House and the Executive Departments. As we will see in chapter 10 a natural antipathy exists between the two, largely because departments and agencies have constituencies and interests of their own. Whatever the promises, Presidents generally resort to using their own (usually reliable) staff rather than risk giving real power to departmental secretaries, and recent history is littered with examples of conflict between powerful staffers or EOP members and departmental heads.

Presidents' urge to reorganize extends to other areas and has included a major reorganization of the EOP by Jimmy Carter, who eliminated seven of the Office's administrative units. And both Jimmy Carter and Ronald Reagan promised to make greater use of their Vice-Presidents. Traditionally the position has meant little in itself, or 'not worth a pitcher of warm piss' as John Nance Garner, one of Franklin Roosevelt's Vice-Presidents, colourfully put it. Walter Mondale was, however, accorded a more central position in the Carter administration than many previous Vice-Presidents, and George Bush, was given an unusual degree of public visibility.

All these efforts demonstrate the increasingly difficult political environment in which Presidents have to work. As we have stressed time and again in earlier chapters, American politics has become increasingly fragmented in the post-war era. Together with the nationalization of political life, this has forced Presidents to manage numerous centres of political power each with its own policy network. As Hugh Heclo has emphasized, staff and other administrative assistance helps, but cannot solve the central dilemma of the office:

> Whoever the President and whatever his style, the political and policy bureaucracies crowd in on him. They are there in his office to help, but their needs are not necessarily his needs. Delegation is unavoidable; yet no one aide or combination of aides has his responsibilities or takes his oath of office. However much the President trusts personal friends, political loyalties, or technocrats, he is the person that the average citizen and history will hold accountable.[21]

21 Hugh Heclo, 'The changing Presidential office', in Arnold J. Meltsner (ed.), *Politics and the Oval Office*, San Francisco, Institute for Contemporary Studies, 1981, p. 177.

Personality

While no one could deny the importance of changes in the nomination process and the political environment as determinants of change in the nature of the Presidency, some observers stress that the most crucial element in the office is the personality of the incumbent. With so much discretion attached to the job and such a premium on leadership skills – persuasion, manipulation, coercion, insight, charisma – personality is undoubtedly important. Indeed even the most casual student of American politics has a cognitive picture of certain Presidents – Truman as feisty and combative, Eisenhower as kind and avuncular, Kennedy as inspirational, Reagan as reassuring, and above all, perhaps, Richard Nixon as devious and insecure. Borrowing heavily from psychology, one political scientist, James Barber, has attempted to formalize the 'Presidential character' by classifying Presidents by personality type.[22] Barber's two dimensions are active–passive and positive–negative. Simplifying somewhat, the former describes how much *effort* Presidents put into the job and the latter how much enjoyment or *satisfaction* they

Table 9.3   Barber's classification of modern Presidents

| | | Energy level in the job | |
		Active	Passive
Emotional attitude to satisfaction from the job	Positive	Franklin Roosevelt Harry Truman John Kennedy Gerald Ford Jimmy Carter George Bush	William Taft Warren Harding Ronald Reagan
	Negative	Woodrow Wilson Herbert Hoover Lyndon Johnson Richard Nixon	Calvin Coolidge Dwight Eisenhower

Source: Adapted from various sources including James David Barber, *The Presidential Character*, and Louis Koenig, *The Chief Executive*, 4th edn, 1981, p. 345.

get from it. The resulting four categories are shown in table 9.3, along with the classification of a number of recent Presidents. The key types are Active/Positives, representing individuals who receive enormous satisfaction from being active in the job and Active/Negatives who put in intense effort but get little emotional reward for their pains. Beware, says Barber, of the Active/Negatives, who are likely to dig in when

22   James David Barber, *The Presidential Character*, Englewood Cliffs, New Jersey, Prentice-Hall, 2nd edn, 1977.

under pressure and display a sometimes paranoid inflexibility. Active/Positives, in contrast, enjoy the cut and thrust of a highly demanding job and are likely to show that spirit of compromise and adaptability which is so essential to the politics of coalition formation. As with all simply psychological theories, Barber's typology is open to criticism.[23] *Events* often mould personality rather than the other way round. Who, after all, would have judged Lyndon Johnson 'inflexible' before he became so fatally obsessed with the war in Vietnam? And in many respects Richard Nixon, the epitome of the Active/Negative type according to Barber, was pragmatic and adaptable. Unlike Woodrow Wilson and Lyndon Johnson he had little moral commitment to causes or higher ideals. Moreover, to put Ronald Reagan in the same category as Warren Harding and William Taft seems misguided, for *every* modern President has to be 'active'. This may not mean working 18-hour days, but it must at least mean being *psychologically* active or aware of events and political priorities.

In sum, Barber's categories are not a very useful guide to Presidential *quality*. Highly successful and 'failed' Presidents are put in the same category (Franklin Roosevelt and Jimmy Carter as Active/Positives, Dwight Eisenhower and Calvin Coolidge as passive negatives),[24] and the changes earlier analysed, especially those associated with Presidential selection, appear to bear little or no relationship to Barber's idea of Presidential quality.

What the typology does do is force us to think more carefully about the impact of personality on the office. There is no disputing that some men have been more suited to the job than others and that, irrespective of events, changes in the selection process and in American society, this simple fact continues to hold true. All the evidence suggests, for example, that Ronald Reagan enjoyed being President and had a talent for handling people around him which most other recent Presidents have lacked. This does not mean to say that history will judge him a great President or even that his record in dealing with Congress and the public will be deemed successful. His casual style and willingness to delegate undoubtedly helped lead to the Iran–Contra affair in 1985 and 1986. But having a personality apparently suited to the job must at least help the incumbent come to terms with what possibly is the most demanding executive position in the modern world.

23   For a good critique, see Alexander L. George, 'Assessing Presidential character', in Aaron Wildavsky (ed.), *Perspectives on the Presidency*, Boston, Little, Brown, 1975.
24   This pairing is particularly inappropriate given recent evidence claiming the high quality of Eisenhower's leadership. See Fred Greenstein, *The Hidden Hand Presidency: Eisenhower as Leader*, New York, Basic Books, 1982.

Assessing the Presidency: Presidential Power in the 1990s

When, in 1960, Richard Neustadt described Presidential power as the 'power to persuade', he accurately captured the need for Presidents to be successful bargainers, negotiators and manipulators.[25] Coalition building, in other words, is the very essential of the President's job, and incumbents must have the personal capacity not only to appreciate this fact (as Jimmy Carter constantly said he did) but also act accordingly (as Jimmy Carter repeatedly failed to do). Coalition-building skills are necessary at every level – within the White House, and in relations with executive departments, Congress, the media, interest groups and the public. Neustadt's famous essay was designed to show that formal command was not enough; that indeed it was sometimes quite limited, unless supplemented by the more subtle political skills involved in the art of persuasion.[26] To reduce almost all of the President's job to bargaining skills is, of course, to oversimplify. Constitutionally, the chief executive has immense power of command – not least as commander in chief – which he can exercise without a finely honed aptitude for bargaining. The Presidencies of Lyndon Johnson and Richard Nixon are proof enough of this. Yet both Presidents are now considered less than successful, and since the early 1970s the number of power centres and policy networks in the American system has increased considerably. Moreover, changes in the selection process, while perhaps not preselecting certain personality types among candidates, has certainly affected the nature of their party and political contacts, and hence their access to major bargaining resources. Add to this the structural changes in society listed earlier and it is easy to appreciate why so many commentators complain of the office being 'overloaded'. While, in such a context, the premium of bargaining and leadership skills is greatly increased, there is also the danger that under such enormous pressures, Presidents will resort to confrontation or to clandestine and possibly illegal acts in order simply to get things done. Such was the case with the later years of the Nixon administration and some aspects of the Reagan administration. As we saw, the veto power is now used more often than in the past, and Presidents are also prone to go over the heads of

25 *Presidential Power*, New York, John Wiley, 1960.
26 Neustadt showed how the commands of Presidents on three occasions – Truman's sacking of General MacArthur, his decision to seize the steel mills in 1951 and Eisenhower's decision to send federal troops to Little Rock, Arkansas in 1954 – were as much a demonstration of failure rather than success, for they represented the failure of persuasion or the bargaining skills so crucial to the office, *ibid.*, chapters 2 and 3.

Congressional leaders with appeals direct to the American people. One thing is sure: no matter how difficult the job becomes or how recent Presidents are judged by a fickle electorate, the position of President of the United States will continue to attract enormous attention both in the USA and abroad. For to repeat the point yet again, alone in a highly fragmented political system, the Presidency is the natural coordinating institution of national leadership. Given the inherent power of the federal government over the lives of many millions of Americans and non-Americans, this must ensure that the very special status of the Presidency will continue.

Further Reading

Louis W. Koenig's *The Chief Executive*, New York, Harcourt Brace Jovanovich, 5th edition, 1986 is among the best of the textbook treatments of the Presidency, but see also Raymond Tatalovich and Byron W. Daynes, *Presidential Power in the United States*, Monterey, Cal., Brooks Cole, 1984. Presidential policy making is analysed in Richard Neustadt, *Presidential Power*, New York, John Wiley, Revised edition, 1976. For accounts of the increasingly public nature of the office, see Sam Kernell, *Going Public*, Washington DC, Congressional Quarterly, 1986, and Roderick P. Hart, *The Sound of Leadership*, Chicago, University of Chicago Press, 1987. Presidential elections are covered in Nelson Polsby and Aaron Wildavsky, *Presidential Elections*, 7th edition, 1988. For an up-to-date discussion of Presidential leadership see Fred I. Greenstein (ed.), *Leadership in the Modern Presidency*, Cambridge, Mass., Harvard University Press, 1988. The most recent study of Presidential bureaucracy is by Stephen Hess, *Organising the Presidency*, Washington DC, Brookings, 3rd edition, 1987.

10

The Federal Bureaucracy

The fully developed bureaucratic mechanism compares with other organizations exactly as does the machine with the non-mechanical modes of production. Precision, speed, unambiguity, knowledge of the files, continuity, discretion, unity, strict subordination, reduction of friction and of material and personal costs – these are raised to the optimum point in the strictly bureaucratic administration.

Max Weber, *Essays in Sociology*

It's time for us to take a new look at our government, to eliminate waste, to release our civil servants from bureaucratic chaos, to provide tough management . . .

Jimmy Carter

Our Government has no special power except that granted it by the people. It is time to check and reverse the growth of government which shows signs of having grown beyond the consent of the governed. It is my intention to curb the size and influence of the federal establishment . . .

Ronald Reagan

Few areas of federal government activity come in for as much opprobrium as does the bureaucracy. As the Weber quote suggests, bureaucracies are supposed to work efficiently. Hierarchy, order, responsibility and professionalism are implied by the model of the 'rational' bureaucrat, yet according to public folklore, typical federal administrators are the very opposite of this. They are overpaid, inefficient and wasteful. Worse, they are often the creatures of special interests and occasionally they are simply corrupt. Surveys have shown, indeed, that the federal government is considered easily the most inefficient of all the major

Table 10.1　Public perception of efficiency of institutions, November 1981 (percentage)

Institution	Not efficient and well run	Efficient and well run	Don't know
Federal government	74	20	6
Local government	49	43	7
Large business corporations	33	56	10
Private voluntary organizations	23	60	17
Small business corporations	20	70	10

Source: Public Opinion, vol. 5, no. 1 (February/March 1982), p. 28. © American Enterprise Institute.

institutions in American society (table 10.1). While some of the more colourful charges levelled at the federal bureaucracy more closely resemble caricature than accurate portrait, the executive branch does seem unusually inefficient, fragmented and complex. So much so, indeed, that every President has pledged himself to simplify the executive branch and to root out wasteful and unnecessary programmes. Promises of this sort are popular with the electorate and no doubt Presidents genuinely believe that they can actually rationalize the bureaucracy. However, in spite of some changes, the complaints – and frustrated attempts at reform – continue. This issue raises a number of questions. Why is it that the executive branch attracts so much criticism? Is the criticism justified? To what extent *can* the federal bureaucracy be controlled and reformed? It may be that the structure and behaviour of the executive departments and agencies reflect other forces in American government which would have to be changed as a prelude to bureaucratic reform. Before we address these questions directly, it is necessary to provide some basic facts about the federal administration in the United States.

The Federal Bureaucracy: Organization and Function

The annual *US Government Manual* produces an organization chart of the government of the United States (figure 10.1). While such charts can be misleading – they imply a hierarchical simplicity and equality between units at the same level which is far from reality – they do reveal the bare bones of the system. The most important distinctions are between the 13 executive departments, the independent establishments

Figure 10.1 The government of the United States

Source: Adapted from *US Government Manual 1987/88*, Washington DC, US Government Printing Office, 1987.

and the government corporations. Executive or Cabinet departments are responsible for the major federal programmes, and their chiefs, the departmental secretaries, are directly answerable to the President. Given the growth in government over the last 50 years, Cabinet departments have not proliferated as might have been expected. In 1988 only six of the 13 departments were creations of the modern era and of these one (Defense) grew out of older departments. In fact successive Presidents have worked hard to reduce the number of departments or to rationalize existing ones. In 1949 the Departments of War, Army, Navy and Airforce were combined in one Department of Defense. In 1971 President Nixon proposed 'the most far-reaching reorganization of the executive branch that has ever been proposed by a President of the United States'[1] by amalgamating seven Cabinet departments into four new ones. His plan was rejected by Congress, but both Jimmy Carter and Ronald Reagan have continued the campaign to simplify the departments. Ronald Reagan went so far as to label the Departments of Education and Energy unnecessary, and during 1982 bills were introduced into Congress proposing their abolition. Both were created by Jimmy Carter – the former because the existing Department of Health Education and Welfare was so large and cumbersome, and the latter as a direct response to the nation's energy crisis. By 1988 they were still in existence, however, demonstrating Congress's resistance to major rationalizations.

Most Presidents prefer a small, compact Cabinet so as to facilitate smooth policy making. Yet the number of departments for which they are responsible is but one of a number of management problems they have to face. Another involves the complexity characteristic of each department. This can be formidable, for with the possible exception of the Department of State (responsible for the foreign service and foreign policy) each department is itself a collection of different agencies and services, each with its own interests and constituents. So the Department of Health and Human Services (HHS) was created in 1979 following an earlier incarnation as the Department of Health, Education and Welfare, which was itself a loose collection of disparate agencies. HHS's present (1987) organization is shown in figure 10.2. Again the apparently simple hierarchical structure belies a reality of considerable complexity and competition – although the sheer number of different programmes does give some sense to the complexity of the department. In almost all Cabinet departments there is a horizontal division of responsibilities

1   Quoted in Otis L. Graham, *Toward a Planned Society: From Roosevelt to Nixon*, New York, Oxford University Press, 1976, p. 209.

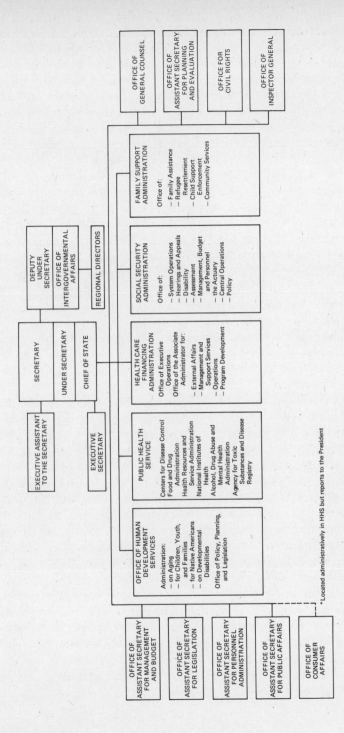

Figure 10.2 Department of Health and Human Services

Source: Adapted from *US Government Manual 1987/88*, Washington DC, US Government Printing Office, 1987, p. 291.

and a vertical division organized geographically. So in figure 10.2 much of the day-to-day work of HHS is carried out at the regional and area levels. There are ten standard federal regions and within these a number of area offices, usually based on large cities. Figure 10.2 also allows us to make some distinction between different sorts of bureaucrats. In the American system, a crucial distinction exists between career officials and political appointees. The latter consist of the executive schedule appointments (Secretary, Under Secretary, Deputy Under Secretary and Assistant Secretary positions as shown in figure 10.2) plus in the other agencies and corporations, administrators, commissioners and so on. About 700 individuals are in this super league but they are assisted by a further batch of political appointees drawn from the 'supergrade' positions in the civil service. Since the passage of the 1978 Civil Service Reform Act these officials have become members of what is known as the Senior Executive Service (SES). This consists of around 8000 employees only 10 per cent of whom can be political appointees. However, the 1978 Act also introduced merit pay awards and other incentives which allow the President and Cabinet secretaries much greater freedom to reward political favourites and punish those not willing to cooperate with Administration policies. As will be developed later, this reform has led to a further politicization of the executive branch.

The independent establishments and government corporations (figure 10.1) include a vast number of agencies performing numerous functions. A very general distinction can be drawn between government corporations (broadly equivalent to nationalized industries in other countries) which include the US Postal Service and the Tennessee Valley Authority, and the regulatory agencies. But there are other institutions which fall into neither category, including the Veterans' administration which, with over 200,000 employees, provides for the medical and other social needs of ex-servicemen, and the General Services administration and Office of Personnel Management which deal, respectively, with the provision of buildings, equipment and other services for the whole executive branch, and the recruitment of staff to the Cabinet departments. It is a little misleading to label all of these institutions 'independent' – the chief administrators (or in a few cases the boards of governors) are appointed by the President, subject to confirmation by the Senate. The President is also a key figure in helping decide the size of their budgets and in some cases he, or his Cabinet secretaries, take a very direct interest in their activities. This is patently the case with the Central Intelligence Agency (CIA) and with the US Information Service, which effectively acts as a propaganda service for the State Department.

However, the regulatory agencies are genuinely more independent as most of them were originally set up by Congress to act as non-partisan organizations responsible for monitoring, controlling or regulating various aspects of economic and social life. Three waves of reform in American politics correspond to the three generations of regulatory agencies which exist. Between 1887 and 1915 a rising tide of reform sentiment led to the creation of agencies designed to tame the unacceptable economic and social activities of large corporations and natural monopolies, mainly the railroads. So during this period the Interstate Commerce Commission and Federal Trade Commission came into being. During the 1930s most of the reforms were inspired by the Depression and its consequences. Hence the Federal Deposit Insurance Corporation underwrites bank deposits to protect the public against bank failures, the Securities and Exchange Commission regulates the stock market and the National Labour Relations Board helps regulate industrial relations. The final wave of reform, during the 1960s and 1970s, was inspired by, among other things, concern at environmental pollution (leading to the Environmental Protection Agency which is, incidentally, *not* an independent agency but a cabinet level organization), civil rights (the Equal Employment Opportunity Commission), election malpractice (the Federal Election Commission) and consumer protection (The Consumer Protection Safety Commission). These agencies have sometimes been given formidable powers by Congress to exercise administrative, legislative and judicial powers over corporations, unions and the public at large. Until the 1960s a common criticism was that they were anything but independent in the use of these powers. Instead the 'regulated controlled the regulators' or, to quote two celebrated cases, the Food and Drugs administration was in the hands of the drug companies and the Interstate Commerce Commission was deferential to the needs of the truckers and railroads.

Although sometimes exaggerated, there is little doubt that many of the regulatory commissions had established a *symbiotic* relationship with what had become their clients.[2] They needed each other, the clients for guidance on how best to operate in (or dominate) the market, and the regulators to ensure political independence and to justify their bureaucratic *raison d'être*. During the 1960s and 1970s much greater public concern at the abuse of corporate power led to the newer agencies (such as the Environmental Protection Agency) establishing a more

2 See Murray Edelman, *The Symbolic Uses of Politics*, Urbana, Illinois, University of Illinois Press, 1964, for a good analysis of this point.

adversarial relationship with the regulated.[3] This, together with limited reforms in the older agencies and a general increase in the amount of regulation in American life – especially of corporations – has led to a backlash by the corporate world and their political allies, the Republicans.

Contrary to popular belief, the burgeoning responsibilities of the federal government, together with greatly increased expenditure, have not been matched by dramatic increases in the *number* of federal employees responsible for implementing programmes and policies. As

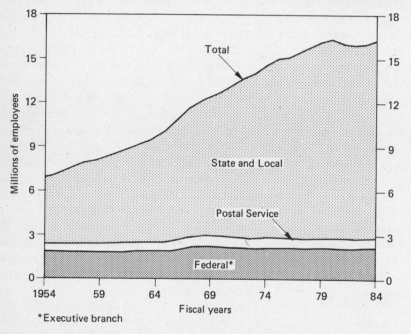

Figure 10.3　Government civilian employment, 1954–1984

Source: Special Analysis Budget of the US Government, 1986, Special Analysis I, Washington DC, US Government Printing Office, 1985, p. I/10.

can be seen from figure 10.3, the number of federal employees has remained roughly the same over the last 30 years, the big increases in total government employment being accounted for by state and local governments. Indeed, starting with the Carter administration and continuing under President Reagan, the absolute number of federal/civilian employees has fallen, reaching around 2,800,000 by

3　For a selection of case studies on regulation, see James Q. Wilson (ed.), *The Politics of Regulation*, New York, Basic Books, 1980.

1985. Recent reductions are part of the continuing campaign against big government, but the general failure of federal employment to rise in the post-war period takes more explaining. Part of the reason, at least until the early 1980s, is the rapid increase in the number and size of grant-in-aid programmes to state and local governments. As we saw in chapter 4, a fair percentage of the general increase in federal spending derives from this source. Devolved programmes increase employment at the lower rather than federal level. Second, increased expenditure does not necessarily require more federal employees – although it has almost certainly led to what is a considerable expansion of the number of professionals in federal employment. Professionals are the middle grade employees – often scientists, or the highly trained personnel who have been increasingly recruited to help run more complex programmes, both old and new. In fact (the Post Office excluded) the federal government employs relatively few less qualified workers. State and local governments employ most of the lower grades (transport, hospital, municipal employees) and lower/middle grades (teachers, social workers, police and firemen). A more professional civil service is harder to control because it can more easily fall back on technical and highly specialized information when challenged by the public, Congress or the President.

The Bureaucracy: How Uncontrollable?

Students of administrative behaviour are quick to identify certain characteristics of bureaucracy which are present whatever the political system involved or governmental function being performed. Some of these characteristics are labelled 'undesirable' – usually because they greatly reduce the accountability of bureaucrats to elected officials – and as government becomes larger and more complex so these undesirable features multiply. There is, of course, no reason to suppose that the United States is exempt from these trends. It is not, and that is problem enough. But critics go much further and argue that US government, and particularly the federal bureaucracy, has a number of additional, and uniquely American features which make the problem of accountability a particularly serious one. Unfortunately, unravelling cause and effect is difficult in this area, especially in a country where 'federal government' and 'bureaucracy' often hold negative connotations. With so many Americans deeply prejudiced against government, it is important to treat with caution some of the more colourful critiques levelled against bureaucracy, regulation, 'Washington' and the civil service.

The task of the remainder of this chapter is, therefore, to outline the major criticisms directed at the federal bureaucracy, to assess their validity and to record the ways in which Presidents, Congress, the courts and the public have attempted to increase their control over administrators.

The Inherent Power of Bureaucracy

Simple theories of both constitutional government and administrative behaviour assign little or no independent power or discretion to administrators. Their job is to implement laws. The legislature passes the laws and the chief executive is responsible for managing and directing the administrators in the implementation process. According to classical theories of administration, bureaucrats can do this effectively if they operate in line with certain basic principles – hierarchical command, specialization and delegation of duties. The elected chief executives are at the apex of this system, they alone give commands; bureaucrats may advise them; but it is not their job actually to give orders. Reality is, of course, very far from this ideal type. In most systems, bureaucrats have two main powers both of which can give them considerable control over the policy system.

Information

Bureaucrats act as administrative gatekeepers. When laws are being framed either by legislatures or executives, it is essential to find out what is achievable and what is not. A new law on lead levels in petrol, for example, needs to be carefully informed about a host of technical questions, including the efficiency of internal combustion engines, pollution levels, the car industry's ability to compete internationally once their products are adapted, and so on. Politicians are obliged to heed the advice of their officials on such technicalities, and the officials themselves can, up to a point, select and organize information according to their own preferences and prejudices, or in favour of one interest rather than another. They may, for example, advise the politicians that certain options are simply not possible for technical reasons. Examples of administrative gatekeeping in highly technical areas may sound understandable, and possibly exceptional. But almost *all* law making and implementation in modern industrial societies is technical and complex. From housing to transport to law enforcement to social security and defence, technical questions are paramount. No single President or

Cabinet secretary can possibly absorb all this information – even with the assistance of professional staffs. They have to rely on their bureaucrats.

Clientelism

Clientelism is the word used to describe the sort of symbiotic relationships between bureaucrats and their customers referred to earlier. Again, it is not unique to American politics; to a greater or lesser extent it occurs everywhere. It is also an entirely understandable phenomenon. Consider the case of defence agencies and defence contractors. In those Western countries with sizeable defence industries (Britain, Germany, France, the USA) intimate relations exist between contractors and officials in defence departments. Defence officials have, therefore, a continuing interest in particular corporations and defence systems – and also, perhaps, in ensuring that defence spending remains at certain levels. These interests may or may not be the same as those of the administrators' political masters. But there can be no doubting the independent political influence of officials in this context. Information is, again, the crucial resource, but it is not merely technical information; it is this plus all the advantages which daily personal contact and shared values give to the official and which are often denied to the politicians.

As government has increased in size and scope, so clientelism has spread. In modern societies all bureaucracies have their customers whose interests and needs must be tended to, whatever the government in power or the values and preferences of elected politicians.

The Bureaucratic Hydra:
A Uniquely American Phenomenon?

Scholars of comparative government often refer to the extent to which different political systems are characterized by 'strong' or 'weak' states. Almost invariably, the United States is categorized as a weak state. In other words, rather than government being unified, resolute and separated from the rest of society, it is fragmented, indecisive and infused with social influence.[4] The aforementioned clientelism is a good

4 For a good comparative analysis see Peter J. Katzenstein (ed.), *Between Power and Plenty: the Foreign Economic Policies of Advanced International States*, Madison, Wisconsin, University of Wisconsin Press, 1978.

indicator of the power and autonomy of the state. Although it exists everywhere, clientelism is likely to be more pervasive in weak state systems. In addition, weak states are likely to be characterized by competition between different parts of the administrative process. So sub-units – individual departments and agencies – display a marked degree of *autonomy* from the centre. They serve different interests and their officials do not all share the same values and policy objectives. We are not referring here to the absolute *size* of government. As noted, in terms of expenditure and function, American government is large by any standards. We are, rather, referring to the extent to which American government is fragmented and simply not amenable to central direction and control.

Much of recent criticism centres on this fact. Critics usually do not put the particular American situation in comparative context, but we have good reason to believe that the United States is different from many other countries; that certain institutional relationships make it especially difficult to exercise central control over public policy. Two basic critiques of American bureaucracy have been made in recent years – the 'iron triangle' and 'issue network' critiques.

Iron triangles

Starting with books written by Douglass Cater and Leiper Freeman in the mid-1960s, came accusations that sub-governments working as iron triangles – congressional subcommittee, administrative bureau and special interest – were the dominant actors in American politics.[5] The analysis was simple: Congressional subcommittees provide the money and monitor regulations, the bureau actually hands over the money or enforces the regulation, and the special interest is the beneficiary. All need each other and the system would break down without equal participation by all. Hence the 'iron triangle' metaphor. Empirical confirmation of sub-governments of this sort was readily at hand, especially in public works, defence, agriculture and water policy. Agriculture became a particularly appealing example with bureaux in the Department of Agriculture handing out subsidies to farmers who in turn had established intimate links with members of the several agricultural subcommittees. The triangle was 'iron' because it was impenetrable. The combined political clout of the leading sub-government actors was

5 Douglass Cater, *Power in Washington*, New York, Vintage, 1964; J. Leiper Freeman, *The Political Process*, New York, Random House, 1965.

formidable, with no individual President, public interest lobby or Congressional leader able to break the pattern of distribution and public expenditure which the triangle had moulded. While the empirical validity of this case was convincing for certain sorts of public policy, it was clearly inappropriate in other areas. Appreciating this fact, Ripley and Franklin refined the thesis in an important book first published in 1976.[6] They pointed out that in what they call re-distributive domestic policy (where resources are taken from one group or class and given to another, as in social welfare programmes), Presidents and top level (politically appointed) officials as well as Congress as a whole play a more important part. And in some regulatory policies, bureaucracy and administration play a relatively small role. Other, more sophisticated refinements, were added by the authors to the sub-government theory, all of which demonstrated that the American administrative and political process is indeed unduly complex and often not amenable to simple, single-model characterizations.

Issue networks

A conceptually much simpler, yet almost certainly more accurate picture of administrative politics in America has been drawn by Hugh Heclo.[7] Heclo argued that as government programmes have grown in size and scope so they have generated new lobbies, interests and, simply, a larger number of active participants in the policy process. Moreover, the networks of politicking and lobbying which develop as a consequence are constantly adapting and changing. So it is very difficult accurately to categorize where the policy system begins and ends:

> The notion of iron triangles and sub-governments presumes small circles of participants who have succeeded in becoming largely autonomous. Issue networks, on the other hand, comprise a large number of participants with quite variable degrees of mutual commitment or of dependence on others in their environment; in fact it is almost impossible to say where a network leaves off and its environment begins.[8]

6 Randall B. Ripley and Grace A. Franklin, *Congress, the Bureaucracy and Public Policy*, Holmewood, Illinois, Dorsey Press, 1976, 3rd edn, 1985.
7 Hugh Heclo, *A Government of Strangers: Executive Politics in Washington*, Washington DC, Brookings Institution, 1977; also his 'Issue networks and the executive establishment', in Anthony King (ed.), *The New American Political System*, Washington DC, American Enterprise Institute, 1978.
8 'Issue networks', ibid., p. 102.

As a result of this much more open and volatile system, no erstwhile secure sub-government can afford to be complacent. The cosy relationships established between corporations and bureaucrats have been challenged by environmentalists, consumer protection advocates and other public interest lobbies (a point to be developed in the next chapter). The sub-governments continue to exist, of course, but they are increasingly buffeted by competing centres of power. Heclo does not view these developments as entirely negative – indeed there may be greater scope for executive leadership when the system is more open. But he does view with alarm the increasing complexity of government and the fact that direct democratic accountability is difficult to achieve when the 'real' decisions are taken, not by President and members of Congress, but by numerous additional political actors including bureaucrats, lobbyists, the media and political consultants.

To the foreign observer, what is interesting about these recent critiques of bureaucratic power, is that they are comments not on administrators and administrative agencies, but also on the whole policy-making system. Many make the *a priori* assumption that more government is by definition a bad thing and that increasing public disenchantment with government derives from the constantly expanding volume of legislation and special regulations. Without commenting on the normative question of whether more government is good or bad, it is obviously the case that government, by whatever definition (number of policies, volume of regulations, amount of public expenditures) has increased in all modern industrial societies over the last 20 years. However, although criticism of big government has occurred in other countries, it has been particularly vocal in the USA – a country where as a percentage of GNP, government, although large, is hardly at the top of the international league table (see chapter 2, table 2.5). No doubt this can partly be explained in ideological terms. As we noted in chapter 2, the USA has a long-established tradition of antagonism to government. But there are also important institutional differences between the USA and most other countries which may help us understand both academic and popular critiques of government in general and bureaucracy in particular.

Easily the most important is the independent role of Congress. Iron triangles and issue networks depend at least in part on an autonomous legislature and, within Congress, little legislatures (committees and subcommittees). Although this has long been appreciated – for example in 1970 Harold Seidman noted that 'meaningful improvements in executive organization and in the management of the Federal system . . . will depend on the final analysis on reorganization of the Congressional committee structure'[9] – it seems to have been partly forgotten amid all the talk of special interest politics, political action committees and the generally more complex and confusing pattern of government typical of the 1980s. Although it could be argued that autonomous legislative power increases accountability, it also greatly facilitates the sort of volatile issue network politics where no single actor in the policy process can ever fully understand what is going on, let alone control events. Arguably, this is the very antithesis of accountability.

A second unique feature of the American system is its openness. Access to Congress and members of Congress, as well as to officials at all levels, is remarkably easy compared with most other countries. Exploiting this fact, Washington has become a political consultants' and lobbyists' paradise. No interest, whether economic (corporations, unions), public interest (environment, consumer protection), or governmental (state and local governments), can afford to drop its guard by failing to make full use of the availability of policy makers. Again openness is at least partly a function of the proliferation of centres of autonomy or power. With subcommittees, bureaux, agencies and even individual officials competing with one another over particular areas of public policy, they are usually only too ready to make use of any resource which will enhance their autonomy further. In essence this means organized interests (together with their technical advisers, the lobbyists and consultants), and the media. A more open system has also, of course, been aided by the cathartic effects of the Watergate scandals. Freedom of information became a major public issue during the late 1960s and early 1970s, and the formal legal access of groups and individuals to government files and information was greatly strengthened as a result.[10] But these formal changes were almost certainly not as important in producing greater access as the changes in Congress, the party system and American society generally which earlier chapters have chronicled.

9   Harold Seidman, *Politics, Position and Power: The Dynamics of Federal Organization*, New York, Oxford University Press, 1st edn, 1970, p. 285.
10   Under the 1966 and 1974 Freedom of Information Acts, Americans have the right to inspect all federal records. Certain information (for example relating to criminal investigation, defence or inter-office memos) can be denied, but citizens can appeal against refusals in the courts. The substantive freedom of access in the USA is dramatically greater than in most comparable countries, and especially than in the United Kingdom.

Reform Attempts

Perhaps the most common recent response to the problem of big government and bureaucratic power is simply to propose a reduction in the size and complexity of government. In his 1982 State of the Union Message Ronald Reagan declared:

> Together, we have cut the growth of new federal regulations in half. In 1981, there were 23,000 fewer pages in the Federal Register, which lists new regulations, than there were in 1980 . . . Together, we have created an effective federal strike force to combat waste and fraud in government. In just six months it has saved the taxpayers more than two billion dollars – and it's only getting started.[11]

As we noted earlier, the number of federal employees has been declining steadily since the late 1970s. Does this mean that Presidents are winning the battle against bureaucracy? Not necessarily. Federal employment may have fallen, but numbers are only loosely related to complexity and autonomy. Similarly, Ronald Reagan's reductions in *new* regulations does nothing to alter the fact of already established regulations, together with their policy networks. 'Waste and fraud' in the federal government undoubtedly exist, but this condemnation is more of a populist rallying cry than an attack on the central problems of complexity and autonomy. As we know, a number of Presidents have attempted to reorganize the executive branch, the most dramatic proposal being Richard Nixon's 1971 plan to create four 'super departments' – Natural Resources, Human Resources, Community Development and Economic Affairs. Other, less ambitious reorganizations have been attempted, some successfully, others not. Sometimes these involve the creation of new departments (HUD in 1965, Health, Education and Welfare (HEW) in 1953, the Department of Energy in 1977, the Department of Education in 1979). More common are *internal* reorganizations usually aimed at simplifying administration and reducing overlapping jurisdictions. Although well intentioned, reorganization is almost always a less than adequate reform measure. For one thing Congress is reluctant to approve reorganizations which affect its own internal distribution of power, and accordingly has vetoed the more far-reaching reforms. Committees and, increasingly, subcommittees, have a vested interest in the continuing autonomy of departments, bureaux and agencies.

11 *Address to Congress*, 26 January 1982, US Embassy Press Release, London, p. 3.

Secondly, internal reorganization often involves 'shuffling the same old drones into new hives' as Robert Sherrill has put it, so no real change occurs.

In fact, Ronald Reagan eschewed the reorganization device, opting instead for more direct control of the executive branch. He did this in two ways: through control of agency and departmental rule-making and through the appointment power. In 1980 Congress passed the Paperwork Reduction Act, a law favoured by the Carter administration and designed to simplify federal regulations. The Act established an Office of Information and Regulatory Affairs (OIRA) within the Office of Management and Budget (OMB). Although not in itself very significant, the Reagan administration used this new unit in combination with two executive orders to screen new agency regulations. In effect, this required the executive departments and agencies to submit any changes in policy to OMB. In turn OMB rejected any rules considered not in line with Administration policy. Not surprisingly, this particularly affected those agencies which in the past the Administration had considered too progressive in such areas as environmental protection, affirmative action, occupational safety and health, welfare, education and social security. These centralized gate-keeping efforts provoked a storm of protest in Congress and almost certainly led to a loosening of regulations in a number of areas. However, as a number of commentators have noted, these changes did not amount to a fundamental shift in policy.[12]

The Reagan administration's use of the appointment power attracted a great deal of publicity because it represented a thorough-going attempt to politicize the executive branch. As well as placing Reagan supporters in the Cabinet departments and regulatory agencies, the Administration centralized the appointment, transfer and promotion of members of the Senior Executive Service. Utilizing the provisions of the 1978 Civil Service Act, the Office of Personnel Management under direct instructions from Ed Meese in the White House promoted, rewarded and transferred Reagan loyalists while punishing those considered liberal or disloyal. At the Cabinet level, some of the Reagan appointees were so out of tune with their departments and with public opinion that they were forced to resign (Anne Burford at EPA; James Watt at Interior).

12   For a review see David McKay, *Domestic Policy and Ideology*, Cambridge, Cambridge University Press, 1989, chapter 7.

Lower down, the politicization strategy was also controversial and led to falling morale and frequent resignations among civil servants.[13]

Again, limits exist to what can be achieved from such a strategy. If Congress establishes an Environmental Protection Agency, its job is to protect the environment. Officials recruited to the EPA will support this basic objective. Changing senior managers can undermine this policy, but they cannot transform it. Congress, moreover, is ever vigilant and keen to exercise its oversight function. This extends to the appointment power and, as noted, several Reagan appointees were rejected or obliged to resign (including the Director of the Office of Personnel Management, Donald Devine).

Other oversight resources have been utilized by Congress in its attempts to control the bureaucracy. The General Accounting Office and Office of Technology Assessment have been more rigorous in providing an information base for evaluation whether the criticism is politicization or not. There has even been some flirtation with 'sunset' legislation. Another symptom of the populist revolt against big government, sunset laws require agencies or programmes to be renewed annually. If they are not fulfilling their purpose, they simply cease to exist. Such measures have not so far been adopted on a significant scale. Finally Congress has been increasingly diligent in securing *information* from the executive branch. Although partly successful, chapter 9 showed that there are technical limits to both the quality and quantity of information which Congress can glean from the executive.

Finally, what of the courts? Surely they are well placed to curb the worst excesses of bureaucratic power. Certainly individual citizens can sue the government if they believe a constitutional right has been violated. It is quite common for the powers of an administrative agency to be delineated by the courts. During the 1978–9 Supreme Court term, for example, the Court outlawed the Federal Communications Commission's directive that cable systems should give citizen groups a certain number of channels (*FCC* v. *Midwest Video*; *ACLU* v. *FCC*). However Congress often gives to administrative agencies quasi-judicial powers. The USA has only a limited system of administrative courts, so recourse to judicial redress is very much up to the aggrieved individual. As we will discover in chapter 12, this can be a long, complicated and expensive process. And of course, much of the criticism

13 For an account of these attempts, see Peter M. Benda and Charles H. Levine, 'Reagan and the bureaucracy: the bequest, the promise and the legacy', in Charles O. Jones, *The Reagan Legacy: Promise and Performance*, Chatham, New Jersey, Chatham House, 1988.

of bureaucracy centres not on administrative wrong-doing or abuse of power but on questions of efficiency, responsiveness and accountability.

Concluding Remarks – and a Word of Caution

This review strongly implies that the Heclo analysis has some validity. The system is characterized by numerous and highly volatile issue networks. These are not impenetrable because a more open policy system allows new forces and interests to influence even the most established 'iron triangles'. Environmentalists now fight the dams and water projects previously approved by the cost triumvirate of bureau (the Army Corps of Engineers), subcommittee and local communities.[14] These networks remain autonomous, however, not in the sense that they constitute closed policy systems, but because they are rarely amenable to central control. Even a determined President intent on imposing radical changes in bureaucratic behaviour could achieve only limited results. Finally, although bureaucrats and administrators continue to attract most of the public opprobrium (and most of the reform attempts), on their own, their powers would be quite limited. Congressional committee and subcommittee autonomy and open access to government are the other absolutely essential conditions which allow the policy network system to flourish.

Fragmentation, autonomy, complexity and openness are all adjectives which can be accurately employed to describe the federal bureaucracy. To the outside observer, however, some really very important characteristics of the policy-making system remain, which can be obscured by the pluralistic confusion which our analysis has so far implied. First, not all of the policy-making sub-systems can be characterized thus. As we will discover in chapter 13, many aspects of foreign policy are made in a very different environment. Second, the distributional consequences of the generally pluralistic policy-making system are far from random. Intuitively, at least, it would be expected that multiple access and overlapping jurisdictions would have egalitarian consequences; all groups, interests, classes and regions would benefit. Yet reality is very different. As we will explore in chapters 11 and 13, increasing access to policy makers does not necessarily result in a more equitable distribution

14 Although the Army Corps of Engineers is quoted as a classic case of a powerful bureau, it was not completely autonomous, for it competed with the Department of Agriculture, the Bureau of Reclamation and the Tennessee Valley Authority over control of water policy. See Arthur B. Maass, 'Congress and water resources', *American Political Science Review*, vol. 44, September 1950, pp. 576–93.

of resources. Indeed in some crucial respects, a system of fragmented political power and open access to government actively discourages redistributive policies or the transferral of resources from one group or class in society to another.

Further Reading

Randall B. Ripley and Grace A. Franklin provide a fascinating insight into the world of sub-governments in their *Congress, the Bureaucracy and Public Policy*, New York, Dorsey Press, 3rd edition, 1985. The best study of senior civil servants is Hugh Heclo, *A Government of Strangers*, Washington DC, Brookings Institution, 1976. A series of case studies is provided by Francis E. Rourke (ed.), *Bureaucratic Power in National Politics*, Boston, Little, Brown, 3rd edition, 1978. Case studies of regulation can be found in Elizabeth Bailey (ed.), *Public Regulation: New Perspectives and Processes*, Cambridge, Mass., MIT Press, 1987. For an account of how Presidents, including Ronald Reagan, have attempted to control the executive branch, see Laurence E. Lynn Jr., *Managing Public Policy*, Boston, Little, Brown, 1987.

11

Organized Interests: The Real Power?

Suppose you go to Washington and try to get at your government. You will always find that while you are politely listened to, the men really consulted are the men with the biggest stake – the big bankers, the big manufacturers, the big masters of commerce . . . The government of the United States is the foster child of special interests. It is not allowed to have a will of its own. It is told at every move: 'Don't do that; you will interfere with our prosperity'.

Woodrow Wilson, *The New Freedom*

Concededly, each interest group is biased; but their role . . . is not unlike the advocacy of lawyers in court which has proven so successful in resolving judicial controversies. Because our congressional representation is based on geographical boundaries, the lobbyists who speak for the various economic, commercial and other functional interests of this country serve a very useful purpose and have assumed an important role in the legislative process.

John F. Kennedy, quoted in Congressional Quarterly,
The Washington Lobby

Throughout American history, concern over the power of organized interests has never been far from the surface. Indeed the growth of the Republic can almost be described in terms of successive waves of populist revolt against the undue influence of organized groups, and in particular private corporations. Woodrow Wilson's characterization (above) came after more than 20 years of public disquiet at the operations of the big companies. During the 1920s corporate power was regarded more benignly, with capitalism flourishing as never before. The Depression transformed this image, however, and it was not until the 1950s that the benevolent view of private power returned. Most recently, the critique has returned to the centre of the political stage, with popular opprobrium directed at those companies responsible for high energy costs, pollution, consumer exploitation and discrimination against women and minorities. Criticism of other organized interests – labour, promotional groups – has been much more isolated and fragmented, although during the 1940s trade unions were under considerable attack with Congress eventually passing union-curbing legislation.

The critique of corporate power has two related strands. First, that large private companies are by their very nature ruthless and exploitative. This mainly populist view considers size to be the main problem. Break up large monopolies and oligopolies, and something approaching 'fair' competition will emerge. Second, corporations have been critized because they exercise power without accountability. They are not, in other words, answerable to democratically elected institutions. They can 'buy' Congressmen, bribe local, state and federal officials, and generally manipulate democratic processes in their favour. We will return to these points later, but note that the most common critique of capitalism in Europe – that the private accumulation of wealth in business is *by definition* exploitative – has been quite rare in the United States.

The quote by John Kennedy represents the second, quite different, judgement on the role of organized interests in America. According to this view, groups are an essential part of the democratic process; that far from undermining representation, they aid it. Advocates of this position point to the multiple access points in the American system and the ways in which myriad organized groups are able to exploit these to their advantage. Crucially, because *all* classes, interests, ideological positions, regions, localities, and social groups *can* organize (even if some actually do not) to defend or promote their positions, the potential for fair or just policies is particularly great in the American system.

Much of the comment and discussion in this chapter will centre on these two contrasting perspectives and how valid they are in the late 1980s and early 1990s. Before we embark on this exercise, it is necessary to provide some basic information on interest groups in the United States.

Interests, Groups and Lobbyists

In all modern industrial societies, citizens band together to form organizations with social, economic and political aims. American group participation is high in comparative terms, with some 62 per cent of the population being members of some voluntary association or other.[1] Of this number many (about one third) are inactive, however, and the organizations with the most active membership tend to be 'non-political' social clubs (youth groups, church related groups, fraternal organizations – Rotary, the Masons, the Lions – and so on), professional societies (representing doctors, lawyers etc.) and educational groups (parent–teacher associations, school and college fraternities). About 8 per cent of the adult population are active in political clubs and organizations – a similar figure to that for most social clubs. The organizations with the highest membership (17 per cent), although by no means the highest active membership, are the labour unions.[2] In addition to voluntary associations with individual membership, a number of groups exist representing corporate and governmental interests, such as trade, commerce and manufacturers' associations and state, local, county and regional government organizations. Finally, a number of single issue groups exist at any one time, ranging from organizations to outlaw abortion, to proponents of a freeze on nuclear arms levels, to local groups created to stop the construction of a particular public works project.

All of these organizations can have a political dimension, obviously so in the case of corporate labour and *ad hoc* groups, but also with most social organizations. Chambers of commerce and professional associations, for example, frequently engage in political activity when laws and regulations affecting their members are introduced or existing laws are changed. As local, state and federal governments have legislated in almost every conceivable area of economic and social life over the last 30 years, it is not surprising that many erstwhile mainly social groups and associations have found themselves at the very centre of political controversy. The debate on gun control intimately involves the National Rifle Association (NRA); environmental pollution controls involve the Audubon Society and Sierra Club, and education cuts and school district consolidations, Parent–Teacher Associations.

Political scientists have long been engaged in the business of trying to classify interest groups and even now no completely satisfactory taxonomy exists. We have already drawn some distinctions (for example between voluntary associations with individual members and corporate groups) but as all of these can engage in political activity this distinction is not necessarily that helpful. For our purposes it is more useful to distinguish between three broad categories of organized group – econ-

1 Sidney Verba and Norman H. Nie, *Participation in America: Political Democracy and Social Equality*, New York, Harper and Row, 1972, p. 41.
2 Ibid.; all figures are from table 2.2, p. 42.

omic, professional and promotional – to which we should add some
comments on political action committees and lobbying.

PAC's

Economic Groups

Business

When discussing business organizations, it is common to distinguish
between the activities of individual corporations and those of peak
associations (trade union confederations, employers' and trade associations). In the United States, corporations tend to be both powerful and
autonomous and frequently they exercise political power as independent
units. So General Motors, the world's largest vehicle manufacturer, is a
political force to be reckoned with in its own right, as is International
Telephone and Telegraph (ITT),[3] the major oil companies or many of
the firms listed in the *Fortune 500*.[4]

In a famous study of business lobbying published in the 1960s, Bauer,
Pool and Dexter concluded that the lobbying activities of individual
firms were not an important influence on public policy.[5] The authors
were, however, primarily concerned with Congress rather than executive
departments and agencies. And state and local governments were not
the subject of their study. Few dispute that corporations do wield
enormous influence on lower level governments. Land, taxation, labour
and public works policies are often moulded by corporate interests
within states. Of course there is also competition between corporate
interests, and between these and other organized groups, but in most
locales business is the single most important influence. The precise
extent of this power varies from area to area, with some states being
effectively dominated by one corporation (such as with the Du Pont
chemical corporation in Delaware); or by a few interests (until recently
cattle and oil in Texas); while in others (New York, Michigan, California,
Massachusetts) individual corporate power is much more diffuse and
ameliorated by union and public interest group activity.

Moreover, since the 1960s there is overwhelming evidence that
individual firms have taken a more active part in public policy making.
Most major corporations now have Washington offices and employ

3   For an account of ITT's political activity, see Anthony Sampson, *The Sovereign State:
The Secret History of ITT*, London, Coronet Books, 1974.
4   *Fortune* magazine produces an annual list of the 500 largest corporations in the USA.
5   Raymond Bauer, Ithiel de Sola Pool and Anthony Lewis Dexter, *American Business
and Public Policy*, New York, Prentice-Hall, 1964.

professional lobbyists to advance and protect their interests. The size of business lobbying can partly be explained as a response to the increasingly strident and successful efforts of the new public interest lobbies devoted to environmental and consumer protection and to affirmative action in employment.[6] Since the mid-1970s, however, a more important spur to corporate political activity has been the rapidly changing economic environment and increasing vulnerability of US corporations to foreign competition. Business now *needs* to ensure that the federal government provides an amenable climate for investments and growth – although, as Charles Lindblom has printed out, only business imposes an *automatic* sanction on society should anti-business policies be pursued, namely, recession and unemployment.[7]

American business peak (or trade) associations have been labelled 'weak' in the past. And certainly the influence of the major single industry associations (representing automobiles, rubber, textiles and so on) as well as the two major cross-industry organizations (the National Association of Manufacturers, and the US Chamber of Commerce) has historically been weak compared with equivalent organizations in such countries as Germany and Japan. Perhaps this should be expected, given the traditional strength of individual corporations in the USA which we noted in chapter 2. Why, after all, should successful individual firms forfeit some of their independence to a trade association? Indeed, as recently as the 1950s both the NAM and Chamber of Commerce were regarded as a marginal influence in Washington. Both adhered to a sometimes unthinking anti-statist philosophy, and were notably less important than the sum of the political efforts of individual corporations. Since then, however, both organizations plus some new ones (notably the Business Round Table which represents the chief executives of the 200 leading corporations) have emerged as more respected spokesmen for corporate interests.[8] This is not to say that American business peak associations have assumed the status of equivalent groups in Germany, Japan or even Britain, but they are now more important than ever before. Again, this revival is linked to the general increase in group activity characteristic of the last 20 years. Before we leave our discussion of business interests, a word of caution should be expressed about any comparison between business activity in government during the 1950s and today. As earlier mentioned, the 1950s were an especially benign period in American politics. For much of the 1950s and 1960s, corpor-

6 See Graham K. Wilson, *Interest Groups in the United States*, Oxford, Oxford University Press, 1981.
7 See Charles Lindblom, *Politics and Markets*, New Haven, Yale University Press, 1977.
8 See Wilson, *Interest Groups*, chapter 4.

ations were highly successful and entered the political arena only when necessary. Government policy was favourable towards them, and particularly towards the larger corporations.[9] Iron triangles and cosy relations with executive bureaux do not require lobbying as such, with all that this implies in terms of attention seeking and publicity. Only when competing or conflicting interests enter the fray is lobbying of the more visible kind necessary.

Trade unions

American unions have traditionally been considered a relatively weak influence in the policy process. In comparative perspective this is undoubtedly true. Only about 18 per cent of the total labour force are affiliated to a union; the unions do not have the unequivocal support of a major political party, and unlike many union movements in Europe they lack ideological cohesion. Almost all the powerful union movements in history have been driven forward by some ideal vision of a new – usually socialist – society. Not so in the case of American unions which, although by no means unideological, are significantly more instrumental than their European counterparts. Interestingly, the period when unions were most ideological in the USA (the 1930s and 1940s), coincided with the years of their most rapid growth and greatest political achievements.

Although relatively weak and divided, trade unions as a whole do constitute one of America's most important organized interests. The USA is, after all, a highly industrialized country and the unions represent more than 20 million workers. However, the relatively high political visibility of the unions has been achieved only slowly. The first unions in America of any significance were craft rather than industry oriented and eschewed any active involvement in politics. Known for the advocacy of 'voluntarism' or 'business unionism', these unions formed the American Federation of Labour (AFL) in 1886 under the leadership of Samuel Gompers. As the name implies, business unionism involved workers perceiving themselves as part of the capitalist environment. The union's job was, therefore, to bargain with employers in line with what employers could or should afford. If a company was doing well, then the workers

9   For example a negative relationship exists between corporate size and taxation levels – the bigger the corporation the lower the tax paid. See Lester M. Salamon and John J. Sigfried, 'Economic power and political influence: the impact of industry structure on public policy', *American Political Science Review*, vol. 71 (1977) no. 2, pp. 1026–43.

would benefit. If it was not, low wages and lay-offs were to be expected. With over a million members, the AFL became an important representative of the skilled worker, but its limited approach became very obvious when the Great Depression struck. Industry wide unions (such as the United Steel Workers and United Mine Workers) formed rapidly during the Depression years and banded together in 1935 as the Congress of Industrial Organization (CIO). In contrast to the AFL, CIO unions saw themselves in an adversarial relationship with employers, and were strongly disposed to use political means to achieve better working conditions and higher wages.

Since the 1930s the CIO (and, following an amalgamation in 1955, the AFL/CIO) has lobbied hard in Washington over the whole range of public policies which affect workers and working conditions – union rights, social security, job training, vocational education, occupational health and safety, overseas trade relations and economic policy generally. Observers generally agree that in terms of organization, staffing and access, the AFL/CIO – mainly through its political organization, the Committee on Political Education (COPE) – has become one of the most coherent and visible of the Washington lobbies. As suggested in earlier chapters, the unions do have links with the Democratic Party, but formal affiliation has always been avoided (although for the first time in 1983, the AFL/CIO endorsed a Presidential candidate, Walter Mondale, early in the campaign). This has almost certainly helped, rather than hindered, the AFL/CIO's public image. In recent years COPE's political interests have widened to include activity on a number of issues not directly related to members' interests, for example foreign policy and civil liberties. Generally – but by no means always – COPE is identified with a liberal political position.

Although the AFL/CIO's national political activities are important, it would be misleading to give the impression that the United States has a centralized and united union movement. In comparison with unions in many countries, the opposite is, if anything, true. Most union structures are highly decentralized, with local and state units often responsible for bargaining over wages and salaries. Moreover, some of the biggest and most powerful unions are not even members of the AFL/CIO, including the Teamsters (truckers) and the largest teachers' union (the National Educational Association).

Over the last 15–20 years, there has been much talk about the decline of the unions as a political force. Certainly their membership (as a percentage of the labour force) has been falling and an occupational structure changing in favour of the tertiary sector has generally weakened the unions whose strength is traditionally rooted in the secondary (manufacturing) sector.[10] In addition, unions suffered from the generally anti-labour policies of the Reagan administrations.

Nonetheless, the unions remain highly visible in the Washington political scene. Graham Wilson has noted that this very visibility is a symptom of weakness, for the unions have so much to do in the pursuit of their interests that they are obliged to take a highly active part in politics.[11] While this is probably true, it should also be stressed that almost *all* interests have become more active at the national level in recent years. In effect the nature of the policy process is now such that no one group or sector can afford not to take part in the Washington bargaining and coalition-building game.

The farmers

In most modern industrial countries, farmers occupy a special place in society. For strategic and/or electoral reasons they often exercise formidable political power, and in recent history American farmers have proved no exception. They are the recipients of massive subsidies designed to raise their incomes to a point at or beyond that necessary to keep production up. As in some other countries (notably within the EEC), this has sometimes resulted in overproduction and the need to destroy or store produce in order to keep prices buoyant. American farms are also among the most efficient in the world, being highly capital intensive and mechanized. Given the high rate of innovation and the general trend towards urban and suburban living over the last 60 years, it comes as no surprise to learn that the farm population declined from over 30 million in 1920 to under 10 million in 1970. Indeed, by 1988 a mere 3.5 per cent of the American workforce were employed in agriculture – a remarkably low figure, given the fact that the United States is easily the largest producer (and exporter) of foodstuffs in the world.

Given this, American farming organizations are perhaps rather less cohesive than would be expected. The largest group, the American

10 Although, since the 1960s, the level of unionization among *government* workers (many of them in manual jobs in hospitals and local government services) has increased, as the phenomenal growth of the American Federation of State, County and Municipal Employers (AFSCME) which now has over 1 million members, shows. For an account of the changing fortunes of American unions, see Michael Goldfield, *The Decline of Unions in the United States*, Chicago, University of Chicago Press, 1987.

11 *Interest Groups in the United States*, chapter 3. For a good account of how the AFL/CIO operates as a lobby, see *The Washington Lobby*, Washington DC, Congressional Quarterly Press, 1979, pp. 97–112.

Farm Bureau Federation (AFBF), has, until recently, actually preached the merits of disengagement of the state from the economy, including presumably the removal of farm subsidies. The National Farmers Union (NFU) has taken a pro-subsidy line, but its membership is smaller and more geographically concentrated (in the West and Mid-West). Nonetheless, the NFU is a lobbying force to be reckoned with and has achieved considerable status in Washington.

As the farm population has declined, so the electoral influence of farmers has fallen. During the late nineteenth and early twentieth centuries, farmers virtually constituted a separate social class in the United States, a fact which helps explain the emergence of farm-based political movements, including the Populists, the Farmers Alliance and the Grange. However, these parties and organizations failed to establish permanent bases of social support and most have now passed into history.[12] More recently, farmers' influence in state legislatures has continued, although even here, re-districting and demographic change has produced a steady decline in the agricultural lobby. The same is true of Congress. At one time, many Congressmen were virtually elected by farmers. Not so today, when in most states and districts the farm vote is but one small voice among many.

In spite of the general weakness of the farming organizations, it would be misleading to suggest that farm interests are politically weak. A more accurate way to charaterize them would be simply to see the larger farmers (or agribusiness, as it is called) as other corporations. Indeed general industrial and financial corporations do own a large number of agribusiness farms. No federal government could afford to see these interests seriously damaged. As with defence industries, food is strategically too important for this to happen. However, smaller farmers, and especially those working marginal land or producing products liable to sharp fluctuations in price, are genuinely weak – a fact shown by the occasional public demonstrations to which smaller farmers are sometimes obliged to resort. In 1985, for example, attempts by the Reagan administration to cut agricultural subsidies aroused fierce opposition from Mid-Western grain farmers. Although the Republicans were 'punished' in the 1988 Presidential election in several farming states (Minnesota, Iowa, Wisconsin), this was not sufficient to make any difference to the eventual result.

12   The Grange remains an important farm lobby. For an account of the vain attempts to build an agrarian populism, see Grant McConnell, *The Decline of Agrarian Democracy*, Berkeley, University of California Press, 1953.

Professional Groups

Although receiving much less public attention than business or unions, professional groups have probably grown and improved their political status more rapidly than any other of the organized interests over the last 40 years. As educational standards have risen and the premium on expertise in a number of areas – particularly the law, medicine and education – has increased, so the professions have prospered. The role of the main lawyers' organization, the American Bar Association (ABA), will be developed in chapter 12. The ABA not only acts as gatekeeper for those practising law, it is also a major source of information on legal standards and procedures. So the nomination of judges and changes in criminal and civil law depend in part on the opinions and position taken by the ABA. With some 500,000 lawyers in the USA, the central importance of the law in policy making, and the great overrepresentation of lawyers among state and federal legislators and officials, the ABA's opinions and interpretations must be taken seriously. As with other professional associations, *expert* opinion gives the ABA its special status. It is true that only about one half of all lawyers are ABA members, but its members include the more successful lawyers, whose expert, non-partisan opinions are highly respected.

The American Medical Association (AMA) performs a similar function for doctors. Again, not all doctors are members, but those who are tend to be among the more successful. For many years the AMA was famous for its fight against federal health insurance (or 'socialized' medicine) and from the 1940s and the 1960s it was one of the most vocal and biggest spending of the Washington lobbies. It eventually lost the battle with the enactment of Medicare (medical insurance for the old) and Medicaid (medical aid for the poor) in 1965,[13] but it remains a major influence on all legislation affecting health care. Its political action committee (AMPAC) was actually the largest spender of all PACs during 1981 and 1982, contributing a total of $1,737,090 to federal candidates.[14] Generally, the AMA's position has been conservative although, since the advent of federal (and state and local) health programmes, it has also sought to improve the position of those members working for governments or receiving government fees. In recent years

13 See Theodore R. Marmor, *The Politics of Medicare*, London, Routledge & Kegan Paul, 1970, for an account of the AMA's battle against Medicare.
14 Quoted in Jeffrey M. Berry, *The Interest Group Society*, Boston, Little, Brown, 1984, p. 163.

the AMA has been overshadowed somewhat by the rise in importance of groups representing medical specialists and consultants. As medicine has become more sophisticated and expensive, so the political strength of the specialists has increased.

Other leading professional groups include some (the American Bankers' Association, the National Association of Home Builders, the National Association of Realtors) whose function is more economic than professional. They are no less important for this, of course. The Realtors (estate agents), for example, contribute large amounts of money mainly to Republican candidates, and generally lobby hard to ensure a growing housing market and low interest rates. At the state and local levels, the Realtors are highly active politically – especially in combating what they consider to be any unnecessary regulation of the housing market – whether it be through restrictive zoning laws, building codes, property taxes or fair housing statutes.[15]

In sum, professional associations often represent the rich and the powerful in American society. This can mean the maintenance of professional standards (as in law or medicine), but it can also mean the advancement of particular economic interests (lawyers, doctors, bankers, Realtors and so on).

Promotional Groups

By promotional group is meant all those organizations devoted to promoting a particular cause or position. This can include a wide variety of groups ranging from the National Rifle Association (NRA), which champions the right of Americans to own firearms, to the National Association for the Advancement of Coloured People (NAACP), which represents Black Americans, to Common Cause, one of the new breed of public interest groups which fights for honesty and efficiency in government. Some of these groups are *ad hoc* and transitory, as with the several organizations which emerged in opposition to the American presence in Vietnam, but most are at least semi-permanent.

In all democratic societies such groups exist, but in America they are particularly numerous and vocal. Why should this be so? One reason is undoubtedly the openness of the policy system. Promotional groups

---

15   The Realtors have made particularly strenuous efforts to prevent the passage of fair housing (anti-race, sex discrimination) laws at the local, state and national levels. See David McKay, *Housing and Race in Industrial Society*, London and New Jersey, Croom Helm, Rowman and Littlefield, 1977.

know that with enough organization, public support and media exposure they can influence members of Congress, executive officials and even judges. So in the 1960s Ralph Nader, the consumer's advocate, went about the business of exposing automobile safety standards with a single-minded determination. Eventually, his methods led to media and later Congressional investigations and culminated in stringent new standards imposed by law. Later, other groups mobilized to launch similar campaigns on environmental pollution, occupational safety and women's rights which led to new, often quite far-reaching, legislation. Common Cause, the 'clean government' public interest group, has supported the reform of the Congressional committee system, votes for 18-year-olds, limits on electoral campaign spending, rationalizing government organization and improvements in voter registration.

Although the sudden blossoming of public interest groups in the 1960s and 1970s has surprised – and even worried – some commentators, it is not so difficult to explain in historical perspective. Middle-class reform movements are, after all, hardly new to the United States. In chapter 4 we saw how reformers attempted to 'clean up' the cities during the nineteenth century, and waves of middle-class moralism have frequently accompanied periods of rapid economic and social change in American history. The 1960s and early 1970s were just such a period, characterized as they were by rapid economic growth, social and political dislocation and, finally, evidence of corruption at the highest level. Moreover, as we chronicled in earlier chapters, this was also a period of party decline, and the increasing atomization of political power. In such an environment, coalition building around such particular issues as environmental protection or clean government became that much easier. This was also a policy context with no parallel in other countries, where, although the same issues have been raised to national prominence, they have tended to do so via political parties or through the operation of a consensus between political and economic elites.

Although public interest groups claim to represent 'the public interest', in reality they are not value free and the policies they promote hardly have neutral distributional consequences. New environmental standards may help produce cleaner air and water, but they can also lead to higher prices. Reforming government sounds admirable enough, but reforms often have unexpected results, as did the nineteenth-century city reforms and campaign finance reforms of the 1970s.

By the 1980s many groups claiming to represent the public interest were as often the champions of special interests. The National Rifle Association (NRA) fights to prevent federal, state and local governments from passing gun control laws. In so doing it claims to represent the public interest. Even more problematical are those organizations whose cause involves moral absolutes. To a 'pro-lifer' (an anti-abortionist), abortion on demand represents a form of judicial murder which clearly cannot be in the public interest. To pro-abortion activists, the free availability of abortion early in a pregnancy represents a basic right of women to exercise control over their own bodies. This too would appear to be in the general or public interest. Clearly the two positions are irreconcilable. Similar dilemmas are raised by such issues as capital punishment, the provision of prayers in public schools and the identification and treatment of AIDS patients.

In recent years, the Christian Right (or fundamentalists) have been making ground on all these issues, but the mere fact that a particular group is well organized and has access to decision makers does not always equal success. As we will develop later, certain groups and interests fail repeatedly. The policy system may be open and complex but it is not neutral.

Political Action Committees

In the sense that particular organized interests have formed Washington committees to fight for or against a particular item of legislation or the electoral success of an individual candidate, PACs are nothing new. Earlier we noted the efforts of the AMA's AMPAC to prevent the passage of Medicare in 1965, for example. Yet since the mid-1970s, PACs have spread to the point where in the 1980 election they contributed $55m of $239m spent by Congressional candidates, and their 1986 contributions reached $139 million (table 11.1). In addition, further vast sums are now spent by PACs in general efforts to defeat candidates or to support candidates separately from their personal campaign organizations. The rise of the 'electoral' PAC can be explained in the main by changes in campaign finance laws which, by putting restrictions on direct contributions by corporations and unions, have encouraged the big contributors to form committees which in turn can raise money from employees and/or members which is then passed on to (mainly) Congressional candidates. (Federal funding of Presidential candidates has reduced PAC influence in Presidential elections.) Fearing that PACs would become simply the 'fat cat' contributors by another name, Congress has amended the 1974 Federal Campaign Act to put further limits on PAC activity. In particular, each PAC cannot contribute more than $5000 to any one candidate's primary campaign, and a further $5000 to his or her general election campaign. While this does not sound very much, it adds up as the figures quoted above for the 1980 and 1986 elections show. Moreover, there are no limits on PAC spending which does not go directly into the campaign coffers of candidates, so PACs can launch their own campaigns against or for particular politicians. In 1982, for example, NICPAC (the National Conservative Political Action Committee) spent $526,000 in an effort to unseat the liberal Senator Edward Kennedy in Massachusetts.[16]

Table 11.1   Contributions by PACs to all candidates for the House and Senate, 1974–1986 (in millions of dolars)

Year end	Corporate	Labour	Member-ship	Non-connected	Other	Total
1974	°	$6.3	°	$ .7	$1.0	$12.5
1976	°	ᵢ8.2	°	1.5	2.8	22.6
1978	$9.8	10.3	$11.3	2.8	1.0	35.2
1980	19.2	13.2	15.9	4.9	2.0	55.2
1982	27.5	20.3	21.9	10.7	3.2	83.6
1984	35.5	24.8	26.7	14.5	3.8	105.3
1986	49.4	31.0	34.4	19.4	5.3	139.4

Source: Frank J. Sorauf, *Money in American Elections*, Glenview, Illinois, Scott Foresman, 1988, table 4.1.

As can be seen from table 11.1 private corporations have donated the largest sums to candidates, followed closely by membership associations (mainly professional groups such as the AMA) and the trade unions. Note also, however, that non-connected organizations raised large sums of money, much of which (not shown in table 11.1) was devoted not to particular campaigns but to raising the salience of a political issue or ideological position, or to painting a positive or negative picture of a candidate. Of these non-connected organizations, two ultra conservative groups were notably successful in the early 1980s – NICPAC and the National Congressional Club which supports the maverick right-wing Senator from North Carolina, Jesse Helms.

Labour PACs contribute mainly to Democratic candidates (predictably) but corporations distribute their largesse more evenly between the two parties (perhaps less predictably). Direct campaign contributions from PACs have generally helped the Democrats rather than Republicans, but the overall impact of PAC activity has almost certainly been to help conservatives. This is mainly because conservative PACs are better organized, generally more professional and can appeal to the strongly felt conservative sentiment so prevalent in many parts of the

16   See *National Journal*, 7 August 1982.

country. However, their efforts began to backfire after 1980. Having been credited with unseating a number of liberal Senators in 1980, they failed to repeat the pattern in 1982, 1984 and 1986.

Whatever the merits and demerits of PACs – and Congress and public interest groups are constantly discussing how they should be reformed – their rise brought out into the open most of the corporate, labour and association political funding which previously tended to be covert and often illegal. Also, by virtue of their ability to make direct appeals to the public on particular issues, PACs have almost certainly aided the rise of single interest politics and have helped further to weaken traditional political party organizations. Perhaps not surprisingly, Democrats have been more vocal in their criticisms of PACs than have Republicans. Indeed, in 1983 both Walter Mondale and Gary Hart announced that they would reject all PAC assistance for their 1984 Presidential campaigns. Similar pledges were made by Michael Dukakis and Jesse Jackson in 1988.

Interestingly, by the late 1980s the growth of PACs peaked

Table 11.2   Growth of PACs, by type: 1974–1986

Year end	Corporate	Labour	Member-ship	Non-connected	Other	Total
1974	89	201	318			608
1975	139	226	357			722
1976	433	224	489			1146
1977	550	235	438	110	28	1360
1978	785	217	453	162	36	1653
1979	950	240	514	247	49	2000
1980	1206	297	576	374	98	2551
1981	1329	318	614	531	109	2901
1982	1469	380	649	723	150	3371
1983	1538	378	643	793	173	3525
1984	1682	394	698	1053	182	4009
1985	1710	388	695	1003	196	3992
1986	1744	384	745	1077	207	4157
1987	1779	382	797	1044	209	4211

Source: Sorauf, *Money in American Elections*, table 4.2.

(table 11.2). Indeed the proportion of total campaign spending accounted for by PACs began to decline. With this decline, the influence of the large conservative PACs has waned. They remain very much part of the Washington political scene, but some of the more dire predictions of their insidious effects seem unlikely to be fulfilled.

The Washington Lobby

We have already referred to the 'traditional' interest groups – labour, business, agriculture, the professional associations – to which are added promotional groups and the activities of political action committees. But the Washington Lobby consists of much more than this. The executive branch itself lobbies Congressmen for support, as do state and local governments, either individually or through the US Conference of Mayors, Council of State Governments and other umbrella organizations (see chapter 4, p. 69). Finally foreign governments lobby Congress and executive alike. A recent *Congressional Quarterly* publication lists the Israeli, Arab, Korean and Taiwan Lobbies as the most significant in recent years.[17] Given that American foreign policy decisions affect virtually every country and also the openness of the American policy system, the presence of such interests should perhaps be expected.

All of these groups and interests employ consultants and professional lobbyists to collect information and to establish links with the key political actors in the policy system. The result is that Washington is a city alive with political activity, where it is difficult to distinguish between the 'insiders' (elected and appointed officials) and the 'outsiders' (lobbyists, media consultants, interest group leaders). Indeed the presence of policy networks with fluid memberships and constantly shifting agendas means that there are really only 'insiders'.

If anything resembles pluralistic decision making, then surely this does. Yet as earlier suggested, openness and accessibility hardly result in neutral policies or a distribution of public benefits which can be considered egalitarian. Let us develop this point further.

Interest Groups: For and Against

Returning to the questions posed at the beginning of this chapter, it is easy to appreciate why, in a society where economic individualism is much admired, a multiplicity of competing interest groups can be regarded as beneficial. In classical economics, equilibrium is reached when demand and supply match each other in a perfectly competitive market. An analogous situation in politics could prevail when groups (analogous to firms) compete with one another in a completely open political environment. The public interest (equilibrium) is hence

17   *The Washington Lobby*, pp. 129–66.

achieved by the balancing of different interests. No policy, according to this theory, is likely to be completely against any one interest because a group's involvement in the system will ensure it modifies or amends policy at least partly in its favour.

These are, in essence, the theoretical assumptions of the 'traditional' group theorists, notably Arthur Bentley and David Truman.[18] Government's role in such a context is to *arbitrate* between competing interests. By implication, government exercises little independent power; it more resembles a cipher or sorting mechanism and ensures that the rules of the game are abided by.

The group theorists never claimed that in reality there was complete *equality* between groups (although that was the ideal), but they did maintain that if the interests of a particular section of society were seriously damaged, they would mobilize, organize and, through access to representative institutions, manage to do something to redress the balance. The rise of trade union power in the 1930s is often quoted as an example of such mobilization. Neither were the group theorists so naïve as to assume that *all* groups had access, even potentially. David Truman, for example, accepted that the position of the American Black population (in the 1950s) was exceptional because they patently lacked access to the policy-making process.

Classical group theory has since been criticized by scholars from almost every school of political thought. Public choice theorists have stressed the tendency in such a system for public expenditure (or the provision of public goods) to spiral ever upwards. The reasoning here is both simple and familiar. With open access to multiple decision-making centres, the potential for log-rolling is enormous. So if one group, sector, region, state or local government is the recipient of a federal programme, all the others will be too. Anthony Downs has put this nicely, labelling it the 'iron law of political disperson': 'All benefits distributed by elected officials will be distributed to all parts of the constituency, regardless of the economic virtues of concentrating them upon a few parts of the constituency.'[19] The result is, in fact, the very opposite of equilibrium or the 'optimal' in economics. Governments end up handing out far too much to various interests which leads to inefficiency and excessive government spending. This particular critique is currently popular. The solution is not to abolish groups, but drastically

18   Although they were never explicit about the analogy with economics. See Arthur Bentley, *The Process of Government*, San Antonio, Texas, Trinity University Press, 1949; David B. Truman, *The Governmental Process*, New York, Alfred Knopf, 1951.
19   Anthony Downs, quoted in David McKay, 'Industrial policy and non-policy in the US', *Journal of Public Policy*, vol. 3, no. 1 (February 1983), p. 45.

to reduce the role of government in economy and society. Predictably, advocates of this position view with alarm the decline of party, and the rise of single issue and special interest politics. Such changes have fragmented the system further and therefore increased the potential for log-rolling and yet more government programmes and regulations. But as we have already noted a number of times in earlier chapters, reducing the size and scope of government is easier said than done, especially given that organized groups and interests are now deeply entrenched in the policy system and most have some interest in maintaining the present pattern of expenditure.

Efficiency in resource distribution is the main concern of this essentially conservative critique. Critics on the left have been more interested in the consequences of the classical view for political, social and economic *equality*. They argue that groups are not just unequal, they are grossly unequal. Or, that there is a bias in the system which some groups are more able to exploit than others.[20] Business or corporate interests, in particular, are advantaged, while labour, the poor and minorities are disadvantaged. This brings us back to the populist condemnation of big business mentioned earlier. How much truth is there to this critique?

First we should note the obvious fact that in terms of its power to move capital, labour and resources around, business is in a unique position among major organized interests. Only government can exercise anything like an equivalent power; none of the other groups can. Instead they are confined to single issues, or particular geographical areas, or they exercise influence over just one sub-group of the population. Even Labour, with its mass membership and finely tuned lobbying machine has relatively few resources compared with business. It is, perhaps, testimony to the power of the corporations that most of them did not even consider it necessary to engage in overt lobbying until relatively recently, because the policy agenda generally favoured them. While the unions and other interests struggled to get items discussed and legislated, business could often sit back and wait until it preceived its interests as threatened.[21] Business is privileged in another sense: it has access to large sums of money which can be used to 'lubricate' the policy-making system to its advantage. This is also true of unions and some other

20 The most eloquent exposition of this view remains E. E. Schattsneider's *The Semi-Sovereign People*, New York, Holt, Rinehart and Winston, 1960.
21 Keeping the policy agenda free of discussion of those issues which threaten the powerful has been called 'non-decision making', and the concept has inspired considerable controversy and empirical application. A good application is by Peter Bachrach and Morton Baratz, *Power and Poverty*, New York, Oxford University Press, 1970. For a theoretical discussion, see Stephen Lukes, *Power: A Radical View*, London, Macmillan, 1974.

groups, but none have access to money in quite the way business has. Recent revelations of corruption in America corporate life (ITT, Lockheed) confirm that, quite apart from legal contributions to candidates, the long-established reputation of American corporations and business generally for undercover financial deals is still very much with us.[22]

Second, if we view society not in terms of discrete groups or organized interests, but in terms of social strata, there is very little evidence that the new politics of openness and accessibility have made very much difference to social and economic mobility. Those groups and classes at the bottom of the social heap 30 or 40 years ago are, generally speaking, still there. Changes in occupational structure have had some impact, but what many have called a 'transformation' of the political system has had little effect. Indeed, it is often the case that the more atomized and complex the decision-making system, the lower the potential for re-distributive policies. The two great social reform periods in recent history which laid the foundations of the welfare state – the New Deal and Great Society – coincided with what was virtually the antithesis of the new politics – strong Presidents, pliant Congresses and a public broadly agreed on the need for reform. To be fair, many re-distributive policies (counter recession and manpower retraining programmes, increased social security spending) where enacted during the Nixon and Ford years and if there is any validity to the public choice critique, greater access should result in more spending, whatever the distributional consequences. This accepted, in a period of fiscal stress, a fragmented political system almost certainly leads to resources being more thinly divided between groups, interests and classes, and those whose need is greatest are likely to find themselves relatively worse off.

Finally, the politics of distribution are now multi-layered and it is not always adequate to perceive the system only in terms of social classes or strata. Environmental controls, equal opportunity for women and improved standards of occupational safety clearly benefit some people more than others, but there is no obvious relationship between the distributional impact of each of these reforms and those which traditional 'class-based' policies (tax reform, welfare, social security) produce. In fact much of the assault on corporate power during the 1960s and 1970s involved policies of this sort. Middle-class reformers, outraged at pollution, consumer exploitation and discrimination, launched the new promotional groups which the corporations were then obliged to engage

22   For a discussion of the ways in which private power has been exercised throughout American history, see Grant McConnell, *Private Power and American Democracy*, New York, Alfred Knopt, 1967; See also Lindblom, *Politics and Markets*.

in battle. Meanwhile, the measures by which it is usual to gauge the living conditions of industrial workers, minorities and deprived social groups – income, access to housing and so on – changed very little. Where moral absolutes are concerned – as with abortion and capital punishment – the distributional consequences are also difficult to measure. This accepted, critics of the conservative position on these issues would claim that the 'victims' are usually the poor – poor mothers, Blacks and other minorities.

It would be wrong to leave our discussion of organized interests without mentioning the serious problems which successive governments have experienced in managing the economy since the early 1970s. Changes in the party system, Congress and the increasing accessibility of myriad groups to the major political institutions have all had consequences for economic management and industrial policy. Chapter 13 will expand on this question and whether meaningful control of the economy can be achieved in this new policy context.

Further Reading

Interest groups and lobbying cover such a wide area of political activity that no one book is a completely adequate guide. For a good account of recent developments see Jeffrey M. Berry, *The Interest Group Society*, Boston, Little, Brown, 1984. Grant McConnell's *Private Power and American Democracy*, New York, Alfred Knopf, 1967, remains one of the most stimulating books on groups in America. For an excellent analysis of the ways in which business has lobbied successive administrations, see Kim McQuaid, *Big Business and Presidential Power: From FDR to Reagan*, New York, William Morrow, 1982. For a discussion of PACs, see Larry Sabato, *PAC Power*, New York, Norton, 1984.

12

The Supreme Court and Judicial Politics

We are very quiet there but it is the quiet of a storm centre.
Oliver Wendell Holmes, Associate Justice of the Supreme Court,
1902–1932

. . . In a democracy, politics is a process of popular education – the task of adjusting the conflicting interests of diverse groups, . . . and thereby to the hostility and suspicion and ignorance engendered by group interests . . . toward mutual understanding.
Felix Frankfurter, Associate Justice of the Supreme Court, 1939–62

In all societies, the courts play some political role. In liberal democracies where the independence of the judiciary is regarded as essential to prevent the exercise of irresponsible executive (and sometimes legislative) power, the political role of the courts as interpreters of the law and as defenders of individual freedoms is well established. In one-party states, courts are political in the quite different sense that they are the instruments of a dominant executive. However, there are also important distinctions within liberal democratic states, the most crucial being the presence or absence of judicial review. As was noted in chapter 3, judicial review is long established in the United States, the Supreme Court being the final arbiter of the meaning of the Constitution. Hence, all laws passed by the state and national legislatures, together with all executive actions, are subject to review by the courts who judge their compatibility with the Constitution. As the final court of appeal, therefore, the Supreme Court has the legal power to declare any action by any other branch of government, unconstitutional. As we will develop later, this apparently formidable power is tempered by a number of factors, but in contrast to many other liberal democracies, there can be no disputing the evidence of what is enormous potential judicial power.

In the United Kingdom, for example, the courts can review executive actions – but only by testing them in relation to the content of Acts of Parliament. This can produce sharp rebukes for governments as happened in the Tameside and Laker Airways cases and there is good reason to believe that the British courts are becoming more active in reviewing executive actions.[1] A Parliament controlled by the executive can, however, always reverse a judicial judgement as sovereignty lies not in the Constitution but in Parliament. In the United States, a decision of the Supreme Court involving the constitutionality of a statute or governmental action can be overturned only by constitutional amendment (or by the court itself, of course) and as was shown in chapter 3, the amendment procedure is cumbersome and rarely used.

In fact, the Supreme Court uses its power of judicial review quite sparingly and much of the day-to-day business of the courts is concerned with interpreting the law, rather than making solemn declarations on the constitutionality of legislation. Even in non-constitutional areas, however, American courts are more active than their British equivalents, for the United States is a highly legalistic society. Recourse to the courts for redress of grievances is swift and ubiquitous in American life. Indeed, the country boasts a staggering half a million lawyers and judges, and among the occupational backgrounds of US Representatives and Senators lawyers outnumber all the other professions put together. A number of reasons could be suggested for this. As we have repeatedly stressed in this book, the USA is a country with a liberal tradition, and the ideology of economic liberalism implies a society made up of individuals rather than social classes, races or other social groups. Distinct and separate individuals acting as self-contained economic units are more likely to defend or promote their interests in the judicial market place rather than, as in many other countries, fall back on social class, family, ethnic group or simply custom and tradition for support. There is a danger of making too much of this, but the tendency for individuals to seek legal redress for poor medical care or a faulty consumer product, or for corporations to sue competitors or suppliers for patent violations or breach of contract is surely related to a pervasive economic liberalism.

In addition, the United States is infused with Constitutionalism. With a written constitution granting certain rights and freedoms to citizens, delineating a separation of powers and guaranteeing a federal system of government, disputes between individuals and government, and

1   For comparisons of the two legal systems and an account of the political role of the British courts, see Ian Budge, David McKay et al., *The Changing British Political System*, London, Longman, 1988, chapter 8.

between branches and levels of government must be arbitrated. Of course, in every political system disputes of this sort have to be resolved, but in few systems are rather rigidly delineated citizens' rights, separation of powers, and federal arrangements married to a strong tradition of legalism and the institution of judicial review. As far as the political role of the courts is concerned, it is the presence of judicial review which marks out the American system as distinctive, and as the Supreme Court is the highest court in the land, it is the Court's judicial review function which has attracted the most attention. The bulk of this chapter will therefore be devoted to this subject.

The American Legal System

For the vast majority of Americans, state courts are what matter, for of the approximately 10 million cases tried in the United States every year, the federal courts account for less than 2 per cent. State, municipal, county and other local courts have jurisdiction over state law – which means that in any one state the vast majority of criminal and civil law cases from mugging to property disputes, to divorce to homicide are initiated and concluded within the state system. As can be seen from figure 12.1, however, federal courts can play a crucial part in state law because, if a decision by the highest state courts of appeal is controversial and if the case involves a federal question then it can be appealed to the US Supreme Court. Effectively, this gives the Supreme Court the power to interpret and judge state law, for 'a federal question' can mean almost anything that is contentious or controversial. In law it means any state court decision which is potentially incompatible with federal law or with the US Constitution. If, for example, a state high court, hands down a decision extending the power of state police to search a suspect's house for evidence, this would have to be compatible with the 4th Amendment of the Constitution which prohibits unwarranted search and seizure. Only the US Supreme Court can judge whether the state law is unconstitutional or not.

In one sense, the Supreme Court's power of judicial review over state law is its most important function. Without it, the country would cease to be a united nation state. Instead, a loose confederacy would prevail with each state going its own way in economic and social affairs. The power to review state high court decisions is part of the *appellate* jurisdiction of the Court. In addition, the Court hears cases on appeal from within the federal court system. As shown in figure 12.1, most federal cases originate in the federal district courts (90 in number)

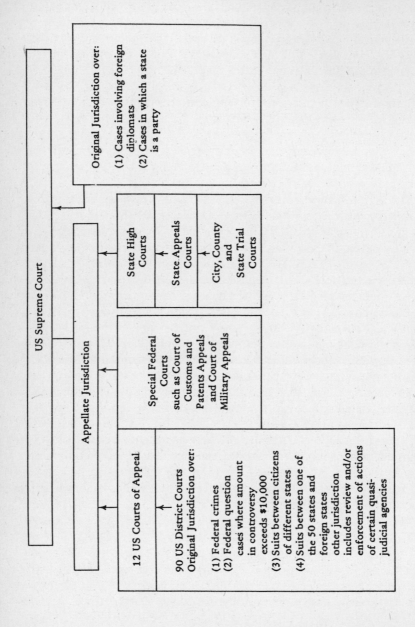

Figure 12.1   Organization of the US court system

whose decisions can be appealed to one of the twelve crucial Courts of Appeal, and thence to the Supreme Court. The Court[2] also has original jurisdiction on a number of minor areas such as cases involving ambassadors.

Most citizens involved in federal litigation, therefore, have contact with the District Courts which are responsible for cases involving federal criminal and civil law. Compared with state law, federal criminal law is limited to a relatively few areas, the most notable being bank robbery, kidnapping, currency forgery, drug trafficking and assassination. Most of the work of the District Courts is in the area of civil law, with taxation, regulation and civil rights and liberty cases dominating. Few of these cases are appealed and those that are, are usually settled in the Appeal Courts which on a day-to-day basis are the most important judicial policy makers in the country.

They are not, however, the key judicial policy makers because their decisions can always be overruled by the Supreme Court.

As can be seen from figure 12.2, the District Courts' caseload has shown an inexorable increase over the last few years, and in the period since about 1966 the number of civil cases commenced has increased particularly rapidly. A greatly expanded federal role in part accounts for this, and although the precise relationship between spreading federal legislation and litigation is hard to establish, there is no doubt that the legislation listed in figure 12.2 has greatly increased the caseload of both the District Courts and Appeal Courts (figure 12.3). By 1978 the overload of the courts had reached crisis proportions and Congress increased the number of district judges from 281 to 398 and appeal judges from 62 to 97. Thus far, the Supreme Court has been immune from such changes in spite of efforts to create a National Court of Appeals to screen petitioners to the Court.

As figure 12.3 shows, the Court has also experienced a sharp rise in its caseload, though not as dramatic an increase as in lower courts. Increases in the number and use of law clerks (each Justice has three clerks assigned to him or her and the Chief Justice four), and improved administration of the Court by the last Chief Justice, Warren Burger, probably account for the institution's ability to manage. As with lower courts, new legislation in civil rights and liberties, and in the general area of federal regulation, largely account for the new demands on the Court.[3] So like the Congress and Presidency, an ever expanding federal

2 For the remainder of the chapter Supreme Court and the Court will be used interchangeably.
3 For a discussion of this point see Richard Hodder-Williams, *The Politics of the US Supreme Court*, London, Allen & Unwin, 1980, chapter 3.

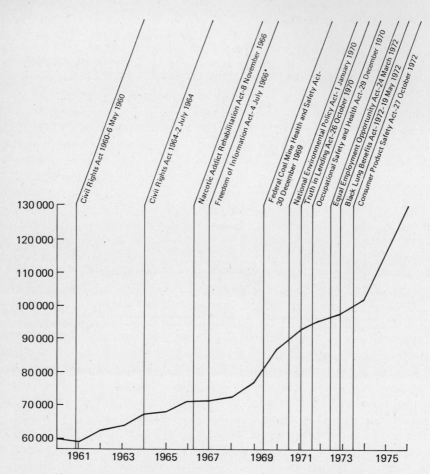

Figure 12.2   Civil cases filed in US district courts, fiscal years 1960–1976

* Effective 4 July 1967.
Source: As reproduced in Linda E. Demkovich, 'The clogged federal courts – who are the culprits?', *National Journal*, 2 November 1978, p. 233. © *National Journal*, 1978.

role has produced new pressures on the Supreme Court which have made its operations more complex and difficult and, crucially, more politically visible.

Figure 12.3   Cases docketed in federal appellate courts per million population

Source: Advisory Commission on Intergovernmental Relations, *The Federal Role in the Federal System: The Dynamics of Growth*, Washington DC, ACIR, 1980, figure 91.

The Supreme Court: Decision Making

Each year about 150 cases are actually decided by the Supreme Court, and while most of these will be of relatively minor political or constitutional import, some will have profound consequences for the American polity and society. Since 1950, for example, the Court has decided that racially separate educational and other facilities are inherently unequal; that almost exact mathematical equality should be applied to the size of state legislative and Congressional districts; that indigent arrested persons should be provided with the services of a lawyer at the government's expense; that tapes of Presidential conversations were not so private as to be protected by executive privilege and therefore could be used in Court against Presidential staff accused of dishonesty; and that the busing of schoolchildren to achieve racial integration is constitutionally required to overcome a historical pattern of legally imposed educational segregation. The very fact that all of these decisions have aroused intense controversy demonstrates their political significance – and the question of how far and in what ways the Court can hand down decisions which are at odds with public opinion or with the other branches of government is a topic we will return to later. Clearly, *how* the Court makes decisions is important. How does it decide which cases to hear? What criteria does it employ when deciding a case?

It is misleading to talk of *the* Supreme Court. Rather than being a unified organic body, the Court consists of nine individuals each with his or her (in 1981 Sandra Day O'Connor was the first woman to be appointed to the Court) quite distinctive view of law, politics and society. Justices are appointed by the President with the advice and consent of the Senate. Unlike other executive appointments, they are appointed for life. Once on the Court then, they are free from the political, financial and other pressures which insecurity of tenure inflicts on most political actors. Of course, only a small percentage of cases coming before the Court are actually heard; most are denied review or, in the language of the Court are denied *certiorari*. *Certiorari* is, simply, that act whereby the losing party in the lower court appeals the record of the case to the Supreme Court so that details of the case can be made 'more certain'.[4] More than 90 per cent of cases are appealed in this way, in most of the remainder the Court is required to hear cases by a statutory appeals process.[5] The granting or denial of *certiorari* is clearly an important decision and the court is legally beholden to no one to justify which cases are heard and which are not. From a strictly legal perspective, the criteria for granting *certiorari* are relatively easy to identify. Loren Beth lists seven:

1   How fundamental is the constitutional (or other) issue presented by the case?
2   How many similar cases have been or are being litigated?
3   Is there a conflict of opinion in the lower courts on this particular issue?
4   Does a lower court decision seem to conflict with an earlier Supreme Court decision?
5   Is there a significant individual right involved?
6   Has the lower court departed significantly from the accepted and usual course of judicial proceedings?

---

4   For a good discussion of this point, see Loren P. Beth, *Politics, the Constitution and the Supreme Court*, New York, Harper and Row, 1962, chapter 3.
5   The most important class of cases here are those where *state* high court decisions declare a federal law unconstitutional, or where the constitutionality of state law is in doubt.

7 Does the case involve the interpretation of a statute never before construed?[6]

At least four of the nine justices have to agree to grant *certiorari* – a fact which strongly implies that the decision is not so clear cut as the list suggests. Indeed, not one of points (1) to (7) is completely unambiguous or not open to serious disagreement or argument. How many cases in the civil rights and liberties areas – a good proportion of the total – do *not* involve a significant individual right? Almost certainly none. Similarly, many cases claim to involve a 'fundamental consti- tutional issue', yet few of these are granted *certiorari*. The fact is that while points (1) to (7) may be a legally correct list of criteria, it tells us very little of the political context in which decisions are taken. Why did it take until the 1940s and 1950s before the Court started regularly to hear civil rights cases? Why did it take to the 1960s for criminal defendants' rights cases to come to the fore, and until 1973 for the Court to deliberate on the constitutional status of bans on abortion?

There are two possible answers here. First, that the philosophy and outlook of the justices changes over time, either as a result of turnover or because individual justices change their minds; and second, that the political and social context in which the Court operates has changed over time, thus forcing certain issues onto the judicial policy agenda which were previously excluded. Taking the second point first it is certain that the Court is influenced by the broader society. In the civil rights area, the Second World War 'nationalized' a number of social issues and brought into sharp focus both for Whites and Blacks the injustices of segregation in the American South. Publicity on conditions in the South was advanced by a number of interest groups, in particular the National Association for the Advancement of Coloured People (NAACP) who also acted as a judicial interest group by providing financial and legal support for litigants involved in civil rights cases.[7]

Although it is impossible to measure the influence on the Court of the 'social and political environment' or of the work of interest groups intent on promoting a particular cause or defending a special interest, the justices are undoubtedly swayed by such factors, at least in terms of letting them influence the policy agenda, or what sort of cases are actually heard.

But it would be misleading to leave the impression of a Court granting *certiorari* only to classes of cases currently subject to public attention.

6 Beth, *Politics*, pp. 31–2.
7 For a good account of the early lobbying efforts of the NAACP see Clement E. Vose, *Caucasians Only*, Berkeley and Los Angeles, University of California Press, 1967.

Many cases are heard when the public pressure is minimal or absent. Re-apportionment, for example, was not a matter of intense public debate when the Court implied in the famous 1962 case, *Baker* v. *Carr*, that the Tennessee State Legislature was constitutionally bound to organize its legislative districts according to the principle of mathematical equality. Later, in *Reynolds* v. *Sims* (1964), the Court made re-districting mandatory. Also, the business of getting a case before the Supreme Court is long and hard. It may be years from the time a case is first filed in the District Court before it eventually reaches the Supreme Court. Such a process does not always lend itself to instant decision making in response to public or interest group pressure.

The judicial agenda is also influenced by the philosophies and attitudes of the justices themselves. Generally speaking, a decision not to hear a case which in some way does meet one or more of the criteria (1) to (7) and which is currently controversial, is a conservative decision. It can reflect a justice's desire to keep the Court out of the 'political thicket' by leaving a lower court's decision or judicial precedent to settle the matter. The fact that the Court did not hear many civil rights cases in the 1920s and 1930s might be explained in this way, as might more recent Courts' reluctance to get involved in cases involving economic policy. We should be wary here, however, for so far discussion has been confined to the influences shaping the Courts' policy agenda, i.e. which cases are heard and which are not. Naturally, the crucial question is, how does the Court decide those cases granted *certiorari*? Even the most conservative justice would have to recommend the issue of a writ of *certiorari* when a Circuit Court of Appeals had decided a case which fundamentally contradicted judicial precedent as represented by an earlier Supreme Court decision. More interesting are those instances when the Court decides to uphold such a radical departure from precedent, or decides that a particular act of Congress or executive action is unconstitutional.

One basic fact must be appreciated when discussing the Court as a political actor: it uses its power sparingly. It exercises *judicial self restraint* (although as we shall see some Courts have been more restrained than others). It follows the doctrine of 'assumption of constitutionality'. In other words, it will use its power of judicial review very selectively, arguing a case on procedural grounds when it can, rather than declaring a law unconstitutional. Indeed, between 1789 and 1937 just 77 national laws were invalidated, although between 1937 and 1977 the rate increased and continued at this accelerated rate through the 1980s. This accepted, as with the granting of *certiorari*, the political and social environment and the judicial philosophy of individual judges will determine the way in which these important decisions go.

As noted earlier, the Supreme Court consists of nine individual justices and the final decision of the Court reflects the interaction of the opinions of these nine people. The formal decision-making process goes like this. Once *certiorari* is granted, the justices first receive written and then hear oral argument from the lawyers on both sides of the case. Later a case conference is convened at which the justices, sitting in private, make a preliminary decision. Five of the justices must agree to constitute a decision and one of these will be assigned to write the majority opinion. If the Chief Justice is part of the majority he or another majority member assigned by him will write the opinion. If the Chief Justice is part of the minority, the most senior member of the majority will make the assignment. Once the assignments have been made, the opinion of the Court is written. This can take many weeks to complete and once published the names of other members of the majority may be added to it. However, some members, while they may agree with the author of the opinion of the Court, may do so for *different* reasons, in which case they will write *concurring* opinions. Finally, those in the minority may choose to write a dissenting opinion, or even a number of dissenting opinions. Usually members will join just the majority or dissenting opinion, but it is quite possible for the Court to publish up to nine separate opinions: an opinion of the Court, four concurring opinions which may support the Court opinion on four different grounds, and four dissenting opinions which dissent on four different grounds. In the celebrated 1978 *Bakke* decision which limited the use of racial quotas to discriminate positively in favour of minorities when admitting them to university courses, the Court published no less than six separate opinions.[8] In this case – and this often applies when the justices are split – the variety of concurring opinions made it difficult to infer the exact meaning of the Court's decision – an outcome possibly preferred by the Court in this politically sensitive and technically complex area.

To the more casual observer of the judicial process, how a justice decides in a particular case may seem obvious. Precedent, and a careful interpretation of congressional statutes would be the immediate answer. Naturally, the justices do refer to precedent and they do spend much of their time interpreting legislation. In this respect their behaviour is little different from that of the British House of Lords (the highest court of appeal in Britain). But even reference to precedent can be

8   For a good account of this and associated cases see Alan P. Sindler, *Bakke, Defunis and Minority Admissions: The Quest for Equal Opportunity*, New York, Longman, 1978.

problematical. What historical precedents are there for cases involving electronic bugging? Or genetic engineering? Or racial quotas, for that matter? Very few that could be considered even vaguely relevant. And interpreting statute law when it involves overruling executive actions can be politically sensitive, to say the least. In both instances the courts have very considerable discretion not only to follow precedent, but to create it; not only to interpret statutes, but to direct the executive branch to change policy. When the formidable power of judicial review is added, the discretion available to the Court widens dramatically. Again, the reflex response to the question 'What guides the Court when it uses judicial review?' is: the Constitution. But as was stressed in chapter 3, there is very little in the Constitution that is unambiguous, and the Supreme Court has reversed itself on a number of occasions when interpreting Constitutional provisions.

If the justices cannot rely on precedent or the literal meaning of statutes or constitutional provisions, what does guide their judicial opinions? This is a complex and difficult question. We have already mentioned the political and social environment and there can be no disputing that the Court has been influenced by pressures from public opinion, Presidents and interest groups. Instances of such pressures will be recorded later. Partly independently of such forces however, different Courts and justices have acquired reputations for being 'conservative' or 'liberal', 'active' or 'passive'. These labels often refer to the jurisprudence or legal philosophy adhered to by different justices. Certainly, no self-respecting Supreme Court justice would rationalize his or her decision in terms of 'political pressures' or 'political expedience' – even if these were truly the main influences. Instead, justices would indeed refer to the Constitution and the ways in which the wording of the Constitution should be interpreted. By so doing they are obliged to look not only at the actual wording of the document but also to the meanings and motives behind the words. If, along with such a 'positivist' approach, the justice also believes that the Court has an unbending duty always to 'discover' the Constitution's true meaning, then an activist Court is implied. For relating the events in a particular case to the true meaning of the Constitution and then testing whether (say) a law on censorship is reconcilable with the Constitution, invites the Court to declare on the constitutionality of that law. Such was the approach of the two outstanding jurists of the early part of this century, Oliver Wendell Holmes and Louis Brandeis. In a number of celebrated cases[9]

9   See Henry J. Abraham, *Freedom and the Courts*, New York, Oxford University Press, 1977.

both argued that some federal and state laws on internal subversion were incompatible with the 1st Amendment's general prohibition of laws abridging freedom of speech – although they accepted that absolute freedom of speech was clearly not intended by the Framers of the Constitution. In Justice Holmes's famous example, 'the most stringent protection of free speech would not protect a man in falsely shouting fire in a theater and causing a panic' they argued that if the 1st Amendment was to mean anything, some principle inherent in the provision must be detected and invoked. By this reasoning, Holmes elaborated the 'clear and present danger test', or 'the question in every case is whether the words used in such circumstances are of such a nature as to create a clear and present danger that they will bring about the substantive evils that Congress has a right to prevent.' Of course, problems remain here – discovering exactly when the danger is clear and present must in part be a subjective exercise – perhaps especially so when Congress (or a state legislature) has passed a law attempting to prevent subversion in time of war. Indeed, Holmes and Brandeis sometimes believed there was a clear and present danger, as they did in the *Schenck* case[10] from which the above quotation is taken. But the very fact of attempting to find some principle inherent in the Constitution implies a legal philosophy which is largely independent of the vagaries of social and political pressures prevailing at any one time.

In marked contrast, one of the most prominent jurists of the 1940s and 1950s, Felix Frankfurter, believed that the representatives of the American people – Congress and President – should be left to interpret the Constitution, the Court's involvement being confined to mediating disputes between the branches or between federal and state governments. Even then, Frankfurter argued, the Court should attempt to *balance* the various competing interests in society rather than search for some 'inherent principle' or 'higher meaning' behind the wording of the document. Clearly, a passive Court is implied by this approach, or one which steers clear of politics, letting representative institutions sort out conflict in society. The activism of Holmes and Brandeis and the passivity of Frankfurter represent two of the more coherent of a number of philosophical positions taken by the Court and the labels 'active' and 'passive' 'liberal' and 'conservative' usually correspond to the perceived philosophy of the Court at a particular time. We should not, however, be deceived into thinking of different Supreme Courts as representing distinct and coherent philosophies. To repeat, nine individuals make the decisions and each may vary quite dramatically in outlook.

10 *Schenck* v. *United States (1919)*.

Some Courts, then, have lacked an identifiable philosophy. More important, it is impossible to separate the decisions of the justices from the political and social environment in which they operate. The 'positivism' of Holmes and Brandeis with its search for a consistency and justice inherent in the Constitution, irrespective of political and social pressures, failed to dominate even the Court on which they sat, let alone be the main approach of subsequent Courts. Like any other political institution, the Court has to interact with society and polity. It is subject to a number of pressures and constraints. What makes the institution so interesting, however, is the mix of judicial philosophy and external constraint which has produced an ever-changing political role for the Court in American history. The remainder of this chapter will be devoted to studying this role, by analysing the constraints on the Court's power and in particular by asking whether the institution can be the equal of the other branches of government.

The Court and Political Power

There can be no doubting that Supreme Court decisions have political impact. From the momentous *Marbury* v. *Madison* decision in 1803 when, by declaring Section 13 of the 1789 Judiciary Act unconstitutional, Chief Justice John Marshall effectively established judicial review, through to the landmark civil rights cases of the last 30 years, the attention of public and polity alike has been riveted by the political implications of the Court's decisions. But as earlier suggested, this does not mean that these solemn judicial deliberations take place in isolation from society. On the contrary, many have argued that the Court rarely deviates from the prevailing weight of political or public opinion; that, in fact, its main function has been to legitimize dominant political influences, and when it has gone against these it has soon found itself in trouble of one sort or another. In one rather obvious sense this is true, for courts depend on their authority rather than naked power. They have no police force or army – or even bureaucrats – to enforce their decisions. For this they have to depend on the other branches of government. Perhaps the most dramatic example of the dangers inherent in fundamentally disagreeing with the other branches of government was the 1857 *Dred Scott* case. In this the Court effectively declared unworkable the 1820 Missouri compromise which gave Blacks free status in those states and territories in the Louisiana Purchase North of the Missouri. If Blacks were to revert to slave status in these Northern territories, a forced extension of the cuture and values of the South was implied, a change completely unacceptable to Lincoln and the dominant Republican Party. The decision was never enforced because the Civil War soon followed, as did the 13th and 14th Amendments which specifically granted equal legal status to all citizens. For the other branches of government simply to ignore the Court is the most serious challenge to its power, for once ignored, its authority and legitimacy are undetermined. Without these it loses all influence. After the Civil War the Court did, in fact, soon reassert its authority and it has never been seriously undermined since. But there have been ebbs and flows of judicial power, crises of confidence and periods of intense controversy. A useful way to study these is to document the constraints or limitations on the court's power, or to record those instances when the scope and substance of judicial decisions have, in one way or another, been circumscribed.

Constitutional amendment

Amending the Constitution to overturn the Court is the ultimate legal weapon available to the other branches and to the states. As we know, however, amendments have been few and far between and just four have been employed to overrule the Court. In one of these – the 26th Amendment ratified in 1971 to extend the vote to 18-year-olds – the Court's *Oregon* v. *Mitchell* (1970) decision was overturned. Another (the 11th Amendment which prohibited a citizen of one state to sue the government of another state) has passed into historical obscurity.[11] Only two amendments stand out as changes crucial to preserve the integrity of the union and the smooth running of government – the 14th Amendment which overturned *Dred Scott*, and the 16th Amendment sanctioning a graduated federal income tax. Ratified in 1913 when the need for increased defence spending was widely perceived as necessary, the 16th Amendment overturned the 1895 *Pollock* v. *Farmers' Loan and Trust* decision which had declared a graduated federal income tax unconstitutional.

Congressional control

The Constitution grants remarkably wide discretion to Congress over

11 Although the Supreme Court decision which sanctioned such cases, *Chisolm* v. *Georgia* (1793), aroused great controversy at the time.

the composition and organization of the federal judiciary. Article 3 states, quite simply: 'The judicial power of the United States shall be vested in one Supreme Court, and in such inferior Courts as the Congress may from time to time ordain and establish.' So Congress has the power to determine the size and administration of the federal machinery of justice. Additionally, the Constitution specifically gives to Congress discretion over the Court's appellate jurisdiction and implicitly, at least, over the number of justices and when the Court should actually sit. Only rarely, however, has the Congress exercised these very substantial discretionary powers. Easily the most important item of legislation in these areas is the 1789 Judiciary Act which established the Courts' power to review state court decisions denying federal rights to citizens. Apart from this, Congress has regularly increased the number of federal judges and courts (the latest increases in District and Appeals Court judges occurred in 1978) in line with population and caseload increases, and the number of Supreme Court justices fluctuated between six and ten until 1870, since when it has remained at nine. During the 1930s, President Roosevelt attempted to increase the size of the Court to overcome opposition to his New Deal legislation, but Congress was disinclined to tinker with the Court in this way (see pp. 257–8 below). By the 1930s the figure of nine justices was regarded as almost a part of the Constitution.

If Congress has been reluctant to alter the Court's composition and jurisdiction, it has shown little hesitation in reversing Court decisions via statutory reversals, or legislating to invalidate a particular judicial interpretation of federal law. Between 1946 and 1968, for example, some 111 roll-call votes in Congress reversed Court statutory interpretations. Few of these were of great import, however, and of course Congress cannot touch those decisions which are based on *constitutional* interpretation.

Perhaps Congress' most important function in relation to the Supreme Court is as a forum for public opinion. Senators and Representatives quite frequently openly attack the Court or even introduce bills designed to curb its power. During the 1950s and 1960s for example, Southerners incensed at the Court's desegregation decisions, and conservatives at its civil liberties and re-appointment decisions, regularly did both. More recently, the 'pro-life' lobby in Congress has attempted to change the law on abortion, following the Court's liberal *Roe* v. *Wade* decision in 1973. Indeed, moral outrage at Court decisions on abortion, obscenity and school prayers inspired no less than 30 bills designed to curb the court's jurisdiction during 1980 and 1981. While these attempts may fail, we cannot claim that constant attacks in the national legislature have no effect on the justices. In some contexts they may well influence the Court, especially if the justices are effectively isolated in their policy position, as was the case in 1937 when few sources of power or influence in American society sided with the Court. Finally, the Senate has to confirm all nominations made to the judicial branch by Presidents. As will be discussed below, this is a power the Senate has used with increased vigour in recent years.

Presidential control

Presidents have two main means whereby they can influence the Court. First and most important, via the appointment power; and second, by appealing to public or Congressional opinion to reinforce their opposition to or support for a particular position. All federal judges are political appointees and the vast majority nominated by a President share his political party label if not his total political and social philosophy. In the case of District and, to a lesser extent, Appeals Court nominations, Presidents used to be guided by the advice and influence of the Senate (via the confirmation power) but also by state and local party leaders and dignitaries. Today, however, both lower court and Supreme Court nominations are very much a matter of Presidential preference. Broadly speaking, Presidents have appointed justices whose political views are similar to their own. This does not mean to say that Presidents deliberately manipulate an appointment in order to change the complexion of the Courts – although often they do – nor does it mean that they are always successful in their attempts to change the Courts' outlook and philosophy.

As far as the Supreme Court is concerned, they are circumscribed by chance, for although a vacancy on the Court has on average come up about every two years, some Presidents have been denied the privilege of receiving their 'quota' of two nominations. In his four years as President, poor Jimmy Carter made no appointments, while in his first three years in office Richard Nixon made four. Interestingly, it was President Carter who explicitly stated an intention to remove political considerations from the appointment of all federal judges, although as far as the Supreme Court was concerned his pledge went untested.

On three occasions in recent history, Presidents have been given and taken the opportunity to try and change the political complexion of the Court. Roosevelt did so after 1937, Nixon after 1969, and Reagan after 1981. In Roosevelt's case, the Court had repeatedly struck down New Deal legislation on the grounds that it was an unconstitutional exercise of the Interstate Commerce Clause and violated 'substantive' due process under the 14th Amendment. In the face of the possible collapse of his economic recovery programme, Roosevelt attempted to 'pack' the Court by asking Congress to increase the number of justices by one for every existing justice over 70 years old, up to a maximum of 15. His strategy was clear – to tip the ideological balance of the Court away from the so-called 'Four Horsemen of Conservatism' (Justices Butler, McReynolds, Sutherland and Van Devanter) towards a more liberal stance. He failed in the Court-packing plan largely because by the time it reached the critical stage in a not too enthusiastic Congress one of the conservatives, Van Devanter, had retired. Roosevelt then proceeded to fill this and other vacancies, which came thick and fast during the next few years, with 'New Dealers' or Justices sympathetic to an enhanced federal role in economy and society. He was remarkably successful. Almost all of his nine appointees toed the New Deal line and the Court kept well out of economic affairs during the 1937–53 period.[12]

The second quite dramatic instance of political use of the appointment power occurred during the first two years of the Nixon administration. One of Richard Nixon's 1968 campaign pledges had been to replace the liberals of the Warren Court with 'strict constructionists' or conservatives less prone to the advancement of civil rights and liberties characteristic of the Warren era. He was given a golden opportunity to do just this, for four vacancies occurred during the 1969–71 period. One of these was for Chief Justice, and the President lost no time in nominating Warren Burger, Chief Judge of the District of Columbia Court of Appeals to the position. Burger, a conservative Republican from Minnesota, remained Chief Justice until 1986.[13] Nixon's next two nominees ran into serious trouble in the Senate. Only rarely in the twentieth century have Supreme Court nominations been rejected, and it is a remarkable testimony to Nixon's political insensitivity that his second and third nominations, Clement Haynsworth and Harrold Carswell were voted down in the Upper Chamber. Both were undistinguished as jurists and Carswell, in particular, had acquired a dubious record on civil rights in the Southern courts from which he hailed. Their

12　And in many respects the Court still keeps out of major economic controversies, especially those relating to federalism (see chapter 4).

13　The Chief Justice position became vacant quite fortuitously for Nixon. President Johnson had nominated Abe Fortas as Warren's successor, but during the Senate hearings into Fortas's suitability it was revealed that, among other things, in 1966 he had received a $20,000 fee from a millionaire who at the time was being investigated (and later was convicted) for fraud. See Bob Woodward and Scott Armstrong, *The Brethren: Inside the Supreme Court*, New York, Simon and Schuster, 1979, Prologue.

rejection illustrates well the simple fact that Presidential discretion over appointments is limited. A President may nominate a conservative or a liberal, but not an incompetent or a bigot. A Senate judiciary committee well versed by the American Bar Association, leading jurists and interested groups will see to that. Richard Nixon did, however, succeed with his next three appointments, Harry Blackmun, Lewis Powell and William Rhenquist. Rhenquist was a solid conservative (but a respected jurist) while the others were known at least as moderately conservative.

The Reagan experience was different again. Sandra Day O'Connor, nominated in 1981, was a respected judge who was chosen largely because she was a woman. A conservative, but no ideologue, O'Connor replaced the moderate Potter Stewart, an Eisenhower appointee. In 1986, when Chief Justice Burger retired, Reagan elevated William Rhenquist to the Chief Justiceship and nominated Judge Antonio Scalia to fill the vacancy. Both moves were highly strategic. Rhenquist was known as a conservative on all major questions. His nomination inspired considerable opposition in the Senate but he was eventually confirmed. Scalia was also known to favour the Reagan agenda, but his nomination met with little resistance.

These controversies pale into insignificance compared with the nomination of Robert Bork following the resignation of Justice Lewis Powell in June 1987. Powell had long held the pivotal vote against the New Right agenda favoured by the Administration involving such issues as affirmative action and abortion. Robert Bork's tenure on the Court of Appeals was marked by a 'strict constructionism' or a consistently conservative interpretation of the Constitution. During the lengthy nomination proceedings Bork worked hard to convince the Senate Judiciary Committee that he was in fact a centrist, rather than an ideologue of the right. It was this inconsistency which helped produce his eventual defeat by the widest margin ever (58 to 42). Reagan's next nominee Douglas Ginsburg was also a conservative but was obliged to withdraw following revelations that he had once smoked marijuana while in law school. Eventually, the Senate confirmed the nomination of Anthony Kennedy, a moderate and pragmatic conservative from California.

At the Appeal and District Court level, Ronald Reagan pursued a more overtly political strategy than any previous president. As one commentator[14] put it: 'The striking feature about Reagan's lower-court judges is that they are predominantly young white upper-class males,

14   David M. O'Brien, 'The Reagan judges: his most enduring legacy?' in Charles O. Jones (ed.), *The Reagan Legacy: Promise and Performance*, Chatham, New Jersey, Chatham House, 1988, p. 75.

with prior judicial or prosecutional experience and reputations for legal conservatism established on the bench in law schools, or in politics.' By appointing large numbers of conservatives to the lower courts, President Reagan almost certainly changed the nature of lower court decisions and therefore the sort of cases which are appealed to the Supreme Court.

There can be no doubt that the Burger Court was very different from the openly liberal Warren Court and that the Rhenquist Court will in turn prove more conservative than the Burger Court. Personnel changes partly account for these shifts, but Presidents can never be sure that, once appointed, a justice will fulfil expectations. Appointed for life to the most respected forum in the land, many justices change their political philosophies once on the Court. Such was the case with Earl Warren, one-time conservative Republican governor of California, expected by his patron President Eisenhower to continue the self restraint of the Stone and Vinson Courts. In civil rights and liberties and re-apportionment he did just the opposite. And although the Nixon appointees generally moved the Court to the right they did not do so in a coherent and consistent manner. Liberal civil rights and liberties decisions did not suddenly cease in 1971, even if they have become infrequent and interspersed with more conservative judgements.[15]

Public and political opinion

So the appointment power must by definition be limited because, even when Presidents have made appointments, they have no direct control over the justices once they are on the Court. They can, of course, appeal to Congress (as with the Court-packing plan) or to public opinion, but once this happens the independent influence of the President is lost. As we noted in earlier chapters, public opinion is hard to define and almost impossible to measure. Scratch beneath the surface and what most commentators mean by public opinion is a particular configuration of political power, expressed either through representative institutions or through organized groups. If we accept this approach, we can confidently state that only very rarely in American history has the Court challenged a dominant climate of opinion. Between the Civil War and 1937, for example, the Court acquired the reputation for defending the

15 See Woodward and Armstrong, *The Brethren*; also Herman Schwartz (ed.), *The Burger Years: Rights and Wrongs in the Supreme Court, 1969–1986*, Harmondsworth, Middlesex, Penguin, 1988.

burgeoning capitalist interests of the period by striking down both state and federal legislation designed to regulate industry or protect workers from exploitation. The regulation of interstate commerce did not, the Court argued, extend to such things as federal laws regulating child labour. Or, more importantly, entitlement of 'due process of law' under the 14th Amendment did not extend to *state* attempts to regulate industrial and commercial life. It applied directly only to federal–citizen relationships. As a result, between 1900 and 1937 some 184 decisions invalidated state regulatory provisions.[16] To be fair, a number of state laws were also upheld during these years, but the general stance of the Court was anti-regulation or anti-government 'interference'. Crucially, however, so generally was public opinion, at least until 1929. Most Presidents, Congress and many state legislatures accepted the Supreme Court's judgements with relative equanimity. It was not until the coming of the Great Depression in the early 1930s that the climate of opinion changed dramatically. And when the Court began regularly to strike down federal New Deal legislation it became politically isolated. Within two years, and following intense pressure from unions, Congress and President,[17] the Court had made its 'switch in time that saved nine' and thereafter followed rather than led the other branches in the general area of economic policy.

During the 1940s and up to about 1957, the Court was deferential to Congress and President on questions of national security. In case after case the Court accepted the restrictions placed on citizens by the 1940 Smith Act, the 1950 McCarren Act and in the case of the Japanese Americans by executive *fiat*.[18] Not until the late 1950s when public fears about communist subversion began to subside did the Court begin to relax the restrictions on communists and others perceived to be subversive.

Even in civil rights it would be difficult to argue that the Court was acting in isolation from broader political and public opinion. *Brown* v. *Board of Education*, the landmark 1954 decision, which argued that racially separate facilities in education and other facilities were inherently unequal, may have been highly unpopular in the South, but it was

16   Quoted in Hodder-Williams, *The Politics of the US Supreme Court*, p. 138.
17   See Beth, *Politics*, chapter 6.
18   The Smith Act made it unlawful to advocate the overthrow of the US Government and the McCarren Act required 'subversive organizations' to register with the Subversive Activities Control Board. In 1942 West Coast Americans of Japanese origin (many of them citizens) were arbitrarily interned in concentration camps by the Governor of California (ironically Earl Warren, later the champion of individual freedom on the Court) as a threat to internal security. The Court failed to hear the cases arising from this until 1944 and then argued them on procedural rather than constitutional grounds.

welcomed in the North by many members of Congress, and was not unpopular with the President. What can be claimed for *Brown*, is that it helped push opinion towards the de-segregation of the South – although enforcement problems apart (of which more later) it was not until 1964 that Congress, goaded on by a determined and proselytizing President, passed the first major federal civil rights act.

The apportionment decisions of the early 1960s, extending the principle of representation according to mathematical equality, first to state legislatures and then to Congressional districts, were probably more widely unpopular with politicians than the civil rights decisions. But they were not unpopular with the public, most of whom stood to gain from a removal of the bias in representation towards rural areas. And how could state and national politicians justify the gross inequities that had accumulated over time? This is not to deny that the Court was a genuine innovator in this area,[19] however, as it was in the realm of criminal defendants' rights. Starting with *Mapp* v. *Ohio* in 1961 and continuing through to Earl Warren's resignation in 1969, the Court handed down a remarkable succession of decisions granting defendants the right to state-provided counsel, access to police files, extending the freedom from unlawful search and seizure and generally providing much greater protection to arrest persons. Coming as they did during the disruptions of the 1960s, these changes were welcomed only by what eventually was a diminishing band of liberals.

Undoubtedly, the Warren Court moved well ahead of public opinion in this area. Perhaps predictably, the Burger Court did not continue the crusading spirit of the Warren era. In both civil rights and liberties it was careful to qualify some of the more dramatic decisions of the 1960s. In one sense, the Burger Court was placed in a much more difficult position compared with the Warren Court, for it had to clarify what were highly complex and difficult questions raised but not settled by Warren. Hence in school desegregation, the thorny problem of distinguishing between *de jure* or legally sanctioned and *de facto* or naturally evolving segregation emerged as the main civil rights issue. Generally, the Court argued that a past pattern of *de jure* segregation should be reversed via busing, but not (as generally prevails in the North) if the segregation is *de facto* in nature. Similarly, on the use of other affirmative action measures such as quotas, the Court had to grapple with the problem of choosing between *individual* rights under the 14th Amendment and the *collective* rights of Blacks and other

19 It is interesting to note that the Burger Court modified the original apportionment decisions to allow community of interest as well as population to determine the size of districts.

minorities who have sought redress for a pattern of past discrimination. Individual rights generally prevailed. In criminal procedural rights, the Court limited the application of the 'exclusionary rule' or the admissibility of evidence culled during unlawful searches and seizures. And in a number of other areas the protection afforded arrested persons was reduced.

Often the Court cannot predict what the impact of its decisions on public opinion will be. The Burger Court, for example, handed down a decision on abortion in 1973 (*Roe* v. *Wade*) which looked like a model of careful, pluralistic judicial decision making. The Court effectively outlawed all state laws which prohibited abortion during the first three months of pregnancy, liberalized them during the next three months and banned abortions during the last ten weeks. This apparently reasonable compromise has, however, been seized by the pro-life anti-abortion special interest groups and branded as a further example of the federal courts undermining public morals and the sanctity of family life. Little doubt exists that the decision precipitated debate and political controversy on an issue whose salience increased enormously during the 1970s and 1980s. The Court's decisions on capital punishment which although laying down pretty strict guidelines have effectively left to the states the final decision on when (and how) a person should be executed, have also aroused great controversy. In both instances, debate on the issues have been passed on to the broader political stage. But they have hardly left the judicial policy agenda. Controversy on where individual rights begin and end must by necessity concern the courts, and given governments' intimate involvement both in granting and denying rights to citizens (indeed in exercising a power over life and death in the two examples cited above), the courts' involvement must also continue.

We can conclude that only rarely has the Court consciously moved against prevailing public and political opinion, and when it has done so, it has not been for long. Two important qualifications have to be applied to this generalization. First, the Court has been reluctant to challenge or has never for long challenged a programme or policy supported by the other branches, and which is perceived to be crucial to the integrity of the union (the status of slavery in the North), national security in wartime or 'emergency' conditions ('subversion' in the two World Wars and afterwards) or to the running of the economy (the New Deal legislation). When, however, there is no consensus on a policy – especially when Congress and President are in serious disagreement – then the Court plays a central role in arbitrating the conflict. We have two dramatic examples of the Court playing just such a role in recent history. In 1952 President Truman seized the nation's steel mills on the grounds that industrial disputes were undermining production and the Korean War effort. The Court quickly condemned the seizure as an unconstitutional infringement on the legislative powers of Congress. In 1974, the Court declared that executive privilege did not protect President Nixon's taped conversations which could be used in the courts and Congress to investigate the Watergate wrong-doings. On both occasions Congress was unsympathetic to the President's position and, significantly, so was broader public opinion.

More recently, the Burger Court showed little reluctance to make deliberations affecting the separation of powers. In *Buckley* v. *Valeo* (1976) some key features of the 1974 Campaign Finance Act were struck down (see chapter 9, pp. 182–3). Later, in *Immigration and Naturaliz-ation Service* v. *Chadha* (1983), the legislative veto was declared unconstitutional. Following this decision, the capacity of Congress to control the discretionary powers given to executive agencies was greatly curtailed. In 1985, the Court effectively established that Congress and the President, rather than the Court and the Constitution, should be the final arbiter of the relationship between the federal government and the states (*Garcia* v. *San Antonio Metropolitan Transit Authority*). Finally, in 1986 the Court declared the mandatory spending cuts required by the Gramm–Rudman–Hollings Deficit Reduction Act an unconstitutional violation of the separation of powers.

The second qualification to the Court's deference to prevailing public and political opinion is that when it does challenge them in areas involving the behaviour of myriad individuals, rather than a few institutions or political leaders, it tends to experience serious problems in enforcing its decisions or in predicting their precise impact on public opinion.

Lack of enforcement powers

As noted earlier, without their own police force, army or bureaucracy, the courts cannot enforce their decisions unless their authority is accepted by those who do exercise coercive powers. Moreover, the Supreme Court depends on lower courts (federal and state) to implement its decisions and these may not always interpret or accept the Court's judgements in an unambiguous fashion. The most celebrated examples of judicial recalcitrance and obstruction involved the enforcement of civil rights in the South. Following *Brown* v. *Board's* 1954 directive that Southern schools should desegregate 'with all deliberate speed', Southern District courts were assigned the job of enforcing the order.

Appointed by Presidents on the advice of local politicians and party faithfuls, District judges reflect local conditions, interests – and prejudices. Very few of the Southern District judges of the 1950s and 1960s were integrationists and most resisted – mainly through delays of one sort or another – the order to desegregate. In fact, not until 1969 in the *Alexander* v. *Holmes County Board of Education* decision – some 15 years after *Brown* – did the Supreme Court finally make it mandatory to desegregate immediately,[20] and by then, of course, the Court was supported by the not inconsiderable weight of the 1964 Civil Rights Act with its array of compliance and enforcement procedures.

More rarely, a state or local political actor may openly defy a Court order as happened in Little Rock, Arkansas, in 1957 when Governor Faubus used the local militia forcibly to prevent Black children from entering a high school. Only the eventual use of federal troops on the instruction of President Eisenhower enabled the Black children to enter the school. Much more common is evasion of the directives of the Supreme Court, not only by other courts or by outright defiance, but through ignorance, deception or the simple fact that complete enforcement is technically impossible to achieve. Such has been the case with criminal law decisions like *Miranda* and *Gideon* which laid down strict procedures for the interrogation of suspects. As research has shown, arrested persons often do not know their rights, police officers are frequently ignorant of the correct procedures, and even when informed can compromise them. Similarly, the decisions of the early 1960s outlawing special prayers and bible reading in public schools (*Engale* v. *Vitale*, *Abington School District* v. *Schempp*) as infringements of the 1st Amendment's freedom of religion clause, have proved very difficult to enforce. Indeed, although neither the Burger nor the Rhenquist Courts had (by 1989) seriously compromised the principles laid down in *Engale* and *Schempp*, both were under considerable pressure to do so.

Conclusion

It is often argued that the greatest limitation on the political power of the Court is 'judicial self restraint' or a conscious decision by the justices to avoid the political thicket by deferring to the other branches (or to public opinion) rather than causing great controversy by departing from

20   For an excellent account of the tactics of Southern District judges see Jack Peltason, *58 Lonely Men*, New York, Harcourt Brace Jovanovich, 1961.

the dominant opinion. Our earlier discussions suggest strongly that this is true, although self restraint is more a matter of political common sense than, as some jurists have argued, something which can be justified solely on philosophical grounds. Judges may search for a 'higher principle' inherent in the Constitution, or they may be convinced that government 'interference' in the economy is always a bad thing. Sooner or later, however, they have to take cognizance of the political and social environment in which decisions are made. As we noted, the Supreme Court is seriously constrained by this environment; it is not an institution apart from politics, but one which is an organic part of the polity and society.

If the Court rarely challenges the dominant political forces in society, what use then is the institution of judicial review? From our discussion we can identify three crucial functions: (a) The Court arbitrates between federal and state law. In terms of the stability and integrity of the union this is undoubtedly its most important function; (b) Judicial review provides the Court with an apparently neutral point of reference (the Constitution) for arbitrating between the different branches of government – although historically this has tended to work only when one branch (the executive) is relatively isolated from Congressional and public opinion; (c) Judicial review can help defend individual freedoms under the Bill of Rights and 14th Amendment. Of course, there have been numerous occasions when the Court has clearly failed to defend such freedoms, as with the internment of the Japanese Americans in 1942. But – and this is the strongest argument in favour of judicial review under bills of rights – the legislative and executive branches would have denied these freedoms even in the absence of judicial review. Its presence is usually beneficial, therefore, in the sense that when it deviates from the other branches it does so by favouring the individual. As the civil rights and especially civil liberties cases of the 1950s and 1960s demonstrate, this can involve quite radical, if sometimes temporary, departures from prevailing political and public opinion.

Finally, how has the Court responded to the much more fragmented polity and society characteristic of the 1970s and 1980s? In a word, uncertainly. As suggested, the Burger Court had to confront questions involving moral absolutes where *any* compromise would have been unacceptable to some. Issue politics, combined with the increasingly technical nature of cases, can produce a situation where the Court hands down decisions which are highly contentious. Issue politics produces odd, unpredictable political coalitions where it is almost impossible to please everybody. The Court's decisions on abortions and capital punishment, for example, involved issues where the subsequent lines of opposition and support were complex and unpredictable. In some other areas – campaign finance for instance – the technicalities of the question are so formidable that the Court has produced decisions whose consequences have been unexpected, and perhaps undesirable. In fact, as mentioned, the Burger Court proved to be quite active on political questions generally, including such issues as federalism and the proper constitutional limits to legislative power. The Rhenquist Court, whose conservatism is likely to be reinforced by any Bush nominations, will face the same dilemmas, and will, above all, find it difficult to make conservative decisions on such questions as abortion and school prayers in the face of a public opinion which is deeply divided.

Throughout all these changes the Supreme Court and the whole judiciary strives to perform what is perhaps its most vital function – the legitimization of the system in the eyes of the citizenry. In the words of Felix Frankfurter:

> A gentle and generous philosopher noted the other day a growing 'intuition' on the part of the masses that all judges, in lively controversies, are 'more or less prejudiced.' But between the 'more or less' lies the whole kingdom of the mind, the difference between the 'more or less' are the triumphs of disinterestedness, they are the aspirations we call justice . . . The basic considerations in the vitality of any system of law is confidence in this proximate purity of its process. Corruption from venality is hardly more damaging than a widespread belief of corrosion through partisanship. Our judicial system is absolutely dependent upon a popular belief that it is as untainted in its workings as the finite limitations of disciplined human minds and feelings make possible.[21]

To perform this function adequately the Court cannot deviate too much from the mainstream of political opinion, a fact which has not been lost on many recent justices, including most on the present Court.

Further Reading

The best single introduction is Henry J. Abraham, *The Judicial Process*, New York, Oxford University Press, 1980. A good non-American interpretation of the Supreme Court is Richard Hodder-Williams, *The Politics of the US Supreme Court*, London, Allen & Unwin, 1980. For

---

21 Quoted in David F. Forte, *The Supreme Court in American Politics*, Lexington, Mass., D. C. Heath, 1972, pp. 93–4.

a vivid journalists' account of how the Court operates, see Bob Woodward and Scott Armstrong, *The Brethren: Inside the Supreme Court*, New York, Simon and Schuster, 1979. Good up-to-date analyses of the Burger Court are Vincent Blasi (ed.), *The Burger Court: The Revolution that Wasn't*, New Haven, Yale University Press, 1983, and Herman Schwartz (ed.), *The Burger Years: Rights and Wrongs in the Supreme Court, 1969–1986*, Harmondsworth, Middlesex, and New York, Penguin, 1988. For a critique of the Burger Court, see Norman Dorsen (ed.), *Our Endangered Rights*, New York, Pavilion, 1984.

13

The Style and Substance of Policy Making

The Reagan Revolution required a frontal assault on the American welfare state . . . It required an immediate end to welfare for the able-bodied poor.

Peter Gottschalk

Today the administration is proposing a national recovery plan to reverse the debilitating combination of sustained inflation and economic distress which continues to face the American economy. Were we to stay with existing policies, the results would be readily predictable: a rising government presence in the economy, more inflation, stagnating productivity, and higher unemployment . . . The program we have developed will break that cycle of negative expectations. It will revitalize economic growth, renew optimism and confidence, and rekindle the nation's entrepreneurial instincts and creativity.

Ronald Reagan

Historically, the test for American statesmanship should therefore be not how long it manages to cling to a deteriorating and overextended hegemony, but how well those liberal domestic and international arrangements it has fostered can adapt themselves to the stresses of the more plural order. In other words, the real test of American statesmanship is whether the postwar world system can survive the relative decline of American Power.

David Calleo, *The Imperious Economy*

It would be easy to infer from earlier chapters that decision making in the American political system is so fragmented and dispersed that the resulting policies are simply not amenable to simple characterization;

that the open and pluralistic nature of the system produces a politics of confusion and unpredictability. While there is no doubt a great deal of truth to this, it would be wrong to leave the analysis without enquiring further into the nature and consequences of policy making in the United States. The purpose of this last chapter is, therefore, to add perspective and balance to earlier conclusions by examining how policy making has developed in three important areas – social, economic and foreign policy. Discussion will particularly focus on the following three questions:

1   To what extent do policy systems differ in style and substance one from the other?
2   How does policy develop over time? How do changes in adminis-tration and the domestic and international environment change the ways in which policy is formulated and implemented?
3   Related is the crucial question of the role that political institutions and processes play in the policy system. To what extent do institutional relationships mould public policies as opposed to broader structural forces in economy and society? This question is important because if institutions' independent role is limited, then so is the potential for institutional reform. In other words, it may be that, whatever the institutional context, governing a large complex industrial society such as the United States would be a difficult business.

Obviously we cannot provide definitive answers to these questions, and obviously our discussion of each of the policy areas must, of necessity, be brief. Because we can only touch on the main issues involved, references to more detailed analyses will be proved when appropriate.

Social Policy in America: Self Reliance and State Dependence

Governments have always been more reluctant to intervene in the general area of social policy in the US than they have in Western Europe. Indeed, it was not until the 1930s that the federal government laid down a framework of law providing for welfare and social security benefits for the poor and the old. Even then, the extent and level of welfare coverage was limited. Contributory earnings-related pensions applied only to certain kinds of workers. Welfare was restricted to families with dependent children (effectively mothers and children) and was distributed through the states on a matching federal–state basis. As a result, great disparities in the provision of welfare from state to state developed – a disparity which remains to this day. Housing and health, moreover, were not considered a legitimate part of federal social policy until the 1960s, and since then housing subsidies have been cut to the point where they are no longer a significant part of social policy. Only education has been universally accepted as a legitimate part of the social policy agenda. But until very recently it was always local and state governments rather than the federal government which provided for elementary, secondary and higher education.

The roots of the American antipathy to anything but limited and selective social benefits are not difficult to identify. They lie in the strongly held notions of self reliance which have been discussed a number of times in earlier chapters. By the 1970s, however, some areas of social policy had become established as proper and legitimate roles for the federal government. Almost all of these involved earnings-related social security benefits for widows, widowers, the disabled, the blind and, above all, the old. Most Americans now consider these benefits as rights, not handouts by the government. There is, in fact, a sizeable 'handout' element in the social security programme, as benefits often bear little resemblance to what has been paid in. In addition, Medicare, the programme providing medical aid for the old, is also now considered a right, even though the re-distributive element in the programme is very considerable. Finally, many Americans, even those on the right, look more benignly on the welfare programme for the old (Supplementary Security Income) than they do on other welfare programmes. Clearly the elderly are given a special status as a group who cannot be expected to help themselves.

The same sympathy is not, paradoxically, extended to children in poor families who, although provided with a range of welfare benefits, do not fare as well as do the old. One reason for this is the problem of ensuring that benefits received by parents do actually reach needy children. Because of this and the belief among many politicians that many of those on welfare can and should be capable of supporting a family through work, the two main welfare programmes, Food Stamps and Aid for Families with Dependent Children, have always been politically vulnerable. Similarly, medical care for the poor (Medicaid) is less well protected than Medicare.

As can be seen from table 13.1, most of the major social policy bills were enacted during the New Deal and the Great Society period of the 1960s. Since then, there have been numerous amendments to the original legislation, but no fundamental reforms. In fact reform attempts have come from left and right, with the most recent assault on the system from the right being led by the Reagan administration during 1981 and 1982. Few question that what is essentially an *ad hoc*, inefficient and inadequate range of benefits is in need of reform. What then accounts

Table 13.1   Major federal social policy legislation, 1935–1971

1935	Social Security Act – established the basic old age, survivors and disabled insurance programme, as well as unemployment insurance and the main welfare programme, Aid for Families with Dependent Children (AFDC)
1937	Public Housing Act – provided limited grants for the construction of municipal housing.
1964	Food stamps – the provision of stamps which the poor can exchange for food
1965	Creation of Medicare (medical care for the old) and Medicaid (medical care for the poor)
1965	Elementary and Secondary Education Act – federal aid for local school authorities in disadvantaged areas
1968	Housing Act – the provision of housing subsidies for the owners and renters of low and moderate income housing
1971	Supplementary Security Income (SSI) – the provision of welfare benefits for older citizens

for the repeated failure to rationalize the system? Both institutional and ideological explanations can be used to answer this question. Let us look at each of these in turn.

Federalism   As far as the welfare programmes are concerned, any reform would have to rationalize the greatly varying benefit levels presently applicable in the 50 states. Such an exercise would prove expensive unless benefit levels in the richer states were to drop in order to pay for higher benefits in the poorer states. Such a strategy would be politically unacceptable. Reforming the 'welfare mess', therefore, would cost a lot of money. Coordinating benefits across programmes would also prove very difficult. AFDC, Food Stamps and Medicaid as well as myriad educational, social service and housing benefits would require rationalization.

Social security and the electoral connection   As earlier suggested, social security has a special status as a protected set of measures in the United States. In 1982 President Reagan attempted to cut benefits but was unable to do so because of fierce opposition from Congress and public opinion generally. Old age pensions are easily the largest item in the social policy budget (table 13.2), and, as entitlement programmes, are effectively uncontrollable. Increasingly, however, benefits for the old which have little or no contributory element (SSI, Medicare and Supplementary Medicare) are also electorally sacrosanct.

Table 13.2 Federal outlays on major social programs in fiscal year 1986 (millions of dollars)

Social insurance, retirement, and disability	
Old-age and survivors insurance	179,572
Disability insurance	20,243
Unemployment	
Unemployment compensation	25,137
Means-tested programs	
Supplemental security income	10,345
Aid to families with dependent children	9,877
Low-income home energy assistance	2,046
Veterans' pensions	3,874
Earned income tax credit	1,415
Nutrition	
Food stamps	11,619
Child nutrition programs	3,820
Supplemental nutrition for women, infants, and children (WIC)	1,578
Miscellaneous	
Coal miners' disability (black lung)	1,612
Health care	
Medicare hospital insurance	49,685
Medicare supplementary medical insurance	26,217
Grants to states for medicaid	24,995

Source: R. Kent Weaver, 'Social Policy in the Reagan Era' in B. B. Kymlicka and Jean V. Matthews (eds), *The Reagan Revolution?* Chicago, The Dorsey Press, 1988, table 1.

The continuing importance of self reliance While the old and disabled are protected, younger, able-bodied citizens are under increasing pressure to take jobs and support themselves. During 1988 Congress passed a new welfare bill designed to force mothers with young children (easily the largest category of welfare recipient) either to take a job or to undergo some sort of job retraining. Opponents of the bill pointed out, however, that this would result in reduced incomes for some women. It would also precipitate a crisis in child care, which is almost entirely a private sector service in the United States. Ronald Reagan's 1981 and 1982 reforms were much more Draconian, involving as they did a return of all welfare benefits to the states. The upshot of this reform would have been to increase the disparities between the states further. As was explained in chapter 4, this New Federalism plan was to come to nothing. In spite of this failure, the level of welfare benefits was reduced during the Reagan years. The President was unable to turn the clock back to the 1920s, but he was able to arrest the steep rise in real benefits characteristic of the 1960s and 1970s.

The Bush administration will have as difficult a job dealing with the social policy agenda as any recent administration. The number of dependent citizens (the old and the poor) is increasing rather than decreasing, and should there be another economic downturn, the total would increase further. In such an event, Congress would be under great electoral and interest group pressure to maintain benefit levels. At the same time, whatever the state of the economy, the elderly will always be a vocal and powerful pressure group for the maintenance and increase in the real value of pensions and medical benefits. As will be discussed below, this combination of pressures does little to help Presidents solve the problem of the budget deficit.

Managing Economic Change

As recently as 20 years ago, a section on economic policy in a textbook on American politics would not have been considered necessary. Today it is essential. Not since the 1930s have economic issues dominated the policy agenda as they do now. Abroad, America's standing has changed in a new and often hostile international economic order. At home, the budget and foreign trade deficits have become perennial problems. It hardly needs stressing that the state of the economy is vitally important, not only for the economic role of governments in society and the ways in which they tax citizens and allocate expenditure, but also for the health of the polity. Small wonder, then, that economic policy has come to dominate the agenda of the 1970s and 1980s. Governments, moreover, are now irrevocably involved in economic affairs. Some 33 per cent of Gross Domestic Product is accounted for by government expenditure; federal regulation of industrial and commerical affairs from environmental protection to anti-monopoly law is widespread; and by manipulating aggregate levels of expenditure and taxation and altering the supply of money in the economy, all federal governments now accept the need to 'manage' the economy. Regulation has been discussed elsewhere (chapter 10), and this section's aim is to study economic management policies and in particular to identify those forces which shape the economic policy-making agenda.

State and economy in the United States

As chapter 2 emphasized, the traditional view of the United States is of a country where the state plays a relatively minor role. In contrast to the burgeoning welfare states and mixed economies of Europe, convention has it that Americans prefer market to public mechanisms to distribute goods and services in society. By most simple quantitative measures this view has some validity. The United States is low on scales measuring the percentage of GNP accounted for by public expenditure and of taxation's share of GNP. Note also, however, that America is closer to such countries as France, Germany and Canada than it is to Japan, so we might be better advised to label Japan rather than the United States as the 'exception'. And although the trend in expenditures has been upwards, there has been no dramatic change since the late 1950s, the increase being from about 27 to 33 per cent of GNP. Of course if a longer time span is taken, then the growth of public expenditure has been dramatic. In 1930 the percentage of GNP accounted for by public expenditure was less than 10 per cent. Much of the increase since then is a result of massively enhanced defence spending and, since the early 1960s, of the partial replacement of defence expenditure with spending on a range of domestic programmes (figure 13.1).

Whatever the relative position of the USA, the sheer size of the government budgets should not be underestimated. In 1988 the federal government alone spent over $1000 billion, and total expenditures of all governments came to over $1400 billion. As table 13.3 shows, the gap between this expenditure and income – the federal debt – has been increasing in recent years, so that by the mid-1980s the size of the deficit had become the number one economic issue. As in every other developed economy American governments – and particularly the federal government – have enormous potential power over economic activity. By increasing spending and lowering taxation the economy can be stimulated. Conversely lower spending and higher taxes can lower the level of economic activity. Used in this way, fiscal policy is a major tool of *macro*-economic policy. Other tools include control over credit and money supply, both of which are currently in fashion as means of fighting inflation.

American government affects the economy in a number of other ways, most of which can be contained under the general description of *micro*-economic policy. Micro-economic policy is concerned not with pulling fiscal and monetary levers to affect the general direction in which the economy moves, but rather with a range of policy instruments which

Figure 13.1   Federal government expenditures as a percentage of GNP, 1962–1987

Source: Figures compiled from *Budget of the United States, Fiscal Year 1989*, Washington DC, Government Printing Office, 1988, tables 3.1 and 3.3, reproduced from Paul E. Peterson and Mark Rom, 'Lower Taxes, More Spending and Budget Deficits', in Charles O. Jones (ed.), *The Reagan Legacy*, Chatham, New Jersey, Chatham House, 1988, p. 217.

Note: The vertical line marking 1981 is the first year of Reagan administration policies.

affect the specific behaviour of individuals, firms, sectors and regions. Hence, industrial policy, labour relations, education, training and regional and urban policy are typical micro-economic tools. Regulatory policy can also be a micro-economic device, although as we saw in chapter 10, it is often motivated by non-economic considerations such as the promotion of equality or the protection of the environment. It hardly needs mentioning that this range of macro- and micro-policies are not perceived by policy makers as a coherent set of interrelated instruments. Neither do they always complement each other according to some coherent economic rationale. If anything, the very opposite applies. Politicians and bureaucrats are not in agreement as to which policy should be applied at any particular time; and the policies themselves often compete with rather than complement one another; or as the economists would put it, *trade-offs* exist between (say) industrial policy and taxation, or between inflation and unemployment.

When attempting to identify the scope and limitations of economic policy in any society both institutional and ideological factors are important. How do these constrain economic policy making in the United States?

Ideology and economic policy

As our discussion in earlier chapters showed, ideology plays an important part in shaping the policy agenda or in influencing which issues or alternative policies are available for debate and discussion at any one time. In most Western countries economic policy has been influenced by three distinct philosophies, each of which has its defenders among economists as well as its political champions. On the right, economic liberals look to the market for salvation. In the centre, Keynesians believe that when the market fails to provide full employment and steady growth, governments should step in and via increased spending and borrowing stimulate demand. On the left socialists place the market in a subordinate position in relation to a public sector which would plan the allocation of resources in society. Socialists solutions are effectively excluded from the policy agenda in the United States and increasingly elsewhere. They carry connotations of collectivism unacceptable in a society so infused with economic individualism. Most debate in recent years has involved clashes between liberals and Keynesians. Much of the politics of economic policy, then, centres on levels of taxation and spending, and on the extent to which credit and the money supply should be controlled. Prior to 1933 liberal economics dominated; it was not until the New Deal and the Second World War that federal governments began to 'borrow and spend their way out of trouble', either to stimulate a depressed economy or to produce war matériel on a massive scale. To the economic liberal high levels of government expenditures are bad enough, even if they are covered by taxation. But deficit spending and loose money supply policies are even worse, for these lead directly to inflation and, so the argument runs, eventually to disaster. Economic liberals' antipathy even to government expenditure adequately financed by taxation derives from their conviction that the market is the only efficient and acceptable allocator of resources. When governments allocate they do so wastefully and inefficiently. Of course, the free marketeers accept that governments have to play some role, especially in defence. But the essence of their philosophy is to reduce what has become a very intrusive role in society and always to ensure that what expenditure remains is recovered by taxation.

During the 1930s and 1940s Keynesian thinking dominated, and successive federal governments ran up large deficits, the peak being reached in 1943 when in one year a $54.8 billion deficit amounted to some 35 per cent of GNP. Interestingly, although most of the post-war period is usually labelled 'Keynesian', total federal debt as a percentage of GNP declined steadily until 1970, although it has risen steadily since. If debt has been increasing, spending has been rising sharply. Moreover, there has been a tendency towards increased domestic rather than defence spending (figure 13.1). To the economic liberal the latter may be justifiable, the former rarely is. The liberal position was given further stimulus by the events of the early and mid-1970s. During the 1971–3 period loose money supply policies were accompanied by steep rises in commodity prices, culminating in the 1973–4 fourfold increase in oil prices. This both fuelled inflation and wrought serious damage on the supply side of the economy. Producers, in other words, found their costs increasing rapidly. Their incentive to produce and invest was greatly undermined, resulting in a drop in output and rising unemployment. The ensuing recession convinced many in the Ford and Carter administrations that the way back to economic health lay in re-creating the right production and investment environment – low taxes, inflation and interest rates. This, they argued, could be achieved only if governments avoided over-stimulating demand through expenditure and borrowing. But neither President was very successful in keeping government spending down, and when elected in 1980, President Reagan made a much stronger pledge to cut expenditure, borrowing and taxes and therefore provide an amenable investment environment. We will examine how Ronald Reagan's new economic programme fared later.

Although by the late 1980s we can conclude that liberal economics are on the ascendant, there is certainly no consensus on policy. Many on the left of the Democratic Party and in the labour unions continued to advocate Keynesian solutions, and most commentators remained wary of the *political* feasibility of exclusively free market solutions, whatever their economic merits. In addition many political leaders are concerned about the social consequences of expenditure cuts. As established in earlier chapters, federal, state and local governments are now irrevocably involved in the business of providing a wide range of economic and social services whether they like it or not. The tension between this plain fact and the prevailing liberal economic philosophy is considerable and unlikely to disappear in the immediate future.

The liberal–Keynesian conflict in economic policy is essentially about macro-economic management. What then of the relationship between ideology and *micro*-economic policy? In some respects, adopting interventionalist micro-strategies to solve economic problems is more of a challenge to liberal ideology than is Keynesian demand management. For industrial or regional policy assumes that governments can and should interfere with individual economic actors or sectors by providing incentives, subsidies, loans or guidance. Perhaps for this reason, the United States has less consciously planned and developed industrial, regional and labour market policies than any comparable country. Indeed there *is* no federal industrial or regional strategy worth the name, and training and manpower policies are more ameliorative *ad hoc* measures than true labour market strategies. Japan and France, by way of contrast, have had highly developed industrial policies involving centrally coordinated resource and investment planning. In Japan's case industrial planning by sector involves close linkages between government, corporations and unions.[1] Such corporatist arrangements are quite alien to the American way of doing things.

Three further points of micro-policy should be noted. First industrial or labour market policies need not involve great expenditure. Economic planning and coordination by sector or region can have profound effects on research and development investment and general economic performance. In the USA, planning of this sort simply is not on the policy agenda; it is not ideologically acceptable. Second, what *is* acceptable in the USA is the regulation of corporations, unions and industries, not primarily in order to enhance economic efficiency or

1 See Peter J. Katzenstein (ed.), *Between Power and Plenty. The Foreign Economic Policies of Advanced Industrial States*, Madison, Wisconsin, University of Wisconsin Press, 1978, chapter by T. J. Pempel.

improve international competitiveness, but to remove unfair competition and monopoly practices, or to promote employment opportunities and protect the environment. From a strictly economic point of view it is probably the case that such regulatory policies inhibit efficiency and prevent the best possible return on investment. Third, although there are no conscious or coherent federal micro-economic policies, there are certainly plenty of policies. In fact, literally hundreds of programmes exist in each of the areas usually accepted under the general heading of micro-economic policy. Crucially, however, most are *ad hoc* in nature, having evolved as a result of the lobbying and bargaining process outlined in earlier chapters. Often the federal government is lured into the area for strategic and political reasons – the rescue of Lockheed and Chrysler during the 1970s come immediately to mind. But more common are the host of policies from loans provided by the Small Business administration to aid for nuclear power development, to employment creation programmes for poor cities and rural areas to investment incentives for commercial and industrial development which may have a specific economic purpose but which are *not* linked one with the other or are part of a broader strategy or design.[2]

Institutions and economic policy

The relationship between ideology and political and social institutions has inspired debate within social science for many years. In American politics, for example, whether federalism is a cause of a limited federal planning and coordinating role in society, or whether it has been maintained as a result of the power of liberal ideology has never been resolved. Whatever the causal directions, there can be no doubting that institutional arrangements continue to have a profound effect on economic policy making. Indeed, some would argue that the institutional constraints are such that no administration can effectively manage the American economy. What are the constraints?

Federalism and localism   Chapter 4 referred to competitive interdependence in US intergovernmental relations and showed how the federal government is now locked in a symbiotic relationship with lower level governments. So, although federal governments hand out vast sums of money to states and localities, it is no easy thing to withdraw this

2   See David McKay, 'Industrial policy and non policy in the United States', *Journal of Public Policy*, vol. 3, no. 1, February 1983.

largesse in line with economic imperatives. State and local governments have multiple channels of access to officials in Washington and formidable political resources can be harnessed to defend federally funded programmes. Of course to a greater or lesser extent this goes on everywhere, but the institution of federalism gives to individual states added legal weight in their efforts to maintain federal funding. Federalism also encourages 'highest common denominator' options when funds are being allocated. In other words, federal governments find it very difficult to discriminate between states according to some rational economic principle. When providing regional economic or research and development aid, for example, who gets what depends more on lobbying, criteria of equity or mere chance than on the needs of economy. The failure to develop a coherent micro-economic strategy must in part be related to this phenomenon.

State and local governments also have independent revenue sources, which can weaken the scope and substance of federal fiscal policy. Federal revenues account for only about 60 per cent of all government income in the USA, the remainder deriving from state and local sales, property and income taxes. Constitutionally, and in marked contrast to the situation in a country like Britain, the federal government cannot *directly* affect these revenues. It is easy to make too much of this point, however. Runaway spending by sub-national governments is uncommon. Many state constitutions prohibit deficit spending and the bulk of government debt in the USA is incurred at the federal level. But in a rather indirect sense the fiscal goings on of state and local governments do affect federal budgets, for their fiscal problems, together with opposition by publics to increased state and local taxes, can lead to calls for federal revenues to fill the gaps left by tax limitation measures. Some commentators have, indeed, pointed to the paradoxical possibility that antipathy towards impersonal government and high taxes will lead to greater centralization at both the state and federal levels.

Separation of powers　　When studying economic policy making in the USA, foreign observers usually look first to the budgetary process and in particular to the conflicts between Congress and President which the spending power produces. Given the American concern with macro-policy and with controlling spending, this is perhaps not surprising. Indeed, as chapters 7–10 showed, battles over spending are the very essence of both Presidential and Congressional politics. Much of the conflict derives from a simple constitutional fact: Congress, and in particular the House of Representatives, was given the power to raise taxes and appropriate monies for the executive branch to spend. As the role of the government has expanded, so the need for institutional mechanisms to coordinate and control spending have also increased. So both President and Congress have improved and streamlined their budgetary bureaucracies, each intent to provide the other branch with a coherent spending and taxing policy.

On the executive side, the first important item of legislation was the 1921 Budget and Accounting Act which created the Bureau of the Budget, a bureaucracy designed to provide improved budget advice and review for the President. At first, the Bureau of the Budget was intended to help control spending – an objective in line with the prevailing *laissez-faire* or liberal philosophy that spending was essentially a bad thing. All changed with the coming of the New Deal, when under the leadership of Franklin Roosevelt the Bureau became a partisan for increased spending in opposition to a sometimes hostile Congress. The Bureau was also formally incorporated into the Executive Office of the President during this period and its staff increased from 40 to over 600. The next significant law was the 1946 Full Employment Act, a piece of legislation which effectively endorsed Keynesian demand management by pledging the federal government to full employment policies. Among other measures, the Act created the Council of Economic Advisers, a further White House innovation but this time designed to encourage Presidents to pursue 'rational economic policies to foster and promote free competition, to avoid economic fluctuations or to diminish the effects thereof, and to maintain employment, production, and purchasing power'. The 1946 Act also mandated the President to produce an annual Economic Report to document economic performance over the past year and to provide Congress with a programme for the coming year.

Since 1946, successive Presidents have experimented further with the budget machinery, usually in order to inject rationality into burgeoning federal budgets. Lyndon Johnson ordered the adoption of planning–programming–budgeting systems, effectively a technique to link spending with preconceived planning priorities. Jimmy Carter, in turn, adopted zero base budgeting, or budget plans organized from the bottom up according to spending limits rather than according to specific programme objectives. The latter adapts spending to (say) the construction of so many miles of interstate highway or to a particular objective in the space programme and thus tends towards expenditure rising incrementally. The point about these and other innovations is that they reflect Presidents' growing concern with the sheer size of the budget and the need to present Congress with a coherent spending plan.

Congress has responded with its own innovations. The 1946 Act, for example, created a Joint Economic Committee consisting of seven

Senators and seven Congressmen to provide Congress with a total view of the economy and aid the legislature's response to Presidential initiatives. More recently, the 1974 Budget Reform Act created a Congressional Budget Office, together with Budget Committees, to provide each House with a coherent view of budget making and instil a sense of spending priority, rather than proceed as had been the case in the past on an incremental basis. Judging by the first few years of the new Budget process Congressional control has improved but the fundamental problems of budget making remain. These are simply that Congress's role is negative rather than positive. Or, as we discovered in chapter 9, 'the President proposes and Congress disposes.' Economic management is first and foremost an executive responsibility. Until the reforms, the role of Congress was confined to trimming, tinkering or otherwise modifying the President's budget on an *ad hoc* basis. After the reforms, the Congressional budget committees played a more prominent role which almost certainly made the budget process more cumbersome. The budget timetable remained effectively the same. In the spring of Year One the departments and agencies submit their expenditure estimates to OMB. OMB then spends several months reviewing – and often cutting – these estimates until the President formally submits the budget to Congress in late January of Year Two. During the ensuing nine months the budget committees work with the legislative and appropriations committees to reconcile competing interests and objectives until a final budget resolution or reconciliation is passed in September before the beginning of the financial year on October 1st. During the first years of the Carter Presidency the system seemed to work moderately well, but then the economy was growing rapidly and deficits actually ended up quite close to the President's projections. Since 1980 the situation has been transformed first by deepening recession, and later by deficits far exceeding expectations (table 13.3). This period has also seen the most radical and frenzied activity in the politics and procedures of Congressional budget making ever experienced.

Table 13.3   Budgeted and actual revenues, budget authority, outlays, and deficits, fiscal years 1976–1988 ($ billions)

	Revenues	Budget authority	Budget outlays	Budget deficit
1976				
President's budget	297.2	385.8	349.4	51.7
First budget resolution	298.2	395.8	367.0	68.8
Second budget resolution	300.8	408.0	374.9	74.1
Actual	300.0	415.3	366.4	66.4
1977				
President's budget	351.3	433.4	394.2	43.0
First budget resolution	362.5	454.2	413.3	50.8
Second budget resolution	362.5	451.6	413.1	50.6
Third budget resolution	347.7	472.9	417.5	69.8
Fourth budget resolution	356.6	470.2	409.2	52.6
Actual	357.8	464.4	402.7	44.9
1978				
Ford budget	393.0	480.4	440.0	47.0
Carter budget	401.6	507.3	459.4	57.8
First budget resolution	396.3	503.5	461.0	64.7
Second budget resolution	397.0	500.1	458.3	61.3
Actual	402.0	500.4	450.8	48.8
1979				
President's budget	439.6	568.2	500.2	60.6
First budget resolution	447.9	568.9	498.8	50.9
Second budget resolution	448.7	555.7	487.5	38.8
Third budget resolution	461.0	559.2	494.5	33.5
Actual	465.9	556.7	493.6	27.7
1980				
President's budget	502.6	615.5	531.6	29.0
First budget resolution	509.0	604.4	532.0	23.0
Second budget resolution	517.8	638.8	547.6	29.8
Third budget resolution	525.7	658.9	572.7	47.0
Actual	520.0	658.8	579.6	59.6
1981				
President's budget	600.0	696.1	615.8	15.8
Revised budget	628.0	691.3	611.5	−16.5
First budget resolution	613.8	697.2	613.6	− 0.2
Second budget resolution	605.0	694.6	632.4	27.4
Third budget resolution	603.3	717.5	661.4	58.1
Actual	599.3	718.4	657.2	57.9

	Revenues	Budget authority	Budget outlays	Budget deficit
1982				
Carter budget	711.8	809.8	739.3	27.5
Reagan budget	650.3	772.4	695.3	45.0
Budget resolution	657.8	770.9	695.5	37.7
Revised resolution	628.4	777.7	734.1	105.7
Actual	617.8	779.9	728.4	110.6
1983				
President's budget	666.1	801.9	757.6	91.5
Budget resolution	665.9	822.4	769.8	103.9
Actual	600.6	866.7	796.0	195.4
1984				
President's budget	659.7	900.1	848.5	188.8
Budget resolution[a]	679.6	919.5	849.5	169.9
		928.7	858.9	179.3
Revised resolution	672.9	918.9	845.6	172.7
Actual	666.5	949.8	851.8	185.3
1985				
President's budget	745.1	1,006.5	925.5	180.4
Budget resolution	750.9	1,021.4	932.1	181.2
Actual	734.1	1,074.1	946.3	212.3
1986				
President's budget	793.7	1,060.0	973.7	180.0
Budget resolution	795.7	1,069.7	967.6	171.9
Actual	769.1	1,072.8	989.8	220.7
1987				
President's budget	850.4	1,102.0	994.0	143.6
Budget resolution	852.4	1,093.4	995.0	142.6
Actual	—	—	—	—
1988				
President's budget	916.6	1,142.2	1,024.4	107.8
Budget resolution	921.6	1,153,2	1,055.5	133.9

[a] Larger figures for authority, outlays, and deficit assumed enactment of programs in a reserve fund.
Source: Ornstein, Mann, Malbin, Schick and Bibby, *Vital Statistics on Congress*, 1987/88 Edition, table 7.3.

This started in the first few weeks of the Reagan administration, when the President submitted major changes for spending in 1982, 1983 and 1984. Large increases in defence spending and cuts in domestic programmes were proposed. Parallel, quite radical cuts in taxation were also introduced into Congress. On the budget side, a new resolution known as Gramm-Latta I (after Delbert L. Latta, the ranking Republican on the House Budget Committee, and Phil Gramm, a leading Democratic conservative on the Committee) actually instructed 15 House Committees and 14 Senate Committees on how their budgets would be slashed over the next three years. The amounts involved – $36, $47 and $56 billion in each of these years – were huge. Finally, the resolution was framed in such a way that any subsequent supplementary appropriations would be very difficult to achieve.[3] In reaction to these Draconian measures, Congressional committees submitted a mass of new legislation designed to reassert traditional Congressional power. The Administration, fearing a sudden increase in spending, accepted a modified resolution (Gramm-Latta II) which was finally passed, very speedily in August.

Although the final bill imposed less extensive cuts than those originally planned, this particular budget experience was almost the antithesis of the slow, incremental, deliberative process for which Congress is famous and which figure 13.2 implies. In retrospect, we can conclude that President Reagan was fortunate to have the support of three key groups in Congress – the conservative Republicans, conservative Southern Democrats (the 'Boll Weevils') and, crucially, moderate Republicans (the 'Gypsy Moths'). It was this coalition which also helped the Administration achieve quite startling tax cuts in the same session. Always a fragile arrangement, signs of collapse were evident even by late 1981, and after 1982 the Administration was much less successful in handling Congress. We can confidently predict that the more Democratic Senate and the solidly Democratic House elected in 1988 will prove as difficult to manage.

Within Congress the 'traditional' centres of budgetary power, the appropriations committes and subcommittees, have begun to reassert their influence. During his last few years in office Reagan found it easier to deal directly with these committees rather than work through the budget committees which were prone endlessly to tinker with the details of the budget. The events of 1981 were, in other words, exceptional. Underneath all the dramatic events of those first few months of the new Administration, the policy networks, clientelism and fragmented and autonomous centres of power which earlier chapters have described did not somehow miraculously disappear. What the 1981 experience does

3   For a full discussion, see Robert W. Hartman, 'Congress and budget making', *Political Science Quarterly*, vol. 97, Fall 1982.

show is that Congress was at least capable of rapid response to Presidential economic initiative. It also demonstrated the growing influence of the Office of Management and Budget which under the leadership of David Stockman, assumed a very central position as both designer and manager of government spending priorities.[4]

Table 13.4   Budget and deficit targets, 1987–1993

	Fiscal years; dollar amounts in billions						
	1987	1988*	1989*	1990*	1991*	1992*	1993*
Budget authority	$1,099.9	$1,175.7	$1,233.2	$1.299.0	$1,375.7	$1,428.8	$1,482.2
Outlays	1,004.6	1,055.9	1,094.2	1,148.3	1,203.7	1,241.0	1,281.3
Revenues	854.1	909.2	964.7	1,044.1	1,124.4	1,139.9	1,258.1
Deficit	−150.4	−146.7	−129.5	−104.2	−79.3	−51.1	−23.3
Gramm–Rudman deficit target	−144.0	−144.0	−136.0	−100.0	−54.0	−28.0	0.0
Difference	6.4	2.7	−6.5	4.2	5.3	23.1	23.3

* estimates.
Source: Congressional Quarterly, *Weekly Report*, 20 February 1988, p. 330.

As can be seen from table 13.4, the Administration's 1981 successes hardly solved the economic problem. On the contrary, deficits continued to increase and did so until 1986. This is partly because the Reagan administration combined hefty tax cuts with more modest reductions in expenditure (and real increases in defence spending). More importantly, certain areas of expenditure are almost impossible to cut. Entitlement programmes (Medicare, social security) increase automatically and to Presidents and Congress alike are almost electorally sacrosanct. And even the more vulnerable programmes – welfare, grants to state and localities – have their champions at all levels. With world recession deepening during the 1981–3 period, the economic and social needs of the population and lower level governments increased, while the capacity of the economy to generate tax revenue deteriorated. Although, after 1983, the economy recovered and both unemployment and inflation fell, the deficit problem remained. Paradoxically, this overspending almost certainly helped the recovery – thus encouraging some to label Ronald Reagan an inadvertent Keynesian.

The problem of dealing with the deficit was sufficiently serious to inspire Congress, under pressure from the Administration, to pass the

4   Although even Stockman's glittering reputation was tarnished somewhat following the publication of a magazine article which revealed his misgivings about the rationality of the policy process. See William Greider, 'The education of David Stockman', *Atlantic Monthly*, December 1981. Stockman was eventually to resign in 1985.

Gramm–Rudman–Hollings Deficit Reduction Act in 1985. By imposing on Congress a timetable for mandatory spending cuts (table 13.4) the law would indeed have solved the budget deficit with major cuts falling on defence and the discretionary programmes. In 1986, however, the Supreme Court declared the mandatory provisions of the law an unconsititutional violation of the separation of powers. As a result what is now an advisory law has produced much smaller cuts than originally anticipated. In 1987 the original targets were revised upwards, and few commentators now believe that the targets set out in table 13.4 will be met.[5]

The economic problems of the 1980s highlight another important institutional relationship which is peculiarly American: the unique political position of the American central bank, the Federal Reserve System. Created in 1913, the Federal Reserve is a 'decentralized' central bank consisting of 12 Federal Reserve Districts governed by a Board in Washington. Congress deliberately gave the Board some autonomy from the President and in recent years, the Chairmen of the Board have asserted their independence to some effect. This is important because the Federal Reserve has special responsibility for implementing monetary policy, and in particular for setting interest rate levels. With budget deficits increasing, the most recent Chairman, Paul Volcker, has insisted on controlling the money supply through a policy of high interest rates. Although at first the Reagan administration accepted the Federal Reserve's policy in this area, by late 1982 serious disagreement had emerged between Volcker and Donald Regan, the Treasury Secretary. Volcker continued to insist on a tight money policy, while some members of the Administration wanted some relaxation to help lift the economy out of recession. Later, Volcker became a vocal critic of the rapidly appreciating dollar, while the administration generally viewed this as a problem for other countries. In these countries central banks, if not the creatures of executives, are significantly less autonomous than the Federal Reserve System.

In many respects the economic policy-making system resembles the social policy system. In both, the chief executive has the major responsibility for policy formulation and implementation, and in both he faces competition from other centres of power – notably Congress, executive departments and agencies, state and local governments and

5   There is some evidence that the deficit problem may not be as serious as some of these figures suggest. The US has a surplus on funds spent by state and local governments, and there is also a substantial surplus in the Social Security Trust Fund used to finance social security payments. Also, if the deficit is expressed as a percentage of GNP it has been coming down during the late 1980s. It is, however, widely *perceived* as a problem.

organized interests. There are, however some important qualitative differences between the two policy areas. Economic policy is obviously more important in the sense that most other domestic and foreign policies depend on it. All parties and politicians have an interest in economic performance and all believe that the federal government has to play a key role in economic management. They may disagree – sometimes radically – on what that role should be but no one disputes the need for economic policy. Social policy, in contrast, is not considered a legitimate concern of the federal government by many on the right. The great paradox of social policy is the incontrovertible fact of dozens of federal programmes existing in the absence of any central coordination and control. Control problems apply to economic policy too, of course, but not in quite the same way. Measures of performance – inflation, growth, interest rate levels, unemployment – exist to provide a focus of activity for policy makers, as does the budgetary process itself. Nonetheless, macro-economic management is shared between at least three major institutions – Presidency, Congress and Federal Reserve – which is highly unusual in comparative context. And micro-economic policy making is as confused and incoherent as social policy. What the two policy systems do share in common is that both are attempting to solve apparently intractable problems. Most other countries are experiencing similar difficulties of economic and social management, but in few are institutional arrangements organized in such an apparently inefficient manner. We will return to this point later.

Managing Foreign Affairs

Over the last 50 years the United States has been transformed from one of six or seven world powers with a standing army of under 200,000 and few foreign alliances or military bases, into a country with a military machine of 3 million men and women under arms (1.5 million of whom are stationed overseas), alliances with nearly 50 countries and an unrivalled military and diplomatic status and capacity. From being isolationist and contemptuous of the 'corruption' and imperialism of the old European powers, the United States is, in spite of recent reverses, now itself in a position to exploit and dominate other countries and, unlike the pre-war powers, literally to determine the fate of all mankind.

The country's political processes and institutions have not always handled these new responsibilities well. Indeed one school of thought argues that a country infused with a past characterized by a combination of isolationism and idealism is ill suited to playing the role of world policeman. Certainly, there have been many foreign and military policy mistakes in the post-war era, including the Vietnam War, which caused serious domestic conflict and terrible suffering and instability throughout Indo-China. This section will not, however, concentrate on normative questions of fortune and folly in American foreign policy. Instead our discussion will focus on the policy-making process and on the constraints imposed on foreign policy by institutional arrangements and public opinion.

The institutional context

As with social and economic affairs, it is somewhat misleading to refer to an American foreign *policy*, for there are at least three distinct types of foreign and defence policy. There is, first, strategic foreign policy or the general stance of the United States in relation to other countries over time. Scholars have been quick to identify two competing themes in the post-war period – realist and idealist. Realism[6] is, simply, the pursuit of 'national self interest' and is associated with international power politics and the implementation of policies which have clear military, diplomatic or, economic benefits. Idealism, in contrast, injects a moral or normative element into policy, as such Presidential rhetoric as 'making the world safe for democracy' or achieving 'peace with honour' in Vietnam implies. We will return to these two characterizations of strategic policy later. Although strategic policy is influenced by the broader society and polity, its main institutional context is the Presidency, National Security Council and State Department.

Second, crisis management is a crucial part of foreign policy. Since the last war, the Berlin airlift, Suez, the Cuban missile crisis, the Gulf of Tonkin incident, a number of subsequent military actions in Indo-China, American reactions to military activity in the Middle East and the Iranian hostage crisis, have all involved the United States in quick crisis management decisions.[7] Generally the Presidency and National Security Council are the institutional focus of these decisions, although the longer the crisis drags on the more likely are Congress and the public to become involved. Just this happened with the year long Iranian hostage crisis in 1979–80.

6 The classic account of the realist position is by Hans J. Morgenthau, *In Defense of the National Interest*, New York, Alfred Knopf, 1951.
7 For a good account of post-war foreign policy, see James A. Nathan and James K. Oliver, *Foreign Policy Making and the American Political System*, Boston, Little, Brown, 1983.

Third, logistical or structural defence policy involves the deployment of billions of dollars worth of matériel and several million personnel around the globe. As we established in earlier chapters, this process entails voters, organized interests (defence contractors), state and local governments and Congressional committees, as well as the more obvious institutions of Department of Defense and Presidency. While this policy system is much more open and accessible than strategic and crisis management policy, it is almost certainly less fragmented and pluralistic than the processes associated with social or economic policy. Oligopolistic defence industries are protected by government contracts,[8] and the defence budget has a powerful base of support in Congress.

These three contrasting institutional settings for foreign and defence policy do impinge on one another. Logistics and weapons system can influence strategic thinking (the Cruise missile) and crisis management (the Iranian hostage crisis, the bombing of Libya), while strategic considerations are obviously important determinants of logistical policy. Similarly, crisis management is profoundly affected by the strategic context. During the Cuban missile crisis, for example, President Kennedy referred constantly to the infringement of an American sphere of influence (the Western hemisphere) which was a long-established part of American foreign policy.

How has decision making in each of these policy areas changed over time? Perhaps obviously, crisis management has always primarily been the prerogative of the President and his closest aides in the National Security Council. Quick response requires tightly knit decision-making structures, and as commander in chief, the President has the constitutional as well as political position to assume the leadership of such structures. Not that this means that the President and his aides, are completely insulated from the outside world during a crisis and make their choices according to strictly rational criteria. As Graham Allison has shown in his brilliant study of the Cuban missile crisis, at least three competing models of decision making can be used to explain the events of the crisis, two of which put great premium on outside information and political and bureaucratic procedures and pressures.[9] But crisis management is, compared with other policy-making processes in Amer-

8 The big eight arms contractors, Boeing, General Dynamics, Grumman, Lockheed, McDonnel Douglas, Northrop, Rockwell International and United Technologies receive almost one third of defence contracts, and most depend on government contracts for their survival. For an account of the defence establishment, see Adam Yarmolinsky, *The Military Establishment: Its Impacts on American Society*, New York, Harper and Row, 1971.
9 Graham T. Allison, *Essence of Decision: Explaining the Cuban Missle Crisis*, Boston, Little, Brown, 1971.

ican government, remarkably free from political and societal pressures.

The main development in strategic foreign policy making has been the gradual centralization of power in President and National Security Council, at the cost of State Department influence. This has shown itself most graphically in the eclipse of some recent Secretaries of State in the shadow of National Security advisers – most notably Henry Kissinger and Zbigniew Brzezinski. As recent research has shown, Presidents have increasingly eschewed State Departments and their Secretaries, because they can represent independent sources of authority and control over particular issues and areas. Certain countries or policy options are championed within the Department and it is simply not convenient for Presidents to have to join battle with the professional bureaucrats when foreign policy is formulated.[10] White House/Departmental antagonism occurs in other areas, of course, but within foreign policy Presidents do at least have the option of, if not ignoring the State Department, at least of by-passing it. For State effectively has no domestic constituency, and its officials are unusually neutral and apolitical, versed as they are in the arts of diplomacy and moderation.[11] So while Presidents may find it almost impossible to disregard the Departments of Defense, Agriculture or Commerce, they can almost do this in the case of State. Foreign policy is also more insulated from the other 'traditional' centres of power in American government. House and, particularly, Senate Foreign Relations Committees are important forums for discussion and criticism, but their function is qualitatively different from (say) those of the Armed Services and Agriculture Committees with their entrenched relationships with big spending bureaux and powerful corporate clients.

In other words, foreign policy decision making is different. Within the White House the NSC is uniquely important, and in theory at least a consistency and coherence is almost certainly more achievable in foreign affairs than in many domestic areas. It may be, of course, that clarity and coherence can lead to greater errors of judgement and strategy, and that more pluralistic arrangements would lead to greater moderation. Perhaps. But it should be noted that in *cross-national context*, American Presidents are *not* particularly free from institutional and political constraints in foreign policy making. Public and Congressional opinion has been exerted on Presidents with increasing intensity since the events of Vietnam and Watergate. Earlier chapters have

10 See Bert A. Rockman, 'America's Department of State: irregular and regular syndromes of policy making', *American Political Science Review*, vol. 75, no. 4, December 1981.
11 Ibid., pp. 924–5.

catalogued some of these constraints, including the 1973 War Powers Act. President Reagan's 1983 remark, when he heard of British Prime Minister Thatcher's carefully disguised visit to the Falklands that he 'couldn't even go to church in secret' reveals a great deal. Presidents and their policy makers are constantly exposed to public scrutiny; they may be able to secrete themselves away in the NSC and plan general strategy. They may also be relatively free from direct and immediate Congressional or bureaucratic pressure. But they still have to operate in the context of the American political system, with all that this applies in terms of openness and accessibility. So individual ethnic groups such as Americans of Polish or Jewish origin constantly monitor the Administration policy towards Poland or Israel. Right-wing caucuses, such as Jesse Helms's National Congressional Club, campaign strongly in favour of a hard line towards Moscow. Since the Vietnam War, the involvement of American troops in counter insurgency wars abroad has become especially difficult because of the ever present potential for serious domestic political opposition.

The openness of the official system has led to the evolution of an 'unofficial' foreign policy system on at least two occasions. Such was the case during 1969–73 when a number of illegal acts were committed in south-east Asia. More dramatic were the events of the Iran–Contra affair which involved the creation of an alternative foreign policy machinery in the White House under the guidance of NSC Advisor John Poindexter, CIA Chief William Casey and Colonel Oliver North. By agreeing to secure the release of American hostages in the Lebanon by selling arms to the Iranians, the proceeds from which would go to help the Contras fighting for the overthrow of the Sandinista regime in Nicaragua, these officials were acting contrary both to the spirit and the letter of the law. President Reagan and Secretary of State George Schultz almost certainly did not know of these events, thus demonstrating the extent to which the President had lost control of this particular policy system during his second term.

But the culprits in the Iran–Contra affair were discovered, thus perhaps demonstrating how much more public and press opinion can do to expose the errors of foreign policy compared with the situation in Britain and France.

American foreign policy under pressure

Turning to the substance of foreign policy, the most striking development of recent years has been the slow demise of the idealist school and its replacement by a more realist vision of America's interests. Although some historians dispute that American foreign policy was ever idealist, the rhetoric of the Kennedy and Johnson years, when the United States role as world policeman was projected as part of a moral crusade, has now largely passed from political debate. Today, and notwithstanding what was President Reagan's sometimes emotional rhetoric, even a conservative Republican administration tended to couch its policies in terms of the country's economic and political interests, and when Presidents do justify policy in terms of moral imperatives – as with American support for Guatemala and El Salvador – it carries little conviction. Not only the rhetoric of politicians but actual policy has changed. The USA now deploys troops in active fighting abroad only very reluctantly. Foreign aid had gradually been reduced and is increasingly tailored to American economic and strategic interests rather than to the needs of recipient states. Even relations with NATO and the European powers have sometimes become strained as officials perceive a conflict of interests between the USA and its allies. These changes parallel the gradual erosion of American political and economic hegemony. No longer is the United States in a position to rescue ailing European economies (as with the Marshall Plan) or to act as military and economic saviour of the Third World. Indeed, many poorer countries view America as an adversary rather than benefactor.

None of this is to deny the enormous power which the United States continues to wield, especially in military affairs. The prospects for world peace remain in Presidents' hands, as the arms limitation agreement with the Soviet Union, signed in 1988, demonstrated. But the period of hegemony is over. The relationship between these changes and the institutional setting of foreign and defence policy is complex. A less dominant world position probably makes the business of crisis management more difficult. Draconian solutions such as those employed in the Lebanon in 1958 and in Vietnam are less viable, as the Iranian hostage crisis and the more recent involvement in the Lebanon showed. This may not, of course, always be a bad thing. Strategic policy making is also likely to be more problematical, for in a more interdependent world where American power is strictly circumscribed, calculating exactly what is in America's best interest becomes a more complex exercise. Policy towards the Middle East, for example, has become immeasurably more difficult since the assertion of Arab oil power. Indeed, it is now often hard to distinguish between military/strategic concerns and economic interest. The performance of the economy affects America's capacity to provide foreign aid or respond to crisis with military force. Perhaps more crucial is that with some 23 per cent of GNP now accounted for by imports and exports, the economy is interlocked with those of other countries as never before. As a result, decisions taken on strictly political or strategic grounds – discouraging Western firms from participating in the Soviet gas pipeline, for example – can have important economic consequences.

This interdependence often makes it difficult to distinguish clearly between different policy systems, and there is no doubt that it makes the business of government more burdensome. Given the external constraints imposed by interdependence and the internal pressures resulting from a fragmented and open political system, it is not surprising that Presidents have sought to centralize decision making in the White House and National Security Council. Unfortunately we cannot easily pass judgement on this development (which, in any case, represents only a relative and partial change towards centralization). For in a world fraught with tensions and dangers, the costs of policy errors and misjudgements can be startlingly high, and the relationship between 'rational' policy making and institutional arrangements is obscure. As Bert Rockman has put it:

> The problem of reconciling 'the persistent dilemmas of unity and diversity' remains to be solved as much in the foreign policy sphere as in the domestic one, especially as the distinction between these areas erodes. In unity lies strategic direction and clarity, but also the dangers of monocled vision. In diversity lies sensitivity to implementation and to nuance, but also the dangers of producing least common denominators.[12]

Coda: The Future of the American Political Economy

Since the mid-1970s an increasing number of commentators have expressed serious doubts about the capacity of the American political system to deal with a world characterized by economic instability, a sometimes ruthlessly competitive international trading environment and an uneasy military balance between East and West. Most of the misgivings have centred on the particular institutional arrangements of American governments or on broader questions of ideology. Both in this and earlier chapters we have made reference to these critiques, which, very generally, can be divided into three related themes.

12 'America's Department of State', p. 925.

1   Politics in the United States is too pluralistic. Open access to multiple centres of power ensures that public goods are distributed inefficiently. Institutionally, this means that the separation of powers, federalism and a weak party system prevent central direction and control. As a result, the sort of tough decisions needed to cope with economic dislocation and world instability cannot easily be made in the American context. Another way of putting this, perhaps, is to argue that the US system is simply too democratic. All social groups, jurisdictions and corporations have *some* influence on policy and need to be 'bought off' before anything actually gets done. This leads to inefficient and often excessive public expenditure.[13] In other countries strong central executives, unitary government and cohesive political parties are better able to direct economy and society decisively and efficiently.[14] Related are claims that the United States has a 'weak state' system, or that government policy is a result of myriad societal influences, rather than being imposed on society by a strong government or by a state which has nurtured a corporatist consensus with leading economic actors within society.[15] This pluralistic indecision and confusion may not be damaging when there is little need for state action. But, so the argument runs, in an interdependent world where governments in all of the competing economies play crucial roles, the United States is at a serious disadvantage, for *strategic* thought and action are all but impossible in a pluralist context.

2   A slightly different critique dwells on the gap between promise and performance characteristic of the American system. In other words, the dominant beliefs and values in the United States – liberty, equality, participation – lead to expectations which cannot be met by the institutional framework of politics.[16] The political system is not particu-

13   See Lester Thurow, *The Zero Sum Society*, Harmondsworth, Middlesex, Penguin, 1981; David Calleo, *The Imperious Economy*, Cambridge, Mass., Harvard University Press, 1982.
14   Although critics on the right advocate the disengagement of government rather than plead for a strong state, see Ezra Solomon, *Beyond the Turning Point: the US Economy in the 1980s*, San Franciso, W. H. Freeman, 1982; also Peter Duignan and Alvin Rabushka, *The United States in the 1980s*, London and Stanford, Croom Helm, Hoover Institution, 1980.
15   See Peter J. Katzenstein (ed.), *Between Power and Plenty*, chapters by Katzenstein and Krasner. For a general comparative perspective on the role of the state in industrial policy, see David McKay and Wyn Grant, 'Industrial policies in OECD countries: an overview', *Journal of Public Policy*, vol. 3, no. 1, February 1983.
16   The most virulent statements of this view are presented in Nathan Glazer and Irving Kristol (eds), *The New American Commonwealth*, 1976, 10th Anniversity Issue of *The Public Interest*, New York, Basic Books, 1976. For a more recent analysis, see Samuel P. Huntington, *American Politics: The Promise of Disharmony*, Cambridge, Mass., Harvard University Press, 1981.

larly efficient at translating the demands which these values encourage into actual policies and programmes. Again, the USA is different from many other countries in this respect. In few countries are egalitarianism and opportunity so deeply embedded in the national culture, and in few do these values persist even when the economy is changing rapidly and the ability of the system to meet public demands is so painfully inadequate. Proponents of this view point to the disintegrating parties, failed Presidents, capricious Congress and, above all, voter apathy and declining trust in government as evidence of the malaise.

3   Critics on the left are more concerned with the consequences of a volatile capitalism and fragmented political system for social and political equality. With even greater pressures for cuts in expenditure and a political system which puts great premium on distributing largesse according to political access and lobby power, rather than according to criteria of social justice or need, the position of those already disadvantaged will surely deteriorate, and the prospects for racial minorities look especially bleak.[17] In partial contradiction of the promise/performance critique, advocates of this position see little prospect for improvement because of the pervasive strength of the dominant ideology which diverts the deprived masses from collective action by immersing them in a culture of shallow consumerism and misguided self reliance.[18]

Although the normative base of each of these three critiques is quite distinctive – the first dwells on questions of economic efficiency, the second on problems of legitimacy and political control, and the third on equality and justice – all are pessimistic about the capacity of American government to adapt to a new domestic and international environment by providing its citizens with an acceptable degree of economic security and social justice. How much credence can be attached to these critiques?

We must, first, acknowledge that the American political system has been experiencing particularly serious problems in recent years. Earlier

17   See Frances Fox Piven and Richard A. Cloward, *The New Class War: Reagan's Attack on the Welfare State and its Consequences*, New York, Pantheon, 1982; also Kenneth M. Dolbeare, *Democracy at Risk: The Politics of Economic Renewal*, Chatham, New Jersey, Chatham House, Revised edition, 1986. Interestingly, the American left is primarily concerned with questions of equality and justice, rather than with more theoretical or abstract issues, thus reflecting the influence of peculiarly American ideas on radical thinking.
18   For a summary of this perspective, see Ira Katznelson and Mark Kesselman, *The Politics of Power: A Critical Introduction to American Government*, New York, Harcourt Brace Jovanovich, 3rd edn, 1987.

chapters catalogued the difficulties which each and every one of the main political institutions has confronted, and our discussion of social, economic and foreign policy confirmed that in a fragmented and open political system, both 'efficent' and 'just' policy making is remarkably difficult to achieve. While acknowledging this, we should be wary of too unqualified an acceptance of these three interpretations. They are, first of all, not always mutually compatible. The radical critique assumes a passivity on the party of the masses which is directly disputed by those who see increasingly strident public demands as the source of social disharmony. In comparative perspective, the latter perspective seems slightly misplaced. By most measures (regime and governmental stability, politically motivated violence, the strength of radical political parties) the USA is remarkably stable, and the populace has accepted economic change and the relative decline of American power with equanimity.[19] Second, problems of economic dislocation and governmental overload are hardly unique to the USA. Indeed, one country, the UK, which with unitary, party government patently lacks some of the institutional disadvantages of America, has expressed a similar crisis. Admittedly, like America, Britain has a liberal tradition which militates against a dominant state, but the relationship between the strength of the state and an 'effective' political and economic system is uncertain. Conservative analyses suggest, indeed, a negative relationship between the strength of the state and economic efficiency – although they provide little realistic guidance on how the state can disengage from its present extensive if often chaotic role.

Discussion of governmental 'effectiveness' involves competing values. A truly successful economy able to adjust to technological change and a highly competitive international trading environment, may be hard to reconcile with a democracy built on equality of opportunity and pluralism. Democracy, participation and accountability are desirable objectives in themselves and, to many, some sacrifice in political or economic efficiency is justified in order to achieve them.

Unfortunately, however, the trade-offs between accountability and effectiveness and between the equality and efficiency are complex and difficult. It may even be that in the context of global economic interdependence and rapid technological change, the fragmented and pluralistic political system which characterizes the United States militates

19 To be fair, this is partly acknowledged by the relevant literature, which stops short of truly pessimistic conclusions. Samuel Huntington, for example follows his own often depressing analysis with a surprisingly encouraging last few pages (*American Politics*, chapter 8). Writing within a culture infused with self reliance and optimism, American critics usually do end on a hopeful, constructive note.

against both efficiency *and* responsiveness and equality. If this is so, radical reform of the American system is urgently needed. While recent experience should lead us to be pessimistic about the prospects for reform, American social and political institutions have, at various times in the past displayed an impressive adaptiveness. The crucial question for the 1990s is whether the individualism and enterprise which have for so long enabled the United States to achieve both economic success and political stability, can continue to facilitate adaptation to change.

APPENDIX

The Constitution of the United States

We the people of the United States, in order to form a more perfect union, establish justice, insure domestic tranquility, provide for the common defense, promote the general welfare, and secure the blessings of liberty to ourselves and our posterity, do ordain and establish this Constitution for the United States of America.

ARTICLE 1 [THE LEGISLATURE]

Section 1

All legislative powers herein granted shall be vested in a Congress of the United States, which shall consist of a Senate and House of Representatives.

Section 2

1. The House of Representatives shall be composed of members chosen every second year by the people of the several States, and the electors in each State shall have the qualifications requisite for electors of the most numerous branch of the State legislature.
2. No person shall be a representative who shall not have attained to the age of twenty-five years, and been seven years a citizen of the United States, and who shall not, when elected, be an inhabitant of that State in which he shall be chosen.

3.   Representatives and direct taxes[1] shall be apportioned among the several States which may be included within this Union, according to their respective members, which shall be determined by adding to the whole number of free persons, including those bound to service for a term of years, and excluding Indians not taxed, three-fifths of all other persons.[2] The actual enumeration shall be made within three years after the first meeting of the Congress of the United States, and within every subsequent term of ten years, in such manner as they shall by law direct. The number of representatives shall not exceed one for every thirty thousand, but each State shall have at least one representative; and until such enumeration shall be made, the State of New Hampshire shall be entitled to choose three, Massachusetts eight, Rhode Island and Providence Plantations one, Connecticut five, New York six, New Jersey four, Pennsylvania eight, Delaware one, Maryland six, Virginia ten, North Carolina five, South Carolina five, and Georgia three.

4.   When vacancies happen in the representation from any State, the executive authority thereof shall issue writs of election to fill such vacancies.

5.   The House of Representatives shall choose their speaker and other officers; and shall have the sole power of impeachment.

Section 3

1.   The Senate of the United States shall be composed of two senators from each state, chosen by the legislature thereof,[3] for six years; and each senator shall have one vote.

2.   Immediately after they shall be assembled in consequence of the first election, they shall be divided as equally as may be into three classes. The seats of the senators of the first class shall be vacated at the expiration of the second year, of the second class at the expiration of the fourth year, and of the third class at the expiration of the sixth year, so that one-third may be chosen every second year; and if vacancies happen by resignation, or otherwise, during the recess of the legislature of any State, the executive thereof may make temporary appointments until the next meeting of the legislature, which shall then fill such vacancies.[4]

1   See the Sixteenth Amendment.
2   Partly superseded by the Fourteenth Amendment.
3   See the Seventeenth Amendment.
4   See the Seventeenth Amendment.

3.   No person shall be a senator who shall not have attained to the age of thirty years, and been nine years a citizen of the United States, and who shall not when elected, be an inhabitant of that state for which he shall be chosen.

4.   The Vice-President of the United States shall be President of the Senate, but shall have no vote, unless they be equally divided.

5.   The Senate shall choose their other officers, and also a President *pro tempore*, in the absence of the Vice-President, or when he shall exercise the office of President of the United States.

6.   The Senate shall have the sole power to try all impeachments. When sitting for that purpose, they shall be on oath or affirmation. When the President of the United States is tried, the chief justice shall preside: and no person shall be convicted without the concurrence of two-thirds of the members present.

7.   Judgement in cases of impeachment shall not extend further than to removal from office, and disqualifications to hold and enjoy any office of honor, trust or profit under the United States: but the party convicted shall nevertheless be liable and subject to indictment, trial, judgement and punishment, according to law.

Section 4

1.   The times, places, and manner of holding elections for senators and representatives, shall be prescribed in each state by the legislature thereof; but the Congress may at any time by law make or alter such regulations, except as to the places of choosing senators.

2.   The Congress shall assemble at least once in every year, and such meeting shall be on the first Monday in December, unless they shall by law appoint a different day.

Section 5

1.   Each House shall be the judge of the elections, returns and qualifications of its own members and majority of each shall constitute a quorum to do business; but a smaller number may adjourn from day to day, and may be authorized to compel the attendance of absent members, in such manner and under such penalties as each House may provide.

2.   Each House may determine the rules of its proceedings, punish its

members for disorderly behavior, and, with the concurrence of two-thirds, expel a member.

3. Each House shall keep a journal of its proceedings, and from time to time publish the same, excepting such parts as may in their judgment require secrecy; and the yeas and nays of the members of either House on any question shall, at the desire of one-fifth of those present, be entered on the journal.

4. Neither House, during the session of Congress, shall, without the consent of the other, adjourn for more than three days, nor to any other place than that in which the two Houses shall be sitting.

Section 6

1. The senators and representatives shall receive a compensation for their services, to be ascertained by law, and paid out of the Treasury of the United States. They shall in all cases, except treason, felony and breach of the peace, be privileged from arrest during their attendance at the session of their respective Houses, and in going to and returning from the same; and for any speech or debate in either House, they shall not be questioned in any other place.

2. No senator or representative shall, during the time for which he was elected, be appointed to any civil office under the authority of the United States, which shall have been created, or the emoluments whereof shall have been increased during such time, and no person holding any office under the United States shall be a member of either House during his continuance in office.

Section 7

1. All bills for raising revenue shall originate in the House of Representatives; but the Senate may propose or concur with amendments as on other bills.

2. Every bill which shall have passed the House of Representatives and the Senate, shall, before it become a law, be presented to the President of the United States; if he approve he shall sign it, but if not he shall return it, with his objections to that House in which it shall have originated, who shall enter the objections at large on their journal, and proceed to reconsider it. If after such reconsideration two-thirds of that House shall agree to pass the bill, it shall be sent, together with the objections, to the other House, by which it shall likewise be

reconsidered, and if approved by two thirds of that House, it shall become a law. But in all such cases the votes of both Houses shall be determined by yeas and nays, and the names of the persons voting for and against the bill shall be entered on the journal of each House respectively. If any bill shall not be returned by the President within ten days (Sundays excepted) after it shall have been presented to him, the same shall be a law, in like manner as if he had signed it, unless the Congress by their adjournment prevent its return, in which case it shall not be a law.

3.   Every order, resolution, or vote to which the concurrence of the Senate and House of Representatives may be necessary (except on a question of ajournment) shall be presented to the President of the United States; and before the same shall take effect, shall be approved by him, or being disapproved by him, shall be repassed by two thirds of the Senate and House of Representatives, according to the rules and limitations prescribed in the case of a bill.

Section 8

1.   The Congress shall have the power to lay and collect taxes, duties, imposts, and excises, to pay the debts and provide for the common defense and general welfare of the United States; but all duties, imposts, and excises shall be uniform throughout the United States;

2.   To borrow money on the credit of the United States;

3.   To regulate commerce with foreign nations, and among the several States, and with the Indian tribes;

4.   To establish an uniform rule of naturalization, and uniform laws on the subject of bankruptcies throughout the United States;

5.   To coin money, regulate the value thereof, and of foreign coin, and fix the standard of weights and measures;

6.   To provide for the punishment of counterfeiting the securities and current coin of the United States;

7.   To establish post offices and post roads;

8.   To promote the progress of science and useful arts, by securing for limited times to authors and inventors the exclusive right to their respective writings and discoveries;

9.   To constitute tribunals inferior to the Supreme Court;

10.   To define and punish piracies and felonies committed on the high seas, and offenses against the laws of nations;

11.   To declare war, grant letters of marque and reprisal, and make rules concerning captures on land and water;

12.   To raise and support armies, but no appropriation of money to that use shall be for a longer term than two years;

13.   To provide and maintain a navy;

14.   To make rules for the government and regulation of the land and naval forces.

15.   To provide for calling forth the militia to execute the laws of the Union, suppress insurrections and repel invasions;

16.   To provide for organizing, arming, and disciplining the militia, and for governing such part of them as may be employed in the service of the United States, reserving to the States respectively the appointment of the officers, and the authority of training the militia according to the discipline prescribed by Congress;

17.   To exercise exclusive legislation in all cases whatsoever, over such district (not exceeding ten miles square) as may, by cession of particular States, and the acceptance of Congress, become the seat of the government of the United States, and to exercise like authority over all places purchased by the consent of the legislature of the State in which the same shall be, for the erection of forts, magazines, dockyards, and other needful buildings; and

18.   To make all laws which shall be necessary and proper for carrying into execution the foregoing powers, and all other powers vested by this Constitution in the government of the United States, or in any department or officer thereof.

Section 9

1.   The migration or importation of such persons as any of the States now existing shall think proper to admit, shall not be prohibited by the Congress prior to the year one thousand eight hundred and eight, but a tax or duty may be imposed on such importation, not exceeding ten dollars for each person.

2.   The privilege of the writ of *habeas corpus* shall not be suspended, unless when in cases of rebellion or invasion the public safety may require it.

3.   No bill of attainder or *ex post facto* law shall be passed.

4.   No capitation, or other direct, tax shall be laid, unless in proportion to the census or enumeration hereinbefore directed to be taken.[5]

5.   No tax or duty shall be laid on articles exported from any State.

6.   No preference shall be given by any regulation of commerce or

5   See the Sixteenth Amendment.

revenue to the ports of one State over those of another: nor shall vessels bound to, or from, one State be obliged to enter, clear, or pay duties in another.

7.   No money shall be drawn from the treasury, but in consequence of appropriations, made by law; and a regular statement and account of the receipts and expenditures of all public money shall be published from time to time.

8.   No title of nobility shall be granted by the United States: and no person holding any office or profit or trust under them, shall, without the consent of the Congress, accept of any present, emolument, office, or title, of any kind whatever, from any king, prince, or foreign State.

Section 10

1.   No State shall enter into any treaty, alliance, or confederation; grant letters of marque and reprisal; coin money, emit bills of credit; make anything but gold and silver coin a tender in payment of debts; pass any bill of attainder, *ex post facto* law, or law impairing the obligation of contracts, or grant any title of nobility.

2.   No State shall, without the consent of the Congress, lay any imposts or duties on imports or exports, except what may be absolutely necessary for executing its inspection laws: and the net produce of all duties and imposts laid by any State on imports or exports, shall be of the use of the treasury of the United States; and all such laws shall be subject to the revision and control of the Congress.

3.   No State shall, without the consent of Congress, lay any duty of tonnage, keep troops, or ships of war in time of peace, enter into any agreement or compact with another State, or with a foreign power, or engage in war, unless actually invaded, or in such imminent danger as will not admit of delay.

ARTICLE 2 [THE EXECUTIVE]

Section 1

1.   The executive power shall be vested in a President of the United States of America. He shall hold his office during the term of four years, and, together with the Vice-President, chosen for the same term, be elected, as follows:[6]

6   See the Twenty-second Amendment.

2.   Each State shall appoint, in such manner as the legislature thereof may direct, a number of electors, equal to the whole number of senators and representatives to which the State may be entitled in the Congress: but no senator or representative, or person holding an office of trust or profit under the United States, shall be appointed an elector.

The electors shall meet in their respective States, and vote by ballot for two persons, of whom one at least shall not be an inhabitant of the same State with themselves. And they shall make a list of all the persons voted for, and of the number of votes for each; which list they shall sign and certify, and transmit sealed to the seat of the government of the United States, directed to the president of the Senate. The president of the Senate shall, in the presence of the Senate and House of Representatives, open all certificates, and the votes shall then be counted. The person having the greatest number of votes shall be the President, if such number be a majority of the whole number of electors appointed; and if there be more than one who have such majority, and have an equal number of votes, then the House of Representatives shall immediately choose by ballot one of them for President; and if no person have a majority, then from the five highest on the list the said House shall in like manner choose the President. But in choosing the President, the votes shall be taken by States, the representation from each State having one vote; a quorum for this purpose shall consist of a member or members from two-thirds of the States, and a majority of all the States shall be necessary to a choice. In every case, after the choice of the President, the person having the greatest number of votes of the electors shall be the Vice-President. But if there should remain two or more who have equal votes, the Senate shall choose from them by ballot the Vice-President.[7]

3.   The Congress may determine the time of choosing the electors, and the day on which they shall give their votes; which day shall be the same throughout the United States.

4.   No person except a natural born citizen, or a citizen of the United States, at the time of the adoption of this Constitution, shall be eligible to the office of President; neither shall any person be eligible to that office who shall not have attained to the age of thirty-five years, and been fourteen years a resident within the United States.

5.   In case of the removal of the President from office, or of his death, resignation, or inability to discharge the powers and duties of the said office, the same shall devolve on the Vice-President, and the Congress may by law provide for the case of removal, death, resignation, or

7   Superseded by the Twelfth Amendment.

inability, both of the President and Vice-President, declaring what officer shall then act as President, and such officer shall act accordingly, until the disability be removed, or a President shall be elected.[8]

6.   The President shall, at stated times, receive for his services a compensation, which shall neither be increased nor diminished during the period for which he shall have been elected, and he shall not receive within that period any other emolument from the United States, or any of them.

7.   Before he enter on the execution of his office, he shall take the following oath or affirmation: 'I do solemnly swear (or affirm) that I will faithfully execute the office of President of the United States, and will to the best of my ability, preserve, protect and defend the Constitution of the United States.'

Section 2

1.   The President shall be commander in chief of the army and navy of the United States, and of the militia of the several States, when called into the actual service of the United States; he may require the opinion, in writing, of the principal officer in each of the executive departments, upon any subject relating to the duties of their respective offices, and he shall have power to grant reprieves and pardons for offences against the United States, except in cases of impeachment.

2.   He shall have power, by and with the advice and consent of the Senate, to make treaties, provided two-thirds of the senators present concur; and he shall nominate, and by and with the advice and consent of the Senate, shall appoint ambassadors, other public ministers and consuls, judges of the Supreme Court, and all other officers of the United States, whose appointments are not herein otherwise provided for, and which shall be established by law; but the Congress may by law vest the appointment of such inferior officers, as they think proper, in the President alone, in the courts of law, or in the heads of departments.

3.   The President shall have power to fill up all vacancies that may happen during the recess of the Senate, by granting commissions which shall expire at the end of their next session.

8   See the Twentieth Amendment and the Twenty-fifth Amendment.

Section 3

1. He shall from time to time give to the Congress information of the state of the Union, and recommend to their consideration such measures as he shall judge necessary and expedient; he may, on extraordinary occasions, convene both Houses, or either of them, and in case of disagreement between them with respect to the time of adjournment, he may adjourn them to such time as he shall think proper; he shall receive ambassadors and other public ministers; he shall take care that the laws be faithfully executed, and shall commission all the officers of the United States.

Section 4

The President, Vice-President, and all civil officers of the United States, shall be removed from office on impeachment for, and conviction of, treason, bribery, or other high crimes and misdemeanors.

ARTICLE 3 [THE JUDICIARY]

Section 1

The Judicial power of the United States shall be vested in one Supreme Court, and in such inferior courts as the Congress may from time to time ordain and establish. The judges, both of the Supreme and inferior courts, shall hold their offices during good behavior, and shall, at stated times, receive for their services, a compensation, which shall not be diminished during their continuance in office.

Section 2

1. The Judicial power shall extent to all cases, in law and equity, arising under this Constitution, the laws of the United States, and treaties made, or which shall be made, under their authority; to all cases affecting ambassadors, other public ministers and consuls; to all cases of admiralty and maritime jurisdiction; to controversies to which the United States shall be a party; to controversies between two or more States; between a state and citizens of another State,[9] between citizens

9 See the Eleventh Amendment.

of different States, between citizens of the same State claiming lands under grants of different States, and between a State, or the citizens thereof, and foreign States, citizens or subjects.

2. In all cases affecting ambassadors, other public ministers and consuls, and those in which a State shall be party, the Supreme Court shall have original jurisdiction. In all the other cases before mentioned, the Supreme Court shall have appellate jurisdiction, both as to law and to fact, with such exceptions, and under such regulations as the Congress shall make.

3. The trial of all crimes, except in cases of impeachment, shall be by jury; and such trial shall be held in the State where the said crimes shall have been committed; but when not committed within any State, the trial shall be held at such place or places as the Congress may by law have directed.

Section 3

1. Treason against the United States shall consist only in levying war against them, or in adhering to their enemies, giving them aid and comfort. No person shall be convicted of treason unless on the testimony of two witnesses to the same overt act, or on confession in open court.

2. The Congress shall have power to declare the punishment of treason, but no attainder of treason shall work corruption of blood, or forfeiture except during the life of the person attained.

ARTICLE 4 [INTERSTATE RELATIONS]

Section 1

Full faith and credit shall be given in each State to the public acts, records, and judicial proceedings of every other State. And the Congress may by general laws prescribe the manner in which acts, records and proceedings shall be proved, and the effect thereof.

Section 2

1. The citizens of each State shall be entitled to all privileges and immunities of citizens in the several States.

2. A person charged in any State with treason, felony, or other crime,

who shall flee from justice, and be found in another State, shall on demand of the executive authority of the State from which he fled, be delivered up, to be removed to the State having jurisdiction of the crime.

3. No person held to service or labor in one State under the laws thereof, escaping into another, shall, in consequence of any law or regulation therein, be discharged from such service or labor, but shall be delivered up on claim of the party to whom such service or labor may be due.

Section 3

1. New States may be admitted by the Congress into this Union; but no new State shall be formed or erected within the jurisdiction of any other State; nor any State be formed by the junction of two or more States, or parts of States, without the consent of the legislatures of the States concerned as well as of the Congress.

2. The Congress shall have power to dispose of and make all needful rules and regulations respecting the territory or other property belonging to the United States; and nothing in this Constitution shall be so construed as to prejudice any claims of the United States, or of any particular State.

Section 4

The United States shall guarantee to every State in this Union a republican form of government, and shall protect each of them against invasion; and on application of the legislature, or of the executive (when the legislature cannot be convened) against domestic violence.

ARTICLE 5 [AMENDMENT PROCESS]

The Congress, whenever two-thirds of both Houses shall deem it necessary, shall propose amendments to this Constitution, or, on the application of the legislature of two-thirds of the several States, shall call a convention for proposing amendments, which, in either case, shall be valid to all intents and purposes, as part of this Constitution when ratified by the legislatures of three-fourths of the several States, or by conventions in three-fourths thereof, as the one or the other mode of ratification may be proposed by the Congress; Provided that no amendment which may be made prior to the year one thousand eight hundred and eight shall in any manner affect the first and fourth clauses in the ninth section of the first article; and that no State, without its consent, shall be deprived of its equal suffrage in the Senate.

ARTICLE 6 [DEBTS, SUPREMACY]

1.   All debts contracted, and engagements entered into, before the adoption of this Constitution, shall be as valid against the United States under this Constitution, as under the Confederation.

2.   This Constitution, and the laws of the United States which shall be made in pursuance thereof; and all treaties made, or which shall be made, under the authority of the United States, shall be the supreme law of the land; and the Judges in every State shall be bound thereby, anything in the Constitution or laws of any State to the contrary notwithstanding.

3.   The senators and representatives before mentioned, and the members of the several State legislatures, and all executive and judicial officers, both of the United States and of the several States, shall be bound by oath or affirmation to support this Constitution; but no religious test shall ever be required as a qualification to any office or public trust under the United States.

ARTICLE 7 [RATIFICATION]

The ratification of the conventions of nine States shall be sufficient for the establishment of this Constitution between the States so ratifying the same.

Done in Convention by the unanimous consent of the States present the seventeenth day of September in the year of our Lord one thousand seven hundred and eighty-seven, and of the independence of the United States of America the twelfth. In witness whereof we have hereunto subscribed our names.

[Names omitted]

ARTICLES IN ADDITION TO, AND AMENDMENT OF, THE CONSTITUTION OF THE UNITED STATES OF AMERICA, PROPOSED BY CONGRESS, AND RATIFIED BY THE LEGISLA-

TURES OF THE SEVERAL STATES, PURSUANT TO THE FIFTH
ARTICLE OF THE ORIGINAL CONSTITUTION.*

*[The first 10 Amendments were ratified 15 December 1791, and form
what is known as the 'Bill of Rights']*

AMENDMENT 1 [FREEDOM OF RELIGION, SPEECH, ASSEMBLY, PETITION]

Congress shall make no law respecting an establishment of religion, or
prohibiting the free exercise thereof; or abridging the freedom of speech,
or of the press; or the right of the people peaceably to assemble, and
to petition the Government for a redress of grievances.

AMENDMENT 2 [RIGHT TO BEAR ARMS]

A well regulated Militia, being necessary to the security of a free State,
the right of the people to keep and bear Arms, shall not be infringed.

AMENDMENT 3 [QUARTERING OF SOLDIERS]

No Soldier shall, in time of peace be quartered in any house, without
the consent of the Owner, nor in time of war, but in a manner to be
prescribed by law.

AMENDMENT 4 [SEARCH AND SEIZURE]

The right of the people to be secure in their persons, houses, papers,
and effects, against unreasonable searches and seizures, shall not be
violated, and no warrants shall issue, but upon probable cause, supported
by Oath or affirmation, and particularly describing the place to be
searched, and the persons or things to be seized.

*   Amendment 21 was not ratified by state legislatures, but by state conventions
summoned by Congress.

AMENDMENT 5 [CRIMINAL PROCEDURAL RIGHTS]

No person shall be held to answer for a capital, or otherwise infamous crime, unless on a presentment or indictment of a Grand Jury, except in cases arising in the land or naval forces, or in the Militia, when in actual service in time of War or public danger; nor shall any person be subject for the same offence to be twice put in jeopardy of life or limb; nor shall be compelled in any criminal case to be a witness against himself, nor be deprived of life, liberty, or property, without due process of law, nor shall private property be taken for public use, without just compensation.

AMENDMENT 6 [CRIMINAL COURT PROCEDURES]

In all criminal prosecutions, the accused shall enjoy the right to a speedy and public trial, by an impartial jury of the State and district wherein the crime shall have been committed, which district shall have been previously ascertained by law, and to be informed of the nature and cause of the accusation; to be confronted with the witness against him; to have compulsory process for obtaining witnesses in his favor, and to have the Assistance of Counsel for his defence.

AMENDMENT 7 [TRIAL BY JURY IN COMMON LAW CASES]

In suits at common law, where the value in controversy shall exceed twenty dollars, the right of trial by jury shall be preserved, and no fact tried by a jury, shall be otherwise re-examined in any Court of the United States, than according to the rules of the common law.

AMENDMENT 8 [BAILS, FINES AND PUNISHMENT]

Excessive bail shall not be required, nor excessive fines imposed, nor cruel and unusual punishments inflicted.

AMENDMENT 9 [RIGHTS RETAINED BY THE PEOPLE]

The enumeration in the Constitution of certain rights, shall not be construed to deny or disparage others retained by the people.

AMENDMENT 10 [RIGHTS RESERVED TO THE STATES]

The powers not delegated to the United States by the Constitution, nor prohibited by it to the States, are reserved to the States respectively, or to the people.

AMENDMENT 11 [SUITS AGAINST THE STATES]

[Ratified 7 February 1795]

The judicial power of the United States shall not be construed to extend to any suit in law or equity, commenced or prosecuted against one of the United States by Citizens of another State, or by Citizens or Subjects of any Foreign State.

AMENDMENT 12 [ELECTION OF PRESIDENT AND VICE-PRESIDENT]

[Ratified 27 July 1804]

The Electors shall meet in their respective states and vote by ballot for President and Vice-President, one of whom at least, shall not be an inhabitant of the same state with themselves; they shall name in their ballots the person voted for as President, and in distinct ballots the person voted for as Vice-President, and they shall make distinct lists of all persons voted for as President, and of all persons voted for as Vice-President, and of the number of votes for each, which lists they shall sign and certify, and transmit sealed to the seat of the government of the United States, directed to the President of the Senate; The President of the Senate shall, in presence of the Senate and House of Representatives, open all the certificates and the votes shall then be counted; The person having the greatest number of votes for President, shall be the President if such number be a majority of the whole number of Electors, appointed; and if no person have such majority, then from the persons having the highest numbers not exceeding three on the list of those voted for as President, the House of Representatives shall choose immediately, by ballot, the President. But in choosing the President, the votes shall be taken by states, the representation from each state having one vote; a quorum for this purpose shall consist of a member or members from two-thirds of the states, and a majority of all the states shall be necessary to a choice. (And if the House of

Representatives shall not choose a President whenever the right of choice shall devolve upon them, before the fourth day of March next following, then the Vice-President shall act as President, as in the case of the death or other constitutional disability of the President.)* The person having the greatest number of votes as Vice-President, shall be the Vice-President, if such number be a majority of the whole number of Electors appointed, and if no person have a majority, then from the two highest numbers on the list, the Senate shall choose the Vice-President; a quorum for the purpose shall consist of two-thirds of the whole number of Senators, and a majority of the whole number shall be necessary to a choice. But no person constitutionally ineligible to the office of President shall be eligible to that of Vice-President of the United States.

AMENDMENT 13 [ABOLITION OF SLAVERY]

[Ratified 6 December 1865]

Section 1

Neither slavery nor involuntary servitude, except as a punishment for crime whereof the party shall have been duly convicted, shall exist within the United States, or any place subject to their jurisdiction.

Section 2

Congress shall have power to enforce this article by appropriate legislation.

AMENDMENT 14 [CITIZENSHIP, DUE PROCESS, EQUAL PROTECTION]

[Ratified 9 July 1868]

Section 1

All persons born or naturalized in the United States, and subject to the jurisdiction thereof, are citizens of the United States and of the State wherein they reside. No State shall make or enforce any law which shall

---

* Superseded by Section 3 of the Twentieth Amendment.

abridge the privileges or immunities of citizens of the United States; nor shall any State deprive any person of life, liberty, or property, without due process of law; nor deny to any person within its jurisdiction the equal protection of the laws.

Section 2

Representatives shall be apportioned among the several States according to their respective numbers, counting the whole number of persons in each State, excluding Indians not taxed. But when the right to vote at any election for the choice of electors for President and Vice-President of the United States, Representatives in Congress, the Executive and Judicial officers of a State, or the members of the Legislature thereof, is denied to any of the male inhabitants of such State, being twenty-one years of age,* and citizens of the United States, or in any way abridged, except for participation in rebellion, or other crime, the basis of representation therein shall be reduced in the proportion which the number of such male citizens shall bear to the whole number of male citizens twenty-one years of age in such State.

Section 3

No person shall be a Senator or Representative in Congress, or elector of President and Vice-President, or hold any office, civil or military, under the United States, or under any State, who, having previously taken an oath, as a member of Congress, or as an officer of the United States, or as a member of any State legislature, or as an executive or judicial officer of any State, to support the Constitution of the United States shall have engaged in insurrection or rebellion against the same, or given aid or comfort to the enemies thereof. But Congress may by a vote of two-thirds of each House, remove such disability.

Section 4

The validity of the public debt of the United States, authorized by law, including debts incurred for payment of pensions and bounties for services in suppressing insurrection or rebellion, shall not be questioned.

* Changed by Section 1 of the Twenty-sixth Amendment.

But neither the United States nor any State shall assume or pay any debt or obligation incurred in aid of insurrection or rebellion against the United States, or any claim for the loss or emancipation of any slave; but all such debts, obligations and claims shall be held illegal and void.

Section 5

The Congress shall have power to enforce, by appropriate legislation, the provisions of this article.

AMENDMENT 15 [THE RIGHT TO VOTE]

[Ratified 3 February 1870]

Section 1

The right of citizens of the United States to vote shall not be denied or abridged by the United States or by any State on account of race, color, or previous condition of servitude.

Section 2　The Congress shall have power to enforce this article by appropriate legislation.

AMENDMENT 16 [INCOME TAX]

[Ratified 3 February 1913]

The Congress shall have power to lay and collect taxes on incomes, from whatever source derived, without apportionment among the several States, and without regard to any census or enumeration.

AMENDMENT 17 [DIRECT ELECTION OF SENATORS]

[Ratified 8 April 1913]

The Senate of the United States shall be composed of two Senators from each State, elected by the people thereof, for six years; and each Senator shall have one vote. The electors in each State shall have the qualifications requisite for electors of the most numerous branch of the State legislatures.

When vacancies happen in the representation of any State in the Senate, the executive authority of such State shall issue writs of election to fill such vacancies: *Provided*, That the legislature of any State may empower the executive thereof to make temporary appointments until the people fill the vacancies by election as the legislature may direct.

This amendment shall not be so construed as to affect the election or term of any Senator chosen before it becomes valid as part of the Constitution.

AMENDMENT 18 [INTRODUCTION OF PROHIBITION]

[Ratified 16 January 1919]

Section 1

After one year from the ratification of this article the manufacture, sale, or transportation of intoxicating liquors within, the importation thereof into, or the exportation thereof from the United States and all territory subject to the jurisdiction thereof for beverage purposes is hereby prohibited.

Section 2

The Congress and the several States shall have concurrent power to enforce this article by appropriate legislation.

Section 3

This article shall be inoperative unless it shall have been ratified as an amendment to the Constitution by the legislatures of the several States as provided in the Constitution, within seven years from the date of the submission hereof to the States by the Congress.*

* Repealed by Section 1 of the Twenty-first Amendment.

AMENDMENT 19 [WOMEN'S RIGHT TO VOTE]

[Ratified 18 August 1920]

The right of citizens of the United States to vote shall not be denied or abridged by the United States or by any State on account of sex.

Congress shall have power to enforce this article by appropriate legislation.

AMENDMENT 20 [TERMS OF OFFICE, CONVENING OF CONGRESS AND SUCCESSION]

[Ratified 23 January 1933]

Section 1

The terms of the President and Vice-President shall end at noon on the 20th day of January, and the terms of Senators and Representatives at noon on the 3d day of January, of the years in which such terms would have ended if this article had not been ratified; and the terms of their successors shall then begin.

Section 2

The Congress shall assemble at least once in every year, and such meeting shall begin at noon on the 3d day of January, unless they shall by law appoint a different day.

Section 3

If, at the time fixed for the beginning of the term of the President, the President elect shall have died, the Vice-President elect shall become President. If a President shall not have been chosen before the time fixed for the beginning of his term, or if the President elect shall have failed to qualify, then the Vice-President elect shall act as President until a President shall have qualified; and the Congress may by law provide for the case wherein neither a President elect nor a Vice-President elect shall have qualified, declaring who shall then act as President, or the manner in which one who is to act shall be selected, and such person shall act accordingly until a President or Vice-President shall have qualified.

Section 4

The Congress may by law provide for the case of the death of any of the persons from whom the House of Representatives may choose a President whenever the right of choice shall have devolved upon them, and for the case of the death of any of the persons from whom the Senate may choose a Vice-President whenever the right of choice shall have devolved upon them.

Section 5

Sections 1 and 2 shall take effect on the 15th day of October following the ratification of this article.

Section 6

This article shall be inoperative unless it shall have been ratified as an amendment to the Constitution by the legislatures of three-fourths of the several States within seven years from the date of its submission.

AMENDMENT 21 [REPEAL OF PROHIBITION]

[Ratified 5 December 1933]

Section 1

The Eighteenth Article of Amendment to the Constitution of the United States is hereby repealed.

Section 2

The transportation or importation into any State, Territory, or possession of the United States for delivery or use therein of intoxicating liquors, in violation of the laws thereof, is hereby prohibited.

Section 3

This article shall be inoperative unless it shall have been ratified as an amendment to the Constitution by conventions in the several States, as provided in the Constitution, within seven years from the date of the submission hereof to the States by the Congress.

AMENDMENT 22 [LIMITATION OF PRESIDENTIAL TERMS]

[Ratified 27 February 1951]

Section 1

No person shall be elected to the office of the President more than twice, and no person who has held the office of President, or acted as President, for more than two years of a term to which some other person was elected President shall be elected to the office of the President more than once. But this Article shall not apply to any person holding the office of President when this Article was proposed by the Congress, and shall not prevent any person who may be holding the office of President, or acting as President, during the term within which this Article becomes operative from holding the office of President or acting as President during the remainder of such term.

Section 2

This article shall be inoperative unless it shall have been ratified as an amendment to the Constitution by the legislatures of three-fourths of the several States within seven years from the date of its submission to the States by the Congress.

AMENDMENT 23 [PRESIDENTIAL ELECTIONS FOR THE DISTRICT OF COLUMBIA]

[Ratified 29 March 1961]

Section 1

The District constituting the seat of Government of the United States shall appoint in such manner as the Congress may direct:

A number of electors of President and Vice-President equal to the whole number of Senators and Representatives in Congress to which the District would be entitled if it were a State, but in no event more than the least populous State; they shall be in addition to those appointed by the States, but they shall be considered, for the purposes of the election of President and Vice-President, to be electors appointed by a State; and they shall meet in the District and perform such duties as provided by the Twelfth Article of Amendment.

Section 2

The Congress shall have power to enforce this article by appropriate legislation.

AMENDMENT 24 [POLL TAX ABOLISHED]

[Ratified 23 January 1964]

Section 1

The right of citizens of the United States to vote in any primary or other election for President or Vice-President, for electors for President or Vice-President, or for Senator or Representative in Congress, shall not be denied or abridged by the United States or any State by reason of failure to pay any poll tax or other tax.

Section 2

The Congress shall have power to enforce this article by appropriate legislation.

AMENDMENT 25 [PRESIDENTIAL DISABILITY AND VICE-PRESIDENTIAL VACANCIES]

[Ratified 10 February 1967]

Section 1

In case of the removal of the President from office or of his death or resignation, the Vice-President shall become President.

Section 2

Whenever there is a vacancy in the office of the Vice-President, the President shall nominate a Vice-President who shall take office upon confirmation by a majority vote of both Houses of Congress.

Senate 3

Whenever the President transmits to the President pro tempore of the Senate and the Speaker of the House of Representatives his written declaration that he is unable to discharge the powers and duties of his office, and until he transmits to them a written declaration to the contrary, such powers and duties shall be discharged by the Vice-President as Acting President.

Section 4

Whenever the Vice-President and a majority of either the principal officers of the executive departments or of such other body as Congress may by law provide, transmit to the President pro tempore of the Senate and the Speaker of the House of Representatives their written declaration that the President is unable to discharge the powers and duties of his office, the Vice-President shall immediately assume the powers and duties of the office as Acting President.

Thereafter, when the President transmits to the President pro tempore of the Senate and the Speaker of the House of Representatives his written declaration that no inability exists, he shall resume the powers and duties of his office unless the Vice-President and a majority of either the principal officers of the executive department or of such other body as Congress may by law provide, transmit within four days to the President pro tempore of the Senate and the Speaker of the House of Representatives their written declaration that the President is unable to discharge the powers and duties of his office. Thereupon Congress shall decide the issue, assembling within forty-eight hours for that purpose if not in session. If the Congress, within twenty-one days after receipt of the latter written declaration, or, if Congress is not in session, within twenty-one days after Congress is required to assemble, determines by two-thirds vote of both Houses that the President is unable to discharge the powers and duties of his office, the Vice-President shall continue to discharge the same as Acting President; otherwise, the President shall resume the powers and duties of his office.

AMENDMENT 26 [VOTE FOR 18-YEAR-OLDS]

[Ratified 1 July 1971]

Section 1

The right of citizens of the United States, who are eighteen years of age or older, to vote shall not be denied or abridged by the United States or by any State on account of age.

Section 2

The Congress shall have power to enforce this article by appropriate legislation.

PROPOSED AMENDMENT [EQUAL RIGHTS FOR MEN AND WOMEN]

[Proposed 22 March 1972]

Section 1

Equality of rights under the law shall not be denied or abridged by the United States or by any State on account of sex.

Section 2

The Congress shall have power to enforce, by appropriate legislation, the provisions of this article.

Section 3

This amendment shall take effect two years after date of ratification.

Index

abortion 50, 94, 120, 125, 233, 256, 263, 266
advertising, electoral campaigns, television 180
age, as voting factor 119
agrarian economy, North 35; population 7, 13
Amendments to Constitution 43, 46, 311–12; 14th 50, 258, 261, 266
America, colonial society 34; military hegemony viii, 2, 269, 289; decline 186; political hegemony viii, 2, 289–90; decline 186
American Federation of Labor 226–8
American Medical Association 230
Annapolis, trade conference 37
Anti-Federalists 44
anti-monopoly laws 59
Appeals Courts 245, 256; judges, appointment of 257
Appropriations Committee (Senate) 145
Armed Services Committee (Senate) 149
Articles of Confederation 36, 43, 58
assembly, freedom of 50
atheists, attitudes to, table 25

Baker, Howard 195
bicameralism 40
'bi-coastal' economy 13
Bill of Rights 44, 48, 50, 266, 313–15
Blacks, civil rights 112, 121, 124, 262, 264; Democratic party adherence 97, 103, 121; lower electoral turnout 105; as nominating convention delegates 179; political behaviour 121; population proportion 11; poverty 18; right to vote 102
Bork, Robert H. 157–8, 259
Brandeis, Louis 252
bribery, of government by large organizations 222
Brock, Bill 91
budget, federal, amounts, tables 284, 285; Congress approval 144, 284–8; deficits 278, 281–6; initiated by President 144
Budget and Accounting Act 281
Budget and Impoundment Control Act 163, 189
Budget Committee, House 149; Senate 145, 149
Budget Reform Act 283
Burger, Warren 245, 258, 260
Burr, Aaron 46
Bush, George, election viii, 79, 93, 120, 174, 176; experience of office 183; Vice-President 180, 196
business associations, influence on government 224–6
Business Round Table 225

Cabinet departments 204
Cabinet, Presidential appointments 80, 192, 195, 204
Camp David agreement 187
candidate voting 116–17

Cannon, Joseph 150
capital punishment 54, 263, 266
capitalism 28, 297
capitation tax 305
Carter, Jimmy, *President*, assessment
  168, 174, 184; and Congress 156,
  185; economic policy 278;
  election 103, 117, 120, 176; energy
  programme 155–6, 173;
  government reorganisation 204,
  208, 217; inexperience of politics
  183; Iran hostages 186; Supreme
  Court 257; unassertive 189
Case Act 189
Catholic voters 79
caucuses, party 88, 91, 151; in party
  elections 176
Central America, US investment in
  187, 294
Central Intelligence Agency 206
centralization, government 186
certiorari 248, 250, 251
checks and balances 39
Chief Justice 245
children, welfare benefits 270, 271
civil liberties 94; Supreme Court
  decisions 245
civil rights 50, 60, 67, 124; for
  Southern Blacks 18, 112, 121, 125;
  Supreme Court decisions 245
civil service, appointments linked to
  political parties 206
Civil Service Reform Act 206
Civil War 50, 81, 83, 85
class, as factor in political adherence,
  lack of 107
cleavage, social, lack of 107
Cleveland, Ohio 71
clientelism, in government
  departments 211, 212; in
  agriculture 212
cloture rule 153
coalition building, by President 199;
  in Congress 164, 191
commerce clause 60
Committee on Political Education
  227
Committees, Congress 138–9, 145–
  50, 162; chairmen, importance of
  149; table 146–7

Common Cause 231
Commons, House of, members, party
  discipline 127; trustees 128
Communists, attitudes to, table
  25
Conference Committees 150
Congress, access to executive
  documents 159; bills, table 165,
  amendments to 153–5, drafting of
  162; budget making process 283,
  286; check on executive 39;
  coalition building 164, 191;
  conservatism 164; efficiency 164;
  elections 302–3; executive
  appointments, investigation of
  157; impeachment, powers of 127,
  159, 301; independence of client
  pressure 214; independence of
  executive pressure 126, 156; key
  institution of government 143;
  legislative power 126, 303–4; limit
  on Presidential power 51, 127,
  144; oversight of executive 156–8,
  159; partisanship 159–60; party
  voting 160, table 161; policy-
  making 153–5, 160, 166, table
  154; powers 304–5; Presidential
  appointments, approval of 144–5,
  157; reform 164, opposition to
  216; relations with President 96,
  127, 166, 189; Speaker 151, 301;
  taxation powers 281, 303
Congress, Committees *see*
  Committees
Congressional Budget Office 283
Congressmen, access to 215;
  accountability of 144;
  constituents 215; election 135–7,
  302; independence 164; payment
  303; privileges 136; representatives
  not delegates 127–8; support
  services 140–2
conscience issues, table 94
Constitution (American) adaptive
  46; constraint on exercise of power
  29; general support for 29;
  independent source of political
  power 33; interpretation 40, 49;
  resilience 33
Constitutionalism 242

Consumer Protection Safety
  Commission 207
consumers 232
Continental Congress 36
Coolidge, Calvin, *President* 198
corporations 222, 279; influence on
  government 222, 224; Washington
  offices 224
corruption, in federal bureaucracy
  201, 207; in political parties 85; in
  state government 75
Council of Economic Advisers 282
Council of State Governors 69
courts, frequent recourse to 242–3
criminal law 245, 314
Cuban missile crisis 172, 187, 290,
  291
currency 37; paper 35

de-alignment, political parties 115
defence industries, undue influence on
  government 211
Defense, Department of 204
Defense, subcommittee (Congress)
  145
Democratic National Commission 91
Democratic Study Group 152
Democrats 85; in Congress 162;
  electoral majority 111–12, 129,
  table 130; of the left 83, 105; as
  party of Southern Blacks interests
  79, 130; reorganization 177; of
  unrepresented groups 97
demonstrations 123
Department of Health and Human
  Services 204, 206, table 205
Depression 20, 60, 207, 221
discrimination, racial 27, 50;
  religious 51
distribution of resources *see* resources,
  distribution
District Courts, 245, 256; judges,
  appointment of 257
Dukakis, Michael 176, 180, 181

economy, American, effect on foreign
  policy 294; government influence
  4, 14; growth 13; market forces
  15; world hegemony viii, 1, 2, 13,
  269, decline of 15, 186

Education, Department of 204, 216
education, high level of 16; state
  provision 271; variations in 272
Ehrlichman, John 192
Eisenhower, Dwight D., *President*,
  assessment 169; personality 112,
  194, 197, 198
Eisenstadt, Stewart 192
elderly, increasing numbers 274;
  provision for 271, 272
elections, Constitutional
  amendments, table 48; municipal
  reform 86–7; Presidential,
  television advertising 180; turnout
  at 106
electoral college 39, 47
electorate, expansion of 47, 101–2;
  mobility 95; property restrictions
  102; volatile, 94
electronic bugging 50, 252
Energy, Department of 204, 216
energy reforms 155–6, 173
Environmental Protection Agency
  207
environmentalists 214
Equal Employment Opportunity
  Commission 207
Equal Rights Amendment 102, 120
equality 26–7, 296, 298
Erwin Committee 158
executive, power over legislation 49
Executive Office of the President
  192, 194, 196; diagram 193
expenditure, government *see* federal
  government, expenditure

factions, definition 40; fear of 83
families, welfare benefits restricted to
  270
Fairness Commission 91
Farmers Alliance 229
federal bureaucracy, autonomy 219;
  complexity 219; fragmentation
  219; function 202; inefficiency
  201; power, misuse of 210;
  relations with president 216; table
  202
Federal Communications
  Commission 218

federal debt 287; as proportion of
Gross National Product 278
Federal Deposit Insurance
Corporation 207
Federal Election Campaign Act 131,
182
Federal Election Commission 207
federal government accountability
298; centralized 50; economy,
management of 274, 287;
efficiency 201, table 202;
employees, number of, table 208;
executive departments 202, table
203; expenditure 61–6, 274, 278,
tables 62, 63; fragmented 207;
intrusiveness 49; popular
confidence in 29; popular dislike
of 209; reform 208, 216; social
pressures on 207; supremacy of
49, 54, 59, 61
federal laws, table 70
Federal Reserve System 288
Federal Trade Commission 207
federalism 41, 54–6, 58, 60, 75; effect
on economic policy 281, 296;
fragmenting power 170
Federalists 44
filibustering 153
Finance Committee (Senate) 149
Food and Drugs Administration,
controlled by drug companies 207
Ford, Gerald, *President*, assessment
168; economy 239, 278; election
175, 183; state governments 69;
Vice-President 180
foreign policy 204, 219, 289;
alternative 293; crisis
management 290, 291; decision-
making 290; economy, effect on
294; public opinion, effect of 293
foreign service 204
foreign trade, deficits 274
Frankfurter, Felix 253
free enterprise 67, 79
Full Employment Act 282
Fundamentalist Christians, right
wing 79, 233

General Accounting Office 158, 218
General Revenue Sharing 67, 69

Goldwater, Barry 117
government, federal *see* federal
government
government files 215
government officials, appointed by
President 80
government, types of, table 57
governments, local *see* local
government
Gramm–Rudman–Hollings Deficit
Reduction Act 166, 264, 288
grants in aid, federal 64, 209
Great Society programmes 67, 139,
239, 271
Gross Domestic Production,
comparison with other countries
276, table 15; proportion spent by
government 274, 275, table 276
group participation by Americans
222

Haldeman, Bob 192, 195
Harding, Warren 198
Health, Education and Welfare
Department 216
Hispanic, characteristics, table 19;
proportion of population 11
House of Commons, British 81, 127
House of Lords, British 251
House of Representatives *see*
Congress
housing, subsidies 270–1
Humphrey, Hubert, *Vice-President*
117, 175, 177, 183
Hunt Commission 91, 178

idealism, foreign policy 290, 293
ideology, as factor in party affiliation
77–8, 110, 117; in relation to
political authority 23–4
immigration 7, 91, 305, table 10;
Hispanic 11; illegal 11;
opposition to 10; selective policy
10; urban 86
Imperial Presidency 188
income tax, federal 48, 59, 60, 318;
state 54, 71
Independents 89, 118, 119
Indians 301
individualism 27

Index

information, freedom of 215
information, possession by
  government bureaucracy as source
  of power 210, 211
integration 115
interest groups 51
International City Management
  Association 69
interstate commerce 305–6;
  relations 310–11; transactions 56
Interstate Commerce Clause 258
Interstate Commerce Commission,
  cointrolled by drug companies 207
Iowa, primaries 176
Iran, hostages 186, 290, 291
Iran–Contra affair 158, 159, 194, 195,
  293
iron triangles 212–13, 214
isolationism 289
issue networks 213, 214, 215, 219;
  politics 184, 185–6, 213, 266;
  voting 116–17

Jackson, Andrew, *President* 85, 170
Jackson, Jesse 174, 179
Jefferson, Thomas, *President* 39, 46
Johnson, Lyndon, *President*,
  assessment 168; Congress,
  Majority Leader 152; Congress,
  relations with 81, 116, 139, 199;
  economy 282; election 117;
  experience of office 183; foreign
  policy 294; personality 198;
  power, abuse of 188; Vice-
  President 180; War on Poverty 67
Joint Economic Committee 283
judicial review 50; Supreme Court
  243
Judiciary Act 256
Judiciary Committee (Senate) 149,
  259
jury trial 310

Kennedy, Edward 175
Kennedy, John F., *President*,
  assessment 169; Catholic 79; and
  Congress 185; election 180;
  foreign policy 294; personal aides
  194; television debate 180; world
  leader 172

Keynesians 277, 278, 279, 287
King, Martin Luther 3
Kissinger, Henry 194, 292

land use planning 54
language, as factor in political
  grouping 77–8
legal system, American, organization
  243–6, table 244
Legislature Reorganization Act 162
Lever Act 170
liberty, right to 38, 296
Libya, bombing 191, 291
life, right to 38
Lincoln, Abraham, *President* 170
local government 34, 57
Locke, John 35, 38
log-rolling 137, 138, 155

McGovern, George 97, 117, 184
McGovern Commission 91
McGovern–Fraser Commission 91,
  97, 177, 178
machine politics 86, 89; Presidential
  election 177
macro-economic policy 275, 279, 281,
  289
Madison, James 38, 41, 42
majoritarianism 28, 39
Majority Leader (House of
  Representatives) 151, 152
manual workers, non-voters 109
Massachusetts rebellion 37
media, influence in politics 51; in
  election campaigns 131, 176, 180
Medicaid 73, 230, 271, 273
Medicare 64, 230, 271, 272, 273, 287
Meese, Ed 195, 217
micro-economic policy 275, 279, 280,
  289
Middle East, American foreign
  policy 294
Minority Leader (House of
  Representatives) 150, 151, 152
Mondale, Walter 103, 117, 121, 174,
  179, 196, 227
money spent in elections 131–2, 176,
  table 176; by Presidential
  candidates 183
money supply 278, 288

Montesquieu, Baron de 38

Nader, Ralph 232
National Association for the
Advancement of Colored People
231
National Association of Counties 69
National Educational Association
237
National Emergencies Act 189
National Governors' Conference 69
national interest groups 123, 223
National Labor Relations Board 207
National League of Cities 69
National Legislative Conference 69
National Rifle Association 223, 231
National Security Adviser 194
New Deal 60, 61, 82, 95, 239, 256,
271, 278; coalition 88, 92, 109,
115; Democratic Party 96
New England 34, 120
'New Federalism' 67, 73
New Hampshire primaries 176
New York City, corruption 85–6;
financial difficulties 71
Nixon, Richard M., *President* 3, 168,
199; economy 239; election 79,
180; executive privilege 159, 264;
government reorganization 204;
law and order 79; New Federalism
67; personality 197, 198; Supreme
Court 257, 258, 259; Vice-
President 180; Vietnam War 181,
186, 188; Watergate 159, 191, 264

O'Connor, Sandra Day 248, 259
Office of Economic Opportunity 67
Office of Information and Regulatory
Affairs 217
Office of Management and Budget
283, 287
Office of Personnel Management
206, 217, 218
Office of Technology Assessment 218
officials, elected, accountability 247;
elections 102
O'Neill, Tip 151
one-parent families 18
organized groups, influence of 221

Paine, Thomas 35
Paperwork Reduction Act 217
patronage 87
pensions, occupational 270
Philadelphia, Constitution
conference 37
plantation economy 35
Plunkitt, George Washington 85
Political Action Committees 131;
election contributions 232–5,
table 234; influence on
Congressional Committees 185,
215
political activity 18; in local
community 122–3
political culture 23
political leaders, awareness of, table
173
political mobilization, parties as
agents of 51
political parties, affiliation factors 77,
78, 90, 110, tables 77, 104;
campaign finance 50; compared to
European 77; decline 98;
development 83, 84, table 84;
functions of 78–83; influence on
legislation 166; moderation 83;
non-ideological 77, 96;
organization 78; popular support
for 29, table 30; Presidential
elections, importance in 178;
programmatic 77; stability 30, 83
political system 6, 30, 31, 78;
fragmentation 25, 219, 269, 297,
298; inefficiency 297; openness
viii, 215, 270, 293, 296
population, ageing 13; composition
11; growth 7, table 8; urban 12
Populists 82, 229
poverty 16, 22, 67; distribution 18;
table 17
President of the United States,
accountability 196; advantages of
incumbency 117, 181, 184; budget
control 187–8, 281–6; and
Congress 189; Constitutional
definition 306–9; election 46–7,
174, 182, 315–16, 322, table 113;
executive privilege 159, 264;
foreign affairs 3, 163, 170, 189,

President of the United States – *cont.*
290; functions 39, 169, 171, 186;
Head of State 169; increased
importance of 170; laws, initiated
by 186; national leader 1, 168,
171, 173, 174, 190–1, 200; party
leader 171–2; party ties 184–5;
personality, importance of 197–8,
table 197; power 169, 308–9,
abuse of 188–9; policy-maker
171; staff 192; succession 320–1;
term of office 320; unifying force
168; veto 188; world leader 171,
174
Presidential appointments 80, 144–5,
157, 172, 206, 217; to Supreme
Court 257, 260
primaries, Congressional 129;
Presidential 87, 175, 177
privacy, right to 50, 51
professionals, as government
employees, 209; as pressure groups,
influence on government 230–1
property taxes, California 71
proportional reprsentation 106; in
Presidential election 177
protest movements 1, 19–20, 30

Quayle, Dan 180

race, as factor in political grouping
77–8
racial discrimination *see*
discrimination, racial
racial tolerance 25
racism 22, 25, 31; in Southern States
21, 23
ratification of Constitution 44, map
45
Rayburn, Sam 151
Reagan, Ronald, *President*, anti-
labour policies 228;
appointments 217, Supreme
Court 257, 259–60; assessment
169, 188, 197; budget deficit 188;
economic policy 164; election 79,
93, 103, 118, 119, 120, 174, 176,
183; federal government, control
of 217, expenditure 278, 286,
reforms in 203, 208, 216, 217; New

Federalism 73, 74; personality
193, 198; popularity 187;
speeches 173; tax cuts, effects
188; welfare benefits 272
Reaganomics 118
recession 69, 73, 278, 287
reformers, urban 86
Regan, Donald 192, 195, 288
region, influence of 21, 77–8, 120–1
regulatory commissions, controlled by
private interests 207
religion 21, 22, 107; factor in political
party adherence 103, 107, table
104; freedom of 50
representation, chief function of
Congress 144
representative government 38
Representatives (Congress),
apportionment between states
301; qualifications 300, 303
republican government 39, 311
Republican National Committee 90,
99, 131–2
Republican Party, electoral
supremacy 112; as party of
Northern industrial workers 79
resources, distribution 219, 239; by
federal government 277,
inefficient 296; Presidential
influence 213
Revenue Sharing 67, 68
Rhode Island 44
Rogers, William 194
Roosevelt, Franklin Delano, *President*
and Congress 185; New Deal 170;
party ties 81; personality 169;
Supreme Court 256, 257, 258
Roosevelt, Theodore, *President* 82
Rousseau, Jean Jacques 35, 38
Rules Committee (House) 145, 149,
153, 162

Securities and Exchange Commission
207
segregation, racial 79, 247, 262
self-reliance 270, 273, 297
Senate 30; committees, table 146;
reforms in 162; *see also* Congress
Senate Finance Committee 145

Senate Foreign Relations Committee 292

Senators, length of term 301, table 134; qualifications 302; status 133

Senior Executive Service 206

separation 39, 52, 281, 296

slavery, abolition 48, 316; Southern economy based on 35; Supreme Court decisions on 59

slaves, census apportionment 41; unable to vote 42

social class 16; as factor in politics .20, 103, 109

social contract 38, 80

Social Democratic Party (British) 77

social issues 177

social policy (welfare) 270, 271, 287, 289, table 64; attitudes to 27–8, 271–2; federal provision, tables 272, 273, 279; reduction 273–4

socialist party, lack of 19, 20

Southern states 21–3; Democratic Party support 120, 121; economy 22, 35; influence in Congress 149, 160; segregation 79; separation from rest of United States 21–3; social class 22

sovereignty, of people 39; of states 52

Soviet Union viii, 191, 294, 295

Speaker of the House 150, 151

special interest groups, influence on federal bureaucracy 201, 215, 223, 239

speech, freedom of 50

stamp duty 35

state courts, importance 243

State Department 206

states, individual, constitutional rights 56–7; control of spending 71; employees, number of 208; expenditure, related to federal government 61, 66; independence 34, 52, 75; limitations on 306; revenues 281

Stevenson, Adlai 112

Stockman, David 194

Sunbelt 12, 13

Supplementary Security Income 271

Supreme Court, authority 254–5,

264, 265, 266; cases, selection 250, table 246; centralizing influence 170, 263; *certiorari see Certiorari*; and Congress 255–7; established under Constitution 309–10; final court of appeal 241; functions 266; interpretation of Constitution 49, 50, 241, 250, 252, 255; judicial review, power of 242; political and social influences on 246, 249, 250, 252, 263, 266, 267; state courts, referral from 243; state law, review of 243

Supreme court decisions 59, 66, 76, 183, 218; decision-making process 248–54; Justices' individual views 250–1; precedents 252; review by Congress 256; written opinions 251

Supreme Court Justices, appointments 157–8, 189, 257–60; by President 39, 257–60; personal legal philosophy 249

Taft, William 198

tax system overhaul 166

television, in Presidential elections 180, 181

ticket splitting 115, 116, table 116

topocracy 69

trade unions 20, 27; as Democrat supporters 112; government regulation 279–80; influence on government bureaucracy 223, 226–8; membership 223; racketeering 158

Truman, Harry, *President*, civil rights 112; and Colngress 263–4; personality 169, 197; Vice-President 180

trustees, Congressmen as 128

unemployment 118, 124, 278, 280

United States, territorial expansion, map 9

urban areas 12; renewal programme 74

urbanization, as factor in Democratic Party support 112

US Information Service 206

Van Buren, Martin 85
veto, Presidential 199
Vice-President, choice of 180;
  constitutional position 309;
  importance of office 180, 196;
  public awareness 173
Vietnam War 3, 92, 118, 124, 140,
  158, 186, 188, 198, 292
violence 30, 31; political 36, 123
Volcker, Paul 288
voluntary associations, participation
  223
voter participation, decline 105, 107,
  119; table 108
voter registration laws 106
voting, electronic 162
voting age 102, 232
voting rights 318, 323, 325
Voting Rights Act 102, 105

Wallace, George 82, 83, 85, 88
War of Independence 34
War on Poverty 67
War Powers Act 163, 189, 293
Warren, Earl 260, 262
'Washington', disillusionment with
  174; lobbyists 236–7; negative
  pulbic image 209
Washington, George 170
Watergate 3, 158, 159, 188, 189, 191,
  194, 215, 264, 292
Ways and Means Committee
  (Congress) 145, 162
wealth, distribution, by country 17
welfare *see* social policy (welfare)
Wendell Holmes, Oliver 252
Whips (House of Commons) 151
Wilson, Woodrow 137–8, 170, 198,
  221
Winograd Commission 91
women, discrimination 18, 27; in
  labour force, table 19; Nominating
  Conventional delegates 179; voting
  pattern 120; voting rights 102,
  130; welfare benefits, restriction
  273
workforce, agricultural 13;
  industrial 13; service sector 13–
  14; women 19
working-class as political movement
  20, 23; Democrat supporters 112

Zeigler, Ron 192

Index by Iris Tapper